THE MAMMOTH BOOK OF
PROPHECIES

DAMON WILSON

CARROLL & GRAF PUBLISHERS
New York

Carroll & Graf Publishers
An imprint of Avalon Publishing Group, Inc.
161 William Street
NY 10038-2607
www.carrollandgraf.com

First published in the UK by Robinson,
an imprint of Constable & Robinson Ltd 2003

First Carroll & Graf edition 2003

ISBN 0-7867-1240-6

Printed and bound in the EU

THE MAMMOTH BOOK OF
PROPHECIES

Also available

The Mammoth Book of Awesome Comic Fantasy
The Mammoth Book of Best New Horror 2003
The Mammoth Book of Best New Science Fiction 16
The Mammoth Book of British Kings & Queens
The Mammoth Book of Celtic Myths and Legends
The Mammoth Book of Comic Crime
The Mammoth Book of Egyptian Whodunnits
The Mammoth Book of Elite Forces & SAS
The Mammoth Book of Endurance & Adventure
The Mammoth Book of Fighter Pilots
The Mammoth Book of Future Cops
The Mammoth Book of Great Detectives
The Mammoth Book of Haunted House Stories
The Mammoth Book of Hearts of Oak
The Mammoth Book of Heroes
The Mammoth Book of Historical Whodunnits
The Mammoth Book of How It Happened
The Mammoth Book of Jack the Ripper
The Mammoth Book of Jokes
The Mammoth Book of Journalism
The Mammoth Book of Legal Thrillers
The Mammoth Book of Literary Anecdotes
The Mammoth Book of Maneaters
The Mammoth Book of Men O' War
The Mammoth Book of Murder
The Mammoth Book of On the Road
The Mammoth Book of Private Lives
The Mammoth Book of Pulp Action
The Mammoth Book of Puzzles
The Mammoth Book of Roman Whodunnits
The Mammoth Book of Seriously Comic Fantasy
The Mammoth Book of Sex, Drugs and Rock 'n' Roll
The Mammoth Book of Sword & Honour
The Mammoth Book of The Science Fiction Century I
The Mammoth Book of The Edge
The Mammoth Book of The West
The Mammoth Book of Travel in Dangerous Places
The Mammoth Book of True War Stories
The Mammoth Book of True Crime
The Mammoth Book of UFOs
The Mammoth Book of Unsolved Mysteries
The Mammoth Book of Unsolved Crimes
The Mammoth Book of Vampire Stories by Women
The Mammoth Book of War Correspondents
The Mammoth Book of Women who Kill

Contents

Part 1   Religious Prophecy   **1**

   Introduction   3
1. The Wisdom of the Oracles   5
2. Gut Knowledge   21
3. The Children of Yahweh   34
4. The Prophets of Yahweh   53
5. Jesus the Preacher   70
6. Jesus the Christ   87
7. The Book of the Apocalypse   104
8. The Final Prophet   119

Part 2   Precognitive Prophecy   **137**

   Introduction   139
9. Old Mother Shipton   141
10. The Life of Nostradamus   154
11. Nostradamus and Astrology   185
12. The Brahan Seer   195
13. Nostradamus and the Seventeenth Century   210
14. Nostradamus and the Eighteenth Century   226
15. Nostradamus and Napoleon   255
16. Nostradamus and the Nineteenth Century   277
17. Nostradamus and the Twentieth Century   308
18. Edgar Cayce – the Sleeping Prophet   353
19. Wolf Messing – Stalin's Seer   370

20. Jeane Dixon – the White House Seer 390
21. Nostradamus and the Future 409

Part 3   Disaster Prophecy 447

Introduction 449
22. *Titanic* 453
23. The Mothman and the Silver Bridge 472
24. 9/11 490

Part 1

Religious Prophecy

Introduction

The study of religious prophecy has always been, by the very nature of the subject, a problematic issue. For a start, the major religions have generally refused to accept the possibility that the beliefs of other, often competing, religions might contain anything but accidental grains of truth. This can hamper a comparative study if one happens to be a follower of a particular faith.

Secondly, different religions define the very concept of prophecy in fundamentally different ways. To a Hindu, for example, it is the prediction of the future by the aid of the gods, often through astrology or dream interpretation; while to a Muslim, prophecy is the correct interpretation of the will of Allah, with any resultant knowledge of future events being a side effect at best.

Taken at the most basic level, one can define the Moslem concept of prophecy as fatalistic – summed up by the Islamic statement of faith: "as it is written, so it shall be". The Hindu idea of prophecy could be said to be pragmatic: the attempted revelation of future events with the aim of best taking advantage of that knowledge. Other religions' concepts of prophecy tend to fall between these two different interpretations.

Finally, there is the problem of the sheer proliferation of human religions over recorded history, balanced against the limited space in any book. Is it fair, for example, to study Christian prophecy, but to leave out Taoism, shamanism or, for the sake of argument, 1940s Polynesian Cargo Cultism?

As an agnostic – one who neither denies the existence of god(s), nor accepts their existence on faith alone – I have taken a historical rather than a theological methodology in compiling this book. Where a fact or theory appears to shed light on the development of the religious prophet, I have included it.

As a result, there are certainly passages in the following section that may shock or even offend believers in the religions discussed. I can only apologize if this is the case, while assuring the reader that this was not my intention. All of the following material is available from other sources, most of unimpeachable standing. I have merely collected it in the following chapters in a form that I hope the reader – whatever their religious outlook – will find enlightening.

I must also apologize for the Mediterranean-centric slant to the study, and can only offer to try to correct it should the opportunity to expand this volume ever arise in the future.

Chapter 1

The Wisdom Of the Oracles

The modern view of the ancient world's pagan prophets tends to be mildly satirical: to many of us they are people who utter dire warnings, like the soothsayer based on Cassandra in the 1970s television comedy *Up Pompeii!*, who always burst on the scene with shouts of "Woe! Woe!" However, in ancient times, prophets were taken seriously because they played a specific role in society – something between a priest and a political adviser. The practice of augury was deliberately institutionalized in most polytheistic (multiple god worshipping) civilizations and, for many of our ancestors, the voice of the oracle (the socially established prophet) was the voice of the gods.

Two of the oldest known oracles in the western world were at Dodona at Epirus, in Greece, and the Siwah oasis in the Libyan Desert. The Greeks believed that two sacred black doves were once dedicated to Isis and released from Egyptian Thebes: one flew to Dodona, the other to Siwah, indicating that the gods especially favoured these places.

The Egyptians, at about the same time, told of two elderly priestesses who, in the service of Isis, travelled and preached as far as their strength would carry them. The place where each finally stopped was dedicated as sacred ground. In an interesting link between the two fables, the word for "dove" in the ancient language of Epirus also meant "old woman".

The temple built at Siwah was dedicated to the goat-headed Theban god of wisdom, Amun, while the ancient grove of oaks at Dodona was dedicated to Zeus – the chief of the Greek gods. A link between the two was always maintained, since the Greeks considered Amun an aspect of Zeus, and when they went to ask his advice at Siwah, addressed him as "Zeus-Ammon".

Alexander the Great, having freed Egypt from the Persians in 331 BC, made a celebratory 200-mile pilgrimage to the Oracle of Siwah. This was no luxurious royal progress: Alexander set off into the trackless desert with only a handful of men and scant supplies. The sheer harshness of the desert conditions took them by surprise and after only a few days, their water ran out. Fortunately, the god indicated his favour by sending a sudden rainstorm that provided just enough water to enable them to reach their destination.

The ritual of the Oracle of Siwah was rather odd. "When an oracle is wanted," Alexander was told, "the priests carry forth the bejewelled symbol of the god in a gilded boat, from whose sides dangle cups of silver; virgins and ladies follow the boat, singing the traditional hymn in honour of the deity." The supplicant would then make his question known, and the god would push the boat in a certain direction: forward meant "yes," backwards "no". (It sounds reminiscent of a modern ouija board.) Furious shaking meant the god thought the questioner was a fool.

Alexander, as liberator of Egypt and a crowned pharaoh, also had the right to speak directly to the deity in a private chamber. Not surprisingly, he decided to forego the bizarre boat ceremony in favour of the latter option, but as such we do not know what he actually asked Zeus-Ammon. Alexander would only say afterwards that he had been given the answer he was seeking. Most historians now believe that he was either asking whether his planned conquest of the vast Persian Empire would succeed or, on a more personal note, if his mother's claim that he was actually the son of a god was true.

As a pharaoh, Alexander was ritually greeted by the head priest as "Son of Amun", and this may well have settled the latter question. His later unshakeable confidence, often in the face of overwhelming Persian forces, suggests that his private audience with the god may have convinced him of the certainty of his eventual victory. Whatever the truth, Alexander later ordered that coins stamped with his head should feature a band or circlet sporting two small goat horns – a possible show of respect or kinship with goat-headed Amun.

It now seems that Alexander may have been duped. Modern excavation has revealed a ten- by twenty-foot chamber off the main courtyard with a secret passage running along the wall. Small holes link the passage with the inner chamber, suggesting that the voice of the god was actually the voice of a priest.

The Oracle at Dodona was less elaborate. It was sited in southern Macedon in the Epirote hills, which were, until the time of Alexander's father Philip, barbaric to the point of savagery. Those who were allowed access by the neighbouring tribes were led up a stream to a grove of oak trees. The oak was sacred to Zeus, and the trees in this grove were said to be especially ancient even for that long-lived species. Tending the grove were oracle-priestesses, usually elderly women trained to read the voice of the god in the whispering sound made by the wind in the trees.

Homer, writing between 750 and 650 BC, describes in the *Iliad* the hero Achilles invoking the chief of the gods as: "King Zeus, Dodonaen, Pelasgian, thou that dwellest afar ruling over wintry Dodona – and around dwell the Selloi, thy prophets, with unwashed feet and crouching on the ground . . ."

The priestesses had to go barefoot, even in the bitter Epirote winters, and were, understandably, filthy and unkempt. Only women were permitted to serve the Oracle of Zeus. The reason may be that the Pelasgians, the original inhabitants who were conquered by the Greeks, were a matriarchal people who worshipped an earth-mother goddess. When the Greeks took over the grove, they replaced the goddess with masculine Zeus, but kept the other traditions of the sanctuary.

Supplicants' questions were written on small tablets and given to the priestess. She would then sit in the grove listening to the sound of the trees and to seven copper bowls hung like wind chimes in the branches of the "voiceful oak" – the tree said to fore-tell the future. Having memorized every rustle and clink, the priestess would then consult the scrolls of ritual, which contained meanings attached to numerous combinations of arboreal sounds.

The stream that ran through the grove was said to be magical – running dry at noon each day and restarting twelve hours later. Since no normal stream behaves in this way, it sounds as if some blocking device was used to divert the stream while the priestesses listened to the sacred trees. In time, this noise-abatement policy was allowed to become one of the mysteries of the sacred grove.

Modern excavations at Dodona have unearthed hundreds of question tablets. Most are mundane to the point of tedium. A local man called Agis asked whether he had lost his blankets and pillows himself, or whether someone had stolen them. Another man asked if the child his wife Nyla was carrying was indeed his own, and a farmer and his wife asked, "By what prayer or form of worship may we enjoy greatest good fortune?"

Others – envoys of powerful men or city-states – came to ask more momentous questions, and were often baffled by the answers. One story tells how emissaries from Boeotia consulted the oracle on some question of grave national importance. Having listened to the grove and consulted the scrolls, the priestess Myrtile advised them that "it would be best for you to do the most impious thing possible". The envoys went into a solemn huddle to discuss the suggestion, then leapt on Myrtile and threw her into a nearby cauldron of simmering water – this being the most impious thing they could think of on the spur of the moment.

Presumably these Boeotian supplicants had already tried the oracle in their native country – or perhaps they had simply decided that a long and dangerous trip to Dodona was preferable to the ordeal of the Oracle of Trophonius. Sited in a deep cave on the Boeotian Hercynos River, this was, quite literally, a "holy terror". The priests of the shrine of Trophonius – dedicated to Apollo the god of light – answered questions by granting "divine visions" to the supplicants themselves: no intermediary oracle was necessary.

The preparation was extremely harrowing. The questioner was first locked in the nearby Temple of Fortuna for three days and nights and made to fast for the whole period. On the fourth night he was led to the Shrine of Trophonius and given two cups of water. The first was from the spring called *Lethe*, and was said to blot out all previous memories for the duration of the oracle. The second was from the stream called *Mnemosyne* (from which we derive the words "memory" and "mnemonic") and was said to help the supplicant to remember the visions that were about to appear.

Visitors were then directed to the cavern beneath the shrine, which involved clambering down a ladder in total darkness; at the bottom of this there was a long narrow tunnel. Having struggled down this grim stretch of cold rock (feet first) the supplicant was placed on a low trolley and handed two sacred honey cakes. The trolley then hurtled away into the darkness at breakneck speed. Quite apart from the risk of falling off, the questioner had to hang on to the cakes no matter what happened, as the penalty for arriving at the other end without them was death.

Timarchus, a disciple of the recently executed Socrates, told how he went to the shrine of Trophonius to ask what he should think of the daimon, a spiritual guide by which Socrates believed himself inspired. After the terrifying descent into the depths of the cavern, he was left alone for a long time in darkness and silence. Suddenly he saw a vision of a lake of fire, dotted with beautiful coloured islands and a voice called:

> Timarchus! The radiant isles that float on the lake of fire are the sacred regions, inhabited by pure souls . . . Those who keep their original purity amid the ordeals of their first experience are clothed in divine radiance by crossing the lake of fire, source of eternal life . . . The soul of Socrates was one of these; always superior to his mortal body, his soul had become worthy of entering communion with the invisible worlds and his familiar spirit, a deputy from them, taught him a wisdom that men did not appreciate and therefore killed. You cannot yet understand this mystery; in three months it will be revealed to you.

The historian Plutarch wrote that Timarchus never recovered from the ordeal. He died three months later "babbling about luminous islands, lakes of fire and holding out his hands to the picture of Socrates who, he said, was coming closer to him."

A modern psychologist may feel that the unnerving ceremonies of the Oracle at Trophonius represent a classic brainwashing technique. Social isolation (in the Temple of Fortuna), starvation, dehydration, prolonged terror and finally sensory deprivation in the depths of the cave: all these (possibly combined with drugs in the cups of water) would be likely to induce powerful hallucinations. We may also see in these rituals typical "rites of passage": physical and mental rigours designed to enhance consciousness and facilitate contact with higher planes of reality.

This argument does not dismiss the "ordeals" of Trophonius as some kind of deception. It could well be that one of the faculties acquired in such states of heightened awareness is that of precognition.

The oracle in Boeotia was named after the architect who designed the shrine above the sacred cave. The same Trophonius, and his brother Agamedes, also designed the temple for the most famous of all soothsayers: the Oracle of Delphi, which was at Phocis in central Greece.

For over a thousand years, kings and commoners from Greece, Asia Minor, the Roman Empire, Egypt and North Africa relied on the Delphic *Pythia* (the oracle-priestess) for accurate predictions of the future. Wars were waged, colonies founded, peace treaties signed and the fates of individuals decided on the "word of the god" pronounced through the medium of the Pythia, who was usually a low-born and uneducated woman. Because of the veneration in which the oracle was held all over the civilized world, Delphi became a nexus of religious and spiritual influence, not unlike the Vatican in the Middle Ages. Greece was transformed from a cultural backwater to the "cradle of Western civilization" largely through the multi-cultural influence of visiting foreign supplicants to Delphi.

Yet the oracle's reputation, and all the riches in offerings that came with it, existed only because its priests knew something nobody else knew: how to choose, train and maintain seers and visionaries.

At the height of its power in the sixth century BC, Delphi – situated on the River Pleistus beneath the awesome ramparts of Mount Parnassus – was a glittering temple of white marble surrounded by a town of the kind that always springs up around tourist attractions. But before the sixth century, it was almost as rustic as the oak grove of Dodona, and had been for about five hundred years.

The Delphic Oracle probably dated back to the period of the Mycenaean Empire, around 1500–1100 BC. In this earlier period of Greek power, sometimes called the Age of Heroes, the nature goddess Gaea (or Gaia) was worshipped as the fount of Delphic prophecies. Later, following the post-Trojan War Dark Age, the religion of Apollo, the masculine god of light, replaced the waning cult of the goddess. The legend tells how Gaea gave birth on

Mount Parnassus to a titanic serpent called Python (after which the species of snake was later named). Apollo slew this monster, which lived in a crack in the ground, and won the right to be worshipped at Delphi; the oracle became known as the *Pythia*, meaning "pythoness".

The original dedication to Gaea came about because the oracle's power came out of the ground – in fact, from the crevice in which the serpent was said to have lived. The Greek historian, Diodorus Siculus, writing in the first century BC, gave the following account of the discovery of the prophetic influence at Delphi:

It was the goats of ancient times that first discovered the divine presence at Delphi – this is why, in our day, the people there still prefer such an animal when they offer sacrifice before consulting the god. The discovery is supposed to have occurred in this fashion. At the spot where the adytum [inner sanctum] of the present temple is, there was once a chasm in the ground where the goats used to graze. Whenever one of them approached this opening and looked down, it would begin skipping about in a startling fashion and bleating in a quite different voice to its normal one. Then, when the goatherds went to investigate this bizarre phenomenon, they too were similarly affected but, in their temporary possession by the god, would prophesy the future. As news of what was happening at the chasm spread across the countryside, many peasants flocked to test its strange power. As each approached the cleft, and breathed the vapour that emerged from the recesses, they would also fall into a sacred trance, through which Apollo would voice the coming of things yet to pass.

Thus, according to Diodorus Siculus, the Delphi fissure itself came to be called miraculous. At first, those who came to commune with the god would proclaim oracles to one another. However, many in their "divine rapture" hurled themselves down the bottomless chasm, so the local inhabitants decided that a single woman should take the burden of the god's possession and speak for all the oracles.

The choice of a woman as the priestess might have been – as at Dodona – a remnant from the pre-historic cult of the Earth

Goddess. A more likely explanation, however, is that in patriarchal Ancient Greek society, women were considered more expendable than men, so it mattered less if a woman threw herself down the hole.

The choosing of a candidate to be the new Pythia was apparently a virtually random affair. Any local woman of the right age, who was willing to take the vow of chastity, was eligible. The testing of an applicant was itself absurdly straightforward. The priests of Apollo would throw buckets of icy mountain stream water on to the woman's bare skin – and could tell from how much she shuddered whether she was both robust and sensitive enough to be the "voice of the God". That was all that was involved, according to contemporary accounts.

This suggests that it was the vapour itself that created the trance in which the woman became the mouthpiece of Apollo. Unfortunately, we cannot test this theory scientifically because the Chasm of Python no longer exists. (That it survived so long in a highly-active earthquake region is in itself rather miraculous.)

Until recently, scientists dismissed the "Delphic vapour" as a myth – possibly concocted to disguise the use of hallucinogenic narcotics to induce the Pythia's oracular frenzies. However, in March 2002, a team of geologists working near Mount Parnassus announced that they had discovered two underground faults in the oil-bearing limestone of the region. These cracks crossed each other's path directly under the site of the oracle temple. It was not only possible, but indeed highly likely the geologists suggested, that petrochemical fumes would have found their way to the surface at that very spot.

One "vapour" that would have issued from the sacred crevice, the team suggested, was *ethylene* – a sweet-smelling gas that was once used as an anaesthetic. In lighter doses, ethylene produces a feeling of "aloof euphoria", according to team head Dr Jelle Zeilinga de Boer, a geologist based at Wesleyan University. As we will see, this phrase is an excellent description of the Pythia in her oracular state.

Becoming the new Delphic Oracle was a doubtful privilege. The lives of the pythia were stressful, pleasureless and usually brief. Although the risk of falling down the fissure was minimized by seating the oracle on a large bronze tripod, the fumes themselves were unhealthy, and shortened their lives. Following an early scandal involving a handsome, virile supplicant and a lonely young pythia, only chaste, middle-aged women were chosen for the task.

Questioners approaching the oracle were first ritually purified, then told to sacrifice a goat to Apollo. They were then led into the sanctuary, but were kept far enough away from the rock cleft to avoid breathing the fumes or disturbing the reverie of the Pythia. The philosopher Apollonius of Tyana (born in the first century AD) described the air in the adytum as "a wonderfully sweet perfume", but admits that incense was burned all around, so we cannot be sure if the sacred vapours smelled as pleasant.

He goes on to describe the effect of the prophetic trance on the Pythia. Her chest heaved, her face flushed then went pale and her limbs shook convulsively. Soon she was foaming at the mouth and her hair was standing on end. Then she gabbled something that Apollonius could not make out, grabbed the sacred woollen fillet from her head and threw it on the ground. At this, the attending male priests, who had carefully transcribed the Pythia's words, hurried Apollonius outside.

Apollonius had asked if his name would live after his death. A priest later handed him a piece of paper carrying a "translation" of the Pythia's holy ranting: *"You shall be spoken of in centuries to come, but only for insults to be levelled against your name."* Not surprisingly, Apollonius tore the prediction to shreds and stamped away in a huff: a reaction he later ruefully noted as being common to those who did not like or understand the Pythia's replies.

We, of course, are in a position to note the accuracy of the prediction. After his death, the early Fathers of the Christian Church selected Apollonius and his Pythagorean beliefs for particular ridicule. Since it is doubtful that the (usually illiterate) oracle knew anything about Apollonius' teachings, it seems unlikely she could have simply guessed such a specifically correct answer.

Not all the Pythia's accurate predictions were induced by the vapour. When Alexander the Great visited Delphi, he is said to have arrived "off-season", during a period when the oracle was not giving predictions. Furious at the priests' flat refusal to prepare the Pythia, Alexander strode into her private chamber and started to haul her out to the sanctuary. Having no idea who he was, but realizing he was too strong to fight against, the Pythia is said to have shouted despairingly: "This young man is unstoppable!" Alexander immediately released her, thanked her politely for the oracle and left to invade Asia. He never lost a battle in his life.

Such clarity of speech – accidental as it may seem in the above case – was a rarity in Delphic oracles. More often than not, the answer babbled by a pythia and transcribed by the priests of Apollo was infuriatingly obscure. (The wilful obfuscation of the meaning of predictions is something we shall often encounter in this study of seers and prophecy.)

In the case of the Delphic Oracle, an element of despair at the inevitability of certain events in the future may be partly to blame. For example, when Polycrates, ruler of the island of Delos – the birthplace of Apollo – asked if a festival he was planning should be named Delian, after the island, or Pythian, in honour of the oracle, the Pythia answered tersely: "It will not matter what you choose to call it."

This apparent self-effacement later turned out to be a strict, if misleading, statement of the truth. Before the festival could be initiated, a Persian satrap captured Polycrates and tortured and crucified him. The event did not need a name because it was destined never to take place.

On another occasion, the people of the island of Siphnos petitioned the oracle to tell them if their recent good fortune would continue. The Pythia replied: "Whenever in Siphnos the town hall becomes white-browed, then wise men ought to beware of an ambush of wood and a herald in red." Siphnos, a fairly small island, had recently become wealthy through the mining of gold and silver. To show off their new wealth, the Siphnians had recently gilded the outside of their town hall, making it appear – in bright sunlight – to be "white-browed". Therefore the warning of immediate danger was plain in the oracle, as was its probable origin: the reference to "an ambush of wood" apparently pointed to the wooden galleys of pirates. In fact, a few days after news of the oracle arrived on Siphnos, the Samian pirates – in ships with red-painted prows – raided the island and kidnapped many important personages. A ransom of 100 talents of gold was eventually paid for them.

The islanders probably breathed a sigh of relief that the prophesied danger had passed, leaving them still comparatively rich; but then the sea broke into the over-extended mine workings and reduced them all to poverty again.

The reason the oracle gave so little information was, in hindsight, readily apparent – the Siphnians might have protected themselves against pirate raids, but no advice could have stopped them from mining, so there was no way of saving their wealth.

On the other hand, a similarly worded oracle once saved all of Greece from conquest. In 480 BC, the Persian king Xerxes led a massive invasion of the Greek mainland, crushing all resistance before him. When it became plain that the Persian army would soon arrive, the Athenians asked the advice of the Pythia. The grim answer was: "Hence from my temple! Prepare for doom."

The Athenians pressed the Pythia for more information. This time she pronounced that the "fortress of Cecrops" – the rock hill at the heart of Athens – must fall, but that "walls of wood unshaken" would save their dear ones. Still baffled, the envoys petitioned a third time and were told: "Stay not to meet the advancing horse and foot that swarms over the land, but turn and flee to fight another day." She added: "Oh blessed Salamis! How many children of women will thou slaughter!"

The envoys now guessed that wooden walls meant ships, and the Athenians trusted the oracle enough to abandon their city to the enemy and fight the Persians at sea in galleys. Greatly outnumbered, the Athenians lured the Persians into the Bay of Salamis, restricting their manoeuvrability and allowing the Greeks to close in for hand-to-hand fighting. The Persian army specialized in cavalry and chariot combat, while the Greek marine hoplites were probably the best foot infantry in the ancient world. The Persians lost 200 ships to the Athenians' forty.

So many men died in the battle that the playwright Aeschylus later described the sea as invisible for broken ships and hacked corpses. With no fleet to back his invasion, Xerxes was unable to consolidate his conquest and was forced to withdraw to Asia Minor.

Again, in 431 BC, when the Spartans asked if they should invade northward into Athenian territory, the Pythia answered: "If you press the war with energy, then victory will be on your side." She added that Apollo – as the god of healing (and disease) – would aid the Spartans. Within days of the launch of the invasion, a plague struck Athens and her Theban allies. Sparta, inexplicably, was not affected.

Sparta eventually won the resulting Pelopponesian War, but at a terrible cost to the whole of Greece. The country's city states were so weakened by the brutal, decades-long conflict that they were easy prey for conquest, first by the Macedonians under Alexander, and later by Imperial Rome. The age of Ancient Greek military pre-eminence in the Mediterranean was over, but their culture still influences us today.

The Delphic Oracle played a major part in the peaceful spread of Greek civilization, for her word was automatically sought whenever a new Greek settlement was planned. It was on the Pythia's advice that the Cretans colonized Sicily, Archias founded Syracuse, the Boeotians built Heraclea in Pontus, the Spartans created another Heraclea in Thessaly, and the city of Byzantium (now Istanbul) was constructed on the Hellespont. These colonizing projects owed much of their success to the belief of the colonizers that Apollo protected them.

It is ironic, but not surprising, that both the later conquerors of Greece – Macedonia and Rome – either aspired to be Greek or believed themselves the spiritual heirs of Greece, the highest aspect of which was the Delphic Oracle. It is impossible to imagine what our western culture would have been like if the Pythia at Delphi had never existed.

The most famous single story about the oracle's prophetic powers dates from 548–547 BC, and is told by Herodotus. The richest country in the eastern Mediterranean at that time was Lydia (situated in present-day northern Turkey) and its king, Croesus, was (and still is) a byword for magnificent wealth.

Croesus had ruled Lydia for eleven years of peace and prosperity, but now faced a major crisis. The Persians, an upstart nation of barbarian horsemen from the eastern hills, had recently conquered his neighbours, the Medes, and Croesus suspected that he would be the next target. It seemed common sense to pre-empt them. Some of Croesus' councillors wanted to attack at once, others argued for caution. Croesus decided to consult an oracle, but could not decide which of them would be the best. So he decided to test them.

He sent ambassadors to Dodona, Trophonius, Siwah, Delphi and dozens of other sanctuaries. All the supplicants were instructed to ask the same question at midday, 100 days after they set out: "What is King Croesus doing at this moment?"

The Pythia at Delphi answered:

I know the number of the sands and all measures of the sea. I understand the dumb and hear the voice that speaks not. A smell comes to my nostrils: strong-shelled tortoise boiled with lamb's flesh in bronze, covered above and below.

Croesus – having decided to do something that nobody could possibly guess – had boiled up some tortoise and lamb meat in a closed bronze pot. Although one of the other oracles is said to have come close to describing the uncommon act of a king cooking his own lunch, it was the Pythia who described it exactly.

The next envoys sent to Delphi took gifts for Apollo and his priests, which included a fortune in gold ingots, gold and silver dishes, jars and vases, a four-and-a-half-foot-high solid gold statue of a woman (known as "Croesus' pastry cook") and two wine bowls, one of gold, the other of silver. Herodotus noted that the gold wine bowl weighed half a ton and could hold over 5,000 gallons. Croesus clearly hoped that he could buy the favour of Apollo; unfortunately he does not seem to have heard about the Greek notion of hubris – the legendary "pride before a fall".

The Pythia was asked three separate questions. The first concerned the issue at hand: "Should Lydia attack the Persians?" The reply was: "After crossing the Halys [the river on the Lydian–Persian border] Croesus will destroy an empire."

The second question concerned the future: "Will Croesus' reign be a long one?" The Pythia replied: "When a mule becomes king of the Medes then flee, soft-soled Lydian, by the pebbly Hermus [another Lydian river]! Stay not, nor feel shame for showing cowardice!"

The final question was personal: "Will Croesus' son [dumb from childhood] ever speak?" To which the reply was: "Croesus, you prince of fools! Hope to be not at home when your son finds his voice. Be far away on that day, for it will not be propitious for you."

Since the first prediction was exactly what he was hoping to hear, Croesus was inclined to find a favourable interpretation for the second two answers. He assumed they meant that he would rule a long time (for how could an animal rule over the Medes?) and that his son would one day regain his voice.

Whether Croesus saw the obvious risk – that the empire he would crush might be his own – is hard to say. Given the growing threat posed by Persian expansionism, he may have already decided that attack was his only defence. If he had known that King Cyrus was born of Persian and Mede parents – and was thus a "mule" of mixed race – he may not have risked the venture.

Croesus and the Lydian army crossed the Halys River in the autumn of 547 BC, and were met by a much larger Persian force led by Cyrus. After a day of fighting, both armies were badly mauled, and neither could claim a decisive victory. At dusk, Cyrus made a tactical withdrawal and Croesus returned to Lydia to gather a stronger army.

If Cyrus had been a less enterprising leader, Croesus might have ultimately won the war – having much greater resources and a number of allies to strengthen him. In the event, Cyrus made a surprise attack into Lydia while Croesus' army was partially disbanded for the winter – the traditional non-campaigning season. The Lydians fought hard, but it was only a matter of time before their capital, Sadis, fell.

As Persian soldiers marched into the Lydian throne room to capture Croesus (who had refused to flee), his son is said to have overcome his speech impediment to shout: "Swine! How dare you lay hands on King Croesus?"

What happened next depends on who we believe. Herodotus says that Croesus was recognized to be a worthy man by Cyrus the Great and later became a trusted adviser in the Persian court. However, a recently-discovered Babylonian message cylinder of that period states bluntly: "Cyrus, king of Persia, has marched into Lydia, killed its king, taken its wealth and left a garrison there."

The oracle's advice did not always lead to disaster. When an undistinguished visitor called Battus sought the counsel of the oracle, she assured him that he would successfully build an empire in Libya. Battus went on to organize an expedition and successfully founded the trading port of Cyrene in 631 BC – the colony went on to flourish for nearly 1,300 years. Battus himself was doubtless rather bemused by the oracle, since he had only gone to Delphi to ask if his stutter could be cured.

On another occasion, the Spartan monarch Lycurgus visited Delphi to ask the god's advice. For some years he had been exiled from his own kingdom, but had now been invited back. Lycurgus asked what he should do and the Pythia replied: "Beloved of God; the commonwealth that observes your laws will be the most famous in the world." Thus encouraged, Lycurgus returned to Sparta and drew up a fundamentally reforming set of proto-republican laws that won the city universal respect for centuries afterwards.

In later years, the oracle was less trusted and consulted. Many people believed that the priests of Apollo were prone to twist their interpretations to please wealthy or powerful patrons. In other cases, where even they seemed unable to comprehend the words of the Pythia, the priests were said to give nebulous and meandering translations that could be understood to mean anything.

The Greek biographer Plutarch, writing in the last century BC, became a Delphic priest himself in the hope of reforming the sanctuary. When he found the task impossible, he retired and recorded his regret in *The Decline of the Oracles*.

Our modern attitude is understandably sceptic; it is tempting to believe that the oracle pronounced obscure nonsense that would take in the ignorant and credulous. The objection to this theory is the consistent reliability of Delphic predictions for over a millennium. As we have seen, many of the oracle's obscure predictions accurately revealed future events, and no amount of educated guesswork could account for this.

The fifth-century BC historian Thucydides – the archetype of the objective chronicler – ruefully admitted that Delphic predictions had repeatedly changed the course of Greek history. This, he could confirm from events in his own lifetime, was because the prophetic answers given by the Pythia were reliable enough to allow the complete redirection of state policies. If a city like Athens or Sparta had followed Delphic advice, later to find it totally inaccurate, historians like the sceptical Thucydides would have been delighted to record the fact, but they never got the opportunity.

The priests of Apollo kept detailed records of all the transactions of the oracle. This Delphic treasure-trove eventually found its way to Constantinople, and remained there for centuries. Sadly, the records vanished following the capture of the city by the Ottoman Turks in 1453.

Like so many prophets, the Delphic Oracle foresaw her own end:

> Aye, if you will hear it, if you endure to know that Delphi's self with all things gone must go. And thus, even thus, on some long destined day shall Delphi's beauty shrivel and burn away. Shall Delphi's fame and fane from earth expire at that bright bidding of celestial fire?

That prediction carried much the same shock value for the Ancient Greeks as Medieval Christians would have felt if someone had prophesied the downfall of the Church.

It was towards the beginning of the second century AD that Delphi faced the growth of this new and hostile religion of the crucified man-god. The early Christian Fathers attacked all previous Greek forms of belief (when they did not covertly - assimilate them). Interestingly, even in their most vitriolic attacks on Delphi, the Christians never questioned the accuracy of Delphic oracles – they simply ascribed them to demonic powers.

However, it was not Christianity, but its own success, that brought about the end of the Delphic Oracle. A young Roman nobleman called Hadrian visited Delphi around the turn of the first century AD and learned that he would one day be the emperor of Rome. On winning the laurel crown in AD 117, Hadrian ordered the oracle closed down and its sacred crevice blocked up. He had no intention of letting any would-be usurper receive such encouragement as he had.

In 362, the Emperor Julian, known as the Apostate because he preferred paganism to Christianity, sent his personal physician to try to revive the oracle at Delphi. But it was too late – the age of oracles had passed. As the *Oxford Classical Dictionary* sadly notes, after the third century AD, "international attention was now confined to tourism and the Pythian games."

Chapter 2

Gut Knowledge

While trusting the mystic predictions of an assessably-accurate oracle remains somewhat understandable to us, one of the oldest forms of divination[1] has become quite incomprehensible to the modern mind. Ancient methods such as astrology, dream interpretation and scrying have survived the millennia and continued to flourish, but "extispicy" – the reading of the future in the ritually-spilled viscera of a dead animal – has largely fallen out of fashion.

Nevertheless, "reading the entrails" was the most popular method of prediction in the cultures around the Mediterranean for thousands of years. Translation of cuneiform texts has shown that ritual evisceration was central to the religion and daily life of the Babylonian civilization (existing from around 1800 BC to 600 BC), and was probably inherited from their cultural forebears, the Sumerians (the first known civilization, dating from around 2800 BC to 1800 BC). We also know that extispicy (from the Latin *exta*, entrails, and *specere*, to inspect) was the chief form of augury in the Roman Empire up to and into the Christian era. In the period separating these cultures – about 3000 years – this practice was zealously followed by virtually all the civilizations of Western Asia and those around the Mediterranean Sea. Indeed, through modern anthropological research, it can be argued that just about every ancient culture worldwide has indulged in some form of extispicy at one time or another, and modern spirit-religions like Santeria and Vodun still do.

It may be difficult for a modern mind to accept, but there are

[1]A magical or religious ritual aimed at divining the future.

numerous recorded incidents of entrail reading successfully predicting future events; indeed, why else would our forebears have continued such an unpleasant custom for so long if they did not see some evidence of it actually working?

The most famous incident of accurate extispicy known today was the prediction that Julius Caesar would die on 15 March 44 BC. It is notable that many modern sources, when describing Caesar's assassination, gloss over just how the soothsayer, Vestricius Spurinnia, came to give the warning: "Caesar! Beware the Ides of March."[2] Perhaps our historians' reluctance to mention this detail is understandable, as many of their readers might find it ridiculous that a goat's liver was the source of one of the best-known prophecies in history.

In Shakespeare's *Julius Caesar*, the doomed dictator contemptuously dismisses the soothsayer as a "dreamer" but, in fact, Spurinnia was both a patrician and a high priest – a man of great respect in Rome. As a *Haruspex* (from the Latin *haruga*, a victim, and *specere*, to inspect), Spurinnia would have been considered a very holy man by most Romans; only certain members of Rome's intellectual elite would have dismissed him as a superstitious fool or a bloody-handed fraud.[3]

On the morning of 14 March 44 BC, Spurinnia was performing the daily ritual sacrifice: a goat had its throat cut as suitable prayers were chanted.[4] When the animal was quite dead, it was laid, belly up, on the altar stone. Temple servants pulled on its legs to keep it steady and the haruspex opened it from ribs to genitals with a sacred knife. He then reached into the steaming cavity, severed the internal organs from their respective anchorages, and carefully arranged the whole stinking mass on the altar stone. While the servants took the empty corpse away, Spurinnia carefully studied the state of the viscera, paying special attention to the liver and intestines – the organs thought most likely to predict the future.

[2]The "Ides" were monthly dates on the Roman calendar, which in March fell on the fifteenth day.

[3]Just over a century before, Cato the Elder had wryly commented: "I wonder how one haruspex can keep from laughing when he sees another." Julius Caesar seems to have shared this depreciatory opinion.

[4]Other animals, such as pigs, geese and sheep, were also "read" by haruspex, but Apollo, god of light and prophecy, particularly favoured goats, so these were usually chosen for sacrifice when important matters were being divined.

To the priest's horror, according to the contemporary statesman Cicero: "there was no head to the liver of the sacrifice. These portents were sent by the immortal gods to Caesar that he might foresee his death . . ." By this we can guess that Spurinnia was either commissioned to make an augury on Caesar's behalf, or that he was curious to know the future of Rome's most powerful politician. Either way, he communicated the bad news immediately to the dictator.[5]

Caesar refused to consider the warning. He had good reason to believe that on the next day, 15 March, he would be proclaimed *Rex* in the Senate House – the first king of Rome in 466 years. Even if he had been a true believer in extispicy, it would have been political suicide to show cowardice on that of all days. Also, as a shrewd political animal, Caesar must have suspected that those who wished to block the coronation might have bribed Spurinnia.

The following day, Caesar met Vestricius Spurinnia as he made his way to the Senate House. Despite the fact that his own wife had dreamt the night before that he would be murdered, Caesar was in buoyant spirits. "Well, Spurinnia," he called, "the Ides of March are come!" "Aye, Caesar," was the gloomy reply, "come, but not yet gone." Less than an hour later, Caesar was dead: stabbed to death by men he had considered friends and colleagues.

The "head", missing from the liver of the goat sacrificed by Spurinnia, was what anatomists now call the *processus pyramidalis*. This is a pointed protuberance found on one side of the organ, containing approximately ten to fifteen per cent of the liver's overall volume. It may therefore seem surprising that despite so much of this vital organ being missing, the goat still seemed healthy enough to be a fit sacrifice. Veterinary research has shown that an animal living in reasonably unstressful conditions can still appear healthy with over eighty per cent of its liver dysfunctional. The fact that the *processus pyramidalis* was actually absent is also less surprising than it may first seem. The liver is not a compact, muscular organ like the heart; various diseases can cause parts of it to literally dissolve away.

If, on the other hand, the liver had been undiseased, complete and a healthy shade of red, the soothsayer would have

[5]Then a term simply meaning the military commander-in-chief, with little of the modern connotation of a tyrant.

proclaimed it a good omen. A complex set of rules and references existed to guide a haruspex. Each section of the liver had traditional, partially descriptive names such as the "Gate" and the "Table"; a particular mark on one of these would indicate a specific portent. This would then be cross-referenced with other signs found on the liver and the other organs. Furthermore, certain areas of the liver were connected with specific portions of the sky – thus creating a link with the sister trade of astrology. All in all, a soothsayer could produce a highly complex prediction from the entrails of a single sacrificial beast, and often many animals were "read" at one time to further honour the god and provide a thorough divination.

The liver and intestines were considered particularly indicative of the gods' influence on the future, largely due to their physical appearance. The intestine of an animal, for example, seems a confused mass of tubing when inside the creature's body, yet, when removed and stretched out, it forms a neat double spiral. From the top of the colon, the intestine curves in a clockwise direction, then doubles back within the first set of coils in an anti-clockwise route to the anus. This finding of order within apparent chaos must have been attractive to men attempting to divine the future.

The intestine was linked with the planet Mercury, whose orbit also seems to double back on itself when viewed from the Earth. Whether the traditional role of the god Mercury – that of messenger and magician – was influenced by the practice of extispicy or, indeed, vice versa, is now a moot point.

The ancients considered the liver the seat of the emotions and home of the immortal soul. Even as late as Shakespeare's day, Elizabethans tended to describe the liver instead of the heart as the originator of non-intellectual reactions. In *Love's Labours Lost*, for example, Biron says in an aside: "This is the liver-vein, which makes flesh deity." The reason that the heart later came exclusively to represent the emotions was simply because an excited person could feel it beating faster. The liver, on the other hand, won its reputation during a period when people tended to do their own butchery and regularly saw an aspect of the organ that is today largely forgotten. When freshly removed, the liver has a glossy, mirrored appearance: a haruspex could literally see his face in it.

Numerous ancient texts refer to the liver as a "mirror of the soul", not least Plato's *Timaeus*:

> God . . . placed the liver in the house of lower nature [the belly] contriving that it should be solid and smooth, and bright and sweet . . . in order that the power of thought, which proceeds from the mind, might be reflected as in a mirror . . . and so might strike terror into the desires.

Plato believed, in other words, that pure, intellectual thoughts originated in the head and were "reflected" in the liver, thus having a controlling influence on the animalistic desires of our "lower nature". "Such is the nature of the liver," Plato went on, "which is placed as we have described in order that it may give prophetic intimations." The liver, he thought, literally reflected the future.

This mirroring aspect of the liver may have been considered as religiously important in the sacrificial cultures outside those of the ancient Mediterranean. Robert Temple, in *Conversations with Eternity*, points out that the Toltec civilization of Mexico sacrificed men to a god called Tezcatlipoca, meaning "Smoking Mirror". The method of killing was disembowelment with an obsidian dagger. Temple suggests that the name of the slaughter god came from the mirror-like aspect of the fresh liver, combined with the "smoke" or steam that would rise from the organ on all but the hottest days. Unfortunately, we do not know enough about the Toltecs (who ruled in Mesoamerica from around 700 to the twelfth century AD) to determine whether they too believed the liver was in any way predictive.

The priests of the Celtic Druid cult of Briton and northern Europe often ritually sacrificed humans and, occasionally, "read" their entrails. The Romans, when they first conquered France and south-east Briton under Julius Caesar, were horrified to discover the Druids practising extispicy on people as well as animals. Although usually tolerant of different religions, the Roman Empire afterwards made several attempts to smash Druidism as a matter of basic human decency. However, the cult survived all violent attempts to destroy it, only withering away when confronted by the peaceful invasion of Christian missionaries into Celtic lands.

Generals of the ancient world often used extispicy as a form of supernatural scouting. For example, when Hannibal and his Carthaginian army ravaged northern Italy in 216 BC, the people of Rome marshalled their troops to counter-attack. At times of national emergency, the city was commanded by two elected consuls. In this case the consuls were called Marcellus and Crispinus, and these opted to lead an army against the Carthaginians before they reached the gates of Rome.

When the opposing forces met, the Romans could not understand why Hannibal – who had arrived in the area first – had not taken the most strategically advantageous position, apparently leaving it for them. Plutarch gives the following account of what followed:

> Now Marcellus determined to ride forward to reconnoitre [the intervening ground], so he sent for a soothsayer and offered sacrifice. When the first victim was slain the soothsayer showed him that the liver had no head [i.e. the *processus pyramidalis* was missing]. On sacrificing for the second time, the head appeared of unusual size, while all the other organs were excellent, and this seemed to set at rest the fear caused by the former. Yet the soothsayers said that they were even more disturbed and alarmed at this; for when, after very bad and menacing victims, unusually excellent ones appear, the sudden change is itself suspicious.

Any modern soldier will wince at the obvious trap the consuls now fell into, but it should be remembered that this was still the era of grand sweeps of massed troops and set-piece battles. Guerrilla war was considered dishonourable – the strategy of a cattle-raider, not a general. Moreover, the vital importance of keeping the army's leaders out of the melee was then rarely considered. Just over 100 years before, Alexander the Great had always taken the point position of the first cavalry charge, and in two battles had come within striking distance of the enemy king himself. Following this example, Roman generals believed that the highest glory was to personally defeat the leader of the opposing army in hand-to-hand combat.

Plutarch goes on:

Marcellus rode forth with his colleague Crispinus and his son, who was a military tribune, in all two hundred and twenty horsemen... On the overhanging crest of the woody hill, a man, unseen by the Romans, was watching their army. He signalled the men in ambush what was going on, so that they permitted Marcellus to ride close to them, and then suddenly burst out upon him, surrounding his little force on all sides . . . Marcellus was pierced through the side with a lance . . . Crispinus [escaped, but] after a few days, died of his wounds. Such a misfortune as this, losing both consuls in one engagement, never before befell the Romans.

In the subsequent Battle of Cannae, the Roman army of 50,000 men was shattered and forced to retreat in disorder. Hannibal lost only 6,700 men in the engagement, but the niggardliness of his countrymen, who refused to send him reinforcements, meant that he could ill afford such a comparatively small loss. Despite their enemy's temporary helplessness, the Carthaginian army was forced to retreat from Italy before it could sack Rome. When the Romans eventually counter-attacked, it was Carthage that fell. Thus the haruspex's prediction apparently came true – a great loss, followed by a great victory.

Through modern archaeological discoveries, it is now possible to trace the traditional development of extispicy. From the Romans, the trail leads to the mysterious Etruscans of western-central Italy. This people, whose few surviving writings have yet to be deciphered, were completely obsessed with augury and specifically extispicy. At the time of the decadent collapse of their empire, it seems that individual Etruscans were unable to make even minor decisions without examining some unlucky creature's innards. The Roman statesman Cicero once commented that: "the whole Etruscan nation [was] stark mad on the subject of entrails."

The origins of the Etruscan people, who apparently colonized Italy sometime before 700 BC, remains a mystery. However, their main cultural influence seems to have been that of the Greeks, and it may have been from this link that their passion for reading livers came.

The Greeks practised extispicy as a matter of religious habit. So, when one reads of the building of the Athenian Parthenon, the preparations before the battle of Salamis or the assembly of ships for the siege of Troy, you can be certain that a priest with knife and a goat was there to divine the gods' will before any strategic decisions were made.

Of course, this sometimes caused dangerous delays, especially if the auspices were consistently unpropitious. In 415 BC, for example, Nicias, the general in charge of the Athenian attack on the island of Syracuse, wasted so much time on the beach waiting for Apollo's sign of favour, that the Syracusians were able to outflank and annihilate his entire army.

Fourteen years later, on the coast of Asia Minor, the Athenian general Xenophon found himself in a similar predicament. His force of 10,000 Greek mercenaries had fought on the wrong side in a Persian civil war and was now being hunted by the victorious enemy army. Bereft of ships and provisions, it was vital that they find food, then march north and cross the Straits of Hellespont to Greece before the Persians were strong enough to crush them.

Before they set out, Xenophon ordered a sacrifice to read the omens. The entrails were unfavourable, so they stayed put for twenty-four hours. The next day the priest sacrificed again, but the sheep's entrails still indicated that they should not move. Xenophon was a young and untried general – elected to the post when his superiors had been captured and tortured to death. He probably would have faced a revolt among his starving troops when he ordered another day's delay, had it not been for the fact that his men believed in extispicy as keenly as he did.

On the third day, all the food was gone. Xenophon later wrote (modestly in the third person): "the soldiers came to Xenophon's tent, and told him they had absolutely no provisions left. He replied that he would not lead them out while the victims were adverse . . . 'The victims,' he said, 'as you have seen, fellow soldiers, are not yet favourable for our departure.'"

Neon, another officer, could not bear to watch his men starving for want of food that could easily be taken from neighbouring villages. So, despite the risk of incurring the displeasure of the gods, he led out a raiding party. However, as soon as they had dispersed to find food, the Persian cavalry attacked and scattered them. On hearing this, Xenophon ordered another sacrifice – this time for the favour of the gods rather than for the auspices – and immediately led out a relief force of veterans. The 500 scavengers were rescued with only a few losses, but no food was secured.

This practical evidence that the Persians were almost ready to attack further demoralized the hungry troops. The priests had by now run out of sheep to sacrifice, and were forced to kill precious baggage oxen. Although the meat of these animals could be eaten following the sacrifice, their deaths only served to make moving all the more difficult. The three-day delay seemed to have doomed them to the same fate as the Athenians on Syracuse.

Finally, on the fourth day, the entrails of the sacrificial ox gave a favourable augury. Within hours, a Greek ship laden with food arrived – completely unexpectedly – and the army got its first full meal since the beginning of the crisis. Xenophon then gave orders to prepare for battle, saying:

> It is better for us to fight now, when we have dined, than tomorrow, when we may be without dinner. The sacrifices, soldiers, are favourable, the omens encouraging, the victims most auspicious. Let us march against the foe.

The Persians were caught on the hop by this sudden advance; they presumably had thought that the Greeks had given up completely and were passively waiting for the deathblow. A Persian tactical withdrawal soon dissolved into a panicked rout and the Greeks found their road home clear (for the time being).

Xenophon did get his army back to Greece, and his account of their long trek through hostile territory, titled *Xenophon's Anabasis* (Xenophon's Campaign), is still required reading in many military schools today. At every major decision point on the 1,500-mile march, he made a sacrifice and had the priests read the entrails: never once, later on, did he feel the omens found therein were false – they were simply confusing now and again.

One general who read Xenophon's account with considerable interest was Alexander the Great. A few decades after the Greek army's retreat from Asia Minor, Alexander led a Macedonian–Greek allied force back across the Hellespont and, often using *Xenophon's Anabasis* as a guide to the territory, annexed the entire Persian Empire. His army conquered as far as North-west India and, by the age of 33, he had conquered the largest empire yet known (only later surpassed by the Mongols under Genghis Khan and the British in Victorian times). Fortunately, Alexander's dream of combining Greek and Persian cultures into one state was greatly aided by the fact that both peoples shared many of the same beliefs, including extispicy.

On their exhausted return from India, Alexander's army headed for Babylon – one of the most ancient cities in the world and, as we have already seen, among the earliest known locations for the practice of extispicy. On the road, a message arrived from the Chaldaean[6] astrologers of the city, warning that a black fate would hang over Alexander's head if he entered Babylon.

The king had been away from his western empire for eight years at this point and now found corruption rife. So he ignored the warning, doubtless thinking that the Chaldaeans – who were city administrators as well as priests – hoped to delay him while they tried to clean up the evidence of their wrongdoings. However, as Alexander approached the famous cyclopean walls of Babylon, a rumour came to him that his own Macedonian governor of the city had made sacrifice and received a hideous omen in the entrails. Setting up camp outside the gate, the king sent for and questioned the priest who had performed the rite. As the historian Plutarch tells:

> The soothsayer answered that the victim's liver had lacked one lobe. "Really!" exclaimed Alexander, "that is a terrible omen!" He did the soothsayer no harm, but regretted that he had not listened to the warning [of the Chaldaeans].

As a devoutly religious man, Alexander was fully schooled in extispicy, and often performed and read sacrifices in person. To try to reduce the threat of the omen, he spent as much time as possible outside the walls of Babylon, but soon caught a fever (or was poisoned) and died in the city.

[6]The Chaldaeans were such acurate prophets that the term was synonymous with astrology up to modern times. Many theologians believe that the "Three Wise Men" of the Christian nativity were Chaldaeans.

Extispicy seems a perfect example of how a ridiculous practice can become a fervently held act of religious faith over the course of generations. A sceptic will say that the above cases of apparent prophecy were actually simple matters of coincidence, magnified by superstition and ignorant beliefs: those times when an entrail reading proved self-evidently false were not recorded, and so comparative study is impossible. Indeed, this argument is often levelled against all forms of religious, magical or scientific faith (excepting, usually, those adopted by the critic himself). However, it is important to consider the point of view of the pre-Scientific Age peoples when trying to understand their need and use of augury.

Our modern world is enthused with the intellectual confidence of scientific assurance. We are educated to believe that where a mystery exists we have, or will find, the mental tools to unravel it. The boundary to this self-confidence may have been set by the quantum physicist who pointed out that: "the subatomic universe is not only weirder than we imagine, it is weirder than we *can* imagine." Nevertheless, even if we accept this intellectual limitation, we are still far beyond our forebears, for whom almost everything was beyond their understanding.

The origins of rain and wind, the inner mechanics of reproduction and disease, the regular movement of the stars and the unpredictability of the sea – all were total mysteries to ancient man and just had to be lived with as best as possible. This was not because they were less intelligent than we are today, but because their civilizations simply failed to record and communicate ideas as consistently as ours has done over recent centuries.

For example, the discovery of the value of *pi*[7] is generally attributed to the Greek philosopher Pythagoras in the sixth century BC. However, a nineteenth-century study of the Great Pyramid at Giza showed that its builders encoded the exact value of *pi* into the structure's dimensions. Since this is highly unlikely to be a coincidence, it seems that the Ancient Egyptians knew the value of *pi* in 2,500 BC. Unfortunately, because they did not pass it on (perhaps because it was a religious secret or maybe because the papyrus scrolls they wrote upon were just too fragile to survive down the millennia) the information was lost until Pythagoras

[7]The ratio of the circumference of a circle to its diameter.

*re*discovered it. Even then, it might have been lost again had it not been for the followers of Pythagoras recording and then actively disseminating his ideas throughout the Mediterranean world.

Some ideas, of course, are universal to all developing civilizations and thus do not need to be communicated – one of the most common being the belief in omnipresent gods and/or supernatural beings.[8]

In the face of great calamity, natural wonder or just plain incomprehension, mankind's typical reaction has been to suspect that somebody somewhere is pulling switches to make it happen. Since, as we will see in this book, acts of precognition and clairvoyance also appear to be regular if inexplicable features of human life, it was only natural that gods would be credited for their occurrence. Here it is important to consider a fundamental aspect of the ancient forms of prophecy: propitiation.

Propitiation was exemplified by practices like extispicy. Mighty gods ran the universe, so offering sacrifice to them was a man's way of bribing them to be on his side: much like making "protection" payments to the Mafia. A natural extension of this idea was the belief that the "insides" of the sacrifice might indicate whether the gods were pleased with the gift or not. If the animal's innards were diseased, it would be easy to guess that the gods would not be pleased by the gift. Unfortunately, until it was killed, such hidden things could not be inspected, and afterwards it was too late. Over time – a sceptical anthropologist might argue – cause-and-effect became confused and it came to be believed that portents on the entrails of the animal specifically indicated future events. The guts of the animal were not bad, thus making the god angry: the god was already angry, and said so by making the guts bad.

Yet, to study extispicy as a practice on its own, separate from the other beliefs of the time, is to misrepresent the people involved. For our ancient ancestors, omens were to be found everywhere. Moreover, they saw apparent evidence of these omens coming true on a daily basis. For them, accurate prophecy was a self-evident, if largely inexplicable, truth – much as magnetism is for you or me. Their argument against modern scepticism would be the existential evidence of their own lives.

The Roman politician Cicero once wrote: "There are two types

[8]This is why priesthood is sometimes said to be the second oldest profession after prostitution.

of divination: one comes from art, and the other from nature." By "art" he meant that the future could be read through intellectual skills such as geomancy,[9] astrology and palm reading. This presupposed that educated observation of the mundane world would lead to clues and insights from the metaphysical sphere. By "nature" he meant dreams, visions and direct contact with supernatural beings that knew the course of future events. Indeed, extispicy may have combined both these aspects. As we will see later, prophets like Nostradamus seem to have induced vision-trances by gazing fixedly into a reflective surface like a bowl of water or a crystal ball. Admittedly, there is little evidence that extispicy relied on visionary skills in the haruspex but, it should be remembered, the craft was sacred to those contemporaries who wrote about it; the inner mysteries may have been a taboo subject for public discussion. Certainly the detailed mechanics of an entrail-reading (what each mark meant and how they were cross-referenced) have not found their way into the historical record.

Before we ridicule the apparently childish beliefs of our ancestors, it is worth remembering that until the discoveries of Sir Isaac Newton, the idea that one could deduce some of the inner workings of the universe by mathematics was at best laughed at and at worst, punishable as heresy. Even in the twentieth century, physicists like Albert Einstein and Niels Bohr found themselves attacked by the more conservative in the scientific community. It should also be remembered that in many ways, we are still as ignorant as to the nature of time as Cicero was in the first century BC.

A fault of modern, scientifically confident mankind is that we all too often decide that if we do not understand a phenomenon, it cannot have happened. However we may rationalize our ancestors' daily use of both oracles and extispicy, we cannot actually prove that such practices did not, in some strange way, predict future events as their practitioners fervently believed. At the very least, we should keep an open mind towards any available evidence of accurate prediction, even if, as with extispicy, we find the actual method deeply repugnant.

[9]Reading the future in the position of landforms.

Chapter 3

The Children of Yahweh

In 1881, a pamphlet was published in Germany with the title *A Word of Warning* (*Ein Wort der Mahnung*). It had no author's name on the title page, and it stated that a tremendous catastrophe was going to be unleashed on the Jews of Germany, and that the disaster would eventually reach as far as Austria. In short, and in retrospect, it seems to have predicted the Nazi Holocaust.

Many German Jews at the time would have seen the pamphlet's attitude as somewhat alarmist. Since about 1800, there had been a new attitude towards the Jews of Germany. Unlike the savage anti-Semitism of Russia and Spain, German Jews no longer felt themselves an oppressed minority, and many felt they were now part of the mainstream of European culture – an argument put forward by Moses Mendelssohn (the grandfather of the composer) in his influential philosophical works.

Germany, in the early 1800s, was a culturally and politically vibrant country of petty kingdoms pulling themselves towards unified nationhood. The Christian Germans generally accepted the Jews' part in this new nation – especially for their artistic and financial gifts. Then, in the late 1870s, a new anti-Semitic movement appeared, inspired by the writings of a fanatic named Adolph Stoecker. It broke like a wave over Germany – the earliest indication of the intolerant spirit that would bring Hitler to power.

At about that time, a Bavarian rabbi named Hile Wechsler began to have a series of dreams, which he believed foretold some great catastrophe for the Jews of Germany. Eventually he published

A Word of Warning, but anonymously, perhaps afraid that the anti-Semites would take their revenge on him or his family.

Wechsler was a highly orthodox rabbi who suffered, and eventually died, from tuberculosis. He spent his life as a schoolteacher and in studying the Torah. Born in 1843, he began teaching in Zell, in Bavaria, at a teachers' training college. However, by the age of 23, he was becoming increasingly tormented by his sexual desires, which focused on his first cousin, Clara Rosenbaum. He was far too shy to speak of this. Then disaster struck when his father died, and Wechsler had to leave home.

When he came back, he learned that his family had chosen a bride for him, and that it was his cousin Clara. Wechsler regarded this coincidence as a special mark of God's favour. He and Clara went on to have fourteen children, of whom seven died. His wife regarded him with such veneration that after his death at the age of 51, she always stood up when his name was mentioned.

A Word of Warning was prompted by a series of remarkable dreams, which Wechsler describes at length. It is clear that he felt that these dreams were messages from his unconscious mind.[1]

Wechsler believed, decades before the dream theories of Freud and Jung became famous, that some of his dreams were messages from the future: "It is clear evidence that in the dream state a higher power is at work, which, as in everything else, uses the natural equipment . . . for its own purposes."

It has been repeatedly observed that those who experience "Jungian" dreams are overwhelmed by a sense of their deep significance, as if receiving a "message from beyond".

A Word of Warning made very little impact during Wechsler's lifetime, and was soon forgotten. It was only after the downfall of Hitler and the Nazis that it was rediscovered and republished in Israel. (Wechsler had urged the Jews to go to the Middle East to escape the catastrophe.)

Wechsler has been discussed at length in a book called *The Reluctant Prophet* by James Kirsch, a Jungian psychiatrist, who clearly regards Wechsler as a genuine prophet whose dreams fore

---

[1]The psychiatrist Carl Jung argued that the "collective unconscious" – the point at which he believed all human minds are telepathically interconnected – lies outside space and time, and can communicate precognitive predictions through our dreams. Jung himself claimed to have had a series of dreams that showed him future events.

told the future. Kirsch also believes that Wechsler defined the idea of synchronicity[2] before Jung did. Kirsch says:

> Wechsler certainly proves to our satisfaction that if a great number of odd and seemingly random phenomena occur, they do belong together. They are not random occurrences, but reveal a meaningful and coherent pattern.

What happens in precognitive prophecy, Kirsch believes, is that the conscious mind is invaded by the unconscious. It happened, he argues, to Herman Melville and Frederick Nietzsche, and led to the publication of the dream-like, allegorical *Moby Dick* and the world-shaking philosophical novel, *Thus Spake Zarathustra*.

This outpouring of the unconscious in *Thus Spake Zarathustra*, Kirsch suggests, had a profound effect on Germany. It became one of the favourite books of the soldiers in the trenches of World War I, and prepared the way for Adolf Hitler's political subversion and corruption of Nietzsche's philosophy. (Nietzsche, it should be remembered, was not particularly anti-Semitic – indeed, he broke off his close friendship with Richard Wagner in protest at the composer's rabid Jew-hating.)

This, in Kirsch's view, is the meaning of prophecy: it is a great explosion from the unconscious, which releases terrifying energies into the world. In one of his dreams, Wechsler was told that he would be sent into the world like the Prophet Elijah. Kirsch has no doubt that this is literally true.

The case of Rabbi Wechsler makes an important prelude to the study of biblical prophecy, for it underlines that men like Isaiah, Jeremiah and John the Baptist did not regard themselves as gloomy predictors of disaster, but as visionaries who could foresee future events. Yet, as we shall see, such prophets often considered their ability to foretell the future quite secondary to their knowledge of the will of God.

There was a logical contradiction at the heart of pre-monotheistic prophetic belief. On the one hand, all the ancient Mediterranean peoples shared the belief that man's fate was preordained. For example, much of Classical Age Greek literature

[2]A word coined by Jung to describe any series of amazing yet significant coincidences.

centred on the inescapability of *Nemesis*: the final and fatal end that, try as they might, the heroes of the stories could never escape.[3]

On the other hand, these same peoples all sought knowledge of the future in the belief that it could somehow help them. From the man who asked the priestesses of Dodona where he had mislaid his blankets and cushions to the desperate Athenians at Delphi seeking to escape destruction at the hands of Xerxes' Persian horde, all hoped to somehow affect future events through the insight of pre-knowledge.

But how could they believe in predetermined fate *and* in the possibility of manipulating the future? The key to the riddle is the multiplicity of gods in the ancient religions. Where one god might have decided your fate one way, another might be called upon to intervene on your behalf – although such divine contests were rarely believed to entirely favour the mortals involved. Odysseus – hero of the Homeric epic *The Odyssey* – is described as spending nine years trying to make a sea voyage that shouldn't have taken him nine weeks, largely because two gods were wrangling over his fate.

This universal belief in deities playing games with human fates extended all the way up to the destiny of nations. The victory of, say, the Greeks over the Persians or the Romans over the Carthaginians, would have been at least partially ascribed – by the defeated and the victors alike – to one pantheon of national gods being stronger than the other.

But even while Homer was writing *The Odyssey*, things were beginning to change. For according to a Semitic people called the *Habiru* (or Hebrews), there was only one god – and He was God with a capital G. To the Hebrews, God was all-powerful and all-knowing. He had made the world, and all other gods were demonic impostors or non-existent bogeymen. "The one true God" was so

[3]The belief in immutable fate seems to have existed from at least the dawn of Indo–European civilization. It is, for example, a key theme in *The Epic of Gilgamesh*, a text that is at least 3,000 years old. It describes the doomed quest for immortality by a Sumerian king who is said to have ruled sometime in the third millennium BC. The earliest date accepted by mainstream academics for the dawn of civilization – that of the Sumerians in what is now Iraq – is around 4,000 BC, although there is now growing evidence that at least one comparatively advanced civilization predated the Sumerians (see chapter 18).

powerful that his followers dared not even speak His name – *Yahweh*[4] meaning "I Am" – and, from the third century BC onward, used code-names like *Adonai, Elohim* or *Jehovah* when praying aloud.

Of course with hindsight it is easy to see the birth of monotheism as an epoch-making event. But for over a thousand years, the Israelites' seemingly self-important claims to worship the "only true God" and to be His "Chosen People" were treated with little better than contempt or mirth by those polytheistic peoples they encountered. For example, the Alexandrian Greeks often got into religiously inspired street fights with the city's Jewish community, while the conquering Roman Empire seem to have regarded the Israelites as irritatingly fanatical eccentrics. But from the point of view of our study of human precognition, the growth and eventual predominance of monotheism has had a profound affect on Western civilization's attitude to its prophets.

Yahweh, being all-knowing, knew the fate of all things, just like the gods of other religions; but being also all-powerful, His decisions could not be affected by any force other than, perhaps, His own rage or compassion.

Followers of a pantheon of gods could always hope that, between the squabbling of their deities, humans might use prayers or actions (inspired by omens and oracles) to nudge the arm of fate, so to speak. Monotheists had no such hope. They had to expect that what their God had fated for them would happen. All that remained was for a chosen "Prophet of God" to tell the people just what God had ordained.

The pantheistic oracle told their questioners what was likely to happen and, as with the Athenians facing the Persian army of Xerxes, an initially negative prophecy might be wangled into a positive prediction. The monotheistic prophet simply told his listeners what God willed – QED Fate, like God, was now to be spelt with a capital letter.

The origin of the Hebrews is hard to pin down, and the same is true of monotheism. Historians think they are probably the Habiru referred to in an Egyptian papyrus of about 1207 BC. The origin of their monotheism is equally obscure – all we can say with certainty is that it took a very long time to develop.

[4]In some translations spelt, *Jahweh*, the name apparently derived from the same source as the Roman god *Jove*, or Jupiter.

The essentials of the Jewish faith are stated in the Pentateuch, the first five books of the Old Testament. This describes the creation of the universe, the expulsion of the first humans, Adam and Eve, from the Garden of Eden, the first murder (of Abel by his brother Cain), the Great Flood (sent to punish humankind) and the life of Abraham, the first patriarch.

In nineteenth-century Germany, a scholar named David Strauss caused a storm with his book *The Life of Jesus Critically Examined* (1835), in which he said that the Gospels were merely "historical myths", which should not be accepted as factually true. The ensuing furore was immense, and cost Strauss a professorship he had just been offered. Nevertheless, his work formed the foundation of a new school of theology that treated the Bible as a work of fiction.

Naturally, both the Jews and the Christians were outraged at this attempt to deprive them of their faith, for as far as they were concerned, every word of the Bible was true. But the new science of archaeology, developed in the previous century by a scholar named Winckelmann, offered hope of refuting the "sceptics", and when, in 1842, an Englishman named Henry Layard began to excavate a mound at a place called Calah, in Mesopotamia (later Iraq), and uncovered the library of the Assyrian king Assurbanipal, that hope began to turn into certainty.

These Assyrians were the same warriors who had "come down like a wolf on the fold" in the second Book of Kings (2 Kings: chapter 18). Soon there were many such confirmations, proving that at least large sections of the Bible were history, not just myth.

One of the most remarkable discoveries was made at Dibon, in Jordan, where Arabs found a large stele inscribed in an unknown language. A clergyman named Friedrich August Klein went to look at the stone and was immensely excited. He took a rubbing of the inscription and tried to buy the stone from the Arabs. They were so suspicious at the sum he offered, which seemed out of all proportion for a mere stone, that they decided that he must be trying to cheat them, and that the stele must be full of gold. So they heated it on a large fire, then poured cold water on it. The stone split into many pieces, leaving the Arabs in no doubt that it contained no gold.

Fortunately, Klein still had the rubbing, and the text could be reconstructed. It proved to be in a language called *Moabite*, from a kingdom situated on the east side of the Dead Sea. It was an inscription by a Moabite king named Mesha, which described a victory over the Israelites some time before 850 BC. The Bible tells the story of the same conflict. Again, the evidence of archaeology supported biblical history. And so, little by little, archaeology was able to confirm some of the major events of the Bible, and the history of the people called the Hebrews.

They were founded, according to their own legend, by a nomadic trader called Abraham, who claimed to be a direct descendant of Shem, the son of Noah, the patriarch who had saved his family (and thus mankind) from the Great Flood. Abraham, the Bible says, was a native of the city of Ur (modern-day Tell al-muqayyar on the Euphrates River) in Sumeria – the earliest known civilization – and was probably born around 1800 BC.

It is important for the modern reader to realize that the Middle East in 2000 BC – and even 2,000 years later in the days of Jesus – was not the rocky, brown-coloured wilderness that now extends along the southern coast of the Mediterranean, but a lush, green land with abundant rainfall. (Even the Great Pyramid was originally surrounded by a green plain.) Millennia of over-farming are largely responsible for the semi-desert, of which the modern Middle East now largely consists.

Abraham saw his wealth increasing as his family grew, and he needed all his many grandchildren to tend huge flocks of sheep. Like all other people on the face of the Earth, the people of Ur worshipped many gods. It would not have been unusual for a man like Abraham to select one of these for special devotion. Yet Abraham went further than that. He decided that his own preferred God, Yahweh was the only god. And since Abraham regarded his own family as the special favourite of Yahweh, he also insisted that his increasing progeny should not marry outside the tribe. So his son Isaac, and Isaac's son Jacob, became the founders of a new race and a new religion. Jacob's life was so hard that he became known as *Israel*, meaning the "struggler with God".

Abraham was arguably the first prophet in the biblical sense. God spoke directly to Abraham, without the intercession of signs or portents, telling him to take himself and his family to the land of Canaan (modern-day Palestine/Israel). After some violent difficulties settling into the new country (including the total annihilation of the towns of Sodom and Gomorrah), God promised Abraham and his family that Canaan would be theirs in perpetuity:

Genesis 13:14
And the Lord said . . . lift up now thine eyes, and look from the place where thou art northward, and southward, and eastward, and westward:

13:15 For all the land which thou seest, to thee will I give it, and to thy seed forever.

13:16 And I will make thy seed as the dust of the Earth: so that if a man can number the dust of the Earth, then shall thy seed also be numbered.

Given the curvature of the Earth's surface, it is unlikely that even if Abraham was standing on a high place on a clear day, he could have seen much more than a few miles in each direction, but the Israelites, as they were named by Abraham's grandson Jacob, took God to mean that the whole of the land of Canaan – what European Christians were to call the Holy Land – was theirs forever. Canaan, for the children of Abraham, became the "Promised Land".

As we shall see, this promise was to form the backbone of Judaic prophecy in the centuries to come, but it was the prediction that the descendants of Abraham would one day be as numerous as the grains of dust on the Earth that was to lead to a more radical line of prophecy.

What initially seems a simple promise that the children of Abraham would prosper and multiply also carried a subtle sub-connotation: logically, any tribe that numbered as many as "the dust of the Earth", would have the sort of manpower that could conquer the world. So it is arguably in Genesis, chapter 13, verse 16, that we see the first seeds of the prophecy of the *Messiah* – for the later Israelites and some modern day Orthodox Jews, a ruler predicted to lead the children of Israel to defeat their enemies and rule as foremost of all the peoples of the Earth.

Abraham's great-grandson, Joseph, was a prophet in the old-fashioned, oracular sense of the word. Exiled to Egypt by a family feud (his brothers sold him into slavery), he made a prediction of future famine, based on his interpretation of a series of dreams that had been puzzling the Pharaoh. When he was proved correct, Joseph was made a favourite of the court, but humbly refused any direct credit, insisting his inspiration came from his God. This is not to say that, like later Jewish prophets, he condemned the use of magical prediction – indeed, in Genesis chapter 44, verse 15, Joseph virtually brags about his skill at divination.

As meticulous as Genesis is on matters of lineage, it does not give any indication as to when the Israelites, and their monotheistic religion, came into existence. Exodus however, the next book of the Pentateuch, gives us more solid clues. Its events, tied to modern archaeological discoveries in northern Egypt, indicate that it is describing happenings from around the beginning of the twelfth century BC.

The beginning of Exodus portrays the Israelites, still just a single family clan rather than a whole tribe, moving to live in Egypt – apparently forgetting their birthright to the land of Canaan, due to the arrival of the famine predicted by Joseph.

Egypt was the greatest power in the Mediterranean at that time, and had been in existence since before 3000 BC. The Bible describes the descendants of Abraham living as humble traders who prospered and greatly increased in number until the jealous Egyptian pharaoh decided to enslave them all. Rediscovered Ancient Egyptian histories, however, seem to tell a different story . . .

Around 1750 BC, a people called the *Hyksos* invaded the Middle East from somewhere in Asia. Around 1630 BC, they invaded Egypt, seized power and ruled for more than a century. Known as "the Shepherd Kings", their style was distinctly rougher than that of the sophisticated Egyptians and, after 108 years, the Egyptians rebelled and drove them out.

Before their conquest by the Hyksos, the Egyptians had been in decline for centuries, but driving out the invaders seems to have revitalized them – or perhaps it was simply that living as a conquered people made them miserable enough to fight back. At all events, the expulsion of the Hyksos around 1520 BC launched the greatest phase in Egyptian history, the New Kingdom, which saw the building of the great temples.

It is possible that the Israelite clan followed the Hyksos armies as Middle-Eastern "carpetbaggers" – abandoning the Promised Land to loot and later stay on in the defeated Egypt. Certainly the 400-odd years between the invasion of Egypt and the events of Exodus would give the necessary time for a family clan to grow into a large tribe, just as the Bible describes.

The upshot after the defeat of the Shepherd Kings was that the descendants of Abraham were enslaved and forced to work in the fields and in the Egyptian temple building. This went on for more than two centuries.

The Book of Exodus describes an angel, in the form of a burning bush, inspiring an Egyptian court favourite called Moses – an Israelite foundling adopted by the Pharaoh's daughter – to free his people. If biblical scholars' present dating of the Pentateuch is correct, the pharaoh in power at that time would have been the arrogant and vainglorious Ramses II – the "Ozymandias, King of Kings" of the Shelley poem – who ruled from 1279–1213 BC. Not surprisingly for a pharaoh this egotistical, he resisted all reasonable attempts to obtain freedom for the Israelites, so Moses, in the name of God, smote the Egyptians with ten plagues.

Here we see a new element being added to the older, polytheistic concept of the prophet: that is, the monotheistic prophet as instigator of world-shattering events rather than simply their predictor. The Oracle of Delphi might curse a supplicant, but she would do so only from her knowledge of probable future events. She was, in effect, doing no more than any of us would be doing when we tell a reckless driver they're bound to have a crash one day. In wielding the direct power of his God, Moses was acting as the avatar (the living embodiment) of Yahweh. Old Testament prophets, as we will see, occasionally smote others with the power of Yahweh, but never to the extent Moses is described as doing in calling down the ten plagues of Egypt.

In recent years, a number of theories have arisen to offer natural explanations for the catastrophic events described in Exodus. If we are to take the series of "plagues" described in the Bible as historically accurate, it is clear that Moses warned the Pharaoh before each happened. Was the prophet actually wielding the power of the "one true God", or was he precognitively predicting a series of natural catastrophes, with the aim of using his fore-knowledge as a political lever to free his people?

The first plague called down on the Egyptians turned the River Nile to "blood". It is probably safe to discount the literal interpretation of this biblical description, as a rotting, 4,000-mile-long black pudding (as a river of blood would quickly become) would have made all the Nile Valley uninhabitable.

Some scholars have suggested that particularly heavy rains in Ethiopia might have washed quantities of red topsoil into the Blue Nile (one of the two rivers that feed the Greater Nile), thus giving the river the appearance of blood. However, it is highly unlikely that enough of this red detritus could have been washed into the Nile to turn it scarlet for its whole length, or to kill all the Nile fish, as Exodus describes.

Another possible, non-miraculous, explanation for the first plague of Egypt might have been what oceanographers call a "red tide". This happens when a red-coloured, waterborne algae called *dinoflagellate* "blooms", vastly increasing its population to the extent that the seawater containing it turns scarlet. Dr John S. Marr, chief epidemiologist for the New York City Health Department, has pointed out that similar blooms are also possible, although very rare, in inland waterways during periods of very hot weather.

Marr suggests that an algae called *physteria* – that attacked waterways in the Carolinas in 1987 – is a likely cause of the Nile turning to "blood". A physteria bloom not only turns water scarlet, but also produces toxic chemicals capable of slowly dissolving fish and other water animals while they are still alive. This would fit with the description in Exodus of all the Nile fish dying in the gory river.

The algal bloom theory might also explain the second, third and fourth punishments that Yahweh, through Moses, inflicted on the recalcitrant Egyptians, the first being a plague of frogs.

A multitude of amphibians – that normally lived in and on the edges of the Nile – might have clambered out of the river during a physteria bloom to escape the lethal chemicals. The unfortunate frogs, trapped between the poisonous river and the surrounding desert (together with its unfriendly human population), would have died out en masse within a few days, leaving a sizable gap in the food chain. The result might have been the plagues of lice and flies that the Bible describes. Freed from a large proportion of their usual predators, these unpleasant pests would have bred with their proverbial vigour.

The fifth plague was the death of the Egyptians' cattle and horses. Given the previous plagues of lice and flies, an outbreak of diseases affecting local livestock is hardly surprising. Dr Andrew Spielman from the Harvard School of Public Health has suggested that a swarm of the African midge called *coolacoidees* might have spread both African horse sickness and the cattle disease known as blue tongue. Both are fatal to infected animals.

Similarly, the plague of boils among the Egyptians might have been caused by the plague of flies. There is a disease called *glanders*, spread by the African stable fly, that would fit the biblical description. The stable fly is, according to Dr Spielman, one of the species of fly likely to have rocketed in population following the death of the Nile amphibian and fish population.

Plague number seven was a storm of hail and fire. Hail storms are obviously rare in Egypt, but they are not unknown. A destructive local hailstorm, possibly causing some house fires, is not beyond the realms of possibility, and would not, necessarily, have needed the intervention of Yahweh to have taken place.

Plague eight was locusts. Unlike hail, swarms of locusts are hardly uncommon in North Africa, especially in the sort of hot weather that might also have caused a red tide of physteria algae in the Nile.

Plague nine was a universal darkness lasting three days. It has been suggested that this might have been a tremendous desert sandstorm – known in Egypt today as a *khamsin*. Again, this is not an altogether unheard-of event in the desert-bounded Nile Valley.

The last plague was the death of all the first-born Egyptian children. This certainly seems miraculous, but even this has been theoretically explained in terms of natural events.

During the plague of locusts, the Egyptians might have buried their stored wheat to save it from the insects. Dr Edwardo Montagnia of the Atlanta Center for Disease Control has suggested that a mould called *Stachybotrys atra* might have grown on the Egyptians' buried grain stocks. This mould produces mycotoxins on the surface of its spores and, if eaten in sufficient quantities, causes a fatal haemorrhaging in the lungs.

The reason that the first-born Egyptians were particularly affected would have been because first-born children were especially valued in Ancient Egyptian society. They were given a bigger helping of food at meal times and, thus, a bigger helping of the mycotoxin poison. The Israelites, as slaves, would not have been given enough food to poison themselves, and thus escaped.

Of course, it is a scientific truism that one cannot explain one inexplicable event by citing another inexplicable event, and it hardly matters (to the historian) whether Moses acted as the avatar of Yahweh, was simply His spokesman, or was using powers of precognition to bamboozle and terrorize the Egyptians into submission; the fact is that it worked. The Israelites were freed, escaping not through the Red Sea, as the Bible is traditionally mistranslated, but over the *Yam Suph* or Sea of Reeds between the Nile Delta and the Sinai Desert. Furthermore, Moses had set a religious precedent for a prophet to be more than just the mouthpiece of a god. Henceforward, the western concept of the prophet would be increasingly interconnected with miracle-working.

However – again leaving the theological debate to others – we are still no closer to an explanation as to why the Israelites took up monotheism. Interestingly, Sigmund Freud – the "Father of Psychoanalysis" and himself a Jew – developed an intriguing theory in his 1939 essay *Moses and Monotheism*. Its main argument rests on the existence of a previous, if short-lived, monotheistic religion founded in Ancient Egypt.

Akhenaton (sometimes called Ikhnaton) was the eighteenth Pharaoh of Egypt and a religious revolutionary. Coming to the throne in 1375 BC under the more traditional moniker of Amenhotep IV, he changed his name, built a new capital city and forcibly changed the ancient polytheistic religion of the Egyptians to a monotheistic creed that worshipped Aton – the ancient name for the Sun before it was associated with the god Ra.

Akhenaton was a religious leader well ahead of his time. The belief he espoused did not insist on the worship of erratic and tyrannical deities, but instead gloried in the love and warmth that Aton – the Sun – bestowed on the Earth. Even Akhenaton's symbol for the sun god – a circle set over rays of light, each ray ending in a hand, open with palm upwards – clearly depicted a kind and giving relationship between the god and men. To Akhenaton, this rapport was also to be mirrored in the relationship between the Pharaoh and his people, and he has been described not only as a benign autocrat, but also as the first of the charismatic, individualist leaders found in recorded history.

Unfortunately, the new and humane religion of Aton lasted no longer than Akhenaton's reign – seventeen years. It is a strange historical fact that new religions that are introduced by those in power are much less likely to succeed than those that spring from "voices in the wilderness". The natural seedbed for a new faith seems to be among the streets and fields of a civilization, not in its palaces.

A revolution, led by disenfranchized priests of the old religion and enthusiastically backed by the common people, shook Egypt. Akhenaton was forced to make his son-in-law his co-regent to try to stabilize the country, but, as so often happens when a supposedly all-powerful leader admits weakness, Akhenaton died very soon afterwards; probably murdered.

In his book *Moses and Monotheism*, Freud suggests that the date of the fall of Akhenaton and the monotheistic religion of Aton – around 1358 BC – and the first appearance of the (also monotheistic) Israelites less than a hundred years later, must be more than a coincidence.

Freud theorizes that Moses was not an Israelite, but an Egyptian aristocrat. An adopted slave – however powerful his foster mother – would have been unlikely to get away with overtly threatening the Pharaoh, regarded as a living god, as Exodus describes Moses doing again and again.

Freud also points out that the name Moses is Egyptian. *Mose* meaning "son of" – as in *Amen-Mose*, meaning "Son of Amen". The name Moses, he suggests, is part of the patronymic of a high-born Egyptian, foreshortened by later generations of Israelites to disguise the fact that their greatest prophet was not a Hebrew.

Freud goes on to suggest that the fallen monotheistic religion of Atonism might well have survived in Egyptian court circles – just as Catholicism was maintained in secret among English aristocrats after the Reformation. Emphasizing, as Atonism did, a kindly and loving god who wished his pharaohs to act likewise, the banned religion might also have spread among the downtrodden Israelite slave class – as Christianity did among the slaves and commoners of the Roman Empire. In that case, asks Freud, how do we explain the brutal and vengeful aspect of Old Testament Judaism – Jehovah as the smiter of cities, the harsh lawgiver and the slayer of first-born children?

Freud suggests that during their forty-year period of wandering in the wilderness, the Aton-worshipping Israelites absorbed other Semitic tribes, together with their more primitive religious beliefs. Although the Sun-worshipping aspect of the Israelite religion was lost, the circumcision (an ancient Egyptian practice) and the monotheism survived, but not in a form that Akhenaton, or even Moses the Egyptian aristocrat, would have countenanced.

Freud (perhaps unsurprisingly) suggests that Moses, the religious father figure, was dead – probably murdered by his own people/ children – by the time the nurturing Aton was transformed in the Israelite mind into the terrifying Yahweh. A living religious leader would not have allowed such a serious deterioration of his faith to occur before his very eyes, but a leaderless horde of illiterate ex-slaves might have had little choice in the matter. They were busy conquering a whole nation and needed a war god, not a celestial social worker.

Freud points to the much later splitting of the nation of Greater Israel into the sub-kingdoms of Judah and Lesser Israel (as will be described in the next chapter) as evidence of a political split, engendered by the only partially successful bonding of mutually incompatible religions under one name: the gentle Atonism with the fear-engendering Yahwehism.

He further suggests that this religious fault line has engendered a cultural psychosis in all Judaism – the reason for both Zionist pugnaciousness and what Freud identified as the Jewish tendency towards unanchored, free-ranging guilt. In effect, he is suggesting that his whole race is in a state of intellectual and emotional denial over what he defines as their contradictory religion.

He suggests that only a return to Judaism/Atonism's earlier, less severe form, dropping much of the Old Testament's "eye for an eye" brutality, could salve the Jewish mindset. Perhaps contro-versially, Freud suggests that evidence of this healing process can be seen in the founding and eventual breaking away of Christianity from Judaism: in effect, Freud is saying that Jesus of Nazareth was an unconscious Atonite.

When Freud was writing in the 1930s, there was apparently no proof that Akhenaton's Atonism and Israelite Judaism were in any way linked. Freud was simply making an intuitive connection between two very similar types of faith that sprang up near to each other during the same period. He was clearly unaware, therefore, of *The Wisdom of Amenemope* – translated and published only in 1923 – that effectively confirmed the basis of his theory.

Amenemope (not to be confused with the pharaoh of the same name) was said to have been an Ancient Egyptian sage whose surviving book of good advice closely resembles what we know of the religion of Akhenaton – indeed, some researchers believe Amenemope and Akhenaton were one and the same author.

Amenemope's sayings are now considered one of the most important finds in Egyptology, simply because they are identical to chapters 15, 17 and 20, chapter 22, verse 17 and chapter 24, verse 22 of the Hebrew *Book of Proverbs* (the twentieth book of the Old Testament). The first psalm of the *Book of Psalms* (the nineteenth book of the Old Testament) is also an Amenemope saying (just as the Ten Commandments were originally from the Egyptian *Book of the Dead*). Amenemope's works existed hundreds of years before Proverbs and the Psalms were written, making it almost certain that the Egyptians influenced the Israelites, and not vice versa.

Whether we accept Freud's theory of Israelite Atonism we have now come to the first archaeological confirmation of the existence of the early Israelites. Evidence found in Palestine points to a brutal invasion taking place in the decades around 1250 BC. Town after town was sacked and burned – just as described in Exodus – and the invaders settled the land that God had promised their ancestor in perpetuity.

Here we come to another theory that may make uncomfortable reading for those married to the more conventional history of Judaism. It is traditionally believed that Moses himself wrote the Pentateuch – the first five books of the Old Testament: Genesis, Exodus, Judges, Leviticus and Numbers. However, since certain events take place in these books that occurred *after* the death of Moses, it is more likely that they were compiled by a number of scholars a number of decades after the Israelite conquest of Canaan.

In commenting on this compilation of the Pentateuch, the highly respected, eleventh-century, French–Jewish scholar, Rabbi Shlomo Yitzhaqi (known as Rashi) made the astonishing claim that the Book of Genesis was actually written to justify the invasion of Canaan. Certainly one might suspect that the frequent divine justifications for the savageries described in Exodus (the ruthless killing of all men of military age and the enslavement of the rest of the hapless Canaanites) might have been the Israelite equivalent of saying: "God told me to do it". But to say that Genesis and, most notably, the divine promises made to Abraham were an exercise in bogus national self-justification is a shattering assertion.

The logical extrapolation of Rashi's statement is that the Israelite people were actually ruthless invaders who, in a fit of guilt after settling down to enjoy their stolen country, re-engineered their own religion to justify their actions. The slaughter and enslavement of the Canaanites was not, in these terms, a reacquisition of a divinely granted birthright, but a callous and hypocritical exercise in what would now be called ethnic cleansing or even genocide. In terms of sinister misinformation, this makes both the Nazi concept of the "Big Lie" and Orwell's "Doublethink" seem downright pedestrian.

Rashi himself was obviously rather nervous of his explosive contention, later going out of his way "to tell my people that they can answer those who claim that the Jews stole the land from its original inhabitants. The reply should be: God made it and gave it to them but then took it and gave it to us. As he made it and it is his, he can give it to whoever he chooses." A lame rationalization of an act of genocide, especially from a Jew who had lived through the anti-Semitic pogroms that broke out in France during the First Crusade.

If Rashi was correct about the invention – rather than the compilation – of the Book of Genesis (and, of course, there is no evidence that he was doing anything more than speculating on the basis of his biblical expertise), it would make the entire concept of the Israelite right to the land of Canaan, plus their position as God's "Chosen People" distinctly questionable. Moreover, it would undermine the teachings of centuries of Jewish prophets whose basic tenets were Yahweh's promises to the Jews, and how these could be made to come to fruition in the future.

When the Israelites invaded the land of Canaan around 1250 BC, they encountered a religion whose frank sexuality appalled their leaders. The temples of the imported Phoenician god Baal and the goddess Astarte were virtually brothels, as well they might have been, since Baal and Astarte were the god and goddess of a fertility cult.

Canaanite and Phoenician virgins had to endure ritual defloration by a stranger before marriage and payment for that sex went into the temple treasury. Nor was this sort of religious harlotry a short-lived fad in the Middle East. The ancient Babylonians followed a similar practice and the historian Herodotus, who lived 484–420 BC, described witnessing a Nasamonian wedding at which the bride was expected to have sex with each of the male guests in turn.

In *The Bible as History,* Werner Keller describes the impact of this sex cult of sensuality on the Hebrews:

What temptation for a simple shepherd folk, what perilous enticement. More than once the Baal religions got a firm foothold and penetrated right into the temple of Yahweh, into the Holy of Holies . . .
Without its stern moral law, without its faith in one God, without the commanding figures of the prophets, Israel would never have been able to survive this struggle with the Baals, with the brothel religions of the fertility goddesses . . .

And this, Keller explains, is why the Hebrew prophets habitually denounced "the abomination of the heathens" over the centuries. When Isaiah denounced Jerusalem as having become "a harlot", he did not mean that the people had slackened their morality and become licentious, he meant they had gone back to the religion of Baal and Astarte.

It is almost impossible for us to grasp what this meant to an Israelite of that period. Their religion was strict and puritanical, due probably to their forty years of enforced chastity in the wilderness – nomadic peoples often have stricter sex taboos than settled peoples, simply because food is always short for wanderers and excess breeding leads inevitably to starvation.

Now the Israelites found themselves in a country where a virgin was expected to offer herself to a stranger before she married, and where the priests at the temple doubled as pimps. The culture shock must have been enormous – rather like a devout Mormon finding himself in the Paris of the 1890s watching a can-can.

The denunciations of the prophets make it clear that many Israelites, settling into their newly-conquered country, were not averse to exchanging the Mosaic Law for something less rigid. Their position could be compared to that of many pious New Yorkers in the 1850s, when a clergyman named John Humphrey Noyes announced that Judgment Day had taken place in heaven in AD 70, and that since that date, adultery was no longer a sin.

Noyes invited his followers to come and live in a community where each man was every woman's husband and vice versa. Among those who founded the Oneida Community were lawyers, doctors, even clergymen. Its success was enormous, both in a religious and commercial sense. It was not until the 1880s that they abandoned their "sexual communism" and returned to a more conventional way of life.

We cannot fully understand the Israelite prophets without understanding the shock induced by the "sexual communism" of the Canaanites. The religion of Yahweh had almost been undermined by the decadent faiths of Baal and Astarte, and thenceforth the prophets saw their main task as the prevention of any more religious and social backsliding.

Chapter 4

The Prophets of Yahweh

The actual term "prophet" is rarely used in the earlier texts of the Old Testament. In the last chapter, I described Joseph as a prophet because he made an accurate prediction about a time of famine, but the actual Pentateuch reserves the title for Moses alone. This again is evidence of the changing attitude taking place among the Israelites. A mere soothsayer like Joseph – however divinely inspired – does not deserve prophetic status. Only those who speak with the direct authority of Yahweh – like Moses – could be termed Prophet of the Lord.

This is not to say that the Israelites had no use for precognitive oracles. In the Book of Numbers, Moses calls together seventy tribal elders and the "Spirit of the Lord" rests upon them and they "prophesied, and did not cease" (Numbers: ch11, v25). Although the Bible does not give details of these prophecies, Moses' attitude to divine precognition is revealed by the following incident. When it was reported to him that two men, who were not of the chosen seventy elders, had been rebuked for giving unofficial prophecies, Moses replied angrily that he did not agree. If he had his way, he said, all the Israelites would have the gift of prophecy: "Would that all God's people were prophets."

Following the conquest of Canaan, the Israelites went through a period of anarchy, with only a loose confederation of tribal "judges" maintaining anything like centralized control. Then the Israelite fortunes of war underwent a change for the worse when they encountered the coastal people called the Philistines. In our time, a "philistine" has come to mean a person without culture, but in fact the Philistines possessed a high degree of culture and invented the basis of the modern European alphabet.[1]

The Philistines continually beat the Israelites in battle – partly because the people of Israel were effectively leaderless, but also because the Laws of Yahweh (handed down by Moses) strictly prohibited any physical activity on a Saturday, the Sabbath, including fighting. The Philistines suffered neither of these handicaps.

Israelite calls for political unity under a single king led to the brief career of the next Prophet of Yahweh, a priest called Samuel. Speaking, like Moses before him, with the direct authority of Yahweh, Samuel told the Israelites that God warned them they would regret it, but if they were fixed on the idea of a king, He wouldn't stand in the way.

This was an uncharacteristically conciliatory stance by God, but He was, of course, proved correct in the long run . . .

A leader appeared in the person of a farmer named Saul, who rallied the Israelites against the Philistines, fought a guerrilla war and was anointed by Samuel as the first king of Israel.

According to the opening books of the Bible (written about five centuries later), Yahweh (and his prophet Samuel) soon had reason to regret choosing Saul. He was a rough diamond, lacked the religious temperament and was prone to fits of violence. In these moods, he was soothed by a young flute player named David, a shepherd boy, whose popularity eventually made Saul jealous and hostile. David was forced to flee for his life.

However, Saul proved a reasonably effective war leader until he was forced into a final, hopeless battle against the Philistines on the slopes of Mount Gilboa. The king was clearly desperate, because he employed the Necromancer of Endor to raise the dead Prophet Samuel in the hope of a word of encouragement. None was forthcoming, however, and Saul and all his sons died in the battle.

Saul is generally considered a failure as an Israelite king, but this is more due to his being overshadowed by his next two successors than to any great fault of his own. Certainly he was more gifted with oracular prophecy than any of the later Israelite kings: once, on meeting a group of wandering *nabi* (oracles who,

[1]The Moabite Stone (see last chapter) was in the Philistine alphabet.

whirling-dervish-like, danced wildly until "the spirit of God came upon them"), Saul hauled off his regal vestments and joined them in dancing, rolling in the dust and crying out prophecies.

The next Israelite king was the ex-fugitive flute player, David. Since David was from Judea (in the northern part of Greater Israel), the Israelites now became known as the *Jews*. It was under David that the Philistines were eventually routed, and the twelve tribes of Israel unified into a single nation. David chose himself a new capital – Jerusalem – and there the Ark of the Covenant[2] was placed in sanctuary on a hill.

During almost forty years on the throne, David proved himself a remarkable general and diplomat. His empire stretched from the Sinai Peninsula almost as far as the River Euphrates.

When David's son Solomon took over the throne (his elder brother Absalom having been killed during an attempt to seize the crown before their father had actually died), he inherited a stable and peaceful empire. He built the Great Temple to house the Ark of the Covenant, instructed his scribes to start writing the chronicles of Israel, and introduced taxes (which his subjects deplored). He enjoyed luxury and had dozens of wives and concubines – not a thousand, as the chronicle claims, but at least eighty.

The most startling thing about Solomon, this most celebrated of Hebrew kings, was that as he grew older, he ceased to regard Yahweh as the only God, and allowed his foreign wives to convert him to the religion of Baal and Astarte. Even the Great Temple itself bore a strong resemblance in design to the temples of Baal. And Hiram of Tyre, the architect of the Temple, was a worshipper of Baal.

In *Outline of History*, H. G. Wells comments unkindly about Solomon:

> The Bible account of Solomon does, in fact, show us a king and a confused people, both superstitious and mentally unstable, in no way more religious than any other people of the surrounding world.

[2]The chest that contained the stone tablets on which Moses had writen the Ten Commandments of Yahweh. (Or the Ten Commandments taken from the *Egyptian Book of the Dead*, if you prefer.)

Nevertheless, this is probably more accurate than the usual view of Solomon as the wisest of men, and it goes a long way to explaining what happened during the next few centuries, and why the prophets spent all their time trying to prevent Israel's plunge into disaster.

Taken in historical terms, it has to be recognized that the biblical descriptions of "Solomon in all his glory" were blatant exaggerations. Solomon was not an emperor or a pharaoh, merely the king of a fairly small and backward nation. His Temple was not some giant building, like the Egyptian temple at Karnak, it was about the size of the average church. In fact, we know it was the size of Rosslyn Chapel, near Edinburgh, for Rosslyn was intended to be a copy of Solomon's Temple.

Solomon's Palace, on the other hand, was reasonably impressive, built with blocks of stone fifteen feet long. Solomon typically spent more on his own comfort than on his God. In his attempts to fill the capacious palace treasury, Solomon almost bankrupted his people with excessive taxation – and all to no purpose, since a few years after his death, in 922 BC, Jerusalem was captured by Sheshonk, Pharaoh of Egypt, who seized all the gold Solomon had accumulated. So Israel was back to square one.

In fact, it was rather worse than square one, for the Israel of Saul and David had been an agricultural economy, and farmers are rarely so badly off that they risk starvation. But Solomon's building projects had turned many farm labourers into building labourers, and when the building came to an end, they became the urban poor. Many of the later prophets – Nahum, Elijah, Amos and Hosea, for example – were also social agitators, providing a voice for the new "proletariat".

The next king, Rehoboam, was even more of a fool than his father Solomon. When his northern subjects (who happened to be the richest) begged him to lighten their tax burden, he told them that, on the contrary, he intended to increase it. Observing his father's self-indulgent extravagance had obviously given Rehoboam delusions of grandeur. These quickly collapsed, however, when one of his tax collectors was stoned to death. King Rehoboam had to flee back to Jerusalem, where he was dissuaded with some difficulty from going to war with his own northern subjects.

It was, in any case, too late; the northerners decided to secede, taking the name Israel with them (for ease of understanding we will refer to their country as Lesser Israel). So Rehoboam had to be content with the smaller remaining portion of the original Israel, which he grudgingly renamed Judah.

King Rehoboam, in all his stupidity and pig-headedness, quite fulfilled the Prophet Samuel's (and Yahweh's) warning that the Israelites would ultimately have cause to regret installing a monarchy.

In 720 BC, two centuries after the schism, the brutal Assyrian Empire conquered the northern state of Lesser Israel, dragging a large proportion of its inhabitants away into slavery. These people were never heard of again – and were ever afterwards referred to as "the Lost Tribes"[3] – but the Kingdom of Judah, and its interpretation of Israelite political and religious history, survived to produce the later books of the Old Testament.

Before this catastrophe, however, another notable Prophet of God appeared in lesser Israel. Elijah added a new concept to the idea of the monotheistic prophet: that of the rebel against ungodly authority.

At that time, 874–853 BC, King Ahab and his Phoenician-born queen, Jezebel, were trying to reintroduce the worship of Baal (originally a Phoenician god) to their subjects. Elijah prophesied a long drought as a punishment from Yahweh, and defeated Baal's priests in a miracle contest (kindling fire on an altar through the power of his God).

The furious Jezebel hounded Elijah into hiding, but there the "still small voice" of Yahweh comforted him, saying that the faithful of Lesser Israel would eventually win out. Returning from exile, the prophet confronted the king and queen, and publicly predicted disaster for both of them.

Shortly thereafter, Ahab was killed in battle against the Syrians; led to that end by the false prophecies given by his soothsayers,

[3]The Lost Tribes suffered their apparent disinheritance from the Promised Land because, Jewish tradition holds, they failed in their adherence to the laws of Yahweh. However, the promise to Abraham is said to be unbreakable so, after a period of suffering under the heels of the gentiles, the Lost Tribes are expected to return to their birthright of Israel. Where they went after their enslavement by the Assyrians can only be guessed. Theories put forward in recent centuries have identified the Lost Tribes as, among others, the Afghans, the Japanese, the Native Americans and the original inhabitants of the British Isles.

who were in turn deceived by a "lying spirit" sent by Yahweh. Jezebel and her son continued to rule for ten years, but were eventually ousted in a coup led by Elijah's disciple, Elisha. Jezebel, while jeering at the besieging rebels from a palace balcony, was pushed to her death by her own attendants. ·

The Prophet Elijah was not there to see Jezebel's literal downfall. He had been taken up to Heaven, still alive, in a "fiery chariot". Elisha, who finally rooted out all the Baal worshippers in Lesser Israel, predicted that Elijah would return one day – a prediction that was perhaps the template for the Christian prophecy of the Second Coming of Christ.

In the Prophet Elijah we see the old and new elements of the monotheistic prophet coalesce. He foretold future events, performed holy miracles, was spoken to directly by Yahweh, spoke with His authority and, finally, heroically stood up to an unjust ruler.

Another "rebel" prophet, Amos, who preached sometime before 760 BC, continued Elijah's tradition of denouncing tyranny, but added the unjust rich to the list of those that Yahweh condemned. This was an early indication of the doctrine of the pre-eminence of the poor and downtrodden in the eyes of God that Jesus of Nazareth would later preach so charismatically. On the other hand, it might also be pointed to as a possible throwback to Judaism's Atonistic roots.

Amos also railed against the extravagant religious rituals of the "children of Israel".[4] Such ceremonies, he said, blinded the worshippers to the truth of Yahweh. The simple rituals of their forefathers were better than any number of expensive burnt offerings, but even better yet was a dedication to harmony, justice and charity. Here Amos is adding yet another layer on to the concept of the monotheistic prophet: that of the living embodiment of the social conscience.

By the time Amos was preaching, however, more than half the Israelites had less than fifty years to worship in whatever way they chose, because the Assyrian king, Sennacherib, swept away the kingdom of Lesser Israel in 720 BC.

---

[4]Some scholars believe that Amos aimed God's diatribe only at the religiously wavering people of Lesser Israel, not Judah, but since he specifically names his audience as the "family brought up from Egypt" (Amos: ch3, v1), he was plainly laying a curse on both their houses.

The Prophet Isaiah had done his best to warn both Lesser Israel and his native Judah of the threat from the Assyrians, but met with frustrating indifference. His long-suffering cry of "How long, O Lord?" has rung down the ages as the exclamation of all those who seek to achieve something in the face of seemingly impossible odds.

King Sennacherib could have taken Jerusalem too, but left the city alone – after being paid a hefty bribe, mostly made up of precious metals looted from the Great Temple itself (2 Kings: ch18, v13–19).

The history given in the Bible says that shortly thereafter "the Lord sent an angel" who destroyed the "leaders and captains" of Sennacherib's army, resulting in a coup in which the defiling Assyrian king was himself killed (2 Chronicles: ch32, v21). However, the rediscovered Assyrian archives mention no such disaster, and Sennacherib is known to have been alive and healthy enough to be still pillaging half a century later in 689 BC.

The Prophet Isaiah was not as delighted as his Judean compatriots at their largely unearned escape from Assyrian conquest – he foresaw that it was only a respite, and that the surviving children of Israel would face invasion again before long.

Now on its own, Judah found itself surrounded by formidable predators – Babylonia, Assyria and Egypt (although the latter was becoming increasingly worn out and decadent). The priests of Judah decided that a return to the religion of their forefathers was indicated, and announced that they had found a document written by Moses and dictated by Yahweh. Everyone was deeply impressed and swore to abide by it, including King Josiah, who decided to make a start by opposing an Egyptian army that had asked to pass through his kingdom on its way to fight enemies to the north.

The result was that Josiah died at the Battle of Megiddo in 609 BC. After five years of holding Judah as a conquest of war, the Egyptians were then defeated at Carchemish by the Babylonian king, Nebuchadnezzar. He then placed what he thought was a puppet king on the throne of Judah. When the "puppet" rebelled, Nebuchadnezzar hastened back into Judah, captured Jerusalem, and dragged off the leading Jews as hostages against further rebellion, including the unfortunate Prophet Ezekiel.

Nebuchadnezzar placed yet another puppet, Zedekiah, on the Judah throne. Unfortunately, ignoring the advice of the Prophet Jeremiah, Zedekiah also rebelled. His patience tried beyond endurance, Nebuchadnezzar returned and burned Jerusalem to the ground, including the Great Temple, killed Zedekiah's sons in front of their father, whom he then blinded, and finally dragged off most of the urban population into captivity.

The Prophet Jeremiah had repeatedly warned of the threat from Babylon, but had not been taken seriously. Indeed, during the siege of Jerusalem, Jeremiah was imprisoned on suspicion of being a Babylonian sympathizer or agent, so accurate had his predictions been. The victorious Nebuchadnezzar freed him and offered to take him to Babylon as an honoured guest, but Jeremiah refused and travelled to Egypt, where he is later said to have died.

The name Jeremiah has become a synonym for gloomy prophecy, but his predictions were not entirely negative. After the Babylonian victory, he said, the Jewish people would be separated, as a farmer does when he separates the good figs from the bad, but after a period of seventy years of bondage, the Gentile peoples of the north (among whom, it is worth noting, he lists the Medes) would invade Babylon and free the children of Judah. Purified by their ordeal, the Jews would return to the Promised Land, where they would be met by the Lost Tribes who were kidnapped by the Assyrians. Then there would follow a golden age for the newly-reformed Israel.

Luckily the captivity of the Jewish upper classes in Babylon lasted only forty-eight years, not the seventy foretold by Jeremiah. In 539 BC, Cyrus the Great, ruler of the new empire of the Persians (that included at its heart the country of the Medes, as predicted by Jeremiah), captured Babylon itself and granted the Jews their freedom. However, it was at that point that the predictions of Jeremiah and Ezekiel began to fail.

Most of the Jews taken from Judah by the Babylonians had died during the decades of captivity, and many of their children had never even seen their nominal homeland and were Babylonians in all but name. Many, unsurprisingly, chose not to return. Those that did were too few in number to fully repopulate Jerusalem, even when combined with those rural Jews who had escaped the Babylonians in the first place. Needless to say the Lost Tribes, taken almost 200 years earlier by the Assyrians, also failed to return home.

In taking the city-dwellers and the Jewish upper classes, the Babylonians had stolen much of the intellectual zest of Judaic society. Now too few of those educated elite had returned, and the cultural vivacity of the rebuilt country – now called Judea – began to decline.

During their exile, the Jews had one basic preoccupation: the coming of the Messiah (*mashiakh*), meaning "the Anointed One", who would lead them out of exile, establish their nation and bring universal peace. On their return from Babylon, a man named Zerubbabel became governor (under the Persians, of course), and, urged on by the prophets Haggai and Zechariah, proceeded to rebuild the Temple. This convinced the Jews that Zerubbabel was the Messiah. But Zerubbabel preferred a quiet life and declined the honour. So did Nehemiah, appointed governor by the Persians about 445 BC; but he at least rebuilt the walls of Jerusalem.

The next candidate was the young Macedonian conqueror, Alexander the Great, who became Lord of Asia (i.e. the Persian Empire) after defeating the Persian King Darius in 332 BC. But Alexander was too busy conquering the world to bother about the religious preoccupations of his Jewish subjects, and then died at the age of thirty-three.

Alexander seems to have liked the Jews, and allowed them a high degree of autonomy as part of his new empire, but the change of nominal overlord did not galvanize Judah to any new creative or religious efforts. This was a time of relative peace for Judea, but it certainly wasn't the golden age predicted by the prophets Jeremiah and Ezekiel.

It may seem odd that no new prophets of God appeared during Israel's long period of peace under the Persians then the Macedonians. It is tempting to surmise that prophets are the product of periods of national self-delusion and/or peril. One of the best descriptions of this aspect of prophecy can be found in Winwood Reade's *Martyrdom of Man*:

Prophets have existed in all countries and at all times, but the gift becomes rare in the same proportion as people learn to read and write. Second sight in the Highlands disappeared before the school, and so it has been in other lands. Prophets were numerous in ancient Greece. In the Homeric period they opposed the royal power and constituted another authority by the grace of God. Herodotus alludes to men who went about prophesying in hexameters. Thucydides says that while the Peloponnesians were ravaging the lands of Athens there were prophets in the city uttering all kinds of oracles . . .

The Jewish prophet was an extraordinary being. He was something more and something less than a man. He spoke like an angel; he acted like a beast. As soon as he received his mission, he ceased to wash. He often retired to the mountains, where he might be seen skipping from rock to rock like a goat; or he wandered in the desert with a leather girdle round his loins, eating roots and wild honey, or sometimes browsing on grass or flowers . . . He not only taught in parables but performed them.

For instance, Isaiah walked naked through the streets to show that the Lord would strip Jerusalem. Ezekiel wore a rotten girdle as a sign that their city would decay, and buttered his bread in a manner we would rather not describe, as a sign that they would eat defiled bread among the gentiles. Jeremiah wore a wooden yoke as a sign that they would be taken into captivity. As a sign that the Jews were guilty of wantonness in worshipping idols, Hosea cohabited three years with a man of the town; and as a sign that they committed adultery in turning from the Lord . . . he went and lived with another man's wife.

Jewish monotheism has always fought hardest to maintain its purity when facing outside or internal threats. Faced with the benevolent conquerors like the Persians and the Macedonians, foreign influences began to creep in – as happened with the religion of Baal after the conquest of the Canaanites.

From Persian Zoroastrianism the Jews picked up a concept of Evil, with a capital E. The Zoroastrians believed that the world was in a constant state of flux in the battle between divine light and demonic darkness. The Jewish attitude to good and evil, on the other hand, had always been more prosaic – enemy nations, corrupt rulers and the forceful incursions of foreign religions had always been their essential idea of evil (not to mention failing to stay on the right side of the ever-irritable Yahweh).

The idea of Evil as a force external to human affairs does not seem to have previously occurred to the Jews. Under the Persians, however, we see them edging towards a belief in a purely spiritual Evil – usually personified as a horde of malicious demons. This process would eventually raise Satan (a petty mischief-maker in the Old Testament) to the position of "the Great Destroyer" in Christian doctrine.

Another inheritance to the Jews from Persian Zoroastrianism and, later, the Greek religion of the Macedonians was a basic curiosity about an afterlife. Previously the religion of the children of Abraham had been strangely deficient on this level – their attitude to the sum of existence could almost be condensed to Woody Allen's laconic axiom: "You're born, life's a bitch, then you die."

In fact this lack of interest in survival after death was probably another inheritance from Egyptian Atonism – combined with the habitual Jewish, down-to-earth attitude to life. In creating his religion of the sun god, Akhenaton left out any notion of life after death; presumably to distance his new creed from the older, after-life-obsessed Egyptian religion.

In the centuries following the introduction of the Persian satrapy, we find some discussion among Jewish scholars about an afterlife, but very little of it finds its way into the Bible until the Christians added their own testament.

Following the release from the Babylonian exile, we see occasional references in Jewish texts to *Gehenna* – now often mistakenly described as the "Jewish Hell" – but these were, in fact, historical not theological images.

Gehenna is a valley, south-west of Jerusalem, where a tribe called the Ammonites once burned children to death as a sacrifice to their god, Moloch (later co-opted by the Christians as an arch demon). The tribes of Israel, after finally driving the Ammonites away from Gehenna, took up the horrific practice themselves – offering their own children, like their forefather Abraham, as sacrifices to Yahweh. The Valley of Gehenna was a place of fiery child-sacrifice from the reign of King Solomon, in the tenth century BC, to the Babylonian invasion over 400 years later. The

Prophet Jeremiah railed against the practice in the final days before the Babylonian invasion (Jeremiah: chapter 19).

During the centuries of the Persian and Greek rule over the tribes of Judea, the Gehenna Valley was used as a rubbish dump – largely to dissuade would-be practitioners of "that old-time religion" – and subsequent Jewish references to the "fires of Gehenna" were primarily illustrations of the horrors of excessive religious zeal, not a living creed about a penitentiary life after death. Only later, when Jesus of Nazareth described Hell as a place of terrible and eternal burning, did the name Gehenna become synonymous with an agonizing afterlife for sinners and non-believers.

The death of Alexander the Great did little to spoil the mood of peaceful, cultural stagnation in Judea. His vast empire, stretching from Egypt to India, immediately fell to pieces as his child heir was murdered and his generals – the Seleucids – settled down to the Greek national sport of fighting other Greeks. From the ashes of his empire there rose numerous petty kingdoms, one of which, Syria, contained Judea, but the Seleucids continued Alexander's policy of letting the seemingly helpless and harmless nation get on with its own business.

This peace was about to be shattered. In 175 BC, a new king, Antiochus IV, came to the throne of Hellenistic Syria. Antiochus called himself "Epiphanes" (Greek for "god manifest") but was called "Epimanes" (Greek for "the mad") by the Jews. Antiochus is probably the template for the Christians' later concept of the Antichrist; but, by his own lights, he was a just ruler who only wished to spread the gifts of Greek civilization and Greek religion to his benighted subjects. In many ways, Antiochus IV resembles the missionary Christian leaders of the British Raj in early-nineteenth-century India – whose well-meaning religious zeal and pompous cultural bigotry touched off the slaughters of the Indian Mutiny.

Antiochus initially maintained a distance from Jewish religious politics, but he happily helped the growing Hellenized Jewish faction in Jerusalem. This led to a Jew, so besotted with Hellenism that he had changed his name to the Greek "Jason", becoming the High Priest of Yahweh (the King of the Jews in all but name). More orthodox Jews were angered when Jason introduced a

Greek-style gymnasium and Greek schools for Jewish youths to Jerusalem, then were infuriated when a quarrel within the pro-Greek faction led to Jason being replaced as High Priest by an even more Hellenistic Jew, Menelaus.

Menelaus was both brutal and corrupt – even allowing his brother to steal from the Great Temple. Where Jason (and probably Antiochus) had been willing to slowly Hellenize the Jews, Menelaus decided to force the issue. He extinguished the holy lamps in the Temple and placed a statue of the Greek god Zeus in the sacred Holy of Holies (the empty room that had, in the Babylonian destroyed Solomon's Temple, contained the sacred Ark of the Covenant). Menelaus then passed edicts forbidding circumcision, observance of the Sabbath and the ownership of Jewish holy books.

Antiochus intervened militarily when Jason, in a coup d'état, regained the High Priesthood. The reinstated Menelaus then seems to have lost all self-control. He ordered Orthodox Jews to be dragged to the altar of Zeus; there they were threatened with death by torture if they refused to eat from a plate of pork (a meat expressly forbidden by Yahweh). Many refused to eat the "unclean" food and were tortured to death – they became known as *Hasidim* (the pious) and were the template for the Christian martyr-saints.

Eventually Menelaus' religious excesses led to a civil war, with the Hellenized Jewish aristocracy on Menelaus' side against the common people, who sided with the Orthodox faction and were led by a man called Judas Maccabeus. Antiochus tried to intervene again, but wars with Seleucid Egypt and Persia stopped him from using his full military might to aid the Hellenist faction.

The anti-Greek faction (called the Maccabees after their leader) won back Jerusalem in 164 BC, relighting the holy lamps in the temple and initiating the Jewish festival of *Hannukkah* (lights). Antiochus died that same year of an illness contracted while campaigning against the Seleucid Persians. His successor was wise enough to keep out of Jewish politics, and so granted Judea religious and cultural freedom, but still maintained overall rule from the Syrian capital, Antioch.

During the Maccabees' revolt there appeared a whole new genre of Jewish religious writing – the *Apocalyptic*, meaning "revelatory" in Hebrew.[5] Influenced by Persian Zoroastrians, Jewish writers began to set down their dreams and visions, searching for evidence of messages from God. Perhaps not surprisingly, the Jewish religious authorities (the faction-split priesthood in Jerusalem) did not appreciate the religious meanderings of a lot of speculative daydreamers, and only one book from that period was considered worthy of inclusion in the Bible as holy writ.

The *Book of Daniel* is unusual in many ways, not least being the fact that it is written about a Jewish folk-hero who had been dead for over 300 years and, indeed, may not have existed at all. Daniel, like Joseph before him, was not considered a prophet, but merely a visionary hero. He was also a prototype Hasidim who suffered at the hands of the wicked King Nebuchadnezzar during the Babylonian exile. In the first six chapters of the book – probably taken down verbatim from an earlier, oral tradition – Daniel and his friends refuse to give up their religion and outdo Nebuchadnezzar's court magicians at accurate dream interpretation (like Joseph at the court of the Pharaoh). As punishment, Daniel is thrown into a lion's den and his friends into a blazing furnace, but all are kept from harm by the power of Yahweh.

In the latter six chapters of the book, the style changes considerably, going from a fast-moving adventure story to the prophecy of a dream-visionary. Daniel is described as dreaming of five creatures being judged by Yahweh – four monstrous and the fifth a glorious human being. The four monsters are representations of the flawed empires of the Babylonians, Medes, Persians and the Macedonian Greeks, while the man is both the future Judea and, at the same time, the "Son of Man" who would lead Judea to pre-eminence amongst the nations of the Earth. (Note that the author of the Book of Daniel does not refer to this future leader as either the "new David" or the "Messiah". On the other hand, he (or she) does not claim that "the Son of Man" is *not* synonymous with these previously prophesied heroes.)

Daniel also dreams of an angel, who tells him that the seventy years of Babylonian captivity predicted by Jeremiah should actually be read as seventy *weeks* of years (i.e. $70 \times 7 = 490$ years).

[5]It was only later, after the writing of *The Revelation of St John the Divine* (called *The Apocalypse of St John the Divine* in its original Greek version) that the word "Apocalypse" came to indicate the catastrophic end of the world.

This would mean that, at the time the Book of Daniel was being written (probably between 167 and 164 BC), there were still another seventy-odd years for the Jews to suffer under Yahweh's displeasure.

The remainder of the Book of Daniel is a description of the reign of terror under Antiochus IV, but becomes historically inaccurate towards the end, perhaps indicating that the author is guessing about future events (thus allowing us to date the writing to the beginning of the Maccabee revolt).

As a historical document, the Book of Daniel shows some intriguing developments over the Old Testament's previous instalments. Firstly, Daniel is the first piece of Jewish political propaganda to find its way into the Bible. Its author's primary purpose seems not to pass on religious instruction, but to rouse the Jews to the Maccabee cause. Secondly, the Book of Daniel shows a literary turn that suggests both Persian and Hellenistic influences – it is, after all, an historical novel as much as it is Holy writ.

In its last chapter, the Book of Daniel offers another golden vision of the future – following the 490 years of Jewish suffering under foreign yokes. As in the books of Jeremiah and Ezekiel, the Jews are depicted as winning back total control of the Promised Land and living under Yahweh's blessing ever afterwards.

Notable, however, is the fact that the leader who is predicted to bring this great deliverance is depicted in Daniel as a semi-divine being. In a very Greek turn of phrase, the prophesied leader is even referred to as the "Son of Man", rather than the more traditional "Messiah" or "new David". There has been constant debate down the centuries as to whether the author of the Book of Daniel was edging towards describing the coming leader of the Jews as "the Son of God" – an outrageously impious concept in Judaism, but a common idea to the polytheistic and hedonistic Greeks.

The Book of Daniel marks yet another, arguably final, point of evolution in the development of the concept of the Jewish prophet – the step beyond the need for a prophet at all. Daniel, as noted above, is not considered a Prophet of Yahweh in the way Moses and Elijah are. He was simply a man of faith who was granted signs, miracles and visions of the future by God. Jewish prophets – like Catholic priests – were seen as the intermediaries between Yahweh and the common people. But the unnamed author of the

Book of Daniel is relaying religious visions without claiming to be a prophet himself. In common with the other authors of the apocalyptic period, he is suggesting that God can speak (through signs, dreams and visions) to any of the Chosen People, without the necessity of an authoritarian prophet as a go-between.

The Book of Daniel was wrong, however, about the immediate future of Judea. Four hundred and ninety years after the Babylonian captivity, the prophesied coming of the Messiah and the promised pre-eminence of Judea seemed as far off as ever.

By 63 BC, the ruling Maccabees were squabbling among themselves and on the verge of civil war. One of the factions made the fatal mistake of inviting the new military power in the Mediterranean, the Romans, to send troops to settle the dispute. Pompey the Great used this excuse to invade Judea, crush both Maccabee factions and declare the country a Roman province. Then – after the Roman civil war between Julius Caesar and Pompey, and the subsequent civil war following the assassination of the victorious Caesar – the Emperor Augustus installed a foreigner, an Edomite called Herod, as King of Judea in 37 BC.

Despite Herod the Great's later paranoid insanity – depicted in the New Testament by the Slaughter of the Innocents – he was, in fact, an excellent ruler. He greatly increased the prosperity and development of the kingdom and, through his popularity at the court of the Emperor Augustus, gave the Jews, for the first time since Solomon, a feeling of being an important power in the world (if still nominally subservient to Rome).

However, that illusion of being the partial rulers of their own destiny was to prove dangerous and, within a hundred years, disastrous for the Judeans. Some began to dream of not only becoming fully independent of Roman control, but actually subverting Rome as the centre of the greatest empire in the known world. After all, hadn't half-a-dozen prophets effectively promised that very thing?

Some of the most influential elements of Jewish society decided to pit their religious zeal against the political and military might of Rome in what became a fight to the death.

It was sometime between the revolt of Judas Maccabeus and the Roman takeover that the Book of Enoch was written. Like the Book of Daniel, it dates itself by its clearly apocalyptic (revelatory) literary influences. Also like Daniel, the Book of Enoch is about a historical figure (in this case the seventh patriarch in the Book of Genesis) and his visions of past and future events.

Although never accepted as Judaic Holy writ, and only briefly adopted by the early Christian Church, the Book of Enoch has survived down the ages and still has a powerful impact on western religious thinking. For example, it is from the visions of Enoch that we first hear of the War in Heaven: the rebellion of the archangel Lucifer to take the Throne of Yahweh, the defeat of the rebel angels and their casting down from Heaven. It is hard to imagine the development of Christian theology without this (very Greek) tale of hubris and nemesis.

Secondly, in giving yet another vision of the coming pre-eminence of the people of Judea, the author of Enoch specifically states that Daniel's "Son of Man" and the Messiah of earlier Jewish prophecies are to be one and the same person. Thus we can be sure that in the decades before the pivotal year of AD 1, at least some elements of Jewish society were expecting the coming Messiah to be something more than a great military leader. They expected the Son of Man to come clothed in a divine light.

Chapter 5

Jesus the Preacher

The Romans were even more impatient about the Jews and their fanatical religious beliefs than the Hellenic Syrians had been, and the result of their oppression was a rash of militant messiahs, whose names are mostly long forgotten: Simon Magus, Judas of Galilee and an Egyptian whose name is not certain, but who led an army of 30,000 within sight of Jerusalem's walls before they were scattered by the Romans. There was also a man called Theudas, who claimed to be a magician who could make the River Jordan divide, but failed to enchant the Roman sword that cut off his head.

The only messiah who is remembered today was called Joshua, but is better known by the Greek form of his name, Jesus of Nazareth. Oddly enough, it is probable that Jesus did not think of himself as "*the* Messiah". When his disciple Peter remarked, "They call you the Christ, the Messiah," Jesus advised him to be silent. The claim apparently embarrassed him, for much the same reason it had embarrassed Zerubbabel and Nehemiah: because the Jews expected the Messiah to be a warrior, like Judas Maccabaeus, who would drive out the Romans. Jesus seems to have been too realistic to expect an end to the Roman occupation. His teaching was quite different.

Study of the scriptures and what he believed was divine inspiration had led him to believe that the world would end within the lifetime of people then alive; in the face of the imminent coming of "the Kingdom of God", the Roman occupation of Judea was probably an utter irrelevance to Jesus.

No other religion has had its founder reinterpreted quite so often as Christianity. From medieval mystery plays to Hollywood epics, the life, actions and preaching of Jesus have been reworked, reconsidered and redepicted so often that many people find themselves surprised and occasionally shocked when they come to read the actual books of the New Testament.

In the Canonized Gospels (the four Church-accepted depictions of his life), the "gentle Jesus, meek and mild" so beloved of Sunday school teachers is also shown as violent (as when he casts out money-lenders from the precinct of the Temple), rude (as when he speaks to his mother at the wedding at Cana), petulant (as when he curses an innocent fig tree for not bearing fruit out of season) and sometimes downright ruthless (as when he describes the flaming, eternal Hell that awaits all who do not believe in his new faith – remember, as a Jew, Jesus was almost certainly brought up with no such image of a penitentiary afterlife).

Christian theologians down the ages have struggled with such apparent inconsistencies in the New Testament – sometimes stretching both their logic and common sense – but the final and all-encompassing answer has always been that Jesus was the Son of God, and was therefore bound to be beyond the shallow understanding of simple human beings. For the purpose of the present study, however, we must consider the historical, rather than the theological, aspect of the founder of Christianity.

As already noted, the monotheistic concept of the Prophet of God had, by the first century AD, evolved from Noah and Abraham – persons blessed by and spoken to directly by God – through Moses – who performed miraculous wonders in Yahweh's name – to the socially reforming prophets like Elijah, then to precognitive Cassandras like Jeremiah, then finally to semi-political visionaries like the author of the Book of Daniel. Where does Jesus fit into this pattern of development?

The answer is that his career contained elements of all the previous prophetic incarnations: he spoke in visionary parables like Daniel, accurately predicted a dire future for Jerusalem like Jeremiah, spoke for justice and the downtrodden like Elijah and Amos, performed miracles to rival those of Moses – and finally, and most importantly, claimed to speak with the direct authority of God.

The question as to whether Joshua-called-Jesus actually existed can be regarded as settled, since independent accounts of events found in the New Testament were written within a century or so of their taking place. Unfortunately, there are only a few of these presently known – possibly because the triumphant early Church is rumoured to have rooted out and destroyed most non-complimentary references to Jesus from the archives and libraries of the Roman Empire.

In 1931, the Austrian historian Dr Robert Eisler published the following startling description of Jesus in his book *The Messiah Jesus*. It, in turn, is reconstructed from the so-called *Lentulus Letter*:

> His nature and his form were human; a man of simple appearance, mature age, dark skin, small stature – three cubits [fourand-a-half feet] high – hunchbacked, with a long face, long nose, and meeting eyebrows, so that they who saw him could be affrighted, with scanty hair with a parting in the middle of his head, after the manner of the Nazirites, and with an undeveloped beard.

The Lentulus Letter was supposedly written by the political superior of Pontius Pilate – the Roman Governor of Judea at the time of the crucifixion. It reprints the above description mainly to refute it. Lentulus goes on to claim that Jesus was a very handsome and striking figure.

In fact the Lentulus Letter itself was a poor forgery, published in AD 311 by someone with too little historical knowledge to know that Pontius Pilate had *no* political superiors other than the Emperor Tiberius. However, Robert Eisler believed the unflattering description of Jesus to be a genuine first-century text. It was said to have been taken from a "wanted poster" issued by the Roman authorities, and was later quoted in the works of a Jewish, pro-Roman historian called Flavius Josephus, who wrote half-adozen decades after the crucifixion.

Unfortunately, some of Josephus' original texts are now lost, and, as we will see in a moment, some people believe the surviving copies of his work to have been doctored out of all recognition – at least where they deal with Jesus. It is, therefore, one of history's ironies that in refuting the "hunchback" description, the Christian forger of the Lentulus Letter in fact enabled its survival.

The Antiquities of the Jews is a surviving Josephus history, originally published in AD 93. It offers four references to early Christian-related events.

First he mentions the great Roman tax census that took place in AD 6 when the Herodian dynasty was deposed in Judea and replaced by a governor sent from Rome. The Gospel of Luke dates the birth of Jesus to this time.

Later, Josephus mentions the death of Jesus' cousin, forerunner and apparent mentor, John the Baptist, at the hands of the Tetrarch (Roman sub-governor) of Galilee, Herod Antipas. Josephus simply describes the Baptist's crime as that of political sedition; no mention is made of John's spirited opposition to Herod's legally incestuous marriage to his half-brother's widow, as stated in the Bible.

Next Josephus gives a brief, but well-rounded, description of the life of Jesus himself:

About this time there lived one Jesus, a wise man, if indeed one should call him a man. For he was one who wrought surprising feats, and was a teacher of such people as accept the truth gladly. He won over many Jews and many of the Greeks. This man was the Christ.

When Pilate, upon hearing him accused by men of the highest standing amongst us, condemned him to be crucified, those who had in the first place come to love him did not give up their affection for him.

On the third day he appeared to them living, for the prophets of God had prophesied these and countless other marvellous things about him. And the tribe of the Christians, so called after him, have still to this day not disappeared.

Given that Flavius Josephus was a devout (if Romanized) Jew, many people have suspected that later, pro-Christian scholars doctored the surviving copies of his *Antiquities* to support their own beliefs. Certainly Josephus' warmth towards what he, as a Jewish priest, should have considered a heretical cult is rather suspicious. If Josephus was really so impressed by the founder of

Christianity, it has been asked, then why did he dedicate such a small section of his exhaustive history of the Jews to Jesus and his teachings?[1]

Whether doctored or not, Josephus' description of Jesus as "the Christ" is not so surprising when one knows just what that phrase meant to an Orthodox, first-century Jew. We will consider this point later.

In his fourth reference to early Christian history, Josephus described the stoning to death of a Christian called James:

> Since [the High Priest] Ananus was that kind of person, and because he perceived an opportunity with Festus [the previous Roman Governor] having died and Albinus [the new Roman Governor] not yet arrived, he called a meeting of the Sanhedrin and brought James, the brother of Jesus (who is called "Messiah") along with some others. He accused them of transgressing the law, and handed them over for stoning.

It has long been Christian doctrine that Jesus had no siblings, but this is based more on the belief that the Virgin Mary, his mother, should have stayed a virgin – there is no biblical evidence to back the suggestion. Almost certainly, Josephus means here that James was Jesus' brother in blood rather than in the religious sense.

Josephus gives no detailed reason for James' execution, but its far-reaching political repercussions are hinted at when he points

---

[1] In *The Messiah Jesus*, Robert Eisler reconstructed what he thought the original, undoctored Josephus text might have looked like, utilizing both the ancient historian's writing style and his habitual hostility to would-be Messiahs:

> Now about this time arose an occasion for new disturbances, a certain Jesus, a wizard of a man, if indeed he may be called a man, who was the most monstrous of men, whom his disciples call a son of God, as having done wonders such as no man has ever done. He was in fact a teacher of astonishing tricks to such men, accept the abnormal with delight. And he seduced many Jews and many also of the Greek nation, and was regarded by them as the Messiah.

> And when on the indictment of the principal men among us, Pilate sentenced him to the cross, still those who before had admired him did not cease to rave. For it seemed to them that having been dead for three days, he had appeared to them alive again, as the divinely inspired prophets had foretold. These and ten thousand other wonderful things concerning him. And even now the race of those who are called "Messianists" after him is not extinct.

out that Ananus had to retire from office as a direct consequence of James' death, and that the Jewish revolt began four years later.

Our next, relatively contemporary, reference to the early Christians comes from the Roman historian Suetonius in his *History of the Twelve Caesars*. In the section covering the life of the Emperor Claudius (who ruled from AD 41–54) Suetonius notes that the Jews were expelled from Rome en masse by Claudius "for making disturbances at the instigation of one Chrestus."[2] An event that could not have endeared the Christians to their orthodox Jewish brethren, the expulsion is also mentioned in the New Testament (Acts: ch18, v2).

Finally, both Suetonius and another Roman historian, Tacitus, mention the first great persecution of the Christians. In AD 64, a terrible fire swept Rome and burned for days. The narcissistic and depraved Emperor Nero was blamed for starting the fire – ostensibly to clear an area in the centre of the city for a new palace. Afraid that the accusations would lead to an uprising, Nero decided that he needed an even more detested scapegoat than himself to shoulder popular calumny. He settled on the Christians.

Suetonius describes the Christians as "a set of people adhering to a novel and mischievous superstition", while for Tacitus they were simply "a class hated for their abominations". This powerful dislike of the Christians was commonplace in Rome during the first and second centuries AD, allowing several emperors to make them scapegoats, as Nero did.

Following the burning of Rome, Nero fed many Christians to the wild beasts in the Coliseum. Others he had crucified, publicly tortured to death or burned alive. In fact he went too far in slaughtering the followers of Christ, and had to stop hastily when the citizens of Rome began to sympathize with the cult. However, the Roman public's antipathy to the Christians soon reasserted itself, and many executions/martyrdoms took place over the next 200 years.

This in itself is rather surprising because the Romans, despite their habitual cruelty and arrogance, prided themselves on their

[2]Most modern historians regard Suetonius' apparent belief that Jesus was alive and preaching sedition in Rome at least ten years after his crucifixion as a simple mistake. But, as we shall see later, Suetonius, (born AD 69) may have known facts that are now all but lost to us.

lack of religious bigotry: provided a cult did not break any laws, the Roman authorities left it alone. So why did the Romans take such a strong aversion to the Christians?

The answer is not, as Hollywood would have us believe, that the gentle Christians shamed the brutal Romans, but because the followers of Christ broke so many Roman social taboos.

To begin with, it struck the Romans as downright perverse that the Christians should worship a convicted criminal who had died by crucifixion. To them, it was the most shameful way to die. (Early Christians adopted the sign of the fish rather than that of the cross, because potential Roman converts found the image of a cross repugnant). An oddly unimaginative people, the Romans seem to have automatically believed that a person sentenced to crucifixion must have been as disgusting as the means of execution itself. Most Romans in the first century AD felt that the sort of people who would worship a crucified criminal must be utter degenerates.

Secondly, Roman snobbery was outraged that the majority of Christian converts were lowly-born proletarians or slaves. It was known that Christian meetings always started with each member of the congregation kissing the others on the mouth, and the Romans felt that carrying on like this with proletarians and slaves was little better than bestiality. No one doubted that the kissing ceremony led to orgies.

Despite our modern image of the Romans regularly indulging in sex orgies, that sort of behaviour was probably no more common then than it is today. Indeed, the attitude of most Ancient Romans toward sex-parties would have pleased a nineteenth century Puritan preacher (the Emperor Augustus, for example, exiled and never forgave his only child, Julia, for indulging in secret orgies) so claims of Christian lasciviousness carried a lot of weight with the average Roman.

Finally – for most Romans who overcame their automatic dislike for the Christians long enough to listen to their teachings – the creeds of non-violence and the pre-eminence of the poor and downtrodden were simply ridiculous, impractical and close to treasonous.

Rome, a society based on slavery, felt that it could ill-afford to follow a doctrine that, against the logical evidence, insisted that the weak and poor were more loved by God than the rich and powerful (although later, in AD 392 when the Emperor Theodosius adopted Christianity as the state religion of the Roman Empire, mass slavery remained largely unchallenged by the Church).

Furthermore, the empire was surrounded by savage barbarians on all sides and depended on the violence of its legions for its very survival. Rome "turning the other cheek" to the Goths or the Parthians seemed just the sort of weakness that would invite invasion. Christians, therefore, faced the same sort of patriotic detestation in Ancient Rome as European conscientious objectors did during the First World War.

Perhaps surprisingly, the Jews were also very negative towards Christianity, especially after the failed Judean revolt of AD 70. One might have thought that Jesus' assurances that he came not to refute the Old Testament, but to enlarge upon it, would have endeared him to the Jews. However, with a few (mostly modern) exceptions, Jesus has never been popular within Judaism.

Although Jesus' career can be seen, in some lights, as a conglomeration of aspects found in the lives of previous Jewish prophets, certain cultural considerations have meant that he could never be called a "Prophet of Yahweh".

Most important is the claim that he was the Son of God. In fact, on the evidence of the Synoptic Gospels (the less esoteric Gospels of Matthew, Mark and Luke), Jesus himself publicly shied away from any such enormous claim – at least before his trial, execution and reported resurrection. It was his followers, especially the fervent St Paul, who heavily stressed this aspect of his being.

For the average first-century Jew, a claim to be the Son of God was both ridiculous and, at the same time, heretical. On the one hand, to claim to be the child of something as all-encompassing and universal as Yahweh would have seemed as silly as somebody today claiming to have been sired by the wind. To the scholarly Jews, divine conception myths were typical of the childish drivel that was to be found in the false religions – like those of the Romans and the Greeks.

There was also, on the other hand, an element of danger in the Christians' claims that angered and probably frightened first-century Orthodox Jews. It was, after all, less than 200 years since the Hellenizing persecutions of Antiochus IV (see last chapter).

The first century Jews, crushed under the heel of a foreign and pagan power, were struggling to maintain both their national identity and the purity of their religion; then along comes a cult that tries to introduce Greek ideas to Judaism – like the fathering of human children by God. Learned Jews would have pointed out that Yahweh had cursed the Chosen People to over 500 years of foreign oppression for just this kind of religious backsliding.

Indeed, the very fact that Christianity's founder chose to be called by a Greek bastardization of his Jewish name (Jesus instead of Joshua) must have been enough to infuriate many traditionalist Jews. So it is not surprising that Jewish authors in the first and second century AD spread their own, polemic, version of the life of Jesus.

Origen, the great defender of the early Church, quotes a now lost text by the anti-Christian Jewish scholar Celsus:

Jesus had come from a village in Judea, and was the son of a poor Jewess who gained her living by the work of her own hands. His mother had been turned out of doors by her husband, who was a carpenter by trade, on being convicted of adultery with a Roman soldier named Panthéra. Being thus driven away by her husband, and wandering about in disgrace, she gave birth to Jesus, a bastard.

Jesus, on account of his poverty, was hired out to go to Egypt. While there he acquired certain magical powers which Egyptians pride themselves on possessing. He returned home highly elated at possessing these powers, and on the strength of them gave himself out to be a god.

Tertullian, another early Christian defender, quotes another lost polemic from the second century, that gives the Jewish reaction to the claimed resurrection of Jesus:

This is your carpenter's son! Your harlot's son! Your Sabbath-breaker! Your Samaritan! Your demon-possessed!

This is he who was struck with reeds and fists, dishonoured with spittle, and given a draught of gall and vinegar!

This is he whose corpse his disciples stole in secret, that they might say: "He has risen!" Or that the gardener quietly removed and buried so that his lettuces might not be damaged by the crowds of visitors!

Needless to say, Christians utterly reject these versions of Jesus' life but, it has to be admitted, can offer no conclusive version of his history themselves. The problem is that, aside from the above scanty (and, in one case, questionable) historical references, there is only the New Testament to give us any direct facts. After the Gospels themselves, most of the New Testament dedicates itself to discussion and re-consideration of Jesus' preaching, miracles and divine origin: for the historical details of his ministry, we are largely restricted to the four Gospels.[3]

This in itself would not be a problem, were it not for the fact that the Gospels themselves are written in such a way as to confound an investigative historian. There are no direct dates, only vague descriptions of historically traceable events, and the geography described in at least one of the Gospels (Mark) is actually nonsensical.

The main reason that the Gospels are so confusing to historians is because they were not written as straight histories; they are actually strings of anecdotes about the life of Jesus, set down with little attempt at historical interconnection. Indeed, most theological historians now believe that the Gospels are the written form of oral histories that were already decades old. The Gospels were therefore unlikely to have been compiled by people who had been witnesses to the events described.

The result is a hotchpotch, to say the least. Some anecdotes are repeated in all four Gospels (the feeding of the 5,000, for example) but most are found in only one or two. The Sermon on the Mount, for example, is found only in the Gospel of Matthew, despite the fact that it is, for most Christians, the essential core of Jesus' teaching.

There are also contradictions between the Gospels. The

[3]Three of the Gospels – Mark, Luke and Matthew – are known as the Synoptic (Greek for "similar viewpoint") Gospels because they are clearly influenced by each other.

The gospel of John is very different to the Synoptic Gospels, being more religiously visionary in style. This is why it is generally believed to have been written much later than the other three, during a period when Christianity had developed further as a religion.

Synoptic Gospels give the impression that Jesus lived only a year after he began preaching, for example, but John mentions Jesus and his disciples celebrating Passover (an annual festival) in Jerusalem no less than three times.

The life of Jesus as a monotheistic prophet is, therefore, hard to map, and the following is a short and conservative approximation.

The date of Jesus' birth is still a matter of debate. In the Gospel of Luke he is described starting his ministry at "about thirty-years-old". We can date the start of his ministry to AD 29/30, because Luke also mentions the appearance of John the Baptist in the "fifteenth year of the reign of [the Roman Emperor] Tiberius Caesar" – that is, AD 28/29 . The Gospels indicate that Jesus started his own ministry about a year later. Thus Jesus should have been born around AD 1 .

However, the Gospel of Matthew specifically places Jesus' birth at the end of the reign of Herod the Great and therefore sometime before 4 BC when Herod died. On the other hand, the Gospel of Luke describes the birth taking place in the year of the great Roman census, which we know was AD 6. The other two Gospels do not mention Jesus' childhood at all, so the date remains impossible to place with any certainty.

AD 6 was the year that the son of Herod the Great, Archelaus I, was deposed as king of Judea for incompetence and unpopularity with his Jewish subjects (who, whatever the Herod dynasty did for them, could never forget that the family were foreign converts to Judaism and therefore unworthy to rule pure-blooded Jews). Archelaus' two brothers, Herod Antipas and Philip, were allowed to remain as tetrarchs (sub-governors) in neighbouring Galilee and Iturea, respectively, but a Roman-born governor was sent to rule in Jerusalem.

If anything, this incensed the Jews even more than the rule of Archelaus. At least he had been a Semite and a practising Jew; a Roman governor – a pagan Gentile – was even less worthy to rule over the Chosen People.

Popular anger was further aroused by the national tax census immediately called for by the new governor. This was actually standard practice in a reorganized Roman province (you can't tax people when you don't know who and where they are) but many Jews, swelled with the pride of nominal self-determination during the reign of Herod I, were furious at the indignity of having to so overtly bend the knee to a Roman overlord.

The freedom-fighting movement who called themselves the Zealots came into existence in AD 6. The Zealots' covert but bloody resistance to Roman rule would shake Jewish politics for the next sixty-four years and would, eventually, lead to the dissolution of Judea as a Jewish nation.

So AD 6 was as important a date to first-century Jews as 1776 was to Revolutionary Americans, so Luke is unlikely to have been mistaken about such an important instance. So why did Luke describe Jesus as "about thirty" only twenty-four years after his birth?

Some have suggested that both Luke and Matthew placed the birth of Jesus at Bethlehem as a piece of propaganda rather than of fact. Bethlehem had been the birthplace of King David and was therefore revered by the Jews. Furthermore, the Old Testament Book of Micah had long predicted that a "ruler in Israel" (Micah: ch5, v2) would be born in Bethlehem. This prophecy had, by the first century AD, become part of Jewish Messianic belief.

It is possible, therefore, that the authors of Luke and Matthew invented the detail about Jesus' birth in Bethlehem to fit him into the Messiah myth. This might also explain why Luke places the birth at least six years too late: he felt that he needed a reason why Mary and Joseph would travel to Bethlehem from Nazareth, and chose the tax census, even though it would confuse the dating of the birth. Given the possibility that the authors of Luke and Matthew had never met Jesus, it is also possible that they did not know his actual birth date, and simply guessed.

More importantly, from a religious standpoint, is the question of Jesus' parentage. Of course all the Gospels proclaim him the Son of God, but those that give the story of the divine impregnation of Mary (again, Matthew and Luke) also describe Jesus as a descendant of King David *through* Joseph, the supposed foster father.

This is a point that Christian theologians generally avoid discussing, but it is all important in the question over whether Jesus was simply a human prophet, like Moses and Elijah, or was God-on-Earth. With the lack of evidence presently to hand, only those with a Christian faith can state the parentage of Jesus with any certainty.

Next to nothing is given by the Gospels about Jesus' childhood. Matthew describes Joseph and family fleeing to Egypt to escape Herod the Great's Slaughter of the Innocents.[4] Certainly Herod, in his later years, was quite capable of such an atrocity – a raving paranoid, he executed most of his close kin before he died. However, there is no mention in the usually punctilious Josephus' histories of such an act of mass murder, so this story is another that has to be taken on faith.

Some have suggested that the sojourn into Egypt might have influenced the young Jesus to believe that foreigners were as worthy of God's love as the Chosen People. Certainly his marked lack of xenophobia was to stand out in his later career.

It has even been suggested that the young Jesus travelled to India, and was influenced there by the Hindu and Buddhist religions – but aside from certain doctrinal similarities between Hinduism, Buddhism and Christianity, there is no evidence to back this theory. Since Herod I died in 4 BC, it is unlikely that Jesus was abroad for very long. His family is described as returning to Nazareth as soon as the old maniac died.

At the age of twelve, according to Luke, Jesus went missing on a family trip to Jerusalem. After three days they found him sitting in the Great Temple, discoursing with the biblical scholars there. He is described as making an excellent impression on the doctors of law, so it is reasonable to assume that Jesus had been well schooled.

This in itself is not so surprising. Leaving aside Luke's suggestion that Jesus was speaking with divine knowledge, it is likely that he would have received a good biblical education. Wood, in forestless Galilee, was a somewhat rare item and Joseph, as a carpenter, would have been a skilled professional with a reasonable income to spend on his children's education.

In around 28 BC, a semi-hermit preacher called John the Baptist appeared in the valley of the River Jordan. He, after Herod I and Archelaus I, is the next confirmable historic character in the Gospels. Josephus, as we saw above, describes John as a political

[4]All the male infants in Bethlehem below two years old were said to have been butchered in an attempt to kill the prophesied Messiah.

rabble-rouser who was executed by Tetrarch Herod Antipas for sedition.

The Baptist was arguably an important influence on Jesus, preaching the coming "Kingdom of Heaven" and beseeching his listeners to repent and "be washed of their sins". As a symbolic sign of this cleansing of his followers' souls, John would baptize them – thrusting them briefly under the water of the River Jordan while praying over them.

Jesus is described as going to John and, when the Baptist recognized him as the Messiah, Jesus insists that John go through with the ceremony of baptism as if he were a normal person. John, we are told in the Gospels, was Jesus' cousin, so this scene clearly has family undercurrents that are not made plain in the text.

John was apocalyptic in the modern sense – preaching absolute repentance, rejection of worldly things and the imminent coming of God's judgment on mankind. Jesus, while agreeing that the Kingdom of God was imminent, stressed that righteous living and everyday life were not incompatible. While John was a prophet in the classic "voice in the wilderness" mould, his cousin Jesus did most of his preaching to townsfolk.

John the Baptist certainly seems to have become an important religious figure in Galilee before he was executed. Later Jewish sources even suggest that, before the Roman dissolution of Judea in AD 135, it was John, not Jesus, who was believed to be the Messiah by many apocalyptic Jews.

Jesus is next described spending forty days living as a hermit in the wilderness. He is tempted by Satan who appears in much the same role as he does in the Book of Job: a demon (or possibly even an angel of God) who tempts the righteous to abandon their faith as a test of their worthiness. It was later, post-crucifixion Christian doctrine that elevated this trickster to the position of arch-enemy of God and all mankind.

On returning from the wilderness, Jesus began his preaching – what the Christian Church describes as his "ministry".

As a historian rather than a theologian, I will not comment he miraculous element to Jesus' career. There is no independent contemporary source to verify that he did actually walk on water, heal the sick or raise Lazarus from the dead and, in any case, Jesus' claimed miracles only served to underline his preaching – surely the most important aspect of his career.[5]

Furthermore, since this section of the book is mainly interested in the development of the concept of the religious prophet, we will not examine Jesus' teachings in detail. Instead we need to look at markedly new elements that he introduced to the prophetic canon – the required surrender of the individual to the manifest will of God, the coming of the Kingdom of Heaven, and a reformed and redefined concept of an afterlife.

While previous Jewish prophets spoke of the will of Yahweh, none insisted, to the extent that Jesus did, that the will of God was an ever-active force in the world. Jesus described himself as the voice and living sign of the divine will, but he also insisted that God was a force that acted on every human being, and that total surrender to His will within the individual's own soul is the only way to obtain salvation.

Jesus' preaching thus introduced a new concept to Jewish religious thinking. Where Moses bewailed the fact that not all the Chosen People could feel and speak the will of God (Numbers: 11), Jesus said that, in fact, everyone *can* and indeed *must* feel the will of God in their everyday lives.

This is the line of belief that would later be expanded by men like John Bunyan, in his novel *The Pilgrim's Progress*, to proclaim that all men are directly in touch with God – without the necessity of an intermediary prophet or priest. Thus some have claimed Jesus as the "first Protestant" – although he himself never suggested the abolition of the priesthood, Jewish or otherwise.

Like John the Baptist, Jesus also preached that the "Kingdom of God" was coming. To many of his listeners, this phrase would have had specific meanings – the coming of the warrior Messiah, the fall of Rome and all other Gentile oppressors of the Jews and,

[5]Josephus describes Jesus as "one who wrought surprising feats" and second-century Jewish polemicist writers depreciated Jesus as a petty magician, but both of these sources wrote many decades after Christian tradition had become both cemented and widely broadcast. From a historian's standpoint, it is impossible to confirm the miraculous events in the Gospels.

finally, the raising of the Chosen People to a place of eternal bliss and pre-eminence in the world by Yahweh.

Jesus, however, meant something much less violent. To him, like the Prophet Amos, justice and the protection of the poor and helpless were God's main interest – so the Kingdom of God would be a heavenly place where the evils of the world would be vanquished. This would come about not by a war, but by the purifying of men's hearts and the following of God's will. Those that failed to heed the will of God, however, would burn in Hell for all eternity.

Hell is the iron fist inside Christianity's silken glove. It is also, as we saw in the last chapter, a distinctly non-Jewish idea. By adding it so specifically to his teachings, Jesus was greatly extending the prophet's role as foreteller of doom.

In Persian Zoroastrianism, the afterlife for the wicked was a stinking pit in which damned souls were forced to wait before they would be finally purified by fire and allowed to return to a perfected Earth.

The Greeks and Romans believed that *all* dead souls (or *shades*) went to Tartarus, the realm of the dark god Hades (or Pluto for the Romans). The shades of those who had offended the gods were eternally tortured by Hades, but for everyone else, Tartarus was said to be a grey, lifeless underworld in which the only consolation lay in drinking the Waters of Lethe – a magical stream that blotted out all memories of a previous life and left the dead shade a shambling automaton for all eternity.

Jesus' definition of Hell[6] seems to embody the grimmer aspects from both the above mythologies: the torment from Zoroastrianism coupled with the everlasting misery of the realm of Hades. As in the Old Testament, the Christian God is a vengeful God, but now His vengeance was defined as everlasting.

Jesus' image of a place of eternal fire might echo the Jewish tradition of the Valley of Gehenna – the place, south of Jerusalem, where the pre-Babylonian-exile Jews burned children to death as a sacrifice to Yahweh.

As we noted in the last chapter, Gehenna was, in Jesus' day, a dump for rubbish as well as a popular icon of monstrous cruelty

[6]Best summed up in Mark (ch9, v43–50), where Jesus repeats three times that Hell is the place where "the worm dieth not, and the fire is not quenched".

and misplaced religious zeal. It is also possible that, because children exclusively were sacrificed in Gehenna, later Jewish parents might have used the story of the valley as an allegorical bogeyman to scare naughty offspring into behaving. Whether any or all three of these concepts can be read into Jesus' warning of eternal Hellfire is a matter for speculation outside the scope of this book. After the birth of Christianity, the word Gehenna swiftly took on the same meaning that Jesus ascribed to Hell.

Jesus' emphasis on continued existence after death was another departure from most previous Jewish prophetic teaching. Extreme critics have accused the Christian Church of being a "death cult", because much of its teaching so often centres on the afterlife, but this is largely unfair. Where Jesus speaks of the Kingdom of God, he is not simply describing the Heaven where good souls will reside after death, but a perfected physical world, inhabited by all – Jew and Gentile, high-born and low-born – who have fully abased themselves to the will of God.

As time and generations of Christians passed, the Church gradually began to emphasize Jesus' promise of a heavenly afterlife for the faithful, but the Gospels make it clear that Jesus also expected some great change in the physical world to take place in the future. This seems to echo the Jewish Messianic belief and, as we shall see in the next chapter, there is evidence that Jesus believed the great change would come within the lifetimes of some who actually heard him preach.

Chapter 6

Jesus the Christ

Not surprisingly, Jesus' journey to Jerusalem for the Passover celebration – and his own execution – takes up a large proportion of all four Gospels. From the point of view of Christian belief, Jesus went to Jerusalem expressly to be sacrificed as the "Lamb of God."[1] However, the political impact of his visit is plain, even though the Gospels seem to try to downplay it.

Two of the Gospels specifically describe Jesus as a descendant of King David. They do not report that Jesus openly proclaimed his bloodline but, on the other hand, they don't say he tried to conceal it. A first-century Jewish population, if aware of Jesus' ancestry, could not help but wonder if he was the Messiah – after all, one of the several names for the prophesied liberator of the Jews was "the new David".

Indeed, Jesus seems to have deliberately fanned such speculation by stopping on his way to Jerusalem and telling his disciples to go find him an ass and a colt. Only when these specific beasts of burden have been obtained does he enter the city. As the Gospel of Matthew points out, a Messianic prophecy in the Old Testament Book of Zechariah (ch9, v9) reads:

"Rejoice greatly, O Zion: shout O daughters of Jerusalem:

---

[1] Jewish Passover involves the ritual slaughter of lambs, in remembrance of the lambs' blood used to mark and protect the dwellings of Jews during the night of the tenth plague of Egypt (the angelic slaughter of the Egyptian first-born). For Christians, Jesus sacrificed himself to protect mankind from the consequence of its own sin.

behold thy king cometh unto thee: he is just and brings
salvation; lowly, and riding on an ass, and upon a colt, the
foal of the ass."

The sight of a popular religious preacher (rumoured to be a cousin
of John the Baptist and also a descendant of King David) riding
into Jerusalem on the eve of the Passover on an ass, and leading a
colt, was a message that the common people read as plain as day:
the Messiah had arrived. They greeted Jesus waving palm fronds
and with cries of "Hosanna!" (Hebrew for "save us, we pray!").

His next action – the casting out of the moneylenders from the
Temple forecourt (Matthew: chapter 21) – must have confirmed
the suspicion that the prophesied leader had arrived. A holy
prophet-king was expected to bring about religious reform and, to
any who had doubts that the gentle carpenter's son had it in him to
be a warlord, the violence of Jesus' attack on the money changers
must have been a welcome sign.

Such blatant self-advertising as the potential Messiah was also,
of course, very dangerous. Christian doctrine stresses that Jesus
was deliberately vexing the authorities – goading them to sacrifice
him. Any unaffiliated observer at the time, on the other hand, must
have suspected that Jesus was playing to the crowd, hoping to gain
enough popular support to raise a rebellion. Judea had no standing
army beyond a few ceremonial guards, so any rebel leader and
would-be-warrior Messiah would have to look to the civilian
populace to fight in the rebellion.

Of course, the Jewish authorities were perfectly aware that
any attempt to pit Jewish civilian rioters against Roman
legionaries would be futile. Little surprise, then, that they moved
quickly to crush what they doubtless believed was a revolutionary faction.

After a final meal with his twelve disciples,[2] Jesus tells them
that he is about to be betrayed, then openly sends Judas Iscariot on

---

[2]The choice of twelve devotees might have been another hint to his fellow Jews
that Jesus believed that he was the Messiah. Before he invaded the land of
Canaan, Moses' proxy – Joshua – sent twelve spies to gather information about the
Canaanites. These spies later became the founders of the twelve tribes of Israel.
Choosing exactly twelve disciples could have appeared the choice of a fledgling
warrior Messiah, poised for war on the Gentiles.

his way. For Christians, Jesus was clearly condoning his own betrayal and surrendering to his fate.

Nevertheless, having retired – or gone into hiding – in the nearby Garden of Gethsemane, Jesus is described as having a crisis of faith: he begs God to "take this cup away."

He was then arrested by soldiers (led there by Judas Iscariot) from the Sanhedrin – the Jewish Supreme Court. This was a politico-religious body that operated autonomously, but with deference to Roman law. At least one disciple tried to attack the troops but, in keeping with his non-violent teachings, Jesus told his followers to stop fighting and went with the soldiers quietly.

Brought before the High Priest, he was asked: "Art thou the Christ, Son of the Blessed?"[3] To which he answers: "I am" (Mark: ch14, v61–2). This is Jesus' first reported public announcement that he is the Son of God,[4] but some doubt its veracity. The Gospels make it plain that the followers of Jesus had gone into hiding the moment he was arrested. So how could they have known what had happened at a secret inquisition?

Moreover since, for a first-century Jew, the idea of a 'Son of God' was heretical as well as nonsensical, a high priest would have been highly unlikely to ask it even as a joke. For whatever reason, Jesus was found guilty of heresy – a sentence that carried an automatic death penalty.

However, further evidence of Jesus' political importance is evidenced by the fact that the Sanhedrin, despite having the right to stone Jesus to death, refrained from doing so. Like a political hot potato, he was tossed to the Roman Governor, Pontius Pilate.

The Gospels explain this odd decision by saying that the Jewish priests were not allowed to execute anyone during Passover, but fail to explain why Jesus was not simply locked up for three or four days, then stoned. Either Jesus was too dangerous to hold (the secrecy of his Jewish trial suggests that the high priests were afraid of a rescue attempt by the citizens) or Jesus had committed political crimes that the Romans would insist came within their jurisdiction. Either way, Jesus was obviously more important

[3] A circumlocution for "Son of God".
[4] Jesus referred to the "Son of Man" occasionally in his preaching, but always either in the third person (Mark: ch13, v26; Matthew: ch4, v27) or as an entity distinctly separate from himself (Mark: ch28, v38; Luke: ch9, v26 and ch12, v8–9).

than the simple preacher of pacifism depicted in the Gospels.

Pontius Pilate, according to Josephus, was a violent and culturally insensitive man who would eventually be recalled to Rome to face trial for his misrule as governor. However, the Gospels show him bending over backwards to try to avoid executing Jesus. Pilate even asked the crowd if they wanted Jesus freed, but when they said they would prefer a thief called Barabas to be released, Pilate literally washed his hands of the matter – a ritual sign of disgust.

So Jesus was beaten, flogged, ridiculed and finally crucified under a sign that, with clumsy irony, declared his crime against Rome as claiming to be "THE KING OF THE JEWS".

Following such brutal treatment it is perhaps not surprising that Jesus died within hours. But since strong, relatively young men could be expected to survive crucifixion for up to a week (death usually came about from dehydration), the Romans became suspicious. Possibly having heard that Jesus, just before he apparently died, had been given a drink of "vinegar" from a sponge on the point of a spear, Pilate ordered that before he was taken down, Jesus should be stabbed to make sure he was actually dead. It therefore seems odd then that a gush of "blood and water" from the wound made in Jesus' side (John: ch19, v34) did not cause the soldiers to check further. Corpses, however fresh, do not bleed very much.

The Gospels' insistence that Jesus actually died on the cross has been questioned. Books like *The Holy Blood and the Holy Grail* (by Michael Baigent, Henry Lincoln and Richard Leigh) and Hugh Schonfield's *The Passover Plot* started the debate in the 1980s. Both suggest that Jesus' death was faked by his followers, emphasizing that he was seen to "die" shortly after being given the drink from the sponge. A powerful sedative could have produced the impression of death.

Schonfield goes so far as to suggest that Jesus deliberately got himself crucified, meaning to escape with the aid of the drug in the sponge. The plan was to use his "return from the dead" as proof that he was the Messiah. The plot backfired, Schonfield suggests, when Jesus died of his wounds, but his followers stuck to the plan anyway, and spread the rumour of his resurrection and ascent into Heaven.

The Holy Blood and the Holy Grail goes even further, arguing that Jesus survived the crucifixion but then (not surprisingly considering his ordeal) retired from public life. He married the reformed prostitute called Mary Magdalene, moved to Gaul and their descendants later became the Merovingian kings of Medieval France.

Startling as these conjectures are, they pale next to theories of the respected Dead Sea Scrolls expert, Dr Barbara Thiering. Over three books – *Jesus the Man, Jesus of the Apocalypse* and *The Book Jesus Wrote (John's Gospel)* – Thiering constructs a fascinating historical detective story. What follows is an attempt – necessarily inadequate – to summarize her views.

We should begin by noting that the political situation in first century Judea was much more complicated than the impression given in the New Testament. The Gospels mention the *Sadducees* and the *Pharisees* (two important sects within the Jewish religious hierarchy) the *Scribes* (a catch-all title for religious teachers) and, of course, the occupying Romans – but little of the Judean political interplay taking place at that time is even hinted at in the New Testament.

The Pharisees were actually an ultra-conservative group of Orthodox Jews who believed that only strict adherence to Yahweh's laws could bring Jewish redemption and, perhaps more importantly, keep Yahweh from cursing the Chosen People again. Despite his insistence that he had no desire to overturn the Old Testament, Jesus was a religious innovator first and foremost, so he would naturally find himself opposed by the Pharisees. They appear in the Gospels as Jesus' chief opponents and plotters of his downfall.

The Sadducees were an older, but more liberal, sect who, at the time of Jesus' ministry, were the dominant force in the Jerusalem Temple's priesthood. Because they were less rigid in their attitude to Gentiles, the Sadducees maintained a generally helpful attitude to the Roman administration. Indeed, traditionalist Jews might have seen them as collaborators and religious backsliders. Nevertheless, the Gospels describe the Sadducees conniving with the Pharisees to destroy Jesus.

Scribes are also mentioned in the Gospels – again in a largely negative role. In Jesus' time they were men who made their living as wandering religious teachers. Jesus' "heresies" might have annoyed this group but, as he was called "Rabbi" by his followers (then a Scribe title) it is possible that he himself was trained as a Scribe.[5]

The Romans – surprisingly from a Jewish Messianic viewpoint – are not the villains in the Gospels. They are certainly seen as foreign oppressors, but are generally kept to the background. When they do feature directly in the story, they are oddly sympathetic. Pontius Pilate tried to save Jesus, against the wishes of the Jewish religious hierarchy and, later, a centurion at the foot of the cross even exclaims: "Truly, this was the son of God!"[6] (Matthew: ch27, v54).

Another Jewish political group mentioned in the Gospels is the Zealots. These were religious fanatics, dedicated to the use of violent means to defeat the Romans and bring about the coming of the warrior Messiah. Jesus' non-violent message would seem to rule out any sympathy with the Zealots, but at least one of his chosen disciples, Simon, was openly called "the Zealot", and the fact that Jesus was crucified by the Romans for political pretensions to kingship suggests they too might have thought he was a member of the Zealot organization.

Finally, a mysterious group called "the *Herodians*" is briefly mentioned as plotting with the Pharisees (Mark: ch12, v13) but nothing much else is indicated about them in the Gospels.

However, as Thiering points out, it is the Herodians and another political movement that the Gospels did not even mention that may point to political agendas deliberately concealed by the early Christians. The Herodians and the *Essenes* were two of the most important factions in Judea during the period of Jesus' ministry, so their non-inclusion is a negative indicator, like the dog in the Sherlock Holmes story, *Silver Blaze*, that revealed the identity of the criminal by *not* barking.

The Herodians were a directly political group, although not nonreligious – no political faction in first-century Judean public life was non-religious. They were a small group of influential, liberal Jews who wished to see Herod the Great's grandson, Herod

[5]It is also interesting to note that, for Jesus' contemporaries, the title "Rabbi" was only applicable to a married man.

[6]Given that the Gospels were written partially to help convert Romans to Christianity, it is perhaps not surprising that the Roman participants were treated so sympathetically in the texts.

Agrippa, placed on the throne of Judea. Despite the deposing of King Archelaus in AD 6, the tetrarchs Herod Philip and Herod Antipas remained in power in neighbouring provinces and – if too old to win the right to rule Jerusalem themselves – they were (somewhat) willing to back their nephew in his attempts to gain the throne of Judea.

Brought up in Rome, Herod Agrippa must have seemed an ideal halfway point for liberal Judeans: he was a devout Jew (if still a foreign-blooded Edomite) and was also a favourite at the court of the Emperor Augustus. Judea's most recent glory days had been under the rule of another of Augustus' pets, Herod the Great. If Herod Agrippa was placed on the throne, the Herodians thought, Judea's good fortunes *must* revive.

Unfortunately Agrippa's mercurial temperament meant that he was regularly both in debt and in trouble. He was exiled from Rome by Augustus' parsimonious successor, Tiberius, and at the time of Jesus' ministry was knocking around Judea trying to find the money and the political backing to return to the emperor's court. As we will see – if we accept Thiering's hypothesis – Jesus' execution provided Agrippa with the latter.[7]

The group mysteriously left out of the Gospels is the Essenes. Not much was known about this monastic sect until 1947, when a large cache of amazingly well-preserved Essene documents were found hidden in hill caves at Qumran, near Palestine's Dead Sea. Some of the so-called "Dead Sea Scrolls" dated back over 2,000 years to the century before Jesus, but others tantalizingly come from around the time of his life, and ran to several decades after his crucifixion. Scholars in the 1940s wondered if further enlightening details of early Christianity might at last be forthcoming.

The first thing that was noticed was that the Essenes were clearly as obsessed with Old Testament law as the Pharisees, but they also espoused a gentler, more humanitarian interpretation of the will of Yahweh. Indeed much, but by no means all of Jesus' teachings echo Essene doctrine, lending weight to the suggestion that he was an Essene.

The Dead Sea Scrolls also revealed that when Judas Maccabeus

[7]Herod Agrippa eventually did become King of Judaea under his old friend the Emperor Gaius (AKA Caligula). After declaring himself the Messiah in AD 44, Agrippa suddenly died of a mysterious illness – probably poisoned.

concluded his highly successful guerrilla war against the Hellenized Jewish followers of Antiochus IV, and finally rededicated the Temple in 164 BC, his brother Jonathan was made High Priest. After Jonathan's death, his brother Simon succeeded him – in short, they had set themselves up as the hereditary rulers of Judea. Eventually, dropping all pretence, the Maccabees declared themselves the nation's kings as well as its high priests.

Although this sounds a fitting reward for the family that had freed the Jews, it outraged the descendants of Zerubbabel, the former Satrap (king/governor) under the Persians. These remembered that their forebear had once been hailed as the Messiah for rebuilding the Temple – although he had declined the title – and they jealously scorned the Maccabee dynasty as little better than the Hellenized Jewish followers of Antiochus IV.

So they withdrew to the wilderness near the Dead Sea, and became the Qumran Essene community. There they lived lives of monastic self-denial – living in spartan conditions, permitting themselves sexual contact only to have children, developing highly elaborate religious ceremonies, studying and teaching scripture, and recording the events of the outside world with a certain level of disdain.

Unfortunately, the Essenes were also habitually secretive in their writings – perhaps not a surprising fact after 500 years of foreign oppression. They frequently encoded their real meanings within biblical and historical riddles. This makes understanding their commentaries difficult and sometimes impossible where we have lost the references that the Essenes took for granted.

The Essenes often wrote in double meanings: so, for example, if they wished to refer to the Roman occupation, they would speak of the "Babylonians" oppressing the Chosen People. To a non-Essene, the scroll would look like a piece of history, not contemporary social comment. They called such political brainteasers *peshers* (Hebrew: meaning "dream interpretations").

Barbara Thiering is an Australian historian who has specialized in studying the pesher riddles in the Dead Sea Scrolls. Over years of study she realized two things: that the only way to understand Essene peshers was to have an in-depth knowledge of Jewish history, and that the Gospels themselves were riddled with peshers.

An example is the story of Jesus' cursing of the fig tree on his way to Jerusalem (Mark: chapter 11). At that time of year – in the Spring – no fig tree could have been in fruit. Yet Jesus curses it "root and branch" when he finds it bare of figs and, later, it is seen to have withered and died. This story is presented in the New Testament as an actual event, not as a parable. So why such uncharacteristically petulant behaviour from a man who preached sweetness and reason?

Barbara Thiering cuts through the complex and largely unsatisfactory theological arguments by explaining a few historical facts. According to Thiering the cursing of the fig tree is an allegory. She points out that the fig tree was an emblem used by the violently anti-Roman Zealot movement – as opposed to the "vineyard", which was a favourite image of the pro-Roman Herodians. In cursing the "fig tree" for not bearing fruit, Jesus is, according to Thiering, criticizing the Zealots, while at the same time, associating himself with the more liberal aspirations of the pro-Roman Herodian "vineyard" party.

Certainly Jesus' parables often utilize the image of a vineyard (Matthew: chapter 20), and he specifically refused to condemn Rome when tempted to do so by his enemies.

Looking at the New Testament as a whole, Thiering argues that an entire history lies hidden beneath a veneer of parables and allegories – that the New Testament itself is effectively one long pesher. To understand this secret history it is necessary to know some fascinating but little-known, facts[8] about Herod's new religion.

During the reign of Herod the Great (37 BC – 4 BC) certain enterprizing Jews realized two things: that more practising Jews lived outside Judea than in (they were known as the *Diaspora*) and that the Roman Empire's rules about foreign religions offered an unimaginably profitable loophole if exploited properly.

The newly-installed King Herod I planned great building and development projects for his new realm, but Judea was a poor and backward nation. On the suggestion of respected Diaspora Jews like Rabbi Hillel (known as Hillel the Great) and Manahem the Essene (founder of the Magian sect), Herod effectively reinvented Judaism to fit his plans.

The Diaspora Jews were extremely rich compared to their Judean kindred – trading, as they did, across the Mediterranean

[8]For full details see Josephus' books *The Jewish War* and *The Antiquities of the Jews*.

and beyond. They were also more cosmopolitan and liberal, and they yearned for the good-old homeland like New York Irishmen on St Patrick's Day. As we shall see later there was also, during that period, a popular belief that the time of the Messiah was approaching.

Taking advantage of all these factors, Herod the Great set up a "mission" to the Diaspora Jews. His representatives preached a new and revivified Judaism, based around Herod as the king who would bring about the Kingdom of Heaven on Earth. Those who wished to join – and thus ensure their place in the new Jerusalem – needed only to pay a regular "tithe" to Herod's agents and undergo the new rebirth ceremony – invented by Herod's advisers – called "baptism". Gentiles were also welcome as converts to the Jewish mission but, of course, had to be circumcized and obey Jewish law as well as be baptized and pay the tithes.

The result was more spectacularly successful than Herod and his advisers could have dreamed. Converts and their money poured in and Herod the Great earned his nickname by transforming Judea into a thoroughly modern state. But this success led some Jews to dream further . . .

Roman law did not interfere in a citizen's choice of religion and, likewise, did not prevent individuals like Herod collecting religious tithes provided they, in turn, paid their taxes to Rome. If the mission could convert a majority of Romans to Judaism – and the stream of Gentile converts made this seem a plausible goal – Judea would become the new centre of the Roman Empire, effectively displacing Rome, like a cuckoo chick taking over a nest.

Optimists involved in Herod's mission wondered if this plan was the prophecy of Jewish world domination coming true before their eyes. Such hopes may sound far-fetched, but we should remember that this was exactly what Christianity would do later when it became the State religion of the Roman Empire.

All the important Judean sects became involved with Herod's mission to differing degrees – for he had plenty of money to give to his friends, while he could be ruthless towards anyone who crossed him. The political control of the Jerusalem Temple swung back and forth between the conservative Pharisees and the liberal Sadducees, but neither party complained at Herod's religious experimentalism and (some might have said) his exploitation of Gentiles and the Diaspora Jews. For the Scribes, Herod offered new and interesting job opportunities outside Judea, spreading news of the mission and collecting the tithes. And the bookish Essenes watched and recorded events with growing hope that it would all lead to the coming of the Messiah and the Kingdom of God. Then Herod died and the roof fell in.

Herod had been the cornerstone of the reformed religion, and it was now split with squabbles. Everyone agreed that what was needed was a new leader: but who? Nobody believed that Herod's inept son Archelaus could fill the role. It was this position, says Thiering, that Jesus aimed to step into thirty-four years after Herod's death.

Herod the Great apparently tolerated Jesus' family, as they were direct descendants of King David. Thiering believes that Jesus' family were actually part of the monastic Essene group that lived in the Qumran community. Joseph, Jesus' father, would have been a highly-respected religious figure at Qumran, deferentially referred to as "the David".[9] According to Thiering, Joseph would also have carried another formal title, indicating his importance and, at the same time, his subordination to Herod: he was called "the Christ".

Certain Dead Sea Scrolls suggest that the Essenes believed in *two* Messiahs – the superior was the member of the Herod dynasty who would eventually bring about the Kingdom of God (via the work of Herod's mission to the Diaspora), while the inferior was a sort of helper-Messiah, who dealt with matters like the Gentiles who wished to become Jews. The superior leader carried the superior title of "Messiah", while the inferior man was given an inferior title of "Christ", which was the Greek word for Messiah. Until the Kingdom of God actually arrived, however, both titles would be handed down in the Herod and David families, from father to son. This would explain why Josephus, a devout Jew, could write that Jesus was "the Christ". For him it would have been just a title, not a statement of faith.

[9]The Gospels describe Joseph as a common carpenter because, Thiering says, whenever he left the monastic retreat to visit the outside world, he would have been expected to earn his living – no matter that he was an immensely important religious figure – because the Essenes were a mendicant (penniless) order. Joseph's profession in such cases was that of a carpenter.

Jesus, according to Thiering, was fathered by Joseph on a female Essene called Miriam (Hellenized later to Mary) – the term used for such Essene "nuns" was "Virgin". Unfortunately, Jesus was conceived between the betrothal of Joseph and Miriam and their wedding, creating something of a constitutional crisis over his entitlement to be the new Christ.

The conservative Pharisees held that Jesus was a bastard (although he was born after the marriage) and that the next son, James, should be the Christ after Joseph's death. The liberal Sadducees, on the other hand, said that Jesus was legitimate, and so was entitled to be the Christ. As power swung back and forth between the Pharisees and the Sadducees in Judea's two-party religious hierarchy, Jesus' position changed accordingly. This doubtless had a marked effect on the young man. Perhaps Jesus became a revolutionary because he had a personal grudge against the religious conservatism that was constantly trying to disinherit him.

Jesus began his ministry as the Christ following Joseph's death. Needless to say, if the Pharisees had been in power at that time, his younger brother, James, would have become "the Christ". Jesus' preaching – which Thiering argues took place in and around the Dead Sea and Qumran, not Galilee[10] – was largely in line with Essene humanitarian beliefs. The Sermon on the Mount, for example, is an echo of many things written in the Dead Sea Scrolls decades before Jesus' birth. Nevertheless, Jesus was undoubtedly a rebel, and many of his teachings would have shocked typical Essenes.

He rejected the strict religious rules about the Sabbath – perhaps on the practical grounds that they had condemned the Jews to permanent foreign occupation by frustrating every attempt to fight off foreigners whose gods allowed them to march, fight and plunder on Saturdays. Jesus also associated with such monastically "unclean" persons as Gentiles, women who were not Essene "virgins" and tax collectors – a stand amounting to a declaration as revolutionary as Gandhi's rejection of the Hindu caste system 2,000 years later.

[10]Thiering points out that many of the distances and much of the geography described in the Gospel of Mark (generally believed to be the first Gospel to be written) are plain wrong. Yet, if Mark's descriptions of Jesus' travels are divided by ten and transposed to the area around the Dead Sea, they fit perfectly.

Most importantly, however, Jesus argued that Gentiles (even Romans) were as beloved by God as the Chosen People. Even under Herod I's mission, converted Gentiles were treated as second-class Jews. Jesus shocked the Essene establishment by arguing the right of every Gentile convert and initiated Jew to act as a priest, because God was close to all of his true followers, regardless of race, sex or profession.

Jesus' crucifixion came about, according to Thiering, because the Roman Governor, Pontius Pilate, needed scapegoats to execute after a Zealot riot in Jerusalem. Herod Agrippa, now rich enough to return to Rome, still needed political backing to get his sentence of exile reversed. So, in return for a favourable letter of endorsement from the Roman governor, Agrippa betrayed the Zealot leader, Simon Magus, to the Romans and threw in Jesus – Simon Magus' friend, if not his fellow Zealot – as well. The Pharisees had just pushed the Sadducees from power, so Jesus was bereft of his political protection and his title as the Christ.

(An interesting aside – Thiering's study of the Dead Sea Scrolls suggested that Pilate needed *three* scapegoats to satisfy his political masters in Rome. The result was that a Zealot friend of Herod Agrippa also had to be betrayed and crucified. That Zealot's name was Judas Iscariot – thus he was the betrayed, not the betrayer.)

Barbara Thiering argues that Jesus survived the crucifixion (drugged by a sedative in the sponge on the spear point). She also suggests that, after his convalescence, he continued his political career, but only in the background. Having been crippled by the nails driven through his hands, he was a less-than-inspiring leader figure and, moreover, the myth of his death and resurrection was too powerful a tool for the early Christian Church to forego.

Jesus himself laid out the policy of sugar-coating the message of the Gospels when he explained to his disciples that the parable stories were mainly a way to reach the "children in Christ". The basic messages of the parables were perfectly valid, but only those informed enough to divine their inner meaning (through the peshers) could understand the veiled history of Jesus' ministry hidden therein. As Jesus proclaimed: "Those who have ears to hear, let them hear!" Everyone else, children and adults, who did not have the necessary training and knowledge ("ears") were designated "Children in Christ", and should not be told of the real history of their movement.

Thiering suggests that Jesus not only dictated the Gospel of John (which she believes was the first to be written and the indirect template for the Synoptic Gospels) but also survived as a guiding force for the early Church up to his death, sometime in his mid-seventies. She cites evidence in the New Testament of the AD 73 wedding and "coronation" in Rome of one Jesus Justus. This, she suggests, was Jesus' son, inheriting the position of the head of the David line.

Following the deaths of many senior Christians during Nero's persecutions and the shattering of most Jewish religious institutions after the failed Judean rebellion in AD 66–70 (including the Judean branch of Christendom and the Essene monasteries), the numbers of "those with ears to hear" fell to effectively zero. Any surviving Christians who recognized the peshers in the Gospels[11] must have realized that it was in the interest of their religion's survival that they did not pass on the knowledge and risk disillusioning future converts. Within a couple of generations the Church passed into the hands of the "Children in Christ", and the deeper meaning of the Gospels was lost.

In AD 325, the Christian Bishops met at Nicaea, in what is now northern Turkey, to debate what Jesus' body was made of. This seemingly innocuous discussion was ultimately to set the path for the Christian Church and finally cut all direct connection with Judaism.

On the one side was Arius, who believed that Jesus was a "created being" of human flesh – a man moved by the will of God, but not a God himself. God was immutable, he argued, and therefore, by definition, indivisible. In other words, Jesus was simply another Prophet of God, like Elijah or Moses. His opponents, led by Bishop Athanasius, disagreed; they said Jesus *was* God, who, since he was omnipotent, could divide himself into Father, son and Holy Ghost without subdividing himself.

It was the orthodox side that won – exiling Arius and declaring his followers heretics. This irrevocably set the path of Church doctrine

[11]Barbara Thiering dates the writing of the four Canonized Gospels to the decade after the crucifixion, whereas most theologians think they were written much later, some even dating John's Gospel to around AD 100.

(and some might say intolerance) for the rest of history. The Judaic roots of the religion were to be quietly ignored, yet, as we saw at the beginning of this chapter, Jesus' career was in many ways an extension of Old Testament prophets like Amos and Daniel.

Even if we reject Barbara Thiering's complex theory, it has to be accepted that Christian theology can no longer exist in a vacuum, refusing to take first-century Jewish political history into account. The Jesus who preached during that period must have been a politician as well as a preacher, otherwise he would not have made such a political impact. This point can be further illustrated if we look at what might be called Jesus' precognitive prophecies.

Like most monotheistic prophets, Jesus' doctrine was mainly based upon knowing the will of God, and preaching the certain results of either following or ignoring that will. However, he did make three specific predictions about the future.

The most striking to his contemporary audience was that the Jerusalem Temple would be destroyed. This indeed happened in AD 70 after the Zealot movement started a general revolt against Roman rule. The Jews did not have a chance of winning, and many of the leaders of the revolt were perfectly aware of this fact, but went ahead anyway. The Zealots so completely believed in Yahweh's promise to protect the Chosen People from ultimate destruction that they embarked on a course that virtually ensured obliteration. Faced with this Hobson's choice, they believed, God would have to send the Messiah and aid the Jews in their holy war. When He failed to sweep the Romans from the land, the Jewish rebels were massacred, committed suicide (as at the siege of Masada) or were driven into hiding or exile. Rome besieged and levelled Jerusalem then declared Judea a pagan province.

Of course, it would not necessarily take precognitive powers in the AD 30s to guess that the Temple might be destroyed in the near future – anyone with enough political common sense to know just how far the Zealots were willing to infuriate Rome could have guessed that the typical Roman reaction would be to destroy Judaism's proudest monument.

It is also possible, at the risk of sounding over-cynical, to explain Jesus' second prophecy – of Christianity's ultimate triumph – as political foresight. He predicted that his own Church would prosper, but would yet contain evil as well as good elements. At the end of the world, a divine cleansing would perfect the Church, allowing the faithful to enter the Kingdom of God. The latter part of this prophecy has, obviously, yet to happen, but it is certainly true that Christianity prospered and grew. But then, we might ask, what founder of a new religion would *not* predict its future success? As to the corrupt elements, surely anyone with a cursory knowledge of human nature could have predicted them.

Yet even if these last two predictions can be dismissed in terms of ordinary political foresight, Jesus' third prophecy takes more explaining. In Luke (ch9, v27) and Matthew (ch16, v28) Jesus predicts that "some standing here will not taste death before they see the Son of Man coming into his Kingdom." Christian doctrine holds this to be a true prophecy, and claims that Jesus was predicting his crucifixion, his resurrection, his ascension to Heaven and his redemption of mankind from the sin of Adam through that sacrifice.

However, to a historian with a little knowledge of first-century Judea, there occurs another possibility as to what Jesus was talking about – one that Jesus' audience would certainly have thought of . . .

We have already looked at how easily the main Jewish religious bodies took to Herod the Great's dabbling in religious doctrine with his mission to the Diaspora and the Gentiles. One of the main reasons for this uncharacteristic liberality was the Jewish calendar. Herod came to power in 37 BC but, of course, this was not the date the Jews would have used. For them it was the year 3903 from the creation of the world, as defined by the Book of Enoch.

At that time it was widely believed that the coming of the Messiah would take place in the year 4000 from the creation of the Earth – ninety-seven years in the future. This Jewish millennialism was one of the reasons why conservative Jews were willing to back the religious experimentalism of a foreigner like Herod – a lot could happen in ninety-odd years, but one thing was certain: Herod would be dead, and therefore could not be the Messiah himself. For them, Herod was only clearing the path for the actual *Jewish* Messiah. Herod I could hint to the worthless Gentiles that he was the future Messiah as much as he liked; God's will would ultimately triumph.

As he was speaking in the AD 30s, Jesus' audience had less than thirty years to wait for the Jewish millennium (that would fall in the Christian year AD 61). When Jesus said "some standing here will not taste death before they see the Son of Man coming into his Kingdom", his audience would certainly have thought that he might be referring to the Jewish year 4000 and the Messiah prophecy. Readers will have to decide for themselves whether that was what Jesus himself actually meant.

When the year 4000 (AD 61) came and went without a sign of the Jewish Messiah, the Temple elders hurriedly reinterpreted their calendar. They removed the 33 years of – the now highly resented – Herod the Great's reign from their calculation, explaining that it was an unclean time of religious backsliding. The new date set for the coming of the Messiah was now 4033 from the creation (or AD 94).

Unfortunately, as we saw above, the total failure of the Jewish rebellion put an end to any hope of a Jewish warlord Messiah in that or any other year.

Ultimately, our study of Jesus' preaching career has thrown up a much more politically active picture of him than that depicted in typical Christian doctrine. It is possible, as Barbara Thiering suggests, that he was fundamentally a religious politician, aiming to restart the charismatic, convert-hunting mission of Herod the Great. On the other hand, he might have been Hugh Schonfield's conniving rebel – who plotted to survive crucifixion in order to reappear as the warrior Messiah and expel the Roman occupiers with a popular revolt. Or he might have been God in human form, come to Earth to offer redemption to mankind.

Whatever Jesus was, however, he was *not* the apolitical, spiritually inclined dreamer so often depicted by modern Christianity.

Whether Jesus was a man or God-on-Earth is a matter for personal opinion and/or faith but, of course, nothing diminishes the importance of his recorded teachings. In the final analysis, it has to be seen that, in terms of religious prophecy, Jesus went far beyond anything seen before. Far more than any previous Mediterranean prophet – monotheistic or polytheistic – he was a religious innovator and reinventor.

Whether or not he was the Son of God, whether he was acting entirely from his own inspiration or was influenced by the teachings of the Essenes and John the Baptist, Jesus set in motion a new form of humanitarian belief that would change the face of the world.

Chapter 7

The Book of the Apocalypse

So how did Jesus, a minor Jewish prophet, whose influence was purely local, succeed in surpassing the fame of all his predecessors?

The answer is that *he* didn't. In fact, in the years immediately after Jesus' death, Christian teaching still had no influence in the Roman Empire and would almost certainly have died out after the destruction of Jewish Judea in AD 70. But an enthusiast called Paul of Tarsus, later known as St Paul, took the minor cult in hand and, with what can only be called a genius for publicity, turned it into a fully-fledged religion.

Paul was a Romanized Jew who changed his name from Saul to Paul when he became a Roman citizen (and not, as usually stated, when he became a Christian convert). He was, at the same time, a fanatically committed Pharisee – the most conservative sect of first-century Judaism. As a result he was given the job of stamping out the more extreme religious sects that were making life difficult for the Temple authorities – he was, in short, an officially condoned inquisitor and thug.

Several years after the crucifixion, Paul was temporarily struck blind while "on the road to Damascus." At that same moment – which some cynics have put down to a severe case of sunstroke – Paul was granted a vision of Jesus glorified in Heaven: an image that changed his life . . . and the destiny of world religion.

His destination would not have been the town of Damascus in Syria – which was outside Judea and therefore outside the scope of his authority – but Qumran, on the shores of the Dead Sea, which was also referred to as "Damascus". Qumran was still, at that time, the home of the sect known as the Essenes (see last chapter).

Probably Paul had been going to Qumran to threaten, arrest or even assassinate a leading member of the Essene community – Jesus' younger brother James, known as James the Just.

James was doubtless startled when the man who had come to Qumran to persecute him instead begged to know all about his brother Jesus. What James – and other members of the community – told him seems to have inspired Paul to create his own religion based upon Jesus. When, in due course, the horrified Qumranians realized what the new convert was actually preaching, they nicknamed him "the spouter of lies".

According to Paul, Jesus was the "Son of God" and had died on the cross to save mankind from the consequences of "original sin" – the eating of the forbidden fruit by Adam and Eve that had doomed all their progeny to suffering and death outside the Garden of Eden.[1]

This version was bound to appeal to Gentiles, particularly those who (like the Romans) highly valued Greek culture. Paul's Jesus was reminiscent of Greek mythology in that Jesus was said to be the son of a deity – like most Greek heroes – and, in keeping with Greek fertility myths, had died and returned to life.

Indeed, some historians point to the inclusion of the halo in early iconic pictures of Jesus as an attempt to link him to the various pagan Sun cults of the day. Such religions often held that the setting of the Sun was the death of the Sun god. The solar deity was said to be travelling through the underworld during the night, and was resurrected to new life, bringing new hope for mankind, the next dawn – a neat parallel with Christian doctrine.

Of course, the promise that Jesus' sacrifice and resurrection guaranteed his followers entry into Heaven was a powerful temptation to convert to the new faith. In fact the image of Heaven, offered by the post-Gospel writers, is very reminiscent of the Greco–Roman

[1]This, like much of Paul's new religion, was an entirely new concept to Judaism. There is no suggestion in the Old Testament that God bears a continuing grudge against humans for the sin of Adam. In Exodus (ch20, v5) Yahweh threatens that his anger might last to the third and fourth generations of a sinner's family, but that's as far as it goes. Likewise, there is no suggestion of original sin in the Gospels themselves and it is possible that Paul was not too certain of the idea himself. Only in his letter to the sect of Roman Christians (ch5, v12–19) does Paul suggest that Jesus' fundamental role was to act as the intermediary of God's forgiveness of the hereditary debt.

otherworld called *Elysium* – the blessed "land of milk and honey". However, pagan Elysium was reserved for dead heroes and for the disporting of the gods themselves – a cross between the Norse Valhalla and a divine holiday camp. Christianity's Heaven was open to all true believers.

James and his followers were known as *Messianists*, because they were still awaiting the coming of the Messiah. This "anointed one" was not, in their eyes, James' brother Jesus – although paradoxically some Messianists apparently believed that the martyred preacher would return from death and lead a military revolt against the Romans as a sort of sub-Messiah. One thing was certain, however: the Messiah they awaited would be an Orthodox Jewish warrior, not Paul's Hellenized demigod.

Possibly the only point on which James and Paul wholly agreed was that the end of the world was at hand, and that their sect – either Messianist or Christian, but not both – would alone be saved.

Paul's Christianity – which he carried abroad to the Gentiles rather than risk the fury of the followers of James in Judea – had a lot more appeal than the inward-looking Messianist[2] version of Jesus' life. In his *Criminal History of Mankind,* Colin Wilson notes:

> This new version of Christianity appealed to gentiles as much as Jews. Anyone of any sensitivity only had to look at the Rome of Tiberius, Caligula and Nero to understand just what Paul meant about the fall of man. These sex-mad drunkards were a living proof that something had gone wrong. And the Roman matron who took up prostitution for pleasure revealed that Eve had fallen just as far as Adam. The world was nauseated by Roman brutality, Roman materialism, Roman licentiousness. Christianity sounded a deeper note; it offered a vision of meaning and purpose, a vision of seriousness. For the strong, it was a promise of new heights of awareness. For the weak, it was a message of peace and reconciliation, of rest for the weary, of reward for the humble. And for everyone, it promised an end to the kingdom of Caesar, with its crucifixions, floggings and arbitrary executions. The Christians hoped it was a promise of the end of the world.

[2]James's faction did not, of course, call themselves Christians, because the word *Christ* was Greek – and they themselves were defiantly Jewish.

It was the Jewish revolt of AD 66–70 which ended in the destruction of the Temple, that led to the triumph of Paul's Christianity over James's Messianism. The insurrection was sparked – according to the Jewish historian Josephus – by the murder of James by the Jewish Orthodox priests in AD 62. The resulting rebellion was so violent that the Emperor Nero was forced to send his best general, Vespasian, to put it down.

When Nero committed suicide in AD 68, following a *coup* in Rome, Vespasian was proclaimed emperor by his troops. Several so-called "barrack room emperors" beat him to the throne, but these killed each other off in short order and Vespasian soon became the first half-decent emperor that Rome had seen in years.

Returning to Rome to take the throne, Vespasian left his son Titus to continue the siege of Jerusalem, which fell in September AD 70. The whole city was burned, the rebels – including the Messianists – were massacred or driven into exile, and the looted treasures of the Temple carried back to Rome in triumph. The Romans declared Judea a "pagan province" and what was left of the independent Jewish authorities collapsed.

Paul's probably enforced decision to preach his own version of the teachings of Jesus abroad now proved to be their salvation. If James' followers had not forced him out, early Christianity would probably been destroyed in the same conflagration that had consumed Messianism. As it was, despite suffering their own persecutions, the Christian communities were soon firmly rooted in pagan lands.

The Judean Jews lived on in what amounted to an occupied police state until AD 132, when they revolted again. The Emperor Hadrian then decided that he had had enough of these troublesome fanatics, and his soldiers slaughtered the rebels, banned circumcision and biblical teaching, and forbade all Jews from entering Jerusalem. With its traditional capital closed to it, Judaism fragmented, and two millennia of wandering began.

Meanwhile the new religion of Christianity, with its creed of the crucified saviour, went on from strength to strength.

One of the reasons Christianity was such a highly successful religion was that it preached the end of the world. Jesus had said that the coming of the "Kingdom of God" – the reformation of the physical world – would take place within the lifetime of some of the people then listening to him. Assuming some of his listeners were children, that meant that the Kingdom of God could be expected not much later than the end of the first century.

Such a close deadline must have concentrated minds wonderfully. Indeed St Paul, sometime in the mid-50s, had to write to a Greek Christian community, warning them to reject those Christians among them who were so certain that the end was near that they had given up working. "If a man will not work," he says grimly, "let him not eat" (2 Thessalonians: ch3, v10).

St Paul and most of the highest-ranking Christians, like St Peter, are traditionally believed to have been killed in Nero's persecutions in the AD 60s. Yet, if the Emperor Nero had meant to wipe out Christianity, Roman popular sympathy and his own insecure political situation prevented him finishing the job.

By the 80s, however, the Christians were again being persecuted, this time by an even more unpleasant emperor than Nero. Vespasian's younger son, Domitian – who almost certainly murdered his good-natured brother Titus to get the throne – insisted that he be addressed as "Lord God" and that the empire's coins all be reminted with this title under his profile.

Pagan Romans shrugged at this affectation – they'd been through it all before with the mad Emperor Gaius-Caligula, and knew it was best to just tug the forelock and keep their thoughts to themselves. The Christians, on the other hand, buoyed by the certainty that the coming of the Kingdom of God could not be more than a few years away, flatly refused to swear allegiance to a human deity, or to handle the idolatrous money. Domitian arrested and killed thousands of them for insulting him. With no likelihood of a back-lash of public opinion, like the one that had ended Nero's persecutions, it looked as if Christianity might be doomed.

Fortunately, Domitian was assassinated in AD 96,[3] but many surviving Christians were now in a vengeful and gloomy mood – hating their pagan Roman persecutors and impatient for the end of the world so they could escape to Heaven.

---

[3]An astrologer had told Domitian that he would die on 18 September AD 96, at a particular hour. When that hour passed, the usually paranoid emperor relaxed, little knowing that conspirators among his servants had deliberately misled him, telling him it was an hour later than it actually was. Convinced he was now safe, Domitian allowed himself to be drawn away from his guards and was stabbed to death . . . at the very moment the astrologer had predicted he would die.

It was around the time of Domitian's persecution of the Christians that the last book of the New Testament was written, and the prevailing atmosphere of the times can be found in every page.

Of all the books of the Bible, *Revelation* has inspired the greatest amount of would-be prophetic interpretation and, it has to be said, a frightening number of doomsday-obsessed, apocalyptic cults.

As we have already seen, the Hebrew word "apocalypse" originally described a revelation from God. Its transformation of meaning under Christianity to indicate the catastrophic end of the world is mainly due to this last book of the New Testament. Originally titled *The Apocalypse of St John the Divine*, subsequent translations of the Bible substituted the word "Apocalypse" in the title to "Revelation", precisely because the former word had so radically changed its meaning for the majority of churchgoers.

The Revelation of St John the Divine claims, like the Old Testament Book of Daniel, to be a work of prophecy in both the religious and precognitive meaning of the word: it spoke with the authority of God, and predicted events in the future.

Its author is traditionally believed to be the Apostle John; the same man who is said to have written John's Gospel and is also believed to have described himself modestly in that text as Jesus' "beloved disciple". However, many modern theologians believe – mainly for linguistic reasons – that "John" was actually the *nom de plume* for at least two different authors.

The message of Revelation owes at least as much to the warnings of John the Baptist as to the teachings of Jesus. As we saw in the last chapter, Jesus' announcement of the coming of the "Kingdom of God" was just as much a call to reform – socially and individually – as a prediction of the end of the physical world.

The Baptist, on the other hand, had foreseen universal destruction falling on all those who had not heard his message, repented and been baptized – the vast majority of humanity, in fact, as his followers were highly unlikely to have numbered more than a few hundreds.[4]

---

[4]An approach that would later lead St Athanasius (AD 293–373) to declare that "all who do not understand are damned". This Church law effectively ruled that not only those who refused to become Christians, but also those who were too slow-witted to avoid committing inadvertent heresies or who had never even heard of Christianity were doomed to eternal damnation. This included, according to Dante in the *Inferno*, everyone who had died before the birth of Christ.

The catastrophes predicted in Revelation, followed by the pitiless "final judgment" of all mankind, smacks of the Baptist's apocalyptic (in both the Hebrew and Christian senses) brand of religion.

Anyone who has even glanced at The Revelation of St John the Divine will probably sympathize with John Calvin, the sixteenth-century Protestant reformer, who said that "anyone who studies [Revelation] is either mad when he starts or is mad when he's finished."

Revelation is made up of a series of strange, but distinctly ordered images, which the author says came to him in a vision sent by God. This dream-like aspect of the book has confounded attempts to find solid, historically specific predictions, and has indeed fuelled insanity in many doomsday spotters.

John opens Revelation in the form of a letter to his fellow Christians in Asia Minor. These were organized into seven churches (bishoprics) and, as we will see, the number seven recurs in the text with repeated and reiterated importance – although why is open to any number of explanations, none in any way conclusive.

John describes Christ appearing to him and telling him to write down what he will shortly see. After passing on lengthy messages to each of the seven churches of Asia Minor, Jesus "opened a door in Heaven" and John is allowed to see God the Father, seated on a throne. God is described: "to look upon like a jasper and a carnelian:[5] and there was a rainbow about the throne, in sight like unto an emerald."

In God's hand is a scroll, sealed with seven seals. Jesus, described as "the Lamb that was slain", opens the first four seals and four mounted men appear. These are the four horsemen of the revelation (later dubbed the Four Horsemen of the Apocalypse): they apparently represent conquest,[6] war, famine and Death, although John only names Death specifically. Death is followed by Hell: "and power was given unto them over a fourth part of the earth."[7] An

---

[5]Brick-red, semi-precious stone, common to the Eastern Mediterranean.

[6]It is interesting to note that the horseman representing conquest was quickly replaced in the popular imagination with "pestilence". This is perhaps because the authorities, throughout history, have always been happy to condemn the wars of others, but consider their own conquests to be "God's will".

[7]John clearly regards Hell to be an entity rather than a place – perhaps like the god Hades, who was ruler of the Greek penitentiary afterlife.

optimist could read this to indicate that only a quarter of humankind are destined to be damned, but commentators on Revelation are rarely so generous in their interpretation.

The fifth seal reveals the souls of all the dead martyrs for Christianity. Having apparently forgotten Jesus' injunction to "turn the other cheek", they clamour to know when God will avenge them. They are told they must wait "a little season", until the preordained number of their fellow martyrs should also be killed.

The breaking of the sixth seal shows the first active sign of God's wrath. There is an earthquake, the Sun is blackened, the Moon becomes as red as blood, the stars fall from the heavens and "the fig tree casteth her untimely figs, when she is shaken by a mighty wind". The sky rolls up like a scroll and the mountains and islands of the Earth are moved from their previous positions.

The opening of the seventh seal reveals, after a "silence in Heaven about the space of half-an-hour", another set of seven: this time seven angels bearing seven trumpets. The blast of each of the first six trumpets inflicts another catastrophe on the Earth: a series of terrible fires, darkness, water pollution and a plague of giant, demonic locusts followed by an invasion of demonic cavalry.

A third of the population of the Earth and most of the plant and animal life are described as being killed off in these divine punishments, but the survivors refuse to either repent or give up their pagan beliefs.

The two "witnesses" – presumably representing leaders of the Christian Church – try to convert pagan humanity with true prophecies. These are no meek and gentle martyrs, however. Any man who tries to harm them is devoured by the "fire [that] proceedeth out of their mouth" (Revelation: ch11, v5).

Nevertheless, after three and a half years, the witnesses are slain by "the beast that ascendeth out of the bottomless pit". Their corpses are left to rot in the streets of a town "called Sodom and Egypt, where also our Lord was killed". Then, after three-and-a-half days, God resurrects the witnesses and a terrible earthquake kills 7,000 people in the town.

Humanity is then described as finally getting the message and, as they start to repent, the seventh trumpet is blown and Christ returns to rule over the Earth.

This is not the end of Revelation. John proceeds, without breaking stride, to continue with the list of catastrophes as if he had not just written that "the kingdoms of this world are become the kingdoms of our Lord, and of his Christ; and he shall reign for ever and ever" (ch11, v15). Whether he is going back and retelling the end of the world from a different point of view, or is describing a new set of God's plagues is not made plain.[8]

A "woman clothed with the sun, with the moon under her feet, and upon her head a crown of twelve stars" is described giving birth to a child. If we assume that John is retelling the events of the end of the world from a different perspective, we can probably also assume that the woman is a representation of Judea – the twelve stars representing the twelve tribes of Israel. This, in turn, might indicate that the child is Jesus. A "great red dragon" attempts to destroy the child as soon as it is born, but the infant is swept up to Heaven, while the woman is given an eagle's wings and flies to a safe place in the wilderness. John identifies the dragon as "that old serpent, called the Devil, and Satan."[9]

Satan then assaults Heaven and is cast down, "and his angels were cast out with him". This clearly seems to be a reference to the War in Heaven described in the Book of Enoch, but it further confuses the timeline. Enoch described the War in Heaven as happening in the distant past, but John seems to be suggesting that it took place either immediately after the death of Jesus or, indeed, that the war has yet to happen.

Theologically speaking, both these interpretations offer problems – the former because it would mean that Satan was still an Angel of God when he tempted Eve, Job and, later, Jesus; the latter because it would mean that Satan is *still* an angel in Heaven, and is therefore unlikely to be "the Great Destroyer" and the instigator of all human evil.

Either way, this passage in Revelation is the first time that Enoch's rebel angel, Lucifer, was specifically identified as Satan,

---

[8]It is at this point – the beginning of chapter 12 – that some theologians believe that another writer takes over from the original "John". Certainly the writing style changes at this point, becoming less Judaicly prosaic and more picturesque, in the Greek style.
[9]*Satan* is the Hebrew word meaning "adversary". However, the Old Testament and the Gospels both fail to make it plain whether Satan is the enemy of God – Yahweh and Satan are at least on speaking terms in the Book of Job – or is, in fact, God's servant, tasked with the adversarial testing of humanity. As God is omnipotent, it might be said to be illogical to describe anything as capable of being His adversary.

the Old Testament tempter, as well as the serpent – presumably the same one who got Adam and Eve thrown out of the Garden of Eden.

In coalescing these three enemies of mankind and God into one, John created a monolithic yet spiritual enemy that would later, ironically, save Christianity from chaos. In the days of the Byzantine Empire, the Papacy heavily emphasized the idea of "Satan the Great Destroyer". In doing this, the priests held up an external threat to distract people's attention from the petty doctrinal squabbles that were threatening to tear the Church apart. Satan was Christianity's ultimate bugbear ever afterwards.

In chapter 13 of Revelation, John becomes yet more dreamily obscure. He sees a terrifying "beast"[10] rise from the ocean with seven heads and ten horns. It is described as mainly resembling a leopard, but has the feet of a bear and has a mouth (singular) like a lion's.

Like the visionary monsters in the Book of Daniel (Daniel: ch7, v2–7), the beast is probably meant to be a representation of an empire. Indeed, its animal features all come from Daniel's four beasts – the Persian leopard, the Median bear, the Babylonian lion and the Greek goat horns.[11] So, John is clearly saying that "the beast" combines all the worst features of those Israel-oppressing empires.

John ends chapter 13 by telling the reader that "the beast" has a number associated with it: 666. The way in which John heavily hints that those with "understanding" will find special significance in this number is reminiscent of the Dead Sea Scrolls' peshers (discussed in the last chapter) that deliberately concealed hidden messages within the text. We will consider possible interpretations of the "number of the beast" later on.

In chapter 14 we are told that only 144,000 people have God's name "written on their foreheads". This may indicate the number of martyrs predestined to die for the Church, mentioned in chapter 6. On the other hand, some have interpreted this passage to indicate the total number of people who are *not* destined to be damned – a very poor lookout for the vast majority of the human race.

[10]Revelation always spells "beast" with a lower case *b*. Thus it is a description rather than a title.

[11]As we saw in chapter 1, Alexander the Great – the founder of the Macedonian–Greek Empire in Asia – was often depicted wearing a diadem decorated with two goat horns: a tribute to his patron god, Zeus-Ammon.

Those that follow and worship the beast are described as being marked with his number on their foreheads and hands. This passage has caused some people to be very nervous of barcode technology after rumours went about in the early 1980s that the number 666 was hidden in every single barcode. Actually, there is no technical evidence for this urban myth, which seems to be based on a combination of a misreading of the codes and a misunderstanding of the technology.

Nevertheless, fears of a future totalitarian (Satanic) regime forcing citizens to have barcodes tattooed on their heads and hands has caused consternation in fundamental Christian circles. Fortunately, however, cheap, paper-thin, silicon chips are likely to replace barcodes in the near future, so this interpretation of Revelation seems to be becoming less likely by the day.

The followers of the beast are certain to be among the damned: "And the smoke of their torment ascendeth up for ever and ever." But eternal burning is not to be the only horror in store for the damned. At the end of chapter 14, angels are (hopefully figuratively) described "reaping" humanity and placing them, like grapes, in a huge winepress. "And blood came out of the winepress, even unto the horse bridles, by the space of a thousand and six hundred furlongs." In other words, a 200 mile shallow lake of human blood.

Chapters 15 and 16 describe seven "plagues", released by seven angels from "vials". This is obviously, in these troubled times, highly reminiscent of biological warfare but, after the first plague that inflicts skin sores on the followers of the beast, the "plagues" are all in the form of natural disasters – the turning to blood of the seas and rivers, a burning heat, a universal darkness, the drying up of the River Euphrates and, finally, a terrible earthquake and a storm dropping sixty-pound hailstones.

Also worth noting in this chapter is the first appearance of an enigmatic companion of the beast: "the false prophet" (ch16, v13). However, John tells us nothing about him (or her) other than, like the beast, the false prophet is capable of vomiting up "unclean spirits".

Chapter 17 gives a closer view of the beast and the "whore" that rides upon it.

Chapter 18 dedicates itself to decrying the iniquities of the "whore", who John makes plain is supposed to be seen as a city, not just an actual woman. Unsurprisingly, God eventually destroys the whore/city in a welter of catastrophe and blood.

Chapter 19 describes the great war at the end of time that has come to be known as the "Battle of Armageddon", although the name Armageddon[12] is not actually mentioned here. It appears only once, back in chapter 16, verse 16, as a place where the kings who follow the beast gather at his command.

Many modern Christians believe that it is at this moment that "the Rapture" will occur – the lifting of all the true faithful into Heaven, leaving everyone else to suffer the "last days". It should be noted, however, that Revelation makes no mention of such an event; belief in the Rapture is a result of modern, North American Christian Millennialism, and has no biblical backing.

Another angelic horseman – also nameless, but referred to by John as "Faithful and True" and "The Word of God" – leads the army of Heaven against the beast and his followers. The beast and "the false prophet" are both captured and cast alive into a lake of burning sulphur. Their followers are all put to the sword and birds feast on their corpses.

Of course, the beast is not the main adversary of God: Satan was the power behind the beast and, in chapter 20, he is captured by an angel and chained up in a sealed pit.

Then Christ returns from Heaven and reigns in peace on Earth. Unfortunately, following the 1,000-year reign of Jesus, Satan is pre-ordained to escape. After gathering a great army from "the four quarters of the earth", Satan attacks the "beloved city", but is defeated when God sends down fire from the heavens. Satan is then thrown into the burning lake to join the false prophet and the beast – there to be "tormented day and night for ever and ever". God himself then appears, "from whose face the earth and heaven fled away" – this presumably meaning that the physical world is banished. The souls of the dead then stand before God, rising from either their graves or from Hell.[13]

---

[12]John specifically points this out to be a Hebrew name – it is thus probably meant to indicate the now-ruined Judean city of Megiddo (*Har* is the Hebrew prefix meaning "hill" – so [H]armegiddo[n] could be read as "the hill of Megiddo"). Sitting, as it did, on a strategically vital pass through the Mount Carmel Ridge, Megiddo has been the site of many battles throughout history, the last between the British and the Ottoman Turks in 1918.

[13]It should be noted that John makes it plain here that, although some souls have been sent to Hell, none have yet been allowed into Heaven. It is only recently hat it has commonly come to be believed that those not destined to be damned can get into Heaven before the Final Judgment.

The Final Judgment takes place: "And whosoever was not found written in the book of life was cast into the lake of fire" – an event similar to the judgment of individual souls described in the Ancient Egyptian *Book of the Dead*. Then the faithful are left to enjoy "a new heaven and a new earth". And both Death and Hell are cast into the burning lake – although what crime they have committed is not made plain.

Finally, after all the visions of savagery and horror, the eternal Kingdom of God, prophesied by John the Baptist and Jesus, has arrived. The last two chapters of Revelation are visions of the delightful world in store for the true believers in Christ. In the last chapter, an angel tells John not to keep his revelations to himself: "Seal not the sayings of the prophecy of this book: for the time is at hand."

As in the rest of the New Testament, Revelation gives little or no indication that, at the very least, almost 2,000 years will need to pass before the arrival of the Judgment Day.

The traditional Church interpretation of "the Beast of Revelation" is that it represents the Antichrist. This is a figure who emerged in the later books of the New Testament (2 Thessalonians and 1 John) and, although never mentioned by Jesus himself, was quickly taken up as Christian doctrine. The Antichrist, as the name suggests, is – or rather will be – the direct enemy of Christ: Satan's attempt to create an avatar on Earth and beat God at his own game, so to speak.

The Antichrist is described as "the lawless one" in 2 Thessalonians, and is prophesied to be a worker of false miracles and a spreader of false doctrine. Indeed, the Antichrist closely resembles the polemic image of Jesus, put about by Jewish authors in the second century AD (see chapter 5).

In the final days before the end of the world, the Antichrist is prophesied to become a powerful ruler. Therefore Antichrist/beast spotting has become the key feature of Christian eschatology – theology regarding the end of the world. However, there is another interpretation of "the Beast of Revelation" that relies on historical knowledge rather than Christian faith.

As we saw in Revelation, chapter 17, an angel allowed John to view the beast in greater detail, and he sees a woman riding the monster. This, John sees from a sign on her forehead, is "BABYLON THE GREAT, THE MOTHER OF HARLOTS AND

THE ABOMINATIONS OF THE EARTH." This, in fact, makes it likely that 'the beast' John is describing is a representation of the Roman Empire.

We know that first-century Jews insultingly referred to the city of Rome as "Babylon", because they felt that Rome was just as much a den of iniquity as the old Babylonian capital. It is possible that John – quite probably born a Jew – might have used the image as a code when writing to others that he knew would be acquainted with the insult.

Chapter 17, verse 9 seems to confirm this assumption: "The [beast's] seven heads are the seven mountains, on which the woman [the Whore of Babylon] sitteth." This would certainly make any first century reader think of the proverbial "seven hills of Rome".

The most famous verse in Revelation has also been cited as a convoluted clue that John was pointing to Rome as "the beast".

Here is wisdom. Let him that have understanding count the number of the beast: for it is the number of a man: and his number is six hundred and three score and six. (Revelation: ch13, v18)

It is fairly clear that John is hinting that those "that have understanding" could work out who or what the beast will be by contemplating the number 666.

Gematria was a Jewish, Kabbalistic technique that reduced Hebrew words, especially names, to numerical equivalents – a procedure intended to reveal secret messages within the Holy Scriptures. Jesus, for example, could be expressed as 888. [The Greek spelling of his name was "*Iesous*". Taking the predefined numerical value of each Hebrew letter and adding them together (10+8+200+70+400+200) gives the number 888.] If John was utilizing Gematria – and we know the technique was in use among Christians as well as Jews in his day – we would need to find a name that equates to 666. Unfortunately, given the scope for variation allowed by a religion that was speaking, in the first century alone, at least three languages (Hebrew, Greek and Roman), there are plenty of candidates for John's beast.

Using convolutions of both spelling and mathematics, different commentators down the ages have accused the Prophet Muhammad, the Emperor Napoleon and Adolf Hitler of being the beast/ Antichrist. Indeed, with a little work and a knowledge of ancient languages, anyone can be labelled 666.

However one possible interpretation of the number stands out. Irenaeus, Bishop of Lyon, writing in the mid-second century AD, is the first known scholar to write a treatise on St John's Revelation. In this work he claims that his former mentor, Bishop Polycarp of Smyrna, had known the author of Revelation personally, so it is possible that Irenaeus had some inside knowledge. Irenaeus suggests that John meant 666 to indicate the Greek word *Lateinos* – meaning "the Latin". Specifically, he says John was pointing to the Romans, whose language and origins were Latin. Using Gematria "Lateinos" adds up to exactly 666, and certainly the Roman Empire was the key threat to Christianity at the time Revelation was written.

If Bishop Irenaeus is right, that could make Revelation, like the Book of Daniel, more of a political commentary on the writer's contemporary period than a prophecy of times to come. (It might also be remembered that where the Book of Daniel predicted events of the Maccabee Revolt that the author believed would happen in the future (Daniel: ch11, v39 to the end of the book), it was, quite simply, wrong.)

If Revelation is an accurate prediction of the end of the world – as opposed to a cryptic fantasy about the Roman persecutors of the Christians being themselves made to suffer – it demands that the present-day reader takes its prophecy purely on faith: none of its predictions have visibly come to pass in almost two millennia. For those lacking a pure Christian faith, Revelation must simply be read as an ancient, surreal diatribe against a long dead empire.

Chapter 8

The Final Prophet

The religion of *Islam* (Arabic: meaning "surrender" – in this case to the will of Allah) was founded in the seventh century AD in Arabia – the desert-bound, million-square-mile peninsula that stands between North Africa and Iran. Despite being at a geographic crossroads between East and West, Arabia's brutal climate long held back Arab cultural development – especially inland of the coasts, where foreign traders and ideas rarely penetrated.

Although a Roman province for several hundred years, very little of the civilizing process that took place in other parts of the empire rubbed off on Arabia. When the Romans left, only the nomadic Arabs, known as Bedouins, saw much worth fighting over in inland Arabia.[1]

Foreign religions did rather better than foreign soldiers. The Arabs still worshipped many gods, and in their land, pagans mixed with Arabian converts to Zoroastrianism, Judaism and Christianity with little rancour. Life in the desert – running trading caravans, breeding camels and raiding back and forth – was hard enough without indulging in religious bigotry.

By the beginning of the sixth century, the Arabs were still largely a nomadic, clan-split society, with only a few ports and market towns scattered across the vast peninsula to offer any fixed centres of commerce, education and religion.

In western inland Arabia, there is a sandy valley, surrounded by

[1]It is ironic that this very land – because of the crude oil beneath it – is today some of the most valuable real estate in the world.

bare hills that afford no shelter from the heat and glare of the Sun, but whose most famous landmark is a well called Zemzem which never runs dry. Around this well sprang up a small caravan trading town called Mecca.

The valley of Zemzem was a holy site long before the creation of Islam. Near the well there stood a cube-shaped temple, known as the *Ka'bah*. This was, of course, a place of worship for the native pagan religion, but might also – before Muhammad – have been a holy sight for Arab converts to Judaism. It housed the sacred Black Stone, which tradition declared to have belonged to Adam, the first man. And even after Mecca ceased to be a great trading centre – because the increased navigation of the Red Sea had greatly reduced the number of caravans – the Ka'bah continued to be a holy place that brought in pilgrims and their money.

The *Koran* (the holy book of Islam) states that the Jewish prophet Abraham built the Ka'bah as a place of worship, aided by his son Ishmael. How Abraham came to be so far from his homeland is a story worthy of a soap opera. The Old Testament says that Abraham's wife, Sarah, was childless. She therefore gave Abraham permission to sleep with her young Egyptian handmaid, Hagar, to produce an heir. When Hagar became pregnant she began to give herself airs so, with Abraham's reluctant permission, Sarah proceeded to mistreat the girl. Terrified, Hagar escaped into the desert and there was visited by an angel. It told her not to fear and that her son would be "a wild ass of a man", who would provide Hagar with many descendants.

So Hagar returned to the house of Abraham and Sarah, and bore Ishmael. Fourteen years later, Sarah – although apparently well past childbearing age – fell pregnant. Upon the birth of her own son, Isaac, she became worried that Abraham might name the illegitimate Ishmael as co-heir. She therefore drove the long-suffering Hagar and her teenage son out into the desert, presumably hoping that they would die there. The pair survived, however, and Ishmael, displaying the strength of a wild ass, went on to become the founding father of all the Arabs – the Semitic people of Arabia. At that point, the Old Testament forgets about them, but the Koran adds that Abraham did not totally abandon his son and mistress to his wife's intrigues, and indeed spent many years living with them in Arabia. It was during this time, the Koran says, that the Ka'bah was built.

Muhammad was born in Mecca sometime around the year AD 570. He had a troubled, if not necessarily unhappy, childhood – his father died several months before his birth and his mother died when he was just six. This may not have been quite such a shattering event for the child, as he had been sent away to be brought up by desert-living, nomadic relatives while he was still a baby, as the air of towns was considered unhealthy for infants.

Returning to Mecca, Muhammad was taken into the house of his grandfather – the leader of the Hashim clan and the closest thing Mecca would have had to an upper class noble. However, the grandfather died when the boy was eight and Muhammad passed into the care of an uncle who ran merchant caravans. Thus the future prophet returned to the travelling life, journeying as far as Syria and witnessing cultures and religions far more complex than those in his backward homeland.

In AD 595, Muhammad married a rich, forty-year-old widow called Khadijah when he was just twenty-five. Certainly money must have been a factor in his decision to marry a woman so much his senior: as a minor when his father and grandfather died, he had been disallowed any inheritance. Nevertheless, the marriage seems to have been a happy one. Khadijah bore him two sons (who died young) and four daughters and, despite polygamy being the Arabian custom, Muhammad took no other wives until Khadijah died, twenty-four years later.

His wife's money allowed Muhammad to set up his own caravan trading business. Always deeply religious – he and Khadijah used to retreat to a desert cave to pray and meditate – Muhammad now became convinced that he was haunted by an evil spirit. He took to wandering out into the hills outside Mecca, pondering religious questions and the state of the society around him.

He was forty years old when, engaged in one of these retreats, he saw a vision. A terrifying figure, whom Muhammad later identified as the Archangel Gabriel, forced him to "Recite: In the name of Allah, the Merciful and Compassionate. Recite: And your lord is most generous. He teaches by the pen, teaches man what he knew not." Before he vanished, the angel also told Muhammad that he was to be "the Messenger of Allah", thus indicating that this was only the beginning of the divine communications.

Muhammad was both shattered and bemused by this revelation. It is likely that "Allah" was one of the native pagan deities then worshipped in the Ka'bah shrine, and that Muhammad would have known the name as one of a number of gods in the Arab pantheon.[2] Yet his vision had spoken of Allah in the way that the Christians and Jews spoke of their own all-powerful deity.

Muhammad was comforted by his wife – who initially failed to see his vision as anything other than a Sun-induced hallucination. As promised, however, the messages from Allah continued. Fortunately there were no more terrifying visions or even voices in Muhammad's head; he would start to perspire heavily (even on a cold day) and occasionally would hear a bell tolling, then the message would leap into his conscious mind as a divine inspiration. The whole process was not without its cost, however. The receiving of the first books of the Koran alone caused Muhammad's hair to turn prematurely grey.

Allah was not, Muhammad discovered through the divine communications, just a local god; he was the one and only God – the monotheistic deity who had created the universe and had inspired both the Jewish prophets and Jesus. These prophets had spoken holy truths, but Muhammad was to be the final and definitive Prophet of Allah – reforming and correcting all that had gone before. Of course, being the Messenger of Allah demanded that Muhammad pass on these tenets to his fellows – so the middle-aged trader started to preach in Mecca.

If Muhammad had begun his prophetic mission 200 years earlier, he might not have made any impact on world history. Then Mecca had been just a desert well with a shrine; often visited by the nomadic Bedouin, but a permanent home for just a few people. The Mecca of Muhammad's day, on the other hand, was an important trading town with enough of a permanent population to provide him with a regular audience and, eventually, fervent followers.

A class of resident Arab traders, known collectively as the

[2]Many Moslems have vehemently denied this possibility. For them, "Allah" is a word contracted from the Arabic *al-'ilah*, meaning "the god", and the religion preached by Muhammad was entirely new. However, it is known that Muhammad's father was called Abd Allah, meaning "worshipper of Allah". Therefore, since there is no evidence of a monotheistic religion of Allah before Muhammad, Allah was almost certainly a pagan god in the native Arabic pantheon. Muhammad himself never denied the fact, stressing instead that Islam was a return to the true worship of Allah after a period of false belief.

Quraysh, had grown up in Mecca – living off the pilgrims to the Ka'bah as much as the now reduced number of trade caravans. These still organized themselves as tribal clans, and were far from the moneyed sophisticates of Byzantium or Alexandria, but their consolidation of trade allowed Mecca to develop into a little city-state, much like Athens, Sparta and Rome had done 1,000 years before.

The Quraysh utilised their contacts with allied Bedouin clans to make Mecca one of the chief trading places of inland Arabia. Also, in a stroke of genius, they declared Mecca a quarterly *haram* – a safe haven period (for three months twice a year) when fighting in the town's environs was forbidden by religious taboo. Given the frequent raiding and feuds endemic to Bedouin life, this offer of a place of sanctuary did much to attract constructive and creative individuals to live in Mecca, further enriching the town's cultural life.

Unfortunately, the Meccan Quraysh suffered one problem that the city fathers of Athens and Rome had avoided: the source of their political strength was their firm alliance with neighbouring Bedouin clans, but this connection also forced the Quraysh to maintain the stratified and unstable clan structure that had so long held Arabia in a state of nomadic barbarism.

It is possible that Muhammad, in his fifteen years of wandering the hills around Mecca – and his previous seventeen years of trading to far-off lands – had realized that if Mecca was ever to become a real power within Arabia, it would have to rise above its petty clan squabbling and in-fighting. Whether the inspiration came from his own mind or directly from Allah, he clearly saw that the Meccans – and Arabia as a whole – needed something to focus their complete allegiance, something greater than the ties of tribe and blood. They needed a unifying religion.

This was why one of the main strands of his early preaching was the *ummah* (Arabic for "community"). Those that followed his reformed (or totally new) religion of Allah were all brothers and sisters within the ummah of Islam, regardless of their tribal loyalties. However, those clan loyalties could remain, provided the convert gave their highest and truest commitment to Allah. Thus the faith of Islam grew quietly at first; converts could maintain their lives as before, and avoided upsetting their clan elders.

But eventual confrontation with the Quraysh was inevitable. Like

Jesus, Muhammad's principal teaching concerned protection of the poor, reinforced by the threat of Allah's Final Judgment and eternal damnation for those who exploited their fellow men. The traders of the Quraysh had turned Mecca into a venal pit of financial exploitation. Free and unpoliced markets had led to price fixing and a ruthless grinding of the poor – especially those not affiliated to a clan – and the wealthy tribal leaders saw little reason to change their habits.

Muhammad was the grandson of a tribal chief and a successful trader in his own right – the Quraysh must have felt that he was turning on his own kind when he publicly attacked their moral standing. Fortunately, Mecca's reputation as a safe haven meant that the growing acrimony between the Quraysh and Muhammad's *Moslems*[3] did not lead to bloodshed – a religious feud might have damaged the valuable pilgrimage trade to the Ka'bah.

This is not to say that there was no trouble at all: the other clans of the Quraysh economically embargoed the entire Hashim clan for three years in an attempt to get Muhammad's own tribe to silence him. The embargo failed when it was realized that everyone's trade was suffering and Muhammad was just as vocal as ever. However, a new head of the Hashim tribe – another of Muhammad's uncles – decided that enough was enough and withdrew the clan's protection from his troublesome nephew. This was a serious matter; without a clan, Muhammad had lost all his protection. His followers stood by him, but it was imperative that he leave Mecca, where his life was in danger.

In AD 619, Muhammad travelled to the town of Ta'if, but his preaching failed to win many of the townspeople over. Ta'if was the seat of worship for the pagan goddess Allat, and the locals saw no reason to change allegiance. It is also possible that Muhammad preached less passionately due to personal grief – his beloved wife Khadijah had died just before the family left Mecca, and their two infant sons died in Ta'if.

The following year, an offer of protection from a different Quraysh clan took Muhammad back to Mecca, but he must soon have realized that his enemies had effectively trapped him. The

[3]The Arabic world "Moslem" (sometimes spelled Muslim) is the active participle of "Islam"; thus it indicates "those who have surrendered to Allah".

Quraysh had seen that he intended to spread his trouble-making creed, and so stopped him leaving Mecca after his return and did their best to silence his public preaching.

Now we see the key feature of Muhammad's character come into play – he was a brilliant diplomat. He realized that he needed a foothold in another town before he could begin to build up the Islamic ummah outside Mecca. The opportunity presented itself in the form of a delegation from the town of Medina (also known as Yathrib). This was split between traditional pagan Arabs and a community of converted Arab Jews. They had failed to settle their many differences between themselves and so needed a neutral arbiter (a *hakam*) to settle disputes.

Muhammad negotiated in secret with the Medinites and seventy of his followers moved to and settled in Medina over the next two years. Then, in AD 622, he and his father-in-law, Abu Bakr, escaped Mecca and made the 275-mile journey to Medina. Moslem tradition holds that they left just in time – the Quraysh had got wind of Muhammad's activities and had finally decided to kill him.

Muhammad used his diplomatic skills to settle many of the feuds in Medina. However, his religious teaching caused him difficulties, just as they had in Mecca. The three Jewish clans in the town seem to have regarded him as a borderline heretic, while the eight pagan clans doubtless felt that they had enough trouble with the Jewish converts – another set of monotheists was the last thing they wanted.

Muhammad initially settled the Medinite Jews' reservations by stressing that they, the Christians and Moslems were all "people of the Book" – that is, fellow believers in the Old Testament. The pagan Arabs he placated by marrying into their families – he now enthusiastically embraced the custom of polygamy, incorporating it into the laws of Islam. He also successfully converted many of the pagans with his charismatic preaching. Also, as a man of the world and an experienced merchant, Muhammad took over control of Medina's main money-making activity: the raiding of caravans on their way from Mecca to Syria.

Three failed caravan raids did not deter Muhammad and, in 624, he fought two pitched battles with large Meccan caravans and won resounding victories. He also took it upon himself to divide the loot after these successful ventures, and did this with such consummate fairness that few complained when he took a straight five per cent tithe – the *zakat* – to be paid into the coffers of the Islamic ummah. As this money was collected specifically to help poor and needy Moslems, most of the town's poor quickly converted to Islam.

By this time Muhammad had cemented his position in Medina. His first successful raid had violated the Meccans' haram – the sanctuary rule. This, and Muhammad's self-evident skill as a leader, caused most of the pagans remaining in Medina to covert to Islam – thereby escaping the threat of pagan taboos by entering the protection of Allah.

Following the second successful raid – which Muhammad had won despite odds of more than two Meccans to every Medinite – he felt established enough to exile a powerful Jewish clan who still refused to follow his leadership. Thereafter he defined both Jews and Christians as second-class citizens who had to pay the Moslem ummah a *jizyah* – a protection fee. (Also at this time, several Medinites who had satirized Muhammad in verse were assassinated, although it is unclear if he himself had a hand in their deaths.)

It was pagans, however, who were still seen as Islam's chief enemy, especially the Meccans who defiled the sacred Ka'bah shrine with false idols. To emphasize the importance of this point, Muhammad now ordered that all Moslems face towards Mecca (and the Ka'bah) when they prayed to Allah. Previously, like the Jews and Christians, they had faced towards Jerusalem.

Muhammad spent much of the rest of AD 624 raiding and counter-raiding the hostile nomad tribes to the north of Medina, but he must have guessed that the Meccans were plotting revenge for his earlier depredations.

On 21 March 625, an army of 3,000 Meccans attacked Medina. If Muhammad had had his way, the Medinites would have withdrawn to several impenetrable forts around the town, but his farmers were horrified to see the Meccans destroying their crops and demanded they be driven off. There followed a set-piece battle in which the Meccan infantry were soon routed, but the Medinite archers failed to protect their victorious infantry's left flank. A counter-attack by the Meccan cavalry thus caused the Moslems severe losses. By the time the Meccans withdrew, it was unclear which side had been most badly damaged.

In fact, both sides suffered more politically than militarily. Muhammad, although he had lost not much more than seventy men, could scarcely afford any loss of face with critics still active within his own camp – in particular the two remaining Jewish clans and a group of Moslem dissidents later derisively nicknamed the *munafiquin* (the hypocrites). At the same time, the Meccans had once again shown that they could not counter the Moslem threat to their caravans, and their trade suffered as a result.

Muhammad moved to further consolidate his position by exiling a second Jewish clan from Medina. He then began a concerted two-year campaign of diplomacy (to bring in allies and potential converts) and raids (aimed at destabilizing Meccan efforts to build an anti-Moslem confederacy). His lack of success at the latter was seen when an army of 10,000 Meccans and their allies attacked Medina in April 627. This time, however, the Moslems were ready. The crops had already been brought in and a deep ditch dug around the town to prevent cavalry charges. Repeated Meccan attempts to cross the ditch were repelled. Meanwhile Muhammad put his diplomatic skill to military use, sending out Moslem secret agents to spread dissent among the besieging army. After a fortnight, the Meccans were so demoralized that a storm of torrential rain was enough to break their spirit. Utilizing a proverbial Bedouin skill, the entire army melted away into the night.

It may seem that the Moslems had simply survived another attack, but the Battle of the Ditch was a decisive moment in the rise of Islam. Mecca, the pre-eminent economic power in inland Arabia, had totally failed to crush their adversaries, and their chances of ever raising another large confederated army were dashed. The new religion had stepped back from the brink of extinction.

The last surviving Jewish clan in Medina had refused to fight at the Battle of the Ditch – and, indeed, may have tried to connive secretly with the Meccans. If they expected to be merely exiled as punishment, like the other two clans of Medina Jews, they were unlucky. Muhammad had all the men killed and the women and children sold into slavery. Medina was now a wholly Moslem town.

This purge behind him, Muhammad set about using his diplomatic skills to win his next goal – access to Mecca. It might have been possible – given the growing numbers of Moslems against the decline in Mecca's military power – that he could eventually have taken the town by force, but Muhammad wanted converts, not subjects.

In 628, Muhammad had a dream in which he saw himself making a pilgrimage to the Ka'bah in Mecca. He took this to be a sign from Allah that he should make the journey. Of course, it would have been suicide for him to go on alone, so he took 1,600 followers with him.

Arriving with this small army he was met on the Meccan border by representatives of the Quraysh. This was actually a very daring move by Muhammad – the Meccan army, although much diminished by the departure of their confederates, could have easily destroyed or scattered the Moslem pilgrims camped on their border. Even if not wiped out, it would have been highly unlikely for any of Muhammad's scattered followers to have made it back to Medina through 275 miles of largely hostile territory. But Muhammad – or his divine inspiration – had accurately assessed the mood of his former townsmen. They were traders, not warriors, after all. They knew that continuing the feud could only cost them lives and money in the long run, so they were willing to fall back on their favourite tactic – haggling.

After three days of tense negotiation, it was agreed that, in return for peace and a cessation of the Moslem caravan raids, the Meccans would allow Muhammad's followers to make pilgrimages to the Ka'bah. The Meccans must have thought they had the best part of the deal – an end to the costly war and more pilgrims to swell their coffers – but they did not have Muhammad's vision.

On returning to Medina, Muhammad immediately launched an attack on a Jewish community to the north – he may have made peace with the Meccans, but many of his followers still demanded regular loot. After besieging the oasis, Muhammad made terms with the defeated inhabitants – as a "people of the Book" they were allowed to stay and maintain their religion, but from now on they must send half their date harvest to Medina. Muhammad obviously realized that an empire (for there can be little doubt that was now his aim) needed a steady income. Raiding was the tactic of a bandit – emperors demanded tribute.

This does not mean that Muhammad was any less possessed by his religious vision – as his personal power grew, he made a point of strengthening the Islamic ummah with new converts. When Medina had been a weak military power, alliances with neighbouring tribes had been more along the lines of non-aggression pacts and mutual protection agreements. Now Muhammad began to insist that

Moslems should only deal with other Moslems (or at worst, other people of the Book). Any tribe that wanted to join his increasingly attractive power bloc had now to convert to Islam en masse, or be rejected as enemies of the faith.

This, combined with a strict law against raiding Moslem co-religionists, turned all of his pocket-empire's military energy outward. That, in turn, made nervous pagan neighbours all the more keen to convert. It also ended the petty feuding and in-fighting that had previously stopped the Arab tribes achieving any significant level of civilization. As he had united Medina in the ummah of Islam (with preaching and diplomacy as well as bloodshed), Muhammad now moved to unite all of Arabia.

Pagan Mecca was the obvious next step. It was a centre of commerce and its (somewhat) educated political elite were just what Muhammad's fledgling empire needed to run its central bureaucracy (Muhammad himself was illiterate). Again, conquest was out of the question. Muhammad needed the Meccans' heart-felt allegiance and, on a more human note, he cannot have relished the idea of attacking his birthplace.

As with his start in Medina, Muhammad utilized the Arab custom of polygamy to gain a diplomatic advantage. He married into one of the most powerful Quraysh clan families and started to negotiate quietly with prominent Meccans who might support his cause.

By late 629, Muhammad was in a strong enough position to use a squabble between some allies of Mecca and a Moslem tribe as an excuse to renounce the treaty. The boot was now firmly on the other foot as he led his army of 10,000 to the border of Mecca and again met with a delegation from the Quraysh. This time they immediately offered him unconditional surrender.

Muhammad then set about putting the town in order. The idols were all removed from the Ka'bah, leaving only the Black Stone of Mecca,[4] and he had a few of his worst enemies executed. He also demanded money from the Quraysh, but distributed this among the poorest of his followers. He did not, oddly enough, demand that the Meccans all convert to Islam, but most of them saw where future prosperity lay and lost no time in converting.

[4] The Black Stone was believed to have been given to Adam on the expulsion from Eden. It is said to have the power to negate sin, and its original pure white shade was lost as centuries of pilgrims had their sins literally drawn out of their penitent bodies.

When Muhammad marched out, just twenty days later, he left a town that was already settling into its new role as the religious and bureaucratic heart of the Islamic Empire. Far from needing to leave an occupation garrison to keep the peace, his army left strengthened by 2,000 Meccan volunteers.

They marched to a place called Hunayn, where a confederacy of hostile tribes had gathered. Part of the Moslem army were routed in the early part of the following battle, but Muhammad and the veteran warriors held their ground and the pagans eventually broke and were driven from the field.

This victory settled beyond a doubt who was the pre-eminent military power in Arabia. The Prophet, as he was now universally known, returned to Medina and received deputations from the remaining non-Moslem tribes. All now wished to ally with him, and all had to convert to Islam to do so. Certainly there were still a few pockets of die-hards who refused to renounce their old religion to join the Islamic Empire, but Arabia was now, nevertheless, a unified nation under one ruler.

It was just twenty years since Muhammad had first begun preaching in Mecca.

Instead of resting on his laurels, the Prophet immediately gathered an army of 30,000 – probably the largest Arabia had seen since the days of the Roman Empire – and struck north. His purpose seems to have been pacification of pro-Byzantine Christian tribes in northern Arabia, because he stopped when he reached the Syrian border. However, the power and zeal of his army was plain to see, and it was probably only old age (he was now sixty) and ill health that stopped him attacking the Byzantine Empire itself.

Muhammad led the now annual pilgrimage – the *haj* – to Mecca in 632. A few months later, on 8 June, he died in Medina, aged sixty-two. Shortly thereafterwards the oral tradition that had passed down his teachings to that point was preserved in written form: the Koran.

Like Alexander the Great, Muhammad had failed to name a successor, and his fledgling empire came close to falling apart the moment he died. Some tribes immediately renounced Islam – their loyalty had been to the Prophet, not the religion – and two Moslem factions put up different candidates as the new leader. However, unlike Alexander's over-extended and unstable empire, the ummah of Islam was still compact enough to survive leadership squabbles.

Later *caliphs* (the Arabic word for "deputy") did not claim to have inherited Muhammad's ability to prophesy the will of Allah, but they and their successors pushed Islamic conquest, at its greatest extent, as far as India in the East, Spain in the West, Central Africa in the South and the European Balkans in the North.

The above account may give the impression that Muhammad was mainly a politician and a warlord: something between Otto von Bismarck and Philip of Macedon. Yet his success as an empire-builder would not have been possible if he had not been, first and foremost, a religious visionary.

Arabia, just before the advent of Islam, was a place crying out for a religion. The Arabs' religion of many gods (and goddesses) was simply unsuited to the increasingly sophisticated lifestyle of new urban populations like that of Mecca. Yet the only alternatives were foreign faiths like Judaism and Christianity; these were not an attractive prospect to a race whose main, if unmarketable, asset was pride. A home-grown monotheism was bound, therefore, to attract the most forward-thinking and self-respecting among the town dwellers. With such men as converts, Muhammad had a stable support base to begin his political career.

Later, for the less-sophisticated Medinite and Bedouin converts to Islam, Muhammad must have seemed a figure much as the Jews had imagined their warrior Messiah – a military genius with the favour of a god to bring him victory. These converts might not have fully understood the finer points of Islam's theological doctrine, but they clearly caught some of the Prophet's passion and fought for him with fanatical ardour.

Throughout the twenty-two years of his public career, Mohammad continued to receive and preach messages from Allah. The practical and sometimes utilitarian nature of many of these revelations have led some cynics to suggest that Muhammad simply made up religious laws to suit himself, as and when his political situation demanded it. Indeed, Muhammad never claimed to have actually been spoken to by Allah, but merely received the rules of Islam as inspirations in his own mind.[5]

[5]Of course, this argument does not necessarily invalidate Islam from a religious standpoint. For example, at her trial for heresy, Joan of Arc was asked if the "voices" she heard in her head – claiming to be from St Michael and St Catherine – might not just be the promptings of her own imagination. To which she replied: "How else does God speak to us?"

The fact remains that Muhammad clearly believed himself to be in communication with the creator of the universe, and acted as he believed that being wished him to act. His extraordinary success was, he doubtless felt, all the proof necessary that his was "the one true religion".

Islam was both derivative from earlier traditions – most obviously the Judaic and Christian – and also innovative. Like the Judaic prophets, Muhammad believed that speaking the will of God was his primary function – he was not an oracle, predicting petty future events, but a messenger of Allah whose main interest in the future lay in preparing mankind for the Final Judgment. Like Jesus of Nazareth, Muhammad preached that mankind's first and foremost duty was to surrender to the will of the creator of the universe. And also like Jesus, he preached that Allah the Merciful's main preoccupations were the condition of the poor and the maintenance of social justice.

However, the teachings of Jesus gave no special rules as to how social responsibility should be enacted (other than dropping hints like the suggestion that the rich would have as difficult a time getting into Heaven as a camel trying to pass through the eye of a needle). Muhammad, on the other hand, placed a religious tax on a Moslem's income (ten per cent on perishable goods and two-and-a-half per cent on money) to aid poor Moslems. (The zakat tithe was strictly enforced in the days of the great Moslem empires, but today is a voluntary contribution to the poor.)

Unlike Jesus and many of the Judaic prophets, Muhammad did not claim to be a miracle worker. While accepting the reality of the miracles described in the Bible, the Prophet rather testily insisted that the only miracle in his life was the continuing miracle of Allah's revelations and the fact that he could remember them with absolute precision (because, of course, he did not know how to write them down). Later tradition attributed miracles to him – for example, to prove the power of Allah, the Prophet "split the Moon in two"[6] but there are no independent contemporary accounts of any of these.

More importantly, Muhammad's teachings intertwined religion and state in a way not seen since the dissolution of Judea. He insisted that the Koran, the direct teaching of Allah, must inform and influence every aspect of Islamic society.

[6]The origin of the sickle-moon emblem of Islam.

Muhammad had presumably seen the workings of Byzantine Christianity in his travels as a young man – a faith torn by doctrinal splits and separated from the common people by Latin-speaking,[7] holier-than-thou priests. This may be why he dictated that Islam was to have no priest class. *Imams*, Moslem scholars who lead the five daily prayers, are not the Islamic equivalent of the Catholic priest and are not allowed to claim any special relationship with Allah.

Instead of appointing a religious hierarchy to guard fellow worshippers' souls, Muhammad insisted that it was the duty of each Moslem to ensure that their every action was in tune with the Koran's teachings – how else could they demonstrate their total and complete surrender to the will of Allah?

Leaving the question of the existence or non-existence of a deity out of the matter, Muhammad, it might be argued, was the sort of religious founder that Jesus might have become if he had lived to relative old age. They certainly shared many of the same attitudes, but it was Muhammad who had the years and the political power to build his beliefs into a structured, fully-functional religion.

This had both good and bad results. On the one hand, compared to the New Testament, the Koran is very straightforward and tends to the pragmatic. One can see in it an attempt to create a blueprint for a working religious state, whereas the numerous (and sometimes conflicting) authors of the New Testament offered nothing so consistent. The Koran is, in effect, a written constitution where the Bible offers only rule by previous precedent and theological interpretation.

The Koran's firmness of rule has served as a constant stabilizing force in Moslem nations – especially during the early days of the Islamic expansion and, later, when suffering the onslaught of the Christian crusades. Since the European Enlightenment in the eighteenth century, however, the inflexibility of Islamic law has proved something of a burden to modernizers within Moslem states.

It is a common western misconception that Moslems are not allowed to question the meaning of the Koran. Indeed, unlike the Bible, the Koran stresses the right of the individual to their own thoughts. However, since the words of the Koran are believed to be the direct utterances of Allah, questioning of the specific rules laid

[7]What came to be known as the Greek Orthodox Church did not split from the Catholic (Latin-preaching) Church until AD 1054.

out by the Prophet is strictly forbidden. One may query the spirit, but never the letter of Koranic law.

As a result, much of Islamic law is actually the product of post-Muhammad debate and compromise among Moslem rulers and scholars – this is called the *ijma'* (Arabic for "consensus"). The theological concept of the ijma' was originally introduced to consider matters that Muhammad had not ruled upon and to standardize legal and social practice in the expanding Islamic empire. Ijma' were not, however, a matter of democratic debate, but rather were rulings handed down by a few Islamic patriarchs or, more often, an absolute monarch.

The various ijma' agreements down the centuries were combined with the unambiguous rulings from the Koran to form *Shari'ah* (literally: "the path to the watering place") law.

As different subjects of ijma' were ruled upon as Shari'ah, they also took on the undeniable aspect of "Allah's will", and all further debate on them was halted. This has meant that many aspects of Islamic life were effectively frozen at the point of history in which their ruling ijma' originated. For example, it was Muhammad who ruled that thieves should have a hand cut off as punishment. Later, during a famine, a caliph ruled that theft from those who hoarded food was allowable – this was not a contradiction of the Prophet, it was argued, just an expansion of the rule, shedding light where Muhammad had not. Enlightened as this particular law may be, it thereafterwards could not be countermanded under any circumstance; only "expanded upon" in its turn.

Little surprise, therefore, that lawyers and scholars in Islamic states eventually began to resemble Christian priests – laying down and enacting laws with the power of both religious conviction and authoritarian absolutism.[8] All too often the Moslem individual's islam (surrender) to the will of Allah was redirected into unconditional capitulation to state authorities. This is the process that has led to the Shari'ah laws that so often shock modern liberal sensibilities. The stoning of adulterers, the repression of women's rights and, above all, the blocking of

[8]Those that do not recognize this image of a Christian priest should peruse the history of seventeenth-century Protestant England, nineteenth-century Orthodox Russia and twentieth-century Catholic Ireland.

democracy all originate in the inflexibility of Shari'ah law when it is carried out to the letter.

It should also be noted that the Koran is only considered holy in its original Arabic – translations are no longer the exact words of Allah, and are therefore considered fundamentally flawed. This has presented a problem for converts who do not speak Arabic and do not have the means to learn it: they are effectively barred from their own sacred book.

Some modernizing Moslem states, like Turkey, Libya and Pakistan, have attempted to separate religion and state, but Muhammad's firm intention that Islam should touch every aspect of a Moslem's life is too fundamental to fully allow this. Ijma' has, in these places, come to indicate liberalization brought about by public (rather than Imam) consensus, but rulers in Shari'ah nations, like many of the Arabian Gulf States, regard such changes as bordering on pagan heresy.

The rigidity of attitude among radical Moslems has combined with one of the few precognitive predictions made by the Prophet to contribute to the creation of the powder keg that is modern Islamic fundamentalism. In chapter 61, verse 9 of the Koran, the Prophet predicted that Islam would one day conquer all other religions:

> He [Allah] it is who has sent His messenger [Muhammad] with guidance and the Faith of Truth, that He may make it [Islam] conqueror of all other religions, much as the idolaters may dislike it.

There is no suggestion, as in Jesus' similar prediction for Christianity, that this process will be one of gentle conversion. Here we are contemplating a prediction of a religious triumph brought about by force.

Surveying the list of monotheistic prophets up to and including Jesus, the reader will probably feel a certain sense of bewilderment. Layer upon layer of different meanings, abilities and purposes were added to the picture of the Prophet of God by succeeding generations of Yahweh's spokesmen: the mouthpiece of divinity became also a miracle worker, then a social reformer, then a precognitive seer, then a political propagandist and poetic visionary then, at last, God in human form.

So, does Muhammad add yet another layer to the seemingly ever-snowballing concept of the monotheistic Prophet of God? Perhaps fortunately, the answer is no. In fact, in Muhammad's career we see many of the more extreme definitions of religious prophecy pared back and even eliminated – he was, in many senses, a back-to-basics prophet.

Muhammad was certainly not the last of the monotheistic prophets, by any means. Many have claimed the title since his day but, with a few notable exceptions – like Guru Nanak, founder of Sikhism, and Joseph Smith, founder of Mormonism – most amounted to little more than cult leaders, were executed as heretics or simply fell into historical obscurity.

However, for the purposes of the present book, Muhammad stands as the perfect example of a non-precognitive prophet. He claimed to see no visions other than the Archangel Gabriel at the beginning of his religious career. He had only one prophetic dream – in which he saw himself going to hostile Mecca – but as he had clearly decided, by that time, that Mecca was his next political objective, such a dream cannot necessarily be considered proof of paranormal powers. Finally, Muhammad also predicted, like Jesus, that his faith would one day conquer the world – but, aside from hinting that force would be necessary, he did not give any indication as to how or when this event might happen. Again, we have to ask ourselves what founder of a new religion has *not* predicted its future success?

In the end, Muhammad has to be accepted – as he demanded himself – as a man who believed that he transmitted the will of the creator of the universe. Any specific prediction of events in the future he left to Allah and His great plan.

Part 2

Precognitive Prophecy

Introduction

The line between religious and precognitive prophecy is thin or, perhaps, nonexistent. Only one of the seers in the next section, for example, was an atheist (and that seems largely to revenge himself on his parents for trying to trick him into becoming a rabbi). All the others were noticeably vocal in attributing their precognitive gifts to God.

Of course, no matter how much Christianity liberalizes, it is unlikely that any future edition of the Bible will add chapters on Nostradamus, Mother Shipton or Jeane Dixon. No matter how much they proclaimed their religious inclinations, they would never be considered prophets in the religious sense, like Moses or Muhammad, because their predictions were mainly involved with mundane matters like wars, disasters and political revolutions. None of the following prophets ever thought they knew what God wanted – or if they did, they kept quiet about it.

The reader will also notice that much of the following section – indeed much of the book – is dedicated to one prophet in particular: Nostradamus. I make no apology for this. Nostradamus was the most prolific of those precognitive prophets whose predictions have survived in print. He is also the most carefully studied non-religious prophet, so it is possible to offer the reader the broadest number of different interpretations of his predictions. And lastly, Nostradamus has been the most influential prophet in European history. Both Napoleon and Hitler felt their "greatness" had caused Nostradamus to predict their careers, and doubtless future Napoleons and Hitlers will do likewise.

Chapter 9

Old Mother Shipton

Sixteenth-century Yorkshire was not a safe place to look or behave like a witch. The religious hysteria that swept Europe in the late Middle Ages led to thousands of people being burned or hanged; England, although somewhat less affected than central Europe, was no exception.

In spite of this, "Mother" Ursula Shipton, one of Yorkshire's most famous daughters, is said to have openly paraded her supernatural powers, and once openly defied the most powerful clergyman in the land. Possibly the fact that she was so surpassingly ugly – she possessed a face like a Halloween mask – explains why she survived into her eighties and died in her bed. No one who has studied the witchcraft trials can doubt that there was a sexual element in the persecutions. If a suspect was reasonably attractive, she was more likely to be stripped and searched for "Devil's marks" than a withered old harridan. Nevertheless, given the evidence, it is tempting to believe that Mother Shipton had the Devil's own luck.

The Yorkshire prophetess was born in Knaresborough around 1488, although accounts differ because several Yorkshire municipalities have claimed her as their own. Ursula's mother was called Agatha Sontheil, and had been orphaned at the age of fifteen with no other living relatives. She inherited her parents' small house, but owned very little else and was often forced to live off the charity of the parish. It was therefore some surprise to her neighbours that, at about the age of sixteen, she began to spend money that nobody had seen her earn or borrow.

It was a sign of the times that, shortly thereafterwards when her belly began to swell, local gossip favoured the belief that Satan was the responsible party. Agatha cheerfully confirmed this rumour, describing a meeting with a very handsome gentleman on the riverbank, and how, after listening to her problems, he offered to banish them all if she would be "ruled by him". Thereafter he visited her cottage regularly, but in secret, and after each dalliance Agatha would find coins scattered about her house. Needless to say, when Agatha became pregnant, the fiend was seen no more.

Whether the father was Beelzebub or just an out-of-town rake, he seems to have had good connections with the Church. Following Ursula's birth, the Abbot of Beverley Minster travelled sixty miles to baptize the babe – a privilege usually reserved for the children of noblemen. The abbot is also said to have maintained a friendly eye on the child in later years, even seeing to it that she received an education (a rarity for peasant girls at that time). The local gossips therefore added his name to the list of suspected fathers.

In his 1997 book *The World's Greatest Unsolved Mysteries*, the Reverend Lionel Fanthorpe suggests that the choice of the name Ursula might offer a clue to the babe's real procreator. *Ursus* is Latin for bear, and Fanthorpe points out that the Bear Clan is a secret bloodline that is supposed to include King Arthur and various other nobles in British history and mythology. Perhaps, Fanthorpe continues, the illegitimate baby was named Ursula to indicate that she was the daughter of a member of the Bear Clan. So perhaps her freedom from persecution was due to the influence of her father's family.

Ursula Sontheil was born late at night during a storm – complete with thunder and lightning. Her physical deformity was immediately apparent, as described in this 1686 pamphlet *The Strange and Wonderful History of Mother Shipton*:

Nor could the Tempest affright the Women more than the prodigious Physiognomy of the Child; the Body was long, but very big-bon'd, great Gogling eyes, very sharp and fiery, a Nose of unproportionable length, having in it many crooks and turnings, adorned with great Pimples, which like vapours of brimstone gave such a lustre in the night, that her Nurse needed no other candle to dress her by.

Although the author has clearly allowed his imagination free rein, all accounts of Mother Shipton agree that her deformity was striking. She was born with a hunchback and, as she grew older and her face developed, her nose and chin both became remarkably long and pointed. Woodcuts of the seeress became common in England following the first publication of a pamphlet about her in 1641. Some scholars have even suggested that these portraits might have been one of the original inspirations for the nineteenth century Mr Punch glove puppet and the archetypal witch portrayed in children's books and cartoons.

During her infancy, she was apparently the centre of a whirlpool of paranormal activity. Her harassed mother was "daily Visited by Spirits in divers shapes and forms" according to the 1684 *Life and Death of Mother Shipton* by Benjamin Harris. She also attracted dozens of stray cats and dogs, and the neighbours had little doubt that these were actually demons in disguise.

Apart from such earthly pests, Ursula's mother was plagued by noncorporeal manifestations:

> The poor woman's work for the major part, was only to rectifie what these Spirits disordered about her house: the Chairs and Stools would frequently march upstairs and down, and they usually plaid below at Bowles with the Trenchers and dishes: Going to dinner, the meat was removed before she could touch a bit of it.

A modern paranormal investigator would categorize the above phenomena as typical, if extreme, poltergeist activity. One widely accepted view holds that such "hauntings" are actually the result of the unconscious telekinetic powers of a disturbed child or teenager. If so, then the young mother herself would seem the most likely "focus". However, since the haunting continued after Agatha left the house for good, we must consider Ursula herself as the most likely catalyst.

Ursula lost her mother when she was still just a toddler. Accounts differ as to whether Agatha simply died or, under the patronage of the Abbot of Beverley Minster, sought peace and redemption in the local convent. Either way, the child was left in the hands of a long-suffering nurse and the haunting continued unabated. Finally, when Ursula was inexplicably found sitting on an iron support bar high up inside the chimney – quite unharmed and laughing happily – the poor woman's nerve broke and the child was sent to a church-run boarding school.

Ursula proved to be an amazingly gifted student. Although classroom jealousy, coupled with her deformity, made her the butt of some cruel teasing, she apparently gave as good as she got. It is said that invisible hands would pinch her enemies until they screamed in terror, while others were struck dumb as they were about to recite aloud in class. Modern parapsychologists would regard this as evidence of a powerful psychic or hypnotic ability in the child. Ursula's contemporaries, however, were in no doubt that she was under the protection of demons.

The Strange and Wonderful History of Mother Shipton tells the following story: a meeting of the important people of the parish was held at the local hostelry, and the teenage Ursula happened to pass through the room on an errand:

> . . . some of them abused her by calling her the Devil's Bastard and Hagface, and the like, whereupon she went away grumbling, but so ordered affairs, that when they was set down to dinner, one of the principal Yeomen, that thought himself spruce and fine, had in an instant his Ruff [a fluffed collar, shaped like a dinner plate] pull'd off, and the seat of the House of Office [a euphemistic name for the toilet] clapt in its place . . . [the man sitting opposite him] had his Hat invisibly convey'd away, and the Pan of a Close-stool [a sort of potty on legs] put instead thereof. A "modest young Gentlewoman" sitting at the table tried to suppress her laughter, but could not, and withal continued breaking of wind backward for above a quarter of an hour together, like so many broadsides in a Sea-fight.

A priest's attempts to exorcise the "demon powers" in Ursula had no effect. By the time she was old enough to leave school, Ursula Sontheil already had a considerable reputation for "second sight" and, reinstalling herself in her mother's little cottage, she was able to make a reasonable living foretelling people's futures. Her main customers were hopeful young maidens who wanted to learn about future husbands. Ursula's skill at such supernatural matchmaking was proved again and again, yet everyone was surprised when Ursula herself landed an excellent husband.

Toby Shipton was a carpenter by trade; a good-natured soul who was clearly devoted to his ugly, but strangely-gifted, wife. Accounts vary as to whether the couple had any children, but the young Ursula soon earned the honorific title "Mother Shipton" out of the respect that her neighbours held for her as a "wise woman".

Even in the late Middle Ages, there was always a place in any village for a wise woman. In the Dark Ages, the Church Fathers had shown a grudging acceptance of such people because – despite being of the female sex and therefore tainted with the sin of Eve – their opinions carried great weight in the community. The local priest often found their influence as strong as his own. Later, as the Church became institutionalized in every town and village, the priests began to undermine and usurp the position and respect previously held by local shamen and wise women.

These village wise women were usually healers and fortune-tellers who had probably learned their skills from their mothers or grandmothers; such skills usually involved charms, and the use of toads and wax figures. These activities were taken for granted, and not regarded as particularly sinister. However, things began to change after 1490, when a village healer named Jehane de Brigue was charged with being a witch, and sentenced to death by the Parliament in Paris; Jehane and a fellow "witch" were burned alive in August 1491.

The previously sporadic witchcraft persecution had turned into a flood after the publication of a book called *Malleus Maleficarum* (meaning *The Hammer of Witches*), by two Dominican monks, Jacob Sprenger and Heinrich Kramer, in 1484. Its emphasis on sexual matters ("the foulest venereal acts are performed by such devils . . .") caused it to be widely read by celibate monks, and the recent invention of the printing press made it Europe's first best-seller. The European witchcraft craze lasted from around 1500 until the early eighteenth century and thousands of people (mostly women) were tortured, then hanged or burned at the stake.

By Mother Shipton's time, at the start of the sixteenth century, the ancient societal power of the local wise woman was only a dim memory in Britain. Nevertheless, women who were expert midwives and who could also cure fevers or foretell the size of the harvest were indispensable in most communities. It was only during the Enlightenment, with the rise of the natural philosophers (later called scientists) that the wise woman became superfluous to requirements and went back to the kitchen sink.

Mother Shipton was born at the beginning of the witchcraft persecutions, but before it had fully spread to England – a good wise woman could still command some respect and, possibly, superstitious fear in her local community. Nevertheless, by the time she became a famous witch, Mother Shipton was also undoubtedly protected by her reputation for integrity . . .

When a young man came to her asking when his sick father would die and pass on his inheritance, Mother Shipton flatly refused to help him. A few days later the father himself arrived and told her that his greedy son had become very ill. When he begged her to foretell if his heir would live, Mother Shipton replied:

> For other Deaths who do gape out,
> Their own unlook't for, comes about:
> Earth he did seek, ere long shall have,
> Of Earth his fill, within his Grave.[1]

As predicted, the young man was soon in the grave. Mother Shipton also foretold public events in the nearby city of York:

> When there is a Mayor living in Minster Yard,
> Let him beware of a stab . . .

The Lord Mayor of York who moved his official residence to Minster Yard was stabbed to death by thieves one night.

> Before Owse Bridge and Trinity Church meet they shall build
> in the day and it shall fall in the night, 'til they get the highest
> stone of Trinity Church to the lowest stone of Owse Bridge.

[1]Note the medieval rhyming of "have" with "grave".

The steeple of the Trinity Church was blown down in a storm and, at the same time, a flood broke the nearby bridge over the River Owse. Efforts to repair the damage went badly, with work by day collapsing again at night. When the bridge was finally repaired, it was noted that some stones from the Trinity spire had accidentally been added to the bridge; indeed, the top of the spire was now part of the base of one of the bridge supports.

If she had confined herself to such local predictions, Mother Shipton would have been forgotten long ago. Her reputation was based on her prophecies about the future of the whole of England, such as:

> Triumphant Death rides London through
> And men on tops of houses go.

We know that this prediction was commonplace outside Yorkshire in 1666 because the diarist Samuel Pepys noted it in his entry for 20 October of that year. He was writing about the arrival, via the Thames, of Sir Jeremy Smith during the Great Fire:

> [Sir Jeremy] says he was on board the *Prince* when news came of the burning of London; and all the [crew of the] *Prince* said that now Shipton's prophecy was out.

The reference to "Death riding triumphant" would have made anyone in the sixteenth century think of the plague, since everyone was familiar with woodcuts of a skeletal Death riding over plague victims. London was ravaged by the plague in 1665 – the Great Fire came the following year. The reference to men climbing to the tops of houses seems an odd anticipation of a city-wide fire – surely a rooftop is the last place one would want to be during a conflagration – until we read of fire-watchers posted to report the direction and spread of the blaze. In that light, the certainty of people at the time that Mother Shipton had foretold the twin disasters becomes more understandable.

The sailors on the *Prince* may have also been thinking of another of Mother Shipton's prophecies:

> A time shall happen, when a ship shall sail up the Thames, till

it come against London, and the master of the ship shall weep, and the mariners of the ship shall ask him why he weeps, since he has made so good a voyage? And he shall say: "Ah! What a goodly city this was, none in the world to compare with it, and now there is scarce left an house that can let us have a drink for our money."

The only other similar catastrophe to befall London was the Blitz of the Second World War.[2]

Mother Shipton became famous for a prediction that came true during her own lifetime. It concerned Cardinal Wolsey, Henry VIII's Lord Chancellor and arguably the most powerful man in the country. Wolsey had also been appointed to the deanery of York but, due to his London schedule, rarely left the capital to visit his diocese.

In the autumn of 1529, Wolsey made preparations to travel to York and sent word ahead to prepare for his coming. Upon hearing this, Mother Shipton publicly proclaimed that the Cardinal would never visit the city again. She was by then notorious enough to attract the attention of several aristocratic members of the Cardinal's faction. These, led by a local gentleman called Beasley, paid the seeress a visit. They were amazed that before they could knock on her door, she called out: "Come in Master Beasley. You lead as their lordships do not know the way."

Once they were inside she greeted each by name and called for refreshments. The Duke of Suffolk replied that she would not be so welcoming if she knew that they were visiting on behalf of the Cardinal. Wolsey, he said, would doubtless burn her as a witch when he arrived in York. Mother Shipton airily replied that if her handkerchief burned then so would she, and threw it straight on to the roaring fire. A quarter-of-an-hour later she picked it out with a poker and handed it round the assembly: all agreed that it was not even singed.

Doubtless rather unnerved, they then asked why she had said that Cardinal Wolsey would never see York again. Mother Shipton replied that, on the contrary, the Cardinal would *see* York, but he would never reach the city.

---

[2]A less grim interpretation of this prediction might suggest an imposition of alcohol prohibition laws sometime in our future (a prospect horrible to a sailor, but probably quite acceptable to the morally upright Mother Shipton).

She then went on to prophesy the fate of each of the visiting lords. Being the reign of the turbulent and execution-prone Henry VIII, it is not overly surprising that most were told that they would suffer early deaths – but it is the accurate detail she is said to have given that impressed later chroniclers. For example, she told Lord Percy that: "Your body will be buried in York pavement and your head will lie in France." At the time Percy made light of this prediction, commenting that his neck would have to stretch a long way. In fact he was later executed and buried in York but, as was the custom with condemned traitors, his severed head was stuck on a public spike as a warning to others. This was then stolen and taken to his relatives who had fled to France.

Cardinal Wolsey spent the last night of his journey at Cawood Castle, within sight of York. He is said to have ascended a tower to look at the city in the evening light, and was there told of Mother Shipton's prophecy. He angrily declared that he would have her arrested and burned, but that same night Wolsey was recalled to London to stand trial for high treason. The fifty-five-year-old priest died of "the flux" on the way back.

Today, Mother Shipton is most famous for her prediction of the developments of the industrial age. The very popular *Life, Prophecies and Death of the Famous Mother Shipton*, published by Charles Hindley in 1862, gives the following version of these prophecies:

> Carriages without horses will go
> And accidents fill the world with woe . . .
> Around the world thoughts shall fly,
> In the twinkling of an eye . . .
> Though hills men shall ride,
> And no horse or ass be by his side,
> Underwater men shall walk,
> Shall ride, shall sleep, shall be seen,
> In white, in black, in green . . .
> Iron in water shall float,
> As easy as a wooden boat . . .
> All England's sons that plough the land,
> Shall be seen book in hand.
> Learning shall so ebb and flow,

> The poor shall most wisdom know . . .
> The world to an end will come
> In eighteen hundred and eighty-one.

Apart from the embarrassingly inaccurate prediction of Armageddon, the rest seems strikingly prescient: trains (or cars), the proliferation of accidents, global communications, the replacement of the horse, submarines and undersea dwellings, metal-hulled ships and even universal education.

Unfortunately, all these "prophecies" were the fictional invention of Charles Hindley – he later confessed as much, admitting he did it to boost the sales of his book. Yet even today books quote this doggerel as genuine prophecies by Mother Shipton.

How many of the other predictions attributed to Mother Shipton were later inventions is now impossible to say. It is only with prophets like Nostradamus or Edgar Cayce, where we are certain that we are reading their own words, that we can be free of doubt.

Most of the prophecies attributed to Mother Shipton seem to concern events during her own lifetime and the 100 or so years following her death. For example, she is credited with predicting that Henry VIII would marry Anne Boleyn, and would then break with Rome:

> When the Cow doth ride the Bull
> Then the Priest beware thy skull.

A cow was part of Henry VIII's personal heraldry, while there was a black bull on the standard of Anne Boleyn's father. The conversion of the state religion from Catholic to Protestant (and the destruction of the power of the monasteries) started during the period of this marriage.

Shipton is also said to have predicted the four decade reign of Elizabeth I and the defeat of the Spanish Armada:

> A Maiden Queen full many a year
> Shall England's War-like sceptre bear.
> The Western Monarch's Wooden Horses
> Shall be destroyed by the Drake's Forces.

The English Civil War and execution of Charles I were foretold in the following verse:

> Forth from the North shall mischief blow,
> And English Hob [the Devil] shall add thereto;
> Mars shall rage as he were wood,
> And Earth shall drunken be with blood.
> But tell us what's next, Oh cruel fate!
> A King Martyr'd at his gate.

Nevertheless, not all her prophecies had such obvious explanations for the seventeenth-century, pamphlet-buying public.

> In time to hereafter,
> Our land will be ruled by two women.
> A child of ours will be contested
> By a child of Spain . . .
> In this time, blood will be shed
> Yet shall the child stay.

This prediction, quoted in Lionel Fanthorpe's *The World's Greatest Unsolved Mysteries*, is believed by some to refer to the 1982 Falklands War between Britain and Argentina. At the time Britain was governed by Prime Minister Margaret Thatcher and ruled by Queen Elizabeth II. Argentina had been a colony of Spain, while Britain developed settlements on the Falkland Islands: both places were therefore "children" of European nations.

A rather odd prophecy seemed to predict a prosperous period, followed by a scarcity of men:

Then may a man take House or Bower, Land or Tower for one and twenty years; but afterwards shall be a white Harvest of Corn gotten by Women. Then shall it be, that one woman shall say to another: "Mother! I have seen a man today!"

One commentator suggests that this is a prediction of British prosperity at the turn of the nineteenth century. This was followed, during the First World War, by the women labouring in fields and factories while their men were slaughtered in great numbers in France.

There are other prophecies of Mother Shipton that continue to defy explanation. Some are too short on comparative detail . . .

> The North shall Rue it wondrous sore,
> But the South shall Rue it for evermore.
> The Time shall come, when Seas of Blood,
> Shall mingle with a greater flood.

Others hardly seem to fit any known historical event up to the time of this writing . . .

You shall have a year of Pining Hunger, & shall not know of the War over-night, yet shall you have it in the Morning, and when it happens, it shall last three years, then will come a woman with one Eye, and she shall tread in many men's blood up to the knee.

> The Fiery Year as soon as 'ore,
> Peace shall then be as before.
> Plenty everywhere is found,
> And Men with Swords shall plow the ground.

> Great noise there shall be heard, Great Shouts and Cries.
> And Seas shall Thunder, louder than the Skies,
> Then shall three Lions fight with three and bring
> Joy to a people, Honour to their King.

Mother Shipton, like many seers, is said to have accurately predicted the time of her own death. A hospitable countrywoman to the last, she invited her friends and relatives to come and see her off, lay down on her bed and promptly passed away. The date is not known, but she is said to have lived well into her eighties, which would make it some time after 1570.

Benjamin Harris' *Life and Death of Mother Shipton* (1684) says of her:

. . . she was generally believed to be a witch, yet all persons whatever, that either saw or heard her, had her in great esteem: her memory to this day is much honoured by those of her own Country.

A stone was erected near Clifton, about a mile from the city of York, from which the following is taken:

> Here Lies she who never ly'd,
> Whose skill often has been try'd,
> Her Prophecies shall still survive,
> And ever keep her name alive.

Chapter 10

The Life of Nostradamus

Michel de Nostredame – known universally as Nostradamus – has had more impact on the world than any other non-religious prophet. His predictions have remained consistently in print since he first published them in 1555. His life and work have inspired novels, plays, Hollywood movies and any number of academic studies and treatises. As a figure of French national pride, he ranks only behind Charles de Gaulle and Joan of Arc. Political leaders since the sixteenth century have seen in his prophecies optimistic portents for their own futures (although few seem to have been prepared to consider any potential warnings of doom from the seer). Indeed, in the public eye, the name Nostradamus has become synonymous with foretelling the future.

Yet we know very little about this man. His background, much of his life, his training, his method of prediction and his reasons for publishing remain largely unknown to us. Everything to do with Nostradamus seems touched with mystery and, as we shall see, this was probably due to the seer's own deliberate policy.

Nostradamus was born in the French city of Saint-Rémy-de-Provence on 14 December 1503. The Nostredame family originally belonged to the Jewish faith, but had been Catholic converts for at least two generations. (The name Nostredame means "our lady", while the pen name *Nostradamus* was a Latinization of his surname.) They made a fortune through trade but, according to Nostradamus' son Cesar, they were also respected as a line of scholars and doctors. Unfortunately, at that time, this combination of money, esoteric training and Jewish roots placed them in a rather dangerous position.

In the fifteenth and sixteenth centuries, many European countries – including France – expelled or executed all Jews who refused to convert to Christianity. The Inquisition – virtually an independent power since the rift with the Protestants – was responsible for widespread persecution of Jewish "enemies of Christ", often blaming them for crop failures and outbreaks of plague. Even those Jews who, like the Nostredame family, were willing to renounce Judaism, lived under continual suspicion. An accusation by a jealous neighbour could lead to a trial for witchcraft and forfeiture of family assets. Nostradamus' favourite pupil, Jean Aimes de Chavigny, later vehemently denied that his master was a Christianized Jew, although he certainly knew better.

Michel de Nostredame showed signs of remarkable intelligence from an early age, so his scholarly maternal grandfather, Jean de Saint-Remy, offered to educate the boy personally. By his early teens, Michel had mastered Latin, Greek and basic medical knowledge. Tradition also holds that his grandfather taught him Hebrew and astrology – both regarded by the Inquisition as bordering on witchcraft.

Many of Nostradamus' commentators believe that his writings reveal evidence of a detailed knowledge of the Jewish esoteric tradition called the *Kabbala*. It is quite possible that he also learned this from his grandfather. If so, this was the most dangerous of his studies, even more so than astrology, for any reference to kabbalism in public could have led to both of them being accused of anti-Christian magic. Fortunately, even when young, Nostradamus knew when to keep his mouth shut.

In his early teens he was sent to study in Avignon, and soon outstripped his classmates in most subjects. As a result, in 1522, Michel went to study medicine at Montpellier – at that time, one of the greatest medical universities in Europe. It took Michel only three years to be granted permission to practise as a doctor. His apprenticeship was probably shortened by an outbreak of plague in Montpellier, when every available doctor battled day and night to halt a form of plague called *le charbon*, which covered the victim's skin with black pustules. By the end of the epidemic, Nostradamus had earned a reputation as a gifted physician.

His pupil, Jean de Chavigny, would later claim that even at this early stage in his medical career, Nostradamus employed anti-plague techniques of his own invention. It has even been implausibly suggested that Nostradamus may have used his power of precognition to anticipate treatments of later centuries, a theory that can be categorically denied, since we have some of Nostradamus' remedies – which he himself noted down – and they were not miracle cures by any definition. They include burning a powder of dried rose petals, cloves, lignum aloes, iris and sweet flag roots to "cleanse the air" (it was believed that plague was caused by "ill humours" in the atmosphere), and concocting pills of the same harmless mixture. The best that can be said is that the vitamin C in the rose petals may have helped his patients.

For more general problems associated with male ageing, Nostradamus prescribed a fabulously expensive ointment containing powdered coral, lapis lazuli and flecks of gold leaf.

> If a man's beard is turning grey, [the ointment] retards that ageing process. It prevents headaches and constipation, and multiplies his sperm to such an extent that a man may enjoy marital pleasures as frequently as he desires without impairing his health. It keeps the four humours in such health that were a man to take it from birth, he could live forever.

This is enough to convince us that, whatever his powers of prophecy, Nostradamus the physician was a typical child of his time.

Even so, there were some respects in which his medical practises seemed an anticipation of the future. He insisted that patients be kept in sunlit, well-ventilated rooms, and be given daily baths – at a time when many people, even the aristocracy, were content with one bath per year. (Nostradamus himself bathed daily.) It is hard for us to appreciate how revolutionary this was; yet it was not until the twentieth century that doctors came to appreciate that patients in sunlit beds tend to recover quicker than those in shadowed beds. In Nostradamus' day, it was widely accepted that sickness travelled in the form of vapour on the air, so it seemed logical to close the windows and doors of the sick chamber.

Even more extraordinary was his refusal to bleed the sick, at a time when bleeding was perhaps the most common remedy for anything from migraine to pneumonia. It was believed that the sick produced excess blood and, since blood was supposed to be the fluid in the body's central heating system, that draining off blood could cure fevers. No one but Nostradamus seemed to notice that bleeding did no good and often killed the patient. To his fellow doctors, he must have seemed as eccentric as we would think a modern doctor who refused to believe in blood transfusion.

Reports of Nostradamus' cures, as well as of his courage in facing the plague (many doctors fled at the first sign of it), led to invitations from other stricken towns. So for a period he practised as an itinerant physician in Toulouse, Narbonne and Bordeaux.

What does this tell us about Nostradamus? Simply that he was a brave man? Surely there is more to it than that. A modern reader finds it quite impossible to imagine what it was like to live in a plague-stricken city (although anyone who wants to find out should read the shattering account in Manzoni's great novel *The Betrothed*). The air was full of the stench of rotting corpses, and since most people believed that this smell carried the plague (and kept scented handkerchiefs pressed to their noses), it required more than courage to remain. It may be simply that, having studied astrology from his eighteenth- to his twenty-sixth year, Nostradamus was convinced that he had a long time to live. But even astrology must seem a doubtful comfort amid the stench of death, and it is surely more likely that Nostradamus simply had a deep and powerful intuition of his own destiny: that fate had something more interesting in store for him than the "black death".

We know that when the plague outbreak receded, some time before 1533, he returned to Montpellier to complete his studies and receive his doctor's degree. He was then invited to teach on the faculty, but his unorthodox ideas seem to have aroused the hostility of his senior colleagues and after two years he decided to resume his travels.

The wandering scholar and doctor returned to his native Provence and to the life of an itinerant doctor. It was at this time that he made a translation of the *Book of Orus Apollo, Son of Osiris, King of Egypt*, which he dedicated to the Princess of Navarre. He must have at least made Her Royal Highness' acquaintance to do this, so we can assume Nostradamus was mixing in the highest circles.

After a year of wandering, Nostradamus decided to settle in Agen, in Aquitaine. De Chavigny believes he chose this town because it was the home of Julius Cesar Scaliger – one of the greatest scholars of the sixteenth century and a man with a strong interest in esoteric lore. It is certainly almost impossible that scholars like Nostradamus and Scaliger can have lived in the same small town without getting to know one another. Some writers have suggested that Scaliger initiated Nostradamus into a secret occult society and showed him forbidden books and methods of prediction, but the truth is that we simply do not know anything about their relationship.

There may be another reason that Nostradamus chose Agen. That pleasant town had belonged to the English crown since 1152, when Eleanor of Aquitaine married Henry II of England, and continued to be English, on and off, for the next three centuries, until the English withdrew at the end of the Hundred Years War (1453). Agen thus had a more international atmosphere than most French cities.

In an article on Nostradamus, James Randi makes the pene-trating comment that many of the quatrains of Nostradamus were "actually political commentaries and justifiable critiques of the activities of the Catholic Church, which was then busily tossing heretics on to bonfires wherever the Holy Inquisition could reach." England became Protestant in 1529, four years before Nostradamus received his degree at Montpellier, so the intellectual atmosphere in Agen was probably freer than in the oppressively Catholic Montpellier. Randi goes on to suggest that Nostradamus was a secret Protestant, basing his theory on revealing letters discovered in the Bibliotheque Nationale. Since his own family had been forced to convert to Catholicism, Nostradamus had no reason to love the Catholic Church. It is, therefore, ironic that Catherine of Navarre – the person most responsible for the St Bartholomew Massacre of Protestants – should later have become Nostradamus' admirer and patron.

Nostradamus married soon after he arrived in Agen – a girl of "high estate" – and fathered two children. Sadly, in 1538, plague broke out in the town, and the great physician was unable to save the lives of his wife and two children. It was a grim year for Nostradamus because he was not only bereaved, but was also caught up in a petty legal row with his late wife's family concerning the return of her dowry – as if her death had somehow placed him in breach of contract.

Worse still, he was accused of heresy. The details are not clear; one version has him watching a workman casting a statue of the Virgin and making some tactless remark about making brazen images, while another has him saying that it was a statue of the devil. Nostradamus is said to have claimed that he meant it was as ugly as the devil. But rather than defend himself before an ecclesiastical court, he set out once more on his travels.

Over the next eight or nine years, he wandered through France, Italy and Sicily. Little is known about this period of his life, but some writers have suggested that he became an initiate of the secret Priory of Sion while he was in Lorraine. The Priory was a heretical Rosicrucian order which, according to modern commentators, taught that Jesus survived the crucifixion, married Mary Magdalene, and moved to France (see chapter 6). As we shall see in a later chapter, it is indeed possible that Nostradamus was an occult "initiate", but whether he was connected with the Priory is unknown.

His pupil, Jean de Chavigny, states that it was during this last period as a wanderer that Nostradamus' gifts as a prophet began to manifest themselves. There is a famous story of how he was riding along a dusty road near the Italian city of Ancona, when he passed a line of mendicant friars, and dismounted and knelt before a young novice. Asked why he abased himself before the youth, he replied: "Because I must kneel before His Holiness." The friar, Felice Peretti, later became Pope Sixtus V.

Another story tells how, when Nostradamus was staying in the Chateau de Fains, in Lorraine, his host, the Seigneur de Florinville, decided to test his guest's gift of foreseeing the future. Pointing to two piglets, he asked what their fate would be. Nostradamus replied that the black one would be eaten for dinner, but that a wolf would eat the white piglet. Florinville then took his cook aside, and told him to kill and roast the white piglet for dinner. After the meal, the cook was summoned and asked to tell Nostradamus the colour of pig he had just eaten. The man looked embarrassed, then admitted that although he had killed the white piglet, as instructed, a pet wolf had stolen it from the kitchen, and he had been forced to kill and roast the black one.

In 1544 there was an outbreak of plague in Marseilles and, forcing his way through a tide of escaping refugees, Nostradamus hurried to the city to help. Two years later he was in Aix-en-Provence doing the same – this time so successfully that he was granted a permanent pension by the city fathers. In Lyon, he fought an outbreak of whooping cough so effectively that he was rewarded with a sack of gold, which he immediately gave to the poor.

In 1547, at the age of forty-four, Nostradamus decided to settle again, this time in Salon-en-Craux (now known as Salon-de-Provence; the French still refer to Nostradamus as "the Seer of Salon"). Here he married a rich and well-connected widow and started a new family. His wife's wealth and his pension from nearby Aix-en-Provence allowed him to devote most of his time to his esoteric studies, the cultivation of his precognitive skill and a new passion: writing.

He had moved with his new wife into a house in a narrow, dark street, whose spiral staircase led to Nostradamus' study on the top floor, from which he could look over the pointed roofs of the town, and at the old castle of the archbishop on a steep rock. Here, surrounded by books and manuscripts, this short, vigorous man, who looked more like a farmer than a sage, meditated upon the future, practised divination and scratched out sheet after sheet with his quill pen. The house can still be seen in Salon.

From 1550, Nostradamus published yearly almanacs – month-by-month diaries of the coming year's events – together with astrological tables of celestial conjunctions. These soon spread his celebrity far and wide. In 1552, he published a description of his "wonder drugs" and his eccentric medicinal theories – such as boiling water thoroughly before drinking. This book also listed a number of feminine cosmetics of his own concoction, as well as the jam recipes that he particularly favoured. The *Traite des Fardemens et Confitures* (Treatise on Cosmetics and Jams) also achieved wide popularity.

At that time, printed volumes were still a novelty, but the spirit of the Renaissance had swept through French society, and new books were bought as quickly as they came off the presses. (These included the works of Nostradamus' contemporary and fellow medical graduate of Montpellier, François Rabelais.) Nostradamus became widely known for his almanacs and his treatise on cosmetics (which had been made popular by Catherine de Medici), so when, on 1 May 1555, he brought out his volume of prophetic quatrains (four line poems) it quickly became something of a best-seller.

The courtier and poet Jean Dorat praised Nostradamus so highly to his students that one of them, Jean Aimes de Chavigny, travelled from Burgundy to Salon to meet the seer. De Chavigny was a distinguished man in his own right, having been mayor of Beaune. He soon settled as a lodger in the house of Nostradamus, and became the prophet's devoted helper and pupil; he also wrote a biography of Nostradamus to which this present account, like all the others, is indebted.

Nostradamus was in his early fifties when he met de Chavigny – an old man by the standards of sixteenth-century Europe. Chavigny described his master as being a

[a] little less than middle height, robust, cheerful and vigorous. His brow was high and open, the nose straight, the grey eyes gentle, though in wrath they would flame . . . a severe but laughing face, so one saw allied with the severity a great humanity. His cheeks were ruddy even into extreme age, his beard thick, his health good.

Nostradamus' *Centuries* was so-called because each book (there were eventually twelve) contained 100 predictions, each consisting of a four-line rhymed verse. In his preface, dedicated to his son Cesar, Nostradamus makes it clear that he was not aiming at a wide audience. His knowledge, he says, derives from "astronomical effects" – that is, study of the heavens – but if he were to tell all he knows of the future, it would cause such offence among "those of the present Reign, Sect, Religion and Faith" that he would be angrily condemned. In spite of which he had decided, for the common good, to speak his mind about the future in "dark, abstruse sentences", and to ignore the advice of St Matthew not to cast his pearls before swine.

Nostradamus succeeded all too well in disguising his meanings
– so well that the first reaction of the unprepared reader is to
dismiss them as some kind of a joke. The two preliminary verses
describe how he sits in his study, looking into a "thin flame"
(presumably a candle) in a brass bowl of water, and using a
divining rod, experiences "divine splendour", which "sits nearby".
Then he plunges straight into obscurity:

> *Quands le littiere du tourbillon versee,*
> *Et seront faces de leurs manteaux couvers,*
> *La Republique par gens nouveau vexee,*
> *Lors, blancs et rouges jugeront a l'envers.*

Translation:

> When the litter is overturned by the whirlwind,
> And faces will be covered by their cloaks,
> The Republic by new men is vexed,
> Then the whites and reds will judge conversely.

The first two lines are an excellent description of litter caught up
by the wind and men covering their faces with their cloaks, but
what Republic is vexed by new men (upstarts?) and who are the
whites and the reds who will pass perverse (or wrong) judgments?
Henry C. Roberts, who translated the *Centuries* in 1937, concludes
that Nostradamus is forecasting the Russian Revolution of 1917,
with its Reds and Whites. But the Reds overthrew the Russian
monarchy, not a republic. Besides, the Russians of 1917 did not
wear cloaks. And if we add that "litter" can also mean a kind of
chair in which wealthy people are carried by their lackeys, we have
to admit that it sounds like a prophecy that applies to
Nostradamus' own country rather than to Russia.

In fact, Nostradamus seems to foresee the future of France more
than that of any other country, so it is unlikely that the quatrain
refers to the Russian Revolution. Which leaves the French
Revolution. The republicans and the royalists were also known as
reds and whites. "*Tourbillon*" can mean a whirlpool or a whirlwind, but since men are holding their cloaks over their faces, a
whirlwind seems the more likely. We have to remember that the

Republic had been established by the time the "new men" – Robespierre, Danton and Marat – gained their power. If the "whites and reds" are royalists and republicans, then the last line means that the reds and whites hold opposite opinions about one another. This is certainly a far more reasonable interpretation than Henry C. Roberts' Russian Revolution theory.

There are a thousand of these verses (plus another thirteen from the two "lost books" 11 and 12), all virtually as incomprehensible as the above quatrain. Just occasionally, a verse seems to score a direct hit on some historical event – as we shall see in the following pages, but for the most part, they are as obscure as the utterances of the Delphic oracle.

Less than four months after the publication of the first *Book of Centuries*, Nostradamus' life was to change dramatically. He was summoned to the court of Henri II, arriving there on 15 August 1555. It was almost certainly the queen, Catherine de' Medici, who was responsible for summoning Nostradamus; her husband was more interested in hunting than in the occult sciences. Catherine was fascinated by astrology and fortune-telling. One of the most calculating and ruthless women of the sixteenth century, she used astrological prediction rather as a modern politician uses polling organizations to help formulate policy. As the wife of the monarch, she could indulge her passion for the occult without fear of the Inquisition, and could offer similar protection to her favourites. Therefore, for Nostradamus, an invitation to the court was the most precious gift his increasing reputation could have brought.

In her excellent novelized biography of Nostradamus, *The Dreamer and the Vine*, astrologer Liz Greene speculates that the real reason Nostradamus was summoned to Paris was that someone had given the queen a copy of the Centuries, and she had seen the one that seemed to foretell her husband's death. *Century I*, quatrain 35, reads:

> *Le Lion jeune le vieux surmontera,*
> *En champ bellique par singulier duelle:*
> *Dans cage d'or loeil il lui crevera,*
> *Deux plays une puis mourrir mort cruelle.*

Translation:

> The young Lion shall overcome the old one,
> In a field by a single duel:
> In a golden cage he shall put out his eyes,
> Two blows from one then he shall die a cruel death.

In fact, the queen was anxious to get a second opinion from Nostradamus concerning a prediction made by another famous seer, Luca Gaurico. This Neapolitan astrologer had warned that the king's stars suggested death or blindness if he fought a duel in an enclosed space in his forty-first year. Catherine was not particularly emotionally attached to her husband – who had numerous mistresses, including his aged childhood nurse – but she was anxious that he should survive until at least 1562, when their eldest son, Francis, would be old enough to legally rule without a regent. Unfortunately, the threat to Henri's life was due to fall between 1559 and 1560.

What Nostradamus told his new royal patrons was not recorded. Tradition states that he gave a copy of *Centuries* to Henri with an offer to explain the meaning of each quatrain, but the king, being no intellectual, refused a privilege that future monarchs would have given fiefdoms for. The same tradition states that the Seer of Salon privately showed Queen Catherine a magic mirror in which she saw three of her seven children attaining the crown of France.

Fantasy or truth, their majesties' known reaction to Nostradamus was in line with these stories: Henri politely ignored him, but Catherine thereafterwards ardently sought his prophetic advice. A Spaniard at the French court, Francisco de Alova, later remarked that Queen Catherine always quoted Nostradamus' words with a confidence "as if citing St John or St Luke". All threat of questioning by the Inquisition receded in the light of such high patronage. Queen Catherine even had Nostradamus lodged in the town house of the Archbishop of Sens. There, a steady stream of nobility visited the seer, who is said to have made a small fortune from medical and astrological consultations. However, Nostradamus had no intention of becoming a court magician, and soon requested, and was given, leave to return to Salon.

It seems unlikely that Nostradamus was altogether candid, at least with the king. The first volume of *Centuries* contained specific predictions that Henri would die in agony and that his children would be the last of the ruling house of Valois. "Ill news is an ill guest", as the saying goes, so if the seer did elucidate these quatrains, we must assume that he was not taken seriously by the queen, or that what he had to tell her did not disturb her unduly.

The event foretold by both Luca Gaurico and Nostradamus, the death of King Henri, occurred in his forty-first year, just as Gaurico had predicted. The "*duelle*" in question was a jousting competition that took place on 10 July 1559. King Henri had already won two jousts that morning. Queen Catherine sent a messenger asking him to "toil no more" as it was "late, and the weather exceeding hot", but the king replied that, as champion of the field, it was his duty to accept three challenges. Gabriel de Lorges – the Comte de Montgomery – was already in the saddle at the far end of the jousting ring and, without another word, King Henri spurred towards him.

They struck and passed each other twice in succession but, as neither was unhorsed, they turned and charged for a third time. To everyone's horror, de Lorges' blunted wooden lance shattered when it struck the king's breastplate and the sharp broken end slammed upward and pierced the visor of Henri's gold embossed helmet. (These were, of course, "two blows in one" pass.) The splintered lance struck and entered just behind Henri's right eye socket, drove through that side of the brain case and exited near the right ear. Amazingly Henri did not die instantly, but suffered ten days of blind agony before a gangrene infection finally put him out of his misery.

The Comte de Montgomery was seven years younger than the king and was commander of his Scottish Guard. Henri II used a lion as his unofficial badge and the emblem of Scotland was, and is, a lion rampant.

Detail for detail, Nostradamus' prediction was exactly correct and many people, especially Queen Catherine, saw it as such. If she was angry that the seer had not given a specific warning to King Henri – which might have saved his life – she showed no sign of it. When somebody suggested that Nostradamus was plainly a sorcerer and should be handed to the Inquisition, she angrily refused, restating that he was under her protection.

The attitude was generous – particularly if she suspected that the meaning of the tenth quatrain of *Century I* related to her children:

> *Sergens transmis dans la cage de fer,*
> *Ou les enfans septaines du Roy sont Pris:*
> *Les vieux et peres sortiront bas de l'enfer,*
> *Ains mourir voir de fruict mort et cris.*

Translation:

> Sergeants sent into an iron vault,
> Which holds the seven children of the King:
> The ancestors and forefathers will emerge from Hell,
> Lamenting to see death of the fruit of their line.

Catherine de' Medici and Henri II had seven children and therefore, in 1555, had some reason to hope that their offspring would continue the line of kings. Unfortunately, this was not to happen. With the death of Queen Margot of Navarre in 1615 – the last of the seven children – the Valois line of kings came to an end.

Quatrain 11 of the sixth volume of *Centuries* seems to be an even more specific prediction of the end of the Valois dynasty.

> *Des sept rameaux à trois seront reduicts,*
> *Les plus aisnez seront surprins par mort,*
> *Fraticider les deux seront seduicts,*
> *Les conjurez en dormans seront morts.*

Translation:

> The seven branches will be reduced to three,
> The older ones will be surprised by death,
> The two will be seduced towards fratricide,
> The conspirators will die while asleep.

Three of Catherine's five sons lived to ascend to the throne of France (under French law, her two daughters were ineligible to rule). Of the seven children, only Queen Margot lived to relative old age, the rest being prematurely "surprised by death" in their teens, twenties and thirties. Two of the brothers, Henri III and François, Duc d'Alencon, became mortal enemies and certainly would have indulged in fratricide hád the opportunity arisen.

Guessing the identity of the conspirators predicted to die in their sleep in the last line of the quatrain is now virtually impossible; sixteenth-century France was full of likely candidates. Some researchers have suggested that it might have been the Guise brothers – co-conspirators with François, later assassinated by Henri III – but, although killed early in the morning, neither was asleep at the time.

Over the next decade, Nostradamus and his second wife lived peacefully in Salon. He never returned to Paris, even after it was generally recognized that he had correctly predicted the circumstances of the death of Henri II. Although he could doubtless have made a fortune at the court of the new king, François II, Nostradamus still declined offers to become the Royal Astrologer. This choice of a quiet life may have been to do with his age and health – by his late fifties he already suffered from severe gout – but it is also possible that he had foreknowledge of the difficult times the French crown would soon undergo.

François II, son and heir of Henri II, was only sixteen when he came to the throne and was easily dominated by the powerful Duc de Guise (just what Queen Catherine had feared might happen if her husband died before 1562). In 1560, after only a year as king, François died and was replaced by his fourteen-year-old brother, who was crowned Charles IX. This time, however, it was Queen-Mother Catherine who dominated her royal son – her intrigues and plots throughout his fourteen-year reign were to split France and sour the sectarian dispute between Protestant and Catholic to the point of massacre and civil war.

Nostradamus was apparently well aware of the tragic events shortly to befall France, because his *Centuries* foretold them in specific, if deliberately obscure, detail. He was visited personally by Catherine and King Charles in 1564, when the royal party went out of its way to pass through Salon. However, if he warned them of the coming massacre of Saint Bartholomew's Day, it failed to influence their later actions.

Two years following this royal visit, on 2 July 1566, Nostradamus died of a massive heart attack, in part brought on by his crippling gout. Following his death, his pupil de Chavigny republished the ten *Centuries* together with two partial volumes and two other posthumous works, *Sixains* (containing sixty-eight quatrains) and *Presages* (containing a further 141 predictions). In this later book, the last quatrain reads:

> *De retour d'Ambassade, don de Roy mis au lieu*
> *Plus n'en fera: sera allé à Dieu*
> *Parans plus proches, amis, frères du sang,*
> *Trouvé tout mort près du lict et du banc.*

Translation:

> On returning from an embassy, the King's gift safely stored
> No more will I labour for I will have gone to God
> By my close relatives, friends and blood brothers,
> I shall be found dead, near my bed and the bench.

Nostradamus had, just before his death, returned from an embassy to Arles, where he had been an official representative for Salon. The "King's gift", also mentioned in the first line, might have been the princely 100 gold Ecus Queen-Mother Catherine had given him, in the name of King Charles, two years before; we know that the seer left his family plenty of money when he died. On the night before his death, Nostradamus called for a priest to give the last rites – although he seemed healthy enough for de Chavigny to be surprised when the seer told him: "You will not see me alive at sunrise."

This was Nostradamus' last prophecy. The next morning, de Chavigny and the seer's family found him dead, lying between his bed and a bench he used to use to help get his gouty foot in and out of bed.

In his biography of his master, de Chavigny tells us that Nostradamus had asked "not to hear feet passing over him when he slept for the last time". Therefore, Nostradamus was entombed upright in a niche in the wall of the chapel of the Convent of Les Cordeliers. The plaque on the tomb reads:

Here lie the bones of the most illustrious Michel Nostradamus,
the only one, in judgment of all mortals, worthy to write with
a pen almost divine, under the influence of the stars, of events to
come in the whole world.
He lived sixty-two years, six months and seventeen days.
He died at Salon in the year 1566.
Posterity disturb not his repose.
Anne Ponsart Gemelle, his wife, wishes her spouse true felicity.

The penultimate line was, not surprisingly, read by many to be a
warning against disturbing the seer's bones. Indeed, quatrain 7,
Century IX was said to be a direct warning against this from the
seer himself:

> *Qui ouvrira le monument trouvé*
> *Et ne viendra le serrer promptement,*
> *Mal lui viendra et ne pourra prouvé,*
> *Si mieux doit estre roi Breton ou Normand.*

Translation:

> He that shall open the discovered monument [tomb],
> And shall not close it again promptly,
> Evil will befall him and no one will be able to prove it,
> Better he were a Breton or Norman king.

There are two tales, possibly apocryphal, concerning the distur-
bance of Nostradamus' tomb. The first states that in the year 1600,
the citizens of Salon decided that their famous seer should be
moved to a more prominent section of the chapel wall. On opening
the tomb, they found Nostradamus' body had been buried with a
lead disc on a chain around its neck. The disk was quite unadorned,
except for the engraved numbers "1600".

Presumably the tomb was quickly resealed, or the bones were
moved *"promptement"* enough for the curse of *Century IX*,
quatrain 7, not to take effect, because no "evil" effects were
reported following this incident.

The same can not be said of the second tradition concerning
Nostradamus' bones. During the French Revolution, some soldiers

are said to have broken into the seer's tomb in the hope of finding the magic mirror they had heard he used to see the future. When they found only his skeleton, they decided to get drunk and one soldier broke open Nostradamus' skull and swigged wine from it. As they were leaving the chapel, a hail of gunfire – fired by whom the legend does not make plain – killed the sacrilegious trooper stone dead.

One fact we know for certain, following the Revolutionaries' ransacking of the Convent of Les Cordeliers, the people of Salon decided that his bones should be moved to the church of Saint-Laurent, where his tomb can still be seen today. Strangely enough, when Nostradamus' original will and testament of 1566 was subsequently discovered, a section of text was noted to have been scored out, but still remained legible. It read:

> In the sepulchre in the collegial church of Saint Laurens of the said Salon, and in the Chapel of Our Lady, in the wall of which it is desired to be made a monument.

A coincidence perhaps, but the fact that Nostradamus asked for a monument to be placed in the very spot where his bones would eventually rest seems in keeping with his reputation for foreseeing the future and his impish sense of humour.

In the remainder of this chapter we shall consider some of the quatrains that seem to have been fulfilled in the lifetime of Nostradamus or soon after. Later chapters will deal with the centuries that follow, and, finally, with those that may reveal our own future.

The main sources I have used are Erica Cheetham's *The Prophecies of Nostradamus*, Henry C. Roberts' *The Complete Prophecies of Nostradamus*, Jean-Charles de Fontbrune's *Nostradamus: Countdown to Apocalypse* and David Ovason's *The Secrets of Nostradamus*. I will cite the theories appropriate to each and, where there is a significant difference of opinion, I summarize the various arguments.

The historical titles are my own. Nostradamus, of course, gave no such clues. The Roman numeral beneath gives the *Centuries* volume, and is followed by the quatrain number.

Due to the seer's unparalleled skill at poetic riddles, no one researcher can claim absolute certainty over the true meaning of *any* of Nostradamus' prophesies, and the reader is always left to think and decide for themselves where any truth may lie. Of course, this indeed may have been Nostradamus' purpose in publishing the *Centuries* in the first place.

Francis II and Mary Queen of Scots: 1558–60

X.55

> *Les malheureuses noces celebreront,*
> *En grand joye, mais la fin malheureuse:*
> *Mary et mere Nore desdaigneront.*
> *La Phybe mort et Nore plus piteuse.*

Translation:

> The unhappy marriage will be celebrated,
> With great joy, but the end will be unhappy:
> Mary will be detested by the mother.
> The *Phybe* dead and the daughter-in-law most piteous.

In 1558, shortly before the accidental death of Henri II, the heir apparent to the French throne, Prince Francis, was married to Mary Stuart – later known as Mary Queen of Scots. Naturally the marriage was celebrated throughout both France and Scotland, but the match was destined to be tragically short.

The mother of Mary (Marie de Guise) and the mother of Francis (Catherine de' Medici) loathed each other: the former referring to Catherine as "the merchant's daughter".[1] Mary's return to Scotland, following the death of King Francis in 1560, dashed any hope of a closer alliance between the two kingdoms.

The reference to "Mary" in line three seems to suggest a prediction of the above events – note that Nostradamus did not use the French spelling, "Marie". Mary is a name rarely found in French history.

But what of "*Phybe*", a name that simply does not exist? This in itself tells us to look for one of Nostradamus' anagrams or words in code. The first syllable "*phy*" suggests the Greek *phi*, the equivalent of our letter F. This is the initial letter of Francis. "*Be*" suggests *beta*, the second letter of the Greek alphabet, so "Phybe" becomes F2, Francis the Second.

[1] A sneering allusion to the unaristocratic roots of the Medici family, whose name means "doctors".

The Conspiracy of Amboise: March 1560

IV.62

> *Un coronel machine ambition,*
> *Se saisira de la grande armée,*
> *Contree son prince faite invention,*
> *Es descouvert sera souz sa ramée.*

Translation:

> A colonel intrigues a plot by his ambition,
> He shall seize upon the best part of the army,
> Against the prince he shall have a feigned invention,
> And shall be discovered under the branches.

Here we have a classic case of different interpretations by different Nostradamus scholars.

De Fontbrune believes this quatrain refers to the 1560 attempt to kidnap Francis II from Castle Amboise. The plotters, many from the army, thus hoped to remove the sixteen-year-old king from the manipulative influence of the Duc de Guise. They were, however, discovered in the neighbouring forest and slaughtered.

Roberts, on the other hand, believes this to be a prediction of the rise to power of Oliver Cromwell, but does not offer any supporting detail.

Erica Cheetham offers a third interpretation: the rise to power of Colonel Gaddafi in 1971 and his overthrow of King Idris of Libya.

Mary Queen of Scots and the "Casket Letters": 1567

VIII.23

> *Lettres trouvées de la roine les coffres,*
> *Point de subscrit sans aucun nom d'hauteur*
> *Par la police seront caché les offres,*
> *Qu'on ne scaura qui sera l'amateur.*

Translation:

> Letters are found in the queen's coffers,
> No signature and no name of the author

> The ruse will conceal the offers,
> So they do not know who the lover is.

Following the death of the teenage Francis II, his widow, Mary Queen of Scots, married the Scottish noble, Lord Darnley. Although the match was at first happy enough to produce a son (later James VI of Scotland, then James I of England), Mary soon came to hate her syphilitic, conniving husband.

In 1567, Lord Darnley died under suspicious circumstances (the house in which he was sleeping exploded – investigators then found Darnley in the garden, strangled to death in his night shirt). The chief suspect in the murder was Mary's close friend, the Earl of Bothwell. This seemed to be confirmed when a silver casket of love letters and sonnets – apparently from Mary to Bothwell – came to light soon afterwards. After a mock trial, however, Bothwell was acquitted and, a few weeks later, divorced his wife and married Mary.

Although they could fix a trial, Queen Mary and her new consort could not control public opinion. The scandalous marital behaviour of the monarch led to a short but decisive civil war in Scotland, at the end of which Mary was forced to abdicate and flee to England. There she was placed under house arrest by her cousin, Queen Elizabeth I. Following an attempt to escape and take the English throne, Mary was beheaded in 1587.

The casket of letters that implicated Bothwell and, indirectly, Mary in Darnley's murder is now thought by some historians to have been a set of forgeries produced by Mary's enemies. Whether this is true or not, however, it was not the casket but the Queen's own shameless remarriage that brought her downfall.

Perhaps it should be noted that Nostradamus almost certainly knew Mary Queen of Scots personally, as both visited the court of Henri II in 1556.

The Turkish Sack of Cyprus: 1570–71

XII.36

> *Assault farouche en Cypre se prepare,*
> *Larme a l'oeil, de ta ruine proche;*
> *Byzance class, Morisque, si grand tare,*
> *Deux differente, le grand vast par la roche.*

Translation:

> A savage attack prepared on Cyprus,
> Tears in my eye, thy ruin approaches;
> Byzantine fleet, Moslems, do great damage,
> Two different ones, the great waste by the rock.

Most sources agree that this quatrain refers to the savage invasion of Cyprus by the Ottoman Army. Byzantium (now Istanbul) has been in Turkish hands since 1453, thus any fleet from there would be (as line three states) Moslem. In 1570, Sultan Selim II ordered the invasion of the island of Cyprus, which was at that time under Venetian rule. The Turkish fleet blockaded towns and landed 60,000 men. When Nicosia fell after forty-five days, 20,000 inhabitants were butchered and the rest were enslaved. Famagusta held out for almost a year before it was forced to surrender; the Venetian governor was tortured then flayed alive, while the Ottoman troops ravaged the town and slaughtered its inhabitants. Repressive Turkish rule on Cyprus continued until 1878.

The Battle of Lepanto: 7 October 1571

III.64

> Le chef de Perse remplira grands Olchades,
> Classe tririme contre gent Mahometique:
> De Parthe et Mede, et pilliers les Cyclades,
> Repos long temps au grand port Ionique.

Translation:

> The lord of Persia shall prepare great Ships,
> A fleet of triremes against the Moslems:
> From Parthia and Media they shall come to plunder the Cyclades,
> A long rest shall come to the great Ionic port.

The idea of a Persian leader sending a fleet against Moslems in the Cyclades (the Greek islands) seems rather odd. If, however, one reads the second line to indicate an opposing fleet attacking the first, a certain famous historical encounter seems to be suggested: the Battle of Lepanto.

Following its successful capture of Cyprus in 1571, the Ottoman Empire launched a fleet to invade the rest of the Aegean islands. This was met by an allied Christian fleet and destroyed in the Gulf of Lepanto (now called the Gulf of Corinth). Although this defeat did little harm to the military strength of the Ottoman Empire, it was of great psychological importance to the Christian states and marked the beginning of a long period of decline for the Turks. Ionian ports (those of the west coast of Asia Minor and the Greek islands) thereafter enjoyed a long period of comparative peace.

The battle of Lepanto is also notable in history as the last in which both sides utilized oared galleys (called triremes in ancient times).

The 1572 Supernova

II.41

> *La grand éstoile par sept jours bruslera,*
> *Nuée fera deux soleils apparior:*
> *Le gros mastin toute nuict hurlera,*
> *Quand grand pontife changera de terroir.*

Translation:

> The great star shall burn for seven days,
> A cloud will make two suns appear:
> The huge mastiff will howl all night,
> When the great pope changes territory.

David Ovason believes that this quatrain specifically indicates the formation of a new star in the summer skies of 1572. This supernova appeared near Cassiopeia and burned visibly, night and day, for 16 months. Thus, says Ovason, two "suns" were visible. He adds that the nova had a distinctly perceptible cloud of stellar gases around it at night.

This astronomical event caused consternation across Europe. Since the Dark Ages, it had been a fixture of Church belief that the "heavenly realm" of the sky was perfect and unchanging. The arrival of a new star was a painful blow to the Church's doctrinal authority just when men like Columbus and Copernicus were already undermining it with their strange theories and discoveries.

The supernova of 1572 highlighted the corrosion of the absolute authority of the Church through the growth of scientific reasoning in European society. It also heralded a new era of invention, reform and bloody conflict.

In Denmark, an alchemist called Tycho Brahe was so amazed by the new star that he dropped all his other work and dedicated his life to the study of the heavens – he was later to be called the "Father of Astronomy".

In Rome, Pope Pius V died during the time of the supernova and was replaced by Gregory XIII – designer of the Gregorian calendar now in almost universal use.

Finally, in Paris, Queen-Mother Catherine de' Medici instigated a slaughter that was to lead to the most savage religious wars in Europe's history.

The St Bartholomew's Day Massacre: 24 August 1572
IV.47

> Le noir farouche, quand aura essayé
> Sa main sanguine par fue, fer, arcs tendus:
> Trestout le peuple sera tant effrayé,
> Voir les plus grans par col et pieds pendus.

Translation:

> The savage black one, when his bloody hand
> Shall have done its worst with fire, sword and bows:
> Then will his people be terror-stricken,
> At the sight of great ones hanged by the neck and feet.

Erica Cheetham suggests that "*noir*" in the first line is a partial anagram for *roi* (French for 'king'). She goes on to speculate that this quatrain refers to the bloody St Bartholomew's Day Massacre that was to escalate the Protestant-Catholic troubles into a savage religious war.

In 1572, Catherine de' Medici – mother of the then King of France, Charles IX – instigated a plot to assassinate Admiral Coligny, the leader of the Huguenot (French Protestant) faction.

The plot failed – Coligny was only wounded – and, while gathered in Paris for the wedding of the king's sister Margot to Henry of Navarre, leading Huguenots demanded an investigation.

King Charles was at first ready to comply, but he soon changed his mind when his mother informed him to whom the trail would lead. With breathtaking cold-heartedness, the king and his mother decided to close the city gates and kill every Protestant their troops could find. Estimates vary, but at least 2,000, possibly even as many as 100,000, men, women and children were butchered on St Bartholomew's Day 1572. The slaughter soon spread to the French provinces and acted as fuel to the religious troubles that were to culminate in the disastrous Thirty Years War, half a century later.

Cheetham suggests that the last line of Nostradamus' quatrain might be a reference to the fate of Admiral Coligny, whose attempted assassination set off the whole terrible chain of events. As soon as the killings began, the violently pro-Catholic Duc de Guise sent men to Coligny's house. The admiral, who had won several campaigns for King Charles, was stabbed to death then hung from a gibbet by one foot. Other Huguenot nobles were hanged by the neck.

On the other hand, Henry Roberts suggests that this quatrain might be a reference to the Italian Fascist (black clad) dictator Mussolini. After helping to instigate World War II and uncounted deaths, Mussolini was himself executed and hung from a lamppost by his feet in 1945.

French Religious Unrest: 1574–76

III.98

> *Deux Royals Freres si fort guerroyeront,*
> *Qu'entre' eux sera la guerre si mortelle:*
> *Qu'un chacun places fortes occuperont,*
> *De regne et vie sera leur grand querelle.*

Translation:

> Two royal brothers shall battle so much one against the other,
> That the war between them shall be mortal:
> Each shall occupy a strong place,
> Their quarrel will concern their kingdom and lives.

Both de Fontbrune and Erica Cheetham agree that this quatrain seems to concern the so-called Fifth French War of Religion.

The Duc d'Alençon, younger brother of King Henri III, was a liberal Catholic who championed the rights of the Huguenot Protestants. This placed him in direct opposition to the (then) anti-Protestant Henri. In 1576, following two years of sectarian unrest and bloodshed, Alençon's faction led 30,000 men to the gates of Paris and forced the king to sign a conciliatory edict. Afterwards an uneasy, well-armed, peace was maintained between the two brothers. With some difficulty, each maintained a rein on his detestation for the other for the greater good of France.

Had sixteenth-century religious differences always been settled in this relatively reasonable fashion, later European history might have been a good deal less bloody. Unfortunately, as Nostradamus seemed to have known, the war between Catholic and Protestant was destined to be "mortal".

The Murder of the Duc de Guise: 23 December 1588
III.51 & III.55

Paris conjure un grand meurtre commettre
Blois le fera sortir en plain effect;
Ceux d'Orléons voudront leur chef remmettre,
Angiers, Troye, Langres leur foront grand forfait.

Translation:

Paris conspires to commit great murder,
Blois shall make it come to pass;
The people of Orléans will replace their leader,
Angers, Troyes and Langres will harm them.

This quatrain seems to deal with an important political assassination that took place in the reign of Henri III.

One of the most influential families of late-sixteenth-century France were the Ducs de Guise – a clan that led the Roman Catholic backlash against the growth of Protestantism. François, the second duke to carry the title, had already tried puppet-mastering the reign of the weakling Francis II (see "the Conspiracy of Amboise", page 172) following the death of Henri II. Eighteen years later his son, Henri de Lorraine, was a close friend and supporter of Henri III. Unfortunately the pair argued over the king's growing favouritism towards the Protestant faction, so Guise formed a "Holy League" of pro-Catholics to counter the king's liberal turn of policy.

King Henri, with the typical ruthlessness of his family, decided to have his friend murdered. The Duc de Guise was invited to the palace at Blois, where several people tried to warn him that his life was in danger, including a beautiful marchioness who spent the night with him for that purpose. They failed because de Guise was too certain that the king would never dare harm him. The king did dare, however; de Guise was asked into a room next to the royal bedchamber and was killed by the king's guards as Henri watched from behind the bed curtains; it was two days before Christmas, 1588.

At the same time, the citizens of Orléans overthrew their governor and replaced him with a relation of the late Duc de Guise. The last line of Nostradamus' quatrain names the other towns that sided with the Holy League and the de Guise faction.

Nostradamus seems to have a second prophecy about the murder of de Guise:

> *En l'an qu'un oeil en France regnera,*
> *La Cour sera en un bien fascheux trouble:*
> *Le grand de Blois son ami tuera,*
> *La regne mis en mal et doubte double.*

Translation:

> In the year when an eye reigns in France,
> The court will be greatly troubled and embarrassed:
> The great one will kill his friend at Blois,
> The reign thrown into evil and double doubt.

Why the king is described as "an eye" is difficult to fathom – although Fontbrune thinks it means a king who has been forced to share power, as Henry III was virtually sharing it with the Duc de Guise. ("Keeping an eye on" and "under someone's eye" also identify the eye with power.) The court was certainly deeply troubled and divided when Henri III had de Guise assassinated, and his reign was plunged into even deeper trouble when the Pope excommunicated him.

The king and the Protestant Henry of Navarre became allies, but another assassination was soon to end that alliance . . .

The Assassination of Henri III: 2 August 1589

I.97

> *Ce que fer, flamme, n'a sceu paracheuer,*
> *La douce langue au conseil viendra faire:*
> *Par repos, songe, le roy fere resuer,*
> *Plus l'ennemy en feu, sang militaire.*

Translation:

> What neither fire, nor iron could achieve,
> A sweet tongue in council shall manage:
> In a sleeping dream, the king will see,
> An enemy, not in war or military blood.

Erica Cheetham sees this quatrain as a clear prediction of the murder of Henri III. If so, it was typical of Nostradamus' habit of concealing the meaning until after the event. No details in the quatrain could have warned Henri, even if he had read it the night before his assassination.

On 30 July 1589, King Henri told friends that the night before, his sleep had been troubled by a strange dream. He had seen the royal ceremonial regalia – the crown, sceptre, sword, spurs and blue cloak – being trodden into the mud by a rabble of common people and monks. Although he was uncertain what this meant, he feared it was a premonition of death.

Three days later, at St Cloud, a young monk called Jacques Clement – who was, in fact, a fanatical anti-Protestant – approached the king. He told Henri that he had news concerning a secret letter and, as the king leaned down for the monk to whisper in his ear, Clement stabbed him in the stomach. Henri struck the monk with his own dagger, and Clement was quickly killed by the guards. After a day of agony, Henri died of peritonitis.

Cheetham points out that the phrase *"douce langue au conseil"* seems to be one of the clever double-meanings of which Nostradamus was so fond. The king, despite his many war-like enemies, was killed in council by a man who pretended to be a friend. She also notes another typical Nostradamian twist: "*douce*" means sweet, as does "Clement".

The Victory of Henri de Navarre: 1589

X.18

> *Le ranc Lorrain fera place a Vendosme,*
> *Le hault mis bas et le bas mis en hault,*
> *Le fils d'Hamon sera esleu dans Rome,*
> *Et les deux grands seront mis en deffault.*

Translation:

> The House of Lorraine shall give place to Vendosme,
> The high shall fall, the low shall be exalted,
> The son of Hamon shall be elected by Rome,
> And the two great ones will be defeated.

Henry III was the last king of the direct Valois line. Although, as Nostradamus predicted, three of Catherine de' Medici's sons inherited the throne, all died without leaving an heir. Catherine herself – the Lady Macbeth of sixteenth century France – died seven months before Henri's assassination and the fall of the dynasty.

The French throne was thus open to any noble who could claim direct descent from the Emperor Charlemagne. The man with the strongest claim to this bloodline was Henri, ruler of the little kingdom of Navarre, but he had virtually no chance in most people's opinion. This was because on one side he had to compete for the crown with the powerful house of de Guise, and on the other, as already noted above, Henri was a Protestant.

Indeed, Henri of Navarre might have been killed in the St Bartholomew's Day Massacre if it had not been for two factors. The first was his immediate conversion to Catholicism when he realized what was happening. The second was his marriage that day to Princess Margot, the king's sister. (This marriage of a Catholic princess to a Protestant prince was, in fact, the very reason so many Huguenots were in Paris at the time of the slaughter.) Henri remained a virtual captive of King Charles until 1576, when he returned to Navarre and reconverted to Protestantism.

Henri immediately claimed the throne on the death of Henri III, but was blocked by a combination of the de Guise family and their Holy League, the Pope – who obviously did not want a Protestant king of France – and the opposition of the predominantly Catholic French population. Despite his brilliant generalship and a string of victories against this coalition, Henri eventually won the crown by converting to Catholicism (again) and thus undermining his opponents' popular support.[2] Thus, in 1593, Henri III of Navarre became Henri IV of France – the first of the Bourbon kings.

The above quatrain predicts the defeat of the "House of Lorraine" – another name of the de Guise clan – by *"Vendosme"* – Henri of Navarre was also Duke of Vendôme. Thus, the second line could be a prediction of the fall of the "high" de Guises and rise of the "lowly" King of Navarre. The "son of Hamon" being chosen by Rome in the third line is a correct prediction that Henri IV's accession would be eventually accepted by the papacy. (Hamon was a heretic, and Henri inherited his Protestant "heresy" from his mother's teachings.) The "two great ones" defeated in the last line were probably meant to indicate the two other main contenders for the throne, the Duc de Guise and the Duc de Mayenne.

Like the prediction of the death of Henri II in a joust, this quatrain was seen – immediately after the event – to be an exactly accurate prediction of an improbable happening. It further cemented Nostradamus' posthumous reputation across Europe as a true prophet.

In fact, if tradition is to be believed, Nostradamus took pains to confirm his premonition that Henri of Navarre would one day be king of France. When, in 1563, Catherine de' Medici visited the ageing Nostradamus, the ten-year-old Henri was taken along in the royal party. During the visit, the seer asked Henri's tutor if he could see the boy naked. Unsurprisingly, the boy flatly refused and his tutor decided not to force the issue. Nevertheless, Nostradamus

[2]Henri cynically summed up his decision to change religion with the phrase: "Paris is worth a Mass."

is said to have gained access to young Henri's bedroom and peeked under his blankets. There he saw the birthmark he had foreseen on the first king of the Bourbon line and was satisfied that his vision had been true.

The Spread of Protestantism in the Late-Sixteenth Century
III.67

> *Une nouvelle secte de Philosophes,*
> *Mesprisant mort, or, honneurs et richesses:*
> *Des monts Germains ne seront limitrophes,*
> *A les ensuivre auront appuy et presses.*

Translation:

> A new sect of Philosophers,
> Despising death, gold, honours and riches:
> They will not be limited by the mountains of Germany,
> They shall have a crowd of followers and much support.

The chief question of Nostradamus' day was the Protestant–Catholic split, later called the Reformation. Racially a Jew, Nostradamus took care to appear a faithful son of the Catholic Church but, as we have seen, his sympathies were possibly with the Protestants. Certainly he was under no illusion – as many of his fellow Catholics and several popes were – that the "Protestant heresy" might one day be stamped out.

Catholic fanatics like the Ducs de Guise and the Holy League aimed to either reconvert all Protestants or – as at the St Bartholomew's Day Massacre – kill them to a man in the name of Christ. This ambition depended, however, on the containment of the Protestant teachings to the Teutonic nations that were at the forefront of championing them. Many Nostradamus scholars believe the above quatrain was Nostradamus' flat prediction that Protestantism would continue to spread and prosper.

The "new sect of philosophers" named by Nostradamus in the first line of the quatrain might well be the Protestants. Quite apart from the seer's habit of disguising identities in his quatrains, he may have used this oblique phrase to avoid trouble with the Inquisition.

Again, the description of the "new sect" as despising gold, honour and riches in the second line may seem odd today, but it should be remembered that Martin Luther's original disgust with the Catholic Church sprang from the hierarchy's obsession with such things. As to despising death, we have already seen how many Protestants were killed and died in the name of their faith.

The last two lines apparently contain the prophecy of the future spread and popularity of Protestantism. Just how prophetic this was in Nostradamus' day is a moot question. By the time he published the *Centuries*, Protestantism had successfully spread from Germany to England, Holland, Scandinavia and large areas of France. One might, therefore, read this quatrain as a statement of political fact as much as a prediction of the future.

Chapter 11

Nostradamus and Astrology

Most portraits of Nostradamus show him holding astronomical instruments, such as an astrolabe or mathematical dividers. The implication – that he obtained his predictions through astrology – seems reasonable, not least because Nostradamus is known to have supplemented his income by casting horoscopes for rich patrons. Yet even a cursory knowledge of the *Centuries* and the seer's life will show that this cannot be the whole explanation.

For example, while Nostradamus was visiting the court of Henri II in 1555, he was lodged in the Parisian townhouse of the Archbishop of Sens. Following his enthusiastic reception by Queen Catherine, it became fashionable for nobles to visit the "Prophet from Provence" to commission astrological birth charts. Yet one visitor was neither rich nor of noble birth: he was a pageboy, in a state of desperation because his master's favourite hunting dog had run away and could not be found. The seer agreed to see him and, before the boy could tell him his problem, announced: "You are worrying about a lost dog. Go and search on the Orléans road. You will find him there on a leash." Sure enough, as soon as the page reached the road leading to Orléans, he met another servant leading the run-away dog on a lead.

Another, rather more whimsical, story tells of the seer taking a walk outside the town walls of Salon. A young woman passed him and said "Bonjour, Monsieur Nostradame," to which he replied "Bonjour pucelle" ("Good day, maiden"). Later that day they passed each other again. The girl again said demurely "Bonjour, Monsieur Nostradame," but this time he replied – with a wry smile

– "Bonjour petite femme," ("Good day little (grown-up) woman"). The story goes on to state that the girl had secretly spent the morning with a young man . . .

Both stories may, of course, be apocryphal, but the fact that both seem to have been in circulation during Nostradamus' lifetime suggests that they were based on fact. They seem to show what seems obvious: that Nostradamus possessed a degree of clairvoyance or second sight.

Even a famous astrologer like Luca Gaurico could only warn Henri II to avoid fighting in an enclosed space (in armour as it turned out) because of a risk to his sight and life. Nostradamus, on the other hand, apparently foresaw minute details of the accidental death of the king. In four short lines (*Century I*, quatrain 35) he gives clues to the colour of the king's armour, the heraldic badge of both men, the position of the fatal wound and the fact that Henri would die an excruciating death. This kind of accuracy points more to an actual vision of the future, than the kind of knowledge gained by astrology, which tends to be less exact. (For example – Astrology: "You will be in mortal danger from wood and iron on such and such a date." Clairvoyance: "Don't walk down the High Street at noon on such and such, or a grand piano, being winched into a high window, will fall and kill you.")

Nostradamus himself gave confusing signals concerning his use of astrology. In the first sentence of his introduction to the first Century, he apparently admits that he used astrology to obtain his predictions:

> Your late birth, Cesar Nostradamus, my son [to whom he was dedicating the book] has caused me to spend much time in continual and nocturnal watchings, so that I might leave a memorial of myself after my death, to the common benefit of mankind, concerning the things the Divine Essence has revealed to me by *astronomical revolutions*. [My italics.]

It should be noted that in Nostradamus' day, astrology was popularly known as "practical astronomy" – astrology's daily usefulness being seen as the only real difference between the related practices. Certainly his contemporary readers would have transposed the two disciplines when reading this sentence –

interpreting it as a direct endorsement of astrology – and there seems little obvious reason for modern readers to do otherwise. Yet, despite his apparently specific backing for astrology as the voice of "the Divine Essence", Nostradamus gives the following warning at the end of *Century VI*:

> *LEGIS CAUTIO CONTRA INEPTOS CRITICOS.*
> *Qui legent hos versus, mature censunto;*
> *Prophanum vulgus & inscium ne attrectato.*
> *Omnesque Astrologi, Blenni, Barbari procul sunto,*
> *Qui aliter faxit, is rite sacer esto.*

Translation:

> INVOCATION OF THE LAW AGAINST INEPT CRITICS.
> Those who read these verses, let them consider with mature mind;
> Let not the profane, vulgar and ignorant be attracted to their study.
> All *Astrologers*, Fools, Barbarians draw not near,
> He who acts otherwise, is cursed according to rite. [My italics.]

Interpretations of this apparently hypocritical statement vary. The simplest is that he actually meant "foolish astrologers" as opposed to "astrologers and fools"; in other words, he was attacking the many charlatans in his profession. This seems unlikely, however: Nostradamus was well versed in Latin and it is hard to believe he could make such an elementary grammatical error.

Another theory is that he was trying to avoid criticism by the Holy Inquisition. However, it was not astrology, but fortune-telling the Church disliked – and Nostradamus was, by any definition, a fortune-teller.

In *Nostradamus – Prophecies of Present Times?* (published in 1985) David Pitt Francis offers a statistical study of the astrological references found in the ten *Centuries*. Of the 942 quatrains he examined, he found only eighty-five that, in his opinion, specifically contained astrological images or references – in other words, less than ten percent of the prophecies. Surely, he argues, if Nostradamus was actually an astrologer, more astrological references would have found their way into the predictions. Francis concludes that Nostradamus probably only dabbled in astrology, utilizing it solely for its poetic imagery – and for making money from courtiers by casting horoscopes, at which he was undoubtedly skilled.

David Francis's theory is partially supported by David Ovason in *The Secrets of Nostradamus* (1997): both agree that Nostradamus' use of astrological imagery in the *Centuries* is not primarily predictive. But where Francis dismisses the material as basically poetic, Ovason sees an occult-dating system that reveals the seer's actual power to foresee the future. In Ovason's words:

> Nostradamus used astrology in a form which is so arcane as to be beyond the understanding of most modern astrologers. There is no evidence that, in the quatrains, at least, Nostradamus used astrology in a conventional way at all, either as a tool for prediction, or as a standard system of symbols for elucidation. In this sense, his quatrains are not astrological predictions. On the other hand, there is a vast body of evidence to show that Nostradamus made use of astrological references to designate specific time-periods in his quatrains.

What Ovason suggests is that Nostradamus did indeed foresee future events, then constructed the quatrains in such a way as to enlighten only those readers with the esoteric knowledge to understand the references he used.[1]

As we have already seen, the seer was very fond of word puzzles. Medieval heraldry, ancient Latin and Greek mythology, sixteenth-century political in-jokes and astrological references were all utilized to construct these wordplays. But he used astrology, Ovason says, for a second purpose: through his remarkable knowledge of planetary conjunctions, he could give his knowledgeable readers very exact clues as to when the predicted events would take place.

[1]Ovason complains that most modern commentators have been prone to judge Nostradamus' astrological references in terms of their own knowledge of the subject: that is, from the viewpoint of the post-nineteenth-century astrology revival. This movement had a tendency to "dumb down" the practice to make it accessible to a newspaper-reading public. The result, Ovason says, is that we fail to understand Nostradamus' use of astrology because he was utilizing it on a much higher level than most of us can ever conceive: we dabble with kindergarten horoscopes while Nostradamus was an initiate of doctorate level.

For example, *Century III*, quatrain 3, reads:

> *Mars et Mercure et l'argent joint ensemble*
> *Vers le midy extréme siccité,*
> *Au fond d'Asie on dira terre tremble,*
> *Corinthe, Ephese lors en perplexité.*

Translation:

> Mars and Mercury and the silver joined together,
> Towards the south extreme drought,
> From the depths of Asia comes report of an earthquake,
> Corinth and Ephesus then in perplexity.

A typically obscure Nostradamus prediction, one might think. But, Ovason argues, with a little astronomical knowledge and historical hindsight, we can see a precise prophecy emerge.[2]

The first line is obviously astrological in meaning. The planets Mars and Mercury are mentioned, and the Moon is implied by the phrase "l'argent". (Any sixteenth-century peasant would have recognized "the silver" to describe the Moon: the two had been connected in popular myth and poetry for time-out-of-mind.)

Mars, Mercury and the Moon align every few years, so the first line does not give a precise date or even a reasonably short list of likely possibilities. Nevertheless, Ovason suggests, the rest of the quatrain allows us to narrow the prediction down to a specific event.

Ovason believes that a fourth astrological reference is hidden in the quatrain. The first word of line two is "*Vers*". Directly beneath it, at the start of line three, is the word "*Au*". The French word "*Versau*" is their name for the zodiac sign of Aquarius. Line two as a whole may also confirm this Aquarian hidden message. In the complex astrology practised by Nostradamus and his contemporaries, Aquarius was considered a symbol of "heat" (thus dryness or drought), as well as being a "*midy*" (southern) sign.

---

[2] Perhaps the most convincing aspect of Nostradamus' predictions is that they seem to have been written with the aid of a modern-day history book. If he could not foresee future events, his defenders argue, how could he have constructed such clever historical puzzles, most of which were totally indecipherable to his contemporaries, only being recognizable after the events described?

Therefore, this might be a typically erudite joke by Nostradamus: an ironic comment that a water sign, also being the representative of southern heat, could be the symbol of "drought". If we accept these riddling references as genuine clues, Ovason suggests that we should look for a time when Mars, Mercury and the Moon align in the House of Aquarius.

The mention of Corinth and Ephesus in the fourth line would have had an ominous meaning for readers in Nostradamus' time: that of the encroaching Turkish Empire. Ephesus was on the Turkish coast, and the Turks had conquered Corinth (with the rest of Greece) almost 100 years before. At the time of the publication of the *Centuries*, the Islamic hordes of the Ottoman Empire were the chief cause of unease in Christian Europe. The nightmare of a mass Turkish invasion hung over the nations of the Mediterranean just as the fear of a pre-emptive nuclear strike did during the Cold War. Any mention of these Turkish-held towns would have caught the reader's attention like a magnet.

The mention of a major earthquake in Asia in line three, Ovason suggests, was a poetic hint that the Turkish Empire would be shaken to its foundations by events in a year of a Mercury–Moon–Mars–Aquarius conjunction. The next such year, following the publication of *Century III*, was 1571. In that year a navy of allied Christian states destroyed that of the Turks at the Battle of Lepanto (also apparently predicted by Nostradamus in *Century III*, quatrain 64 – see last chapter). This unexpected defeat shook the Ottoman Empire to its roots. As a direct result, the Turkish armies became less aggressively expansionist and their empire began a centuries' long process of collapse.

In passing, it should also be noted that the Battle of Lepanto took place in the Bay of Corinth. Afterwards, commerce in the Turkish ports of Corinth and Ephesus suffered as Christian pirates became bolder in the eastern Mediterranean; a "perplexity" possibly reflected in the fourth line of the quatrain.

Apart from Nostradamus' preference for riddles, there may have been a second reason for his use of astrology to suggest dates: it is possible that he knew that the calendar familiar to his readers would soon become redundant.

In 1582, sixteen years after Nostradamus' death, Pope Gregory XIII reformed the Christian calendar. The previous system, the

Julian calendar (instituted by Julius Caesar), was eleven minutes and fourteen seconds longer than the solar year. This apparently negligible miscalculation had accumulated, year on year, since 45 BC. By the mid-sixteenth century, all dates were ten days later than they should have been. The calendar 20 June, for example, was not the longest day of the year – that had taken place ten days earlier. The Church was embarrassed that religious festivals were beginning to fall in the wrong season, and so decided on reform.

Pope Gregory realized that the Julian method of calculating leap years – by simply nominating one year in four – was the root of the problem.[3] The new Gregorian system decreed that if the first year of a century was evenly divisible by 400, it was a leap year. Thus AD 1600 was a leap year, but 1700, 1800 and AD 1900 were not. This effectively removed several days every 400 years and balanced the Julian discrepancy.

To begin the new calendar, the ten-day discrepancy had to be removed. This was achieved by the simple expedient of "jumping back" ten days in 1582, then continuing as normal. Nostradamus seems to have known that this would happen because in *Century I*, quatrain 42, he wrote:

> *Le dix Kalende d'Avril de faict Gothique,*
> *Resuscité encor par gens malins:*
> *Le feu estaint assemblé diabolique,*
> *Cherchant les os du d'Amant et Pselin.*

Translation:

> The tenth of the Calends of April calculated Gothic,
> Resuscitated by the wicked people:
> The fire put out, a diabolical assembly,
> Seek for bones of the demon of *Psellus*.

We will look at the magical significance of this strange quatrain in a later chapter, but for now we are only interested in the first line. The "Calends" was the first day of the month in Ancient Rome.

[3]The solar year (the time it takes the Earth to travel around the Sun) is actually 365 days, 5 hours, 48 minutes and 45.5 seconds long. To rectify the discrepancy a "leap year" (with an extra day in February) needed to be added at correct intervals.

During the date conversion in 1582, the tenth of April and the first of April became the same day, but only in Catholic countries. Protestant nations obstinately stuck to the Julian calendar, in some cases for centuries, while the Orthodox Church is still using it today. In Nostradamus' day, the most notably Protestant nations were the Germanic states of central Europe: the so-called "Gothic" states. Therefore, we might paraphrase the first line to read: "The Julian tenth of April, as the Protestants of Germany will calculate it . . ."

Sceptics will point out that the problem of the calendar was widely debated in Nostradamus' day, so this line hardly proves him a prophet; still, his recognition that the normally progressive Gothic nations would be slow to follow suit is altogether harder to dismiss.

Whether through precognition or through a common sense certainty that the calendar must soon lose ten days, Nostradamus must have known that any date he gave in the quatrains would have been incorrect, either for his own day or for post-Julian readers. So the use of astrological conjunctions as a dating system would certainly have solved the problem.

Before leaving the subject of Nostradamus' use of astrology, I would like to add a personal experience that may support David Ovason's theory.

Several years ago I noticed that *Century II*, quatrain 5, might reflect an event then featuring high on the international news. It reads:

> Qu'en dans poissan, fer et lettres enfermée,
> Hors sortira qui puis fera la guerre:
> Aura par mer sa classe bien ramée,
> Apparoissant pres de Latine terre.

Translation:

> In a fish, iron and letters are enclosed,
> He goes out and will then make war:
> His fleet will have travelled far across the sea,
> Appearing near the *Latine* shore.

The word "fish" in the first line has often been translated as a submarine. For example, Henry Roberts (in *The Complete Prophecies of Nostradamus*) suggests that the quatrain predicts the secret preparations by General Mark Clark, prior to the invasion of North Africa in World War II. Other commentators, who translate "iron and letters" as "weapons and documents", suggest the quatrain is darkly reminiscent of atomic submarines: these carry codebooks to translate radio orders to launch their nuclear missiles.

Erica Cheetham, on the other hand, suggests that "iron" may indicate the planet Mars (also the god of weapons) and "letters" may indicate the planet Mercury (god of messengers). The "fish" might therefore be the zodiac sign of Pisces. She suggests that the quatrain may indicate the beginning of World War III – on a date when Mars and Mercury are both in the House of Pisces.

In *The Prophecies of Nostradamus* (1974), Cheetham noted that the next such conjunction was due on 26 March 1996. I read this explanation during mid-March 1996, when one of the main topics in the news was the up-coming Taiwanese General Election, due to be held on the 26th of that month.

Taiwan is a large island, south-west of Japan and only a few miles off the coast of China. For centuries the island's sovereignty has been a bone of contention between Japan, China, the European Imperial powers and Taiwanese nationalists. In 1949, the anti-communist Chinese leader Chaing Kai-shek was driven out of mainland China, so set up a new independent government on Taiwan. The Red Chinese would certainly have gone on to invade the island, but the United States quickly signed a treaty with Taiwan, effectively guaranteeing war if Communist China attacked their escaped enemy. Since that time, China has loudly maintained its right to reabsorb its old province but, to avoid starting a third world war, has limited its actions to bellicose posturing and military exercises in the Strait of Taiwan.

The Taiwanese general election in 1996 was considered highly significant across the world, because the Chinese government had virtually promised to invade the island if an anti-Chinese-leaning government was voted in. Since this seemed highly likely, considering Taiwanese public opinion, the Chinese sent a huge war fleet to "conduct war games" within sight of the Taiwanese coast. America, reacting to protect a major trading partner and to honour their treaty commitments, sent most of the US Pacific Fleet, also to "conduct war games" near Taiwan.

Since Taiwan was, at that time, one of the most productive economies in the world, it seemed to me that the word "*Latine*" in the fourth line of *Century II*, quatrain 5, might have been a reference to the island. In Nostradamus' day, the most prolific traders were unquestionably the Latin cities of Genoa, Venice and Florence. It therefore seemed possible that Nostradamus might have used the term "*Latine*" not to indicate Italy, but a major trading nation for which he think of no other representative reference.

Of course, the above interpretation is open to doubt; yet the fact that a major trading nation was brought to the brink of war when Mars and Mercury were conjunct in Pisces was a worrying coincidence.

Fortunately, the international incident did not escalate. Although an anti-Communist government was returned on the island, China decided that diplomatic loss-of-face was preferable to a major war. The only "*guerre*" to be seen in the incident were the fleet war games and the diplomatic posturing on both sides.

Chapter 12

The Brahan Seer

Coinneach Odhar, the Brahan seer – whose Anglicized name was Kenneth Mackenzie – is the most famous of the Scottish sooth-sayers. In a nation with a traditional place by the fire for the village prophet – whether a minister from the kirk or a descendant of Macbeth's demonic hags – Coinneach Odhar's accuracy of prediction won him a reputation to rival that of Nostradamus in France.

The Brahan seer became known to folklorists fairly late. Stories about him were collected in the nineteenth century by writers like Andrew Lang and Hugh Miller, more than two centuries after his death around 1662 (although some had been chronicled by Alexander Cameron of Lochmaddy soon after that date). So, as we might expect, they lack the authenticity of records by actual contemporaries. Nevertheless, the consensus appears to be that he was born of a peasant family in the parish of Uig, on the Isle of Lewis, sometime in the early seventeenth century (some say as early as 1600). When he later became a bondsman of the clan Mackenzie, he moved to their estate at Castle Brahan, near Dingwall, on the coast of the Cromerty Firth.

The Brahan seer's first prediction is said to have saved his own life. Mackenzie's father was a peasant farmhand, whose status was little better than that of a medieval serf. Even his surname, Odhar, simply meant "mud-coloured". However, his son was not content with a life of virtual slavery, and could be sharp tongued about the failings of his betters. The story goes that when he was bonded to a local farmer, he so infuriated the farmer's wife that she decided to murder him. She waited until her husband sent Odhar off on his own to cut peat in a distant part of the farm. Since it was too far away for him to return for his midday meal, she knew that he would have to go without. So she prepared a bowl of milk and oats (and a noxious herb that would kill him before he could reach help) and took it to him by her own hand.

She found Odhar lying fast asleep on a low hill, known in local folklore as a fairy mound. Rather than wake him, and be invited to share the poisoned meal, the woman laid the bowl beside his shoulder and hurried away. Coinneach awoke, found the food and was about to wolf it down when he felt a cold pressure against his heart. Reaching into his shirt he found a small, pearly white stone with a natural hole through the middle. (In Celtic mythology, "water-bored" stones were considered particularly lucky). Holding the stone, Coinneach turned again to the bowl and suddenly knew that the food was poisoned. Lifting the stone to his eye, he even saw the farmer's wife preparing the dose. He tested his suspicion by offering the food to his dog, which ate ravenously and promptly died. The legend does not say what revenge, if any, Odhar managed to exact, but the power of his first vision is said to have robbed him of sight in one eye.

It is said that Odhar could, if he wished, summon the power of second sight by peering through the hole in the stone, but that most of his prophecies came to him unbidden. This places him firmly within the Celtic tradition of the *taibhsear*: one who sees visions.

In Gaelic Scotland, the taibhsear was seen as a creature to pity as much as to respect or fear. His – or her – visions might descend at any moment and were often horrific. Far from cultivating second sight (or "the sight" as it was simply known), many taibhsears lived in hermit-like isolation, afraid that company or travel might spark ghastly revelations.

The visions themselves were said to slip into the seer's awareness as smoothly as an optical illusion. One Scottish author, a Dr Beattie, has speculated that the sight of the play of sun- or moonlight over the broad landscapes of the Highlands might trigger psychic ability much as flashing lights can cause epileptic fits. Traditionally, the taibhsear would close his eyes and bend double if he came upon something that he suspected might be present only to his inner eye. If the vision was still there when he straightened up, then he knew it was real.

Second sight was generally thought to be hereditary, but might also be a gift from God, the Devil or some other supernatural agency. It is interesting to note that Coinneach Odhar is said to have had his first vision after sleeping on a "fairy mound". Such protuberances in the landscape are found across the Celtic and Scandinavian countries and usually consist of a prominent hump or an oddly-shaped hill. The fairies said to live within were not the charming and childish "little-folk" that Victorian authors claimed "lived at the bottom of the garden", but were powerful and dangerous magical beings. Their widely-feared bad temper led their human neighbours to refer to them as the "Good-Folk" or "the Gentry", since even a slightly derogatory remark might lead to anything from a minor accident to violent death. Even today, some farmers refuse to plough over fairy mounds because they believe it will bring bad luck.

Historian Elizabeth Sutherland has suggested that the belief in fairy mounds might date back to the pre-Druidic ancestor worship of the Celts. These people buried their dead in man-made hillocks called barrows, where they would also offer sacrifices, both out of fear of the spirits and hope of their favour. Moreover, many beliefs involving spirit or ancestor worship – such as Japanese Shinto, Cuban Santeria and the Spiritism of Brazil – accept that the dead are able to induce visions of the future.[1]

However, where Odhar was concerned, common sense suggests that his gifts came neither from the dead nor from the fairies, but that he was born with them. The story of the fairy mound is fairly certainly a later accretion, as is another tale to the effect that Odhar's pregnant mother happened to be passing a cemetery when she saw all the dead leaving then, later, returning to their graves. She placed her stick over the grave of the last to return to bar access. The latecomer proved to be a beautiful girl who identified herself as the King of Norway's daughter, and who presented the

[1]These are not necessarily momentous – in fact, may be amusingly trivial. On 12 April 1923, at a seance in London, the young medium Stella Cranshaw (better known as Stella C) described the front page of the *Daily Mail* dated 19 May – five weeks hence. She said that she glimpsed the words "Andrew Salt", with a picture of a small boy, and a white powder being poured from a bottle or tin. On that date, half the front page of the *Daily Mail* was taken up with an advertisement for Andrew's Liver Salt showing a small boy pouring the white powder from a tray – an advertisement that, as the makers confirmed, was prepared after the date of the seance.

seer's mother with the pierced stone in exchange for allowing her back into her grave. This story has since proved to be an Icelandic legend that had been recruited for service in Odhar's biography.

So we are probably safe to assume that, like so many of his countrymen, the Brahan seer possessed second sight, which he probably inherited, and that tales of murderous farmers' wives and Norwegian princesses are irrelevant.

In due course, Odhar's reputation as a prophet came to the attention of the lord of the clan Mackenzie, Kenneth Cabarfeidh (meaning "Staghead") Mackenzie, first Lord of Kintail, who lived in Brahan Castle on the mainland, north-west of Inverness. He summoned Odhar around 1622, but died shortly thereafter, and was succeeded by his son, who became the First Earl of Seaforth in 1623. The seer was then living in a farm cottage and working as a labourer, and this hard existence continued throughout the lifetime of both the First and the Second Earl. So Odhar slaved throughout two generations, until the Third Earl of Seaforth, whose name was also Kenneth Mackenzie, succeeded to the title. He was roughly the same age as the seer, and seems to have liked him – enough, in fact, to allow him to retire.

The new life plainly agreed with Odhar, and, as his fame spread across Scotland, he was invited to visit the homes of other clan leaders. From then onward, the seer is said to have spent much of his life wandering across the Highlands from one castle to another.

There were apparently those among Odhar's acquaintances who felt that the gloom that characterized his predictions sprang out of his own rather dour temperament: but historical retrospect suggests that it was due rather to the fact that the centuries following his death were among the grimmest in Scotland's history.

Clan power enjoyed a brief renaissance during the rebellion under Bonny Prince Charlie in 1745, when the Highland clans rose against the English in an attempt to restore the Jacobite crown. They initially enjoyed considerable success, winning several battles with the terrifying Highland charge – a rush of berserk men armed with round shields, axes and claymores. Then at Culloden Moor near Drummossie in 1746, the English employed a newly-invented weapon: the bayonet.

Due to the time it took to reload their weapons, Redcoat musketeers were virtually defenceless once they had fired their first volley.

At Culloden, however, with a fixed blade on the end of their muskets, the English soldiers were, in effect, armed with a heavy spear as well as a rifle. The Highlanders were slaughtered in huge numbers.

At some point, the Earl of Seaforth "lent" Odhar to a gentleman of Inverness, who recorded many of his predictions. Crossing the moor of Culloden, the seer cried out:

> Oh Drummossie! Thy bleak moor shall, before many generations have passed away, be stained with the best blood in the Highlands. Glad I am that I will not see that day, for it will be a fearful time. Heads will be lopped off by the score and no mercy shall be shown or quarter given by either side.

This was duly recorded by the gentleman of Inverness.

After the defeat of Bonnie Prince Charlie, the English repression was long and harsh, culminating in the wholesale "clearances" in the nineteenth century, when thousands of Highland crofters were driven from their farms to allow aristocratic landowners to farm sheep or raise deer for hunting. If this was the future glimpsed by the Brahan seer, his gloomy disposition is understandable.

Coinneach Odhar has never developed an international reputation like that of Nostradamus, but this is not because he was any less accurate in his predictions – if anything the taibhsear's plainness of language makes confirmation of his prophecies easier than for the enigmatic Frenchman. Yet where Nostradamus described occurrences outside the borders of his own country, Odhar stuck only to events within Scotland, and, usually, to whatever area he happened to be viewing at the time. This made his predictions both personal and poignant to his listeners, but less interesting to non-Scots.

The Rev. John Macrae of Dingwall recorded the following story of the Brahan seer. Asked by Macrae's kinsman, the elderly Duncan Macrae of Glenshiel, by what means he would end his days, Odhar replied that he would die by the sword. That seemed unlikely, since the clan wars – in which Macrae had fought bravely – had long been over. But in 1654, during the English Civil War, General Monck led a troop of Parliamentary soldiers to Kintail, and Macrae encountered a company of them in the hills behind his house. Addressed in English, which he did not understand, Macrae put his hand to the hilt of his sword, and was cut down – the only casualty of Monck's expedition.

On another occasion, Odhar announced that "a Lochalsh woman shall weep over the grave of a Frenchman in the burying place of Lochalsh." Again, it seemed unlikely, since there were no Frenchmen that far north. Later, the Third Earl learned that a Lochalsh woman had, in fact, married a French footman, who had died young, and that since then she had been inconsolable, weeping by his grave in Lochalsh.

The seer also made long-term predictions, stating that in the village of Baile Mhuilinn, in west Sutherland, a woman named Annabella Mackenzie (Baraball n'ic Coinnich) would die of measles. Two centuries later, in 1860, a woman of that name lived in the village, but since she was 95, seemed more likely to die of old age than disease. However, Odhar proved to be correct, and she died of measles.

Another startling prediction concerned an eight-ton stone that marked the boundary of the estate of Culloden and Moray. The seer spoke of the day when the "Stone of Petty" would be moved from dry land to the sea in Petty Bay. In a great storm on the night of 20 February 1799, the stone was uprooted and was swept 250 yards out to sea.

One prediction seemed so absurd it led a local who had been writing down the seer's utterances to burn his notes. Standing in Inverness, Odhar gazed up at the neighbouring hill of Tomahurich and said (in his native Gaelic, the only language he spoke):

"Strange as it may seem to you this day, time will come, and it is not far off, when full-rigged ships will be seen sailing east and west by the back of yonder hill."

One hundred and fifty years later the Royal Navy constructed the Great Caledonian Canal, running from the North Sea diagonally south-west to a spot near Glasgow on the opposite coast. The link from the Moray Firth to the head of Loch Ness passed behind Tomahurich Hill.

Another geographical prediction began: "The day will come [his favourite preamble] when the hills of Ross-shire will be strewed with ribbons, and a bridge on every stream." The seer was plainly talking about roads. In his day, and for some time after, the only Highland roads were rough cattle tracks. Anybody who has read

Robert Louis Stevenson's Highland adventure novel, *Kidnapped,* will recall that the heroes spend most of their time wading knee-deep in trackless heather. It was not until the late eighteenth century that roads and bridges began to appear in the Highlands.

Odhar is also quoted as saying that there would be "a mill on every stream and a white house on every hillock". The "mill on every stream" sounds like a prediction of the Industrial Revolution. The mention of white houses must have struck his contemporaries as odd, since Gael houses in Odhar's day were invariably black – being roofed with turf and sooted with peat smoke inside and out. However, with the later influx of Lowlanders and English settlers, the white-washed cottage has become the typical Highland home.

While Odhar's view of Scotland's future gave grounds for optimism, his predictions concerning his countrymen were less optimistic: "The people will degenerate as their country improves and the clans will become so effeminate as to flee from their native country before an army of sheep."

This was hardly tactful. The Highland clans of the time were both powerful and proud; for Odhar to describe their descendants as "effeminate" might have been regarded as biting the hand that fed him. In Scottish histories dating from the early- to mid-nine-teenth century, the prediction is listed as "unfulfilled", but from the late nineteenth century, the "Highland clearances", the eviction of crofters to make way for sheep farms owned by absentee land-lords, suddenly revealed its accuracy. Thousands of legally unrep-resented people faced either starvation or emigration. What was left of clan power, following the 1745 rebellion, now vanished forever. With the clearances came a steady drop in Scotland's population that has only showed signs of reversal in the second half of the twentieth century.

Odhar also predicted that:

The ancient proprietors of the soil shall give place to strange merchant proprietors, and the whole of the Highlands will become one huge deer forest; the whole country will become so desolated and depopulated that the crow of a cock shall not be heard north of Druim-Uachdair . . .

This again sounds like a reference to the clearances.

> The people will emigrate to islands as yet undiscovered or unexplored, but which shall yet be discovered in the boundless oceans. Afterwards the deer and other wild animals in the huge wilderness shall be darkened and exterminated by horrid black rains. The people will then return and take undisputed possession of the lands of their ancestors.

This "black rain", it has been suggested, was the industrial soot of the nineteenth century – although it could also refer to the nuclear fallout from the Chernobyl meltdown or the environmental and economic changes brought about by the exploitation of North Sea oil. Many Scots emigrated to Australia or New Zealand, "undiscovered" at the time of Odhar's prediction. After the discovery of North Sea oil, many Australians, New Zealanders, Texans and Canadians of Highland descent returned to work on the oil rigs.

Among his contemporaries, Odhar's reputation was based on minute but accurate details he scattered through his prophecies. For example, the Laird of Raasay, of the MacGille-challum holdings on the Isle of Skye, once asked Odhar about the future of his clan. The seer's answer was depressing:

> When we shall have a fair-haired Lochiel, a red-headed Lovat, a squint-eyed, fair-haired Chisholm, a big, deaf Mackenzie and a bow-crook-legged MacGille-challum, who shall be the great-grandson of John Beg of Ruiga: he shall be the worst MacGille-challum that ever came or ever will come. I shall not be in existence in his day and I have no desire that I should.

The other families named were the owners of lands around the Macgille-challum clan's own. At the later birth of a clan heir – who also happened to be a grandson of a John Beg of Ruiga – delight was mixed with a certain amount of misgiving. The physical description of the neighbouring lairds given by Odhar, and the bow-legs of the young MacGille-challum, were accurate. He turned out to be the last Laird of Raasay; a wild spendthrift who bankrupted the clan.

As we have seen, many of Odhar's predictions seemed improbable to the point of absurdity. One concerned the village of Strathpeffer, which stands in a valley a few miles from the western end of the Cromarty Firth (a long, narrow inlet of the North Sea). To a visitor standing on the hills above the village, the valley bottom appears to be below sea level: only a hilly ridge at its seaward end seems to protect it from flooding. Visiting the valley, Odhar prophesied: "When five spires rise above Strathpeffer, ships will sail over the village and hitch cables to their tips."

So seriously did locals take this prediction, that in the early years of the twentieth century, when an Episcopal rector proposed building a church, a petition was raised to beg him not to include a spire on the building. The spire, of course, would bring the number of such edifices to Odhar's fateful five. The rector, knowing that the valley bottom was actually at least three or four feet above sea level, ignored the petition and added a spire to his church.

Shortly before the First World War, a small blimp airship was hired to make an appearance at the Strathpeffer Games. By accident, the ship's grapnel line became entangled with the spire of one of the five churches. This seems to have fulfilled the prophecy in an unexpectedly unproblematic way but, with the threat of global warming and of rising sea levels, a threat still hangs over Strathpeffer.

Odhar had another prophecy concerning Strathpeffer relating to its sulphurous waters, which locals shunned as poisonous:

Uninviting and disagreeable as it now is, with its thick crusted surface and unpleasant smell, the day will come when it shall be under lock and key, and crowds of pleasure and health seekers shall be thronging its portals in their eagerness to get a draught of its waters.

In 1818, Strathpeffer became a fashionable spa, and the pump room of its sulphur spring was kept locked.

An equally unlikely prediction was of a disastrous flood from a loch "above Beauly", a small town at the head of the Beauly Firth – there was no loch anywhere near. But in the twentieth century a dam was built across the River Conon at Torrachilty, a few miles from Beauly, and in 1966 it overflowed and destroyed farm build-ings and hundreds of sheep and cows in the village of Conon Bridge, "above Beauly".

Odhar also seems to have predicted the coming of the steam train to the Highlands:

When there shall be two churches in Ferrintosh, a hand with two thumbs in I-Staina, two bridges in Conon and a man with two navels at Dunean: a black bridleless horse will bring soldiers through the Muir of Ord. I should not like to be alive then.

Local tradition affirms that all these conditions had been met when the railway was laid through the Muir of Ord in the nineteenth century. Whether it has ever carried soldiers is not recorded.

With such a naturally dismal and depressing prophet, it is not surprising that certain of his recorded predictions strike some modern readers as warnings of environmental disaster:

A dun hornless cow will appear in the Minch [an area of sea off Carr Point near Gairloch] and make a bellow which will knock six chimneys off Gairloch House.

Gairloch House was a fortified structure in Odhar's day; its other name, *Tigh Dige*, meant "house of the ditch" and came from the defensive ditch that ran around it. This prediction caused con-fusion for some generations, since the house had *no* chimneys. Its subsequent replacement with a manor house (with the same name) has caused some disquiet, because the new building has six chimneys. As to the "dun hornless cow", environmentalists have suggested that it might be a nuclear submarine, and that the "bellow" powerful enough to wreck six stone chimneys could be a nuclear explosion.

Eventually, the seer's second sight would lead to his own down-fall. The instrument of that downfall was Isabella Mackenzie, third Countess of Seaforth. Shortly after the Restoration of King Charles II in 1660, Kenneth the Earl of McKenzie-Seaforth was sent by the king on a mission to Paris, leaving his wife Isabella to mind the clan and property. As time went by and neither the Earl, nor any word of him, returned to Brahan, the Countess grew increasingly worried. Eventually she sent for Coinneach Odhar and asked him to scry out the truth. The taibhsear replied that he was only occasionally able to force the sight to come, but when he gazed through the hole in his seeing-stone he broke into one of his rare smiles.

"Madam," he is said to have announced, "there is no need to worry concerning your husband's welfare. He is well and merry." When the Countess pressed him further, the seer replied that the Earl was staying in a luxurious house with fine company in a foreign place he could only assume was Paris. As she asked for further details, any man of common sense would have claimed he could see nothing more, or at least asked to speak to the Countess alone – for this encounter took place among a large gathering of family and principal retainers. Instead, he seems to have allowed himself to succumb to his customary testiness, and told the Countess that her husband was "on his knees before a fair lady".

She was naturally furious. Tradition has it that she was an unpopular mistress, and also, that she was herself "wanton". If Odhar's "sight" could reveal her husband's infidelity, it might come to rest on her own . . .

Whatever the reason, she used her power as her husband's authorized representative to condemn Odhar to death as a witch, and ordered that the seer be burned alive in a barrel of tar. Her decision had to be ratified by the elders of the Kirk, but they knew better than to cross the Countess – or perhaps they genuinely felt that Odhar's powers came from the Devil. (Although the accession of Charles II brought a dramatic reduction of witch trials in England, in Scotland they had yet to reach their high point.) So they upheld the death sentence, and the seer was taken to the Presbytery at Chanonry Point, on the Moray Firth, for execution.

Awaiting death, the seer made the following prophecy:

I look into the future and I see the doom of the race of my oppressor. The long-descended line of Seaforth will, ere many generations have passed, end in extinction and sorrow. I see a chief, the last of his house, both deaf and dumb. His four sons will go to the tomb before him, one dying on the water, and he shall die in misery, knowing that his line is extinguished. No more Mackenzie men will rule over Brahan and Kintail.

His possessions will be handed to a white-hooded lass from the east, and she will kill her own sister.

It shall be known that these things are coming to pass by the existence of four great lairds – Gairloch, Chisholm, Grant and Ramsey – of whom one will be buck-toothed, another hare-lipped, another half-witted and the fourth a stammerer.

There would also, he said, be a "stag-like" Laird of Tulloch, who would kill four of his wives, although a fifth would survive him. "When the last Laird of Seaforth looks around him and sees his neighbours are these men, he will know his sons are doomed and his line ended."

It is said that he then hurled the "seeing stone" into Loch Ussie. When the Countess vindictively told him that he would never go to Heaven, Odhar replied:

I think I shall, but you will not. After my death, a raven and a dove shall meet above my ashes. If the raven lands first, you are right. If the dove, my word is truth.

When the barrel of tar – and the seer – had been reduced to ashes and cooled down, a dove and a raven were seen hovering over the remains; the dove, according to witnesses, landed first.

The seer was executed – probably in 1662 – near the modern Chanonry Point lighthouse, by the road from Fortrose to Fort George ferry, and the place is marked with a stone slab. What happened to the Countess and her errant husband is, unfortunately, not recorded.

The history of the next century and a half bore out the seer's prophecies. In 1715, the Seaforths took part in the Jacobite risings against the Hanoverians. In the subsequent defeat, the clan lost their titles, but these were restored in 1726. The Seaforths became staunch Hanoverians and prospered during the following decades. Although title ceased to exist in 1781 when its holder died without an heir, the position of head of the Clan Mackenzie passed to a second cousin, Francis Humberstone Mackenzie. It was he who gave his name to the Seaforth Highlanders regiment, which he raised to fight in the revolutionary wars with France, which began in 1793. In 1797 he was created Baron Seaforth of Kintail, became Governor of Barbados, and was a patron of Sir Humphrey Davy and the painter Sir Thomas Lawrence.

Yet this apparent favourite of fortune was deaf, as a result of an outbreak of scarlet fever in his boarding school when he was 12; later in life his speech became affected and he would only communicate by writing notes. As the seer predicted, he was deaf and dumb.

All four of Francis Humberstone Mackenzie's sons died: the first, William, as a baby; the second, George, at the age of 6; the third, Francis – a midshipman in the Royal Navy – in a skirmish at sea ("dying on the water"); the last, William Frederick – an MP for Ross – in 1814, of a particularly lingering and painful disease. At one point, when it seemed that William Frederick might pull through, an old family retainer was heard to comment: "Na, na, he'll nay recover. It's decreed that Seaforth must outlive his four sons." The grief-stricken Baron Seaforth would, in fact, die in the following year, 1815.

The *Edinburgh Daily Review* pointed out in its obituary that Francis Humberstone Mackenzie's neighbours were the buck-toothed Sir Hector Mackenzie of Gairloch, the hare-lipped Chisholm of Chisholm, the retarded Laird Grant, and the stammering MacLeod of Raasay.

As Odhar foretold, Mackenzie's eldest daughter, Mary, who had married Admiral Sir Samuel Hood, returned from the East Indian station where her husband had just died, to take over her father's estate, and her formal mourning dress included a white hood. One day, she was driving her younger sister, the Hon. Caroline Mackenzie, through the woods when the ponies bolted and the trap overturned; she was only injured but her sister died.

The Laird of Tulloch, mentioned by the seer, was a well-known ladies' man, and he might be said to have killed four of his wives in that they died in childbirth, presenting him, between them, with eighteen children. Because he was known as having fathered also thirty illegitimate offspring, he was known as "the stag". (Odhar called him "stag-like".)

The widow Hood eventually married a man called Stewart and, over the decades, the Seaforth lands were gradually sold off by the

Stewart-Mackenzies. In 1921 it seemed that Odhar's prophecy of the end of the Seaforth line might be inaccurate, when James Mackenzie-Stewart was created Baron of Seaforth and Brahan, but sadly he died without issue two years later and the title became extinct once again.

In 1877, the respected historian Alexander Mackenzie published *The Prophecies of the Brahan Seer*, which quickly became a best-seller in Scotland. In this book he freely admitted that almost all of his source material came from oral traditions, but added that since most Highland history has been passed down this way, he felt justified in its serious presentation.

In her conclusion to the 1977 edition of Mackenzie's book, the historian Elizabeth Sutherland hypothesized that Coinneach Odhar might never have existed as an actual individual. Instead, she suggested, he might be a conglomeration of hundreds of years of taibhsear folklore – much as some historians believe the myth of King Arthur might be based on the exploits of several real warlords of post-Roman, Dark Age Britain. Understandably, most Scots reject the idea with contempt, just as Englishmen reject the notion that King Arthur never existed.

Yet Elizabeth Sutherland mentions one intriguing piece of evidence for her theory. After pointing out that there is no record that the Countess Isabella ever had a man burned to death, she suggests that the story may spring from a confusion with the case of Lady Catherine Munro of Foulis, seventy years earlier.

Lady Catherine was publicly tried for murder, attempted murder and witchcraft in 1590. The Crown's accusation was that thirteen years earlier, Catherine had tried to murder her stepson and her sister-in-law, first through the spells of several local witches, then by poisoning. In the course of testing the dosage of ratsbane to be used on her relatives, she was also said to have killed two servants. An Edinburgh jury packed with her relatives acquitted her, but the confessions of her magic-dabbling co-conspirators tainted her reputation for life.

We might feel justified in dismissing this identification of Countess Isabella with Lady Catherine Munro as far-fetched, but Elizabeth Sutherland supports it by pointing out that one of the male witches said to have aided Lady Munro, and who was later executed for dealing with the Devil, was named Coinneach Odhar.

Against this "collective" hypothesis we can set the fact that so many of the predictions of the Brahan seer are highly specific and concern contemporaries connected with his part of the Highlands – and, of course, that so many of them later came true. With such a legacy, the Brahan seer's place in the history of prophecy is assured.

Chapter 13

Nostradamus and the Seventeenth Century

The following are some of the quatrains that Nostradamus scholars have attributed to the events of the seventeenth century. The reader should keep in mind the fact that Nostradamus deliberately obfuscated the meaning in his quatrains. Even the most erudite translator can only guess at the poems' possible meanings and implications.

Sceptics have claimed that Nostradamus did this to hide the fact that he could not actually foresee the future. The quatrains, they argue, are a poetic version of Rorschach inkblots. These are symmetrical ink stains that psychiatric patients are asked to contemplate and describe as if they were pictures with some specific meaning. The viewer's imagination "translates" the image and a trained psychiatrist can deduce aspects of a patient's psyche from listening to the process. For example, a healthy person might see a butterfly or a tree; a sex-maniac might see genitalia or a bloodstain.

The obscurity of most of Nostradamus' quatrains certainly demands imaginative "filling" by the translator, and the scholar's own interests can colour the result. For example, Henry C. Roberts (in *The Complete Prophecies of Nostradamus*) attributes many of the quatrains to events in the twentieth century. Erica Cheetham (in *The Prophecies of Nostradamus*) disagrees with Roberts on the translation of a number of these quatrains, finding pre-twentieth-century historical events to match their nebulous descriptions. Neither can claim to have positive proof to back any of these translations.

Yet most people who have studied the *Centuries* closely believe that there is more to Nostradamus' predictions than the desire of the reader to see their own historical interests reflected in the riddles of a sixteenth-century doctor. As we will see in this chapter, some quatrains contain partially hidden historical details that later appeared to be stunningly accurate predictions of real events after the seer's death. Of course, it is still possible to put these down as mere coincidences, but in some cases this explanation strains credibility to its limit.

The Catholic Church's Persecution of Astronomers in the Early Seventeenth Century

VIII.71 & IV.18

> *Croistra le nombre si grand des Astronomes,*
> *Chassez, bannis et livres censurez,*
> *L'an mil six cens et sept par sacre glomes,*
> *Que nul aux sacres ne seront asseurez.*

Translation:

> The number of Astronomers shall grow great,
> Driven away, banished and books censured,
> The year one thousand six hundred and seven years by *glomes*,
> None shall be safe from the sacred.

By the early seventeenth century, the Catholic authorities were growing increasingly uneasy. Attacked by Protestants on one hand and undermined by freethinking "natural philosophers" on the other, church leaders began to show increasing signs of paranoia. The most obvious evidence of this malady was the growing power of the Inquisition and the active participation of the church in the European witch-hunting craze.

Students of the fledgling science of astronomy were under particular suspicion during this period. However, the date Nostradamus gives – 1607 – is not particularly significant as far as we can now discover.

In 1600, the Inquisition burned the philosopher and astronomer Giordano Bruno. In 1633, the astronomer and mathematician Galileo was sentenced to life imprisonment by the same authority.

Between these dates, we know that the Inquisition acted against many of the thinkers that the ecclesiastical authorities felt were overstepping the mark in their research. Perhaps the date 1607 may refer to one of these, but the key to understanding may be, of course, contained in the mysterious and unknown word "*glomes*" in the third line.

> *Des plus lettrez dessus les faits celestes,*
> *Seront par princes ignorans reprouvez,*
> *Punis d'edit, chassez comme celestes,*
> *Et mis a mort la ou seront trouvvez.*

Translation:

> The most learned in the celestial sciences,
> Will be found at fault by ignorant princes,
> Punished by edicts, chased like criminals,
> And put to death where they shall be found.

This prediction fits several periods of history since Nostradamus' day. In the twentieth century alone, it may refer to both the Nazi and Stalinist mass execution of "subversive" intellectuals, Mao Tse-tung's "Cultural Revolution", Pol Pot's Cambodian "Killing Fields" or even the "Atom Spy" trials in Britain and America at the beginning of the Cold War. However, the use of the word "princes" suggests that Nostradamus may have meant the "Princes of the Church", and had in mind the Church's persecutions of astronomers and astrologers in the seventeenth century.

There is an unmistakable hint of personal bitterness in both the above quatrains. It is worth remembering that Nostradamus' family had lived in fear because of their Jewish roots and that the seer himself had undergone investigation by the Inquisition in 1538. Given that Nostradamus was a practising astrologer and, almost certainly, an initiate of "occult sciences", he had no reason to love the Catholic Church's authoritarian stance on the subject.

The Execution of Giordano Bruno: 17 February 1600

IV.31

> La Lune au plain de nuict sur le haut mont,
> Le nonveau sophe d'un seul cerveau l'a veu:
> Par ses disciples estre immortel semond,
> Yeux au midi, en seins mains, corps au feu.

Translation:

> The Moon at full by night upon the high mount,
> The new sage alone with his brain has seen it:
> Invited by his disciples to become immortal,
> His eyes to the south, his hands on his chest, body in the fire.

Arthur Prieditus, in his book *The Fate of Nations*, suggests that this obscurely occult quatrain refers to the death of the brilliant Italian philosopher, Giordano Bruno.

Bruno was a young Dominican monk who independently, through his own astronomical observations, came to the same conclusion as Nicholas Copernicus and Tycho Brahe – that the Earth revolved around the Sun and not, as the Church insisted, vice versa. However, being more of a poet than a scientist, Bruno used his discovery as a basis of a new pantheistic philosophy. He identified the order in the universe as the "world soul" or God. All material things, he said, were manifestations of the world soul.

Naturally enough, he felt his new, "heretical" beliefs invalidated his vows as a monk and fled the Inquisition to the Protestant countries of northern Europe. After many years travelling and discussing his ideas, he was invited to return south to Italy under the patronage of a Venetian nobleman called Giovanni Mocenigo. Bruno was at first reluctant to return to the heartland of the Inquisition, but eventually allowed the enthusiasm of his Italian disciples to persuade him.

On Bruno's arrival in 1592, Mocenigo treacherously denounced the philosopher to the Inquisition. The Church incarcerated Bruno for eight years, tore his tongue out and finally burned him at the stake. However, his Neoplatonic philosophy lived on and, through its influence on Baruch Spinoza, won Bruno acclaim as the father of modern philosophy.

The Assassination of Henri IV: 14 May 1610

III.11

> *Les armes battre an ciel longue saison*
> *L'arbre au milieu de la cité tombé:*
> *Verbine, rongne, glaive en face, Tison*
> *Lors le monarque d'Hadrie succombé.*

Translation:

> The weapons battle in the sky for a long season
> The tree fell in the midst of the city:
> The sacred branch is cut, the sword opposite Tison
> Then the monarch of *Hadrie* succumbs.

Henri IV of France (formerly Henri of Navarre) was preparing for a major war in the spring of 1610. A disagreement over the succession in the otherwise insignificant state of Julich-Cleves had set him at odds with the House of Hapsburg – the most powerful royal line in Europe, ruling both Spain and the Holy Roman Empire. Neutral observers feared the conflict would set the whole of Europe ablaze.

On 14 May, Henri was attacked and stabbed to death on the Rue Ferronnierre, in the centre of Paris. The murderer was a pro-Spanish Catholic called Francois Ravaillac. He was caught and tortured to death. Despite the likelihood that Ravaillac was put up to the assassination by the Hapsburgs, Henri's widowed queen immediately made peace with her husband's enemies, and thus ensured peace in Europe (at least for a few more years).

The first line of Nostradamus' quatrain suggests an air war to modern minds, and thus apparently places the prediction in the post-1900 era. However, the other three lines seem to be specifically about the death of Henri IV.

The "tree" that fell in the "middle of the city" and the "sacred branch" are both poetic images of Henri – the last person related to the Valois family tree to rule France and, following his anointing and coronation, a sacred person. Ravaillac stabbed him on a street that adjoined Rue Tison, thus the "sword opposite Tison". Finally, the nickname Hadrie appears in several other

Nostradamus quatrains – all apparently dealing with Henri of Navarre.

In fact, records from the time of Henri's death actually mention sightings of a ghostly army in the sky over France (like those seen over English Civil War battlefields and over the Battle of Mons in World War I). Popularly considered a portent of the death of kings, this phenomenon may be what Nostradamus was referring to in the mysterious first line of the quatrain.

The Thirty Years War: 1618–48

V.13

> Par grand fureur le Roi Romain Belgique
> Vexer vouldra par phalange barbare:
> Fureur grinsseant chassera gent Libyque
> Despuis Pannons jusques Hercules la hare.

Translation:

> In a great rage the king of Roman Belgium
> Vexed with barbarian warriors:
> Gnashing fury will chase the Libyan people,
> From Hungary as far as the Straits of Gibraltar.

Erica Cheetham argues that this quatrain describes the broad outline of the Thirty Years War. By 1618, the smouldering hatred kindled between the Catholic and Protestant nations of Europe exploded into war. On the Catholic side were Spain and France, loosely allied with Ferdinand II, the Holy Roman Emperor. On the Protestant side were Germany, Holland, Denmark, Norway and Sweden. Cheetham suggests that Belgium is mentioned in the quatrain because it was the geographical centre-ground between these factions. She adds that the terms "barbarian" and "Libyans" in the quatrain both describe the Protestant forces – all outlanders and heretics in the eyes of the Catholic Church.

For over thirty years, up to the 1648 Peace of Westphalia, the war ravaged central Europe, killing and displacing thousands of people from eastern Hungary to western Spain

The Last Days of Cardinal Richelieu: 1642

VIII.68

> *Vieux Cardinal par le jeune deceu,*
> *Hors de sa change se verra desarmé,*
> *Arles ne monstres double soit aperceu,*
> *Et Liqueduct et le Prince embausmé.*

Translation:

> Old Cardinal by the young one deceived,
> Shall find himself disarmed,
> Arles does not show the double is perceived,
> And *Liquiduct* and the Prince embalmed.

The most famous European Cardinal since the time of Nostradamus was Richelieu of France.[1] Erica Cheetham suggests that this quatrain accurately describes his final days.

In 1642, the fifty-seven-year-old Cardinal Richelieu – who had effectively run French national policy for over a decade – suddenly found himself supplanted in King Louis XIII's favour by the twenty-two-year-old nobleman, Henri de Cinq Mars. Richelieu was quickly forced into retirement (politically "disarmed"). However, while he was staying in the town of Arles, the Cardinal's spies provided him with a copy of a treaty that had been treacherously made between Cinq Mars and the King of Spain. Although very sick, Richelieu travelled to Paris by barge to denounce his enemy ("*Liquiduct*", from line four, literally means "led by water"). Cinq Mars was beheaded, but Richelieu and Louis XIII also died within the year. Both were embalmed.

The Age of the Sun King: 1643–1715

X.89

> *De brique en marbre seront les murs reduits*
> *Sept et cinquante années pacifiques,*
> *Joie aux humains renoué L'aqueduict,*
> *Santé, grandz fruict, joye et temps melifque.*

---

[1]The villain in Alexandre Dumas' *The Three Musketeers*, but also the man whose various political intrigues ultimately cemented over 100 years of power and prosperity for his country.

Translation:

> The walls shall be turned from brick to marble,
> Seventy-five years peace,
> Joy to humanity renewed the aqueduct,
> Health, abundant fruit, joys and mellifluous times.

This glowing picture of three-quarters-of-a-century of happiness and plenty certainly fits the reign of Louis XIV – the "Sun King" of seventeenth-century France. De Fontbrune points to the beautiful Palace of Versailles as the explanation of the first line. Built by Louis between 1661 and 1701, much of it faced with marble, it was the wonder of its day. Louis XIV's reign from 1643 to 1715 was the longest in European history, just three years short of Nostradamus' "seventy-five years".

On the other hand, the reign of Louis XIV – although generally prosperous – was far from peaceful. Mainly for his own glorification, the king involved France in a series of foreign wars throughout the course of his life. In this light, it might be more optimistic to place this prediction among those yet to be fulfilled.

The Fall of Charles I of England and the Rise of Oliver Cromwell
III.80 & III.81

> *Du regne Anglois l'indigne dechassé,*
> *Le conseiller par ire mis à feu:*
> *Ses adhera iront si bas tracer,*
> *Que le batard sera demi receux.*

Translation:

> From the English kingdom the unworthy one is driven away,
> The counsellor through anger will be burnt:
> His followers will stoop to such depths,
> That the bastard will be half received.

Judging from the *Centuries*, some scholars believe that Nostradamus was rather emotionally involved in his visions of the English Civil War. His apparent descriptions of Oliver Cromwell drip with loathing and hatred – much as one might expect from an ardent royalist contemplating a regicide. Nevertheless, if we accept Erica Cheetham's reading of the above quatrain, Nostradamus fully understood that King Charles' downfall was mostly of his own doing. Charles showed himself "unworthy" of remaining king through his obsessive and irrational belief in his "divine right" to rule, and his refusal to recognize Parliament as a force that needed diplomatic handling.[2]

Two of Charles's councillors were executed for treachery – Lord Stafford was beheaded and Archbishop Laud was burned at the stake (as line two seems to predict). The followers who stooped "to such depths" in the third line might have been the Scots – to whom Charles surrendered himself in the hopes that they might join him, but who instead handed him over to the Parliamentary forces. Finally, the "bastard" of the final line was probably Cromwell. Following the arrest and execution of King Charles, Cromwell had himself made Lord Protector – a king in all but name. However, he was never fully accepted by the people and, following his death, the British monarchy was restored.

> Le grand crier sans honte audacieux,
> Sera eseu gouverneur de l'armee:
> La hardiesse de son contentieux,
> Le pont rompu, cité de peur pasmee.

Translation:

> The great shouter shameless and proud,
> Shall be elected governor of the army:
> The audacity of his contention,
> The broken bridge, the city faint from fear.

This quatrain is the subject of some debate among writers on Nostradamus, but most believe it to refer to the rise to power of Oliver Cromwell. The prediction that the demagogue described in the first line will be "elected" to leadership of the army is important to this argument. Few military commanders since the days of Ancient Rome have been elected rather than appointed to the position, but the radical Roundhead Parliament insisted on voting on every major decision.

[2] An attitude that was also to doom Tsar Nicholas of Russia 250 years later.

Cromwell was certainly an audacious commander and the frightened city of the broken bridge, mentioned in the last line, could be Pontefract – a Royalist stronghold that suffered two grim sieges during the war. The Latin for bridge is "*pons*", and "*fractus*" means broken: thus Pontefract equals "bridge broken" – a typical Nostradamus wordplay.

The Execution of Charles I: 30 January 1649

IX.49

> Gand et Bruceles marcheront contre Envers
> Senat du Londres mettront à mort leur Roi
> Le sel et vin lui seront à l'envers,
> Pour eux avoir le regne en dessarroi.

Translation:

> Ghent and Brussels march against Antwerp,
> The Senate of London shall put their King to death
> Salt and wine oppose him,
> That they may have the kingdom into ruin.

In 1648, Parliament brought Charles I to trial and found him guilty of wantonly shedding his people's blood by starting the Civil War. On 30 January the following year, he was publicly beheaded in front of Whitehall.

During this time, Philip IV of Spain made great efforts to maintain the Spanish hold on Holland. Several attacks were made on rebellious Antwerp (as mentioned in line one) but the effort would ultimately prove fruitless. The salt and wine and the national ruin mentioned in the last two lines are explained by de Fontbrune as a warning of the economic difficulties England would suffer following the Civil War – during which both luxuries and basic necessities were scarce.

This is one of the most striking and oft-quoted quatrains of Nostradamus. Not only does it predict that an English Parliament would commit regicide – an unthinkable event in Nostradamus' day – but also its numbering (Quatrain 49) seems to be a hint to the year (1649) in which the execution would take place.

The Protectorate of Cromwell: 1653–58

VIII.76

Plus Marcelin que roi en Angleterre
Lieu obscure nay par force aura l'empire:
Lasche, sans foi, sans loi saignera terre,
Son temps approche si presque je soupire.

Translation:

More Butcher than king in England,
Born in obscure place by force shall rule the empire:
Coward, without faith, without law the land bleeds,
His time approaches so close that I sigh.

If we assume that Nostradamus considered "close" to be within a hundred years of his own death, the only candidate for this gloomy prediction is Oliver Cromwell.

Although a good strategist, Cromwell was also ruthless in battle and may therefore be described as a "butcher" (the Irish certainly thought so). However, to call Cromwell a "coward without faith" (in line three) seems very unfair, as does the suggestion that he ruled "without law". In fact Cromwell, as a dyed-in-the-wool Puritan, was very keen on strict laws. He even went so far as to close all the theatres, fight a minor civil war in the southern counties to prevent the frivolous celebration of Christmas, and pass laws to "reform manners".

On 16 December 1653, Cromwell was elected Lord Protector of the Commonwealth for life – a role that gave him almost sovereign powers. Born a gentleman (but of a relatively poor family), Cromwell was popular with the people, but his political power always rested on his control ("force") of the army.

Following Cromwell's death in 1658, his son Richard took over as Lord Protector. He was not up to filling his father's boots, however, so Richard Cromwell resigned in 1659 and Charles I's son was invited to return and renew the monarchy. Charles II ruled from 1660 to 1685.

The Wreck of the French Fleet: 1655

III.87

> *Classe Gauloise n'approches de Corsegne,*
> *Moins de Sardaigne tu t'en repentiras:*
> *Trestout mourrez frustrez de l'aide grogne,*
> *Sang nagera, captif ne me croiras.*

Translation:

> French fleet, do not come near to Corsica,
> Much less Sardinia or you will regret it:
> You will all die frustrated help from the pig's snout,
> Swimming in blood, captive you will not believe me.

In 1655, much of the French fleet was wrecked in a storm in the Gulf of Lyons while sailing past the islands of Corsica and Sardinia. Erica Cheetham notes that the odd sounding end of the third line contains a typical Nostradamus double meaning. "Grogne" could mean both "pig's snout" and "cape" in sixteenth-century French and, in fact, many sailors from the fleet drowned trying to swim to the Cap de Porceau (Cape of the Pig). The "captive" in the last line may have been the fleet's pilot, Jean de Rian, who had, earlier in his career, been enslaved by Algerian pirates.

This quatrain, like many others in the Centuries, reads like a dire warning. Yet here Nostradamus used the same riddling style, devoid of specific details, as elsewhere. Even if Jean de Rian had read the quatrain and believed its warning, he would have had no information with which to save the fleet.

The Great Plague of London: 1665

II.53

> *La grande peste de cité maritime,*
> *Ne cessera mort ne soit vengée*
> *Du juste sang par pris damné sans crime,*
> *De la grand dame par feincte n'outragée.*

Translation:

> The great plague of the maritime city,
> Shall not cease until the death be revenged
> Of the just blood by price condemned without crime,
> Of the great dame not feigned outrage.

Most commentators believe this quatrain refers to the great plague outbreak in London in 1665. Although de Fontbrune suggests it might, in fact, have been a prediction of the 1720 plague outbreak in Marseille, the former interpretation seems more likely because the third line echoes Nostradamus' indignation concerning the execution of King Charles I. The disease arrived on trading vessels and killed thousands before it died out. All those that could walk or ride left London, and to survivors it must have seemed that the wrath of God had struck the city. The outrage of the "great dame" could be a reference to the old St Paul's Cathedral, to which some "unclean" plague victims fled for succour.

The Great Fire of London: 1666

II.51

> *Le sang juste à Londres fera faulte,*
> *Bruslés par fouldres de vingt trois les six:*
> *La dame antique cherra de place haute,*
> *Des mesme secte plusieure seront occis.*

Translation:

> The blood of the just will be required of London,
> Burnt by fire in three times twenty and six:
> The ancient dame shall fall from her high place,
> Of the same sect many shall be killed.

As the reader may have noticed, many of Nostradamus' quatrains are vague to the point of total obscurity. No amount of historical knowledge can help a researcher when the references given by the seer are both nebulous and highly poetic. Therefore, the above quatrain, with its clearly-stated date (66), stands-out in the *Centuries* as plainly as a light in the fog. It is often quoted as one of the most convincing pieces of evidence for precognition.

As with *Century II*, quatrain 53 (see above), divine vengeance for the execution of Charles I seems to be regarded by the seer as the cause of a catastrophe befalling London: in this case the Great Fire of 1666.

This blaze, started by accident in a bakery on Pudding Lane, went on unabated for four days and destroyed 13,200 homes. Although amazingly few people were killed, this was due in part to the fact that so many had already died in the previous year's plague outbreak.

The figure given in the second line $(3 \times 20 + 6)$ is remarkably accurate, and it should be noted that no other great fire has raged in London during the sixty-sixth year of any century since the time of Nostradamus.

Most commentators agree that the "ancient dame", mentioned in the third line, is the old St Paul's Cathedral – burned during the fire along with eighty-seven other London churches (perhaps these being those "of the same sect" Nostradamus notes in the last line). Ovason points out that the Bank of England (the "Old Lady of Threadneedle Street" was also burned.) Ovason also suggests that the blood of the just was not that of King Charles, but of the Protestant martyrs burnt by Bloody Mary in 1555 and 1556, during the seer's own lifetime.

The Rise of the British Sea Empire:
Mid-Seventeenth Century to Mid-Twentieth Century

X.100

> *Le grand empire sera par Angleterre,*
> *Le pempotam des ans plus de trois cens:*
> *Grandes copies passer par mer et terre,*
> *Les Lusitainns n'en seront pas contens.*

Translation:

> The great empire will be in England,
> The all-powerful for three hundred years:
> Great armies will travel by land and sea,
> The Portuguese will not be content.

Another remarkable, and this time quite unambiguous, prediction by the seer. England was a third-rate power in Nostradamus' day. In both military and economic strength, the country lagged behind France and Portugal and was even further behind Spain and the Holy Roman Empire. Indeed, Nostradamus' readers in the sixteenth century might well have laughed at this quatrain, much as a Victorian European would have laughed at the idea of Japan becoming a world power.

Many historians date the rise of the British Empire from the reign of Queen Elizabeth I. On the other hand, it is arguable that the foundations of the empire were not properly laid until after the English Civil War. If we use this more conservative dating, Nostradamus' 300 years would take us to the late 1940s and the end of the British Raj in India – the date most historians would give as the end of Britain as a first-rank world power.

The final line of the quatrain may seem odd today, but this is only because Portugal has been so eclipsed by other nations in the last 400 years. In Nostradamus' day, Portugal was a powerful trading state and had been awarded sovereignty over half the world by the Catholic Church. It might have been more accurate for the seer to predict that Spain – so long harried by British pirates – would be discomforted by the rise of the British Empire but, all things considered, naming Portugal was not too inaccurate.

James II, William of Orange and the "Glorious Revolution": 1688–9

IV.89

> *Trente de Londres secret conjureront,*
> *Contre leur Roi sur le pont entreprinse,*
> *Lui, satalites la mort degousteront.*
> *Un Roi esleu blonde, natif de Frize.*

Translation:

> Thirty Londoners will secretly conspire,
> Against the King on a bridge the plot is made,
> He and his courtiers will not choose death.
> A blonde King elected, native of Holland.

Although some students of Nostradamus believe this quatrain predicts the Guy Fawkes gunpowder plot, the last line seems to link it more firmly with the "Glorious Revolution" of 1688–9.

Following the death of King Charles II in 1685, his brother ascended the throne as James II. However, the new king was unpopular with his largely Protestant subjects from the start because he was a Roman Catholic convert. His haughty and occasionally ruthless behaviour only served to make matters worse.

In 1688, a group of lords secretly asked James's Protestant sister Mary and her husband, William of Orange, to take the throne. William sailed with his Dutch army in November and, on landing and marching to London, found the city open and welcoming. James's troops had, it turned out, deserted him and the king and his close courtiers had fled to France rather than face imprisonment or death. Following a vote in Parliament, William of Orange was crowned William III of Great Britain – the only king in European history to have been elected ("*esleu*").

Erica Cheetham offers an ingenious explanation of the odd-sounding second line. She suggests that the word "pont" might also indicate a sea crossing – she points out that William of Orange insisted on the English rebel lords secretly crossing to Holland, to sign a document of support, before he would undertake the usurpation of James's throne.

The word "blonde" in the last line has proved confusing for many scholars, because William had brown hair. However, David Ovason points out that the word "blonde" derives from the old Germanic word for "yellow" – so Nostradamus could have been deviously indicating William's title: "Orange".

Chapter 14

Nostradamus and the Eighteenth Century

For all his confusing obscurity, Nostradamus offers at least some notion of the time frame he has in mind – that is, how far into the future his prophetic visions would stretch. *Century I*, quatrain 48, reads:

> *Vingt ans du regne de la lune passez,*
> *Sept mil ans autr tiendra sa monarchie:*
> *Quand le soleil prendra ses jours lassez,*
> *Lors accomplit et mine ma prophetie.*

Translation:

> Twenty years of the reign of the Moon having passed,
> Seven thousand years another will hold its monarchy:
> When the Sun ends his tired days,
> Then fulfilled and ends my prophecy.

The astrological "great lunar year" is equivalent to 320 solar years. Erica Cheetham points out that the great lunar cycle during which Nostradamus wrote the *Centuries* began in 1535. Thus 1535 plus twenty years (as mentioned in the first line) gives the year 1555 – the date in which the first book of *Centuries* was published. The second line, adding 7,000 years, therefore gives us the date AD 8555.

On the other hand, *The Prophecies and Enigmas of Nostradamus* (editor Liberte E. LaVert) suggests the reader should multiply the twenty by the 320 years of the great lunar year. The result is 6,400. If we add 555 (1555 minus the thousand which Nostradamus himself would often leave out in the quatrains) we get 6,955 . . . just 45 years short of AD 7000.

Of course, neither of these arguments can claim to be conclusive, but unless readers expect to live another five or six thousand years, the debate is rather academic. The one certainty about the above quatrain is that Nostradamus claims his prophecies stretch many millennia into the future.

If one expected the quatrains to be evenly spread over a 7,000-year period, one could expect an average of thirteen or fourteen predictions to correspond to each hundred years. However, as the reader will doubtless have already realized, Nostradamus had his own ideas about distribution, and did not adhere to such a simple set of rules.

Nostradamus scholars claim to recognize "clusters" of predictions, concentrating on periods of history involving the seer's main obsessions: France, regicide and the fate of the Christian Church. So it is hardly surprising that a disproportionate number of quatrains have been assumed to be about the last twelve years of the eighteenth century: the period of the French Revolution, the execution of Louis XVI, the suppression of the Catholic Church in France and the rise of Napoleon. Of 952 quatrains, at least sixty have been claimed to cover the period between 1789 and 1800.

Nostradamus' introduction to *Century VII* is an open letter to Henri II (the king whose death he had unobtrusively predicted in *Century I*, quatrain 35). Couched in the sycophantic tones that were expected of a writer addressing his royal patron,[1] and full of unusually obscure predictions – even for Nostradamus – the letter contains a sentence that leaves the reader feeling slightly stunned:

> Then the beginning of that year shall see a greater persecution against the Christian Church than ever was in Africa,[2] and it shall be in the year 1792, at which time everyone will think it a renovation of the age.

---

[1]"I have been ever since perpetually dazzled, continually honouring and worshipping that day, in which I presented myself before [Henri's 'immeasurable Majesty']." Introduction, *Century VII*.

[2]Probably a reference to the Vandal persecution of Orthodox Christians in North Africa during the fourth- and fifth centuries AD.

Of course, 1792 was the turning point of the French Revolution. It was the year that saw the unsuccessful attempt to change France from a monarchical dictatorship to a democracy headed by a constitutional monarch – an attempt that soon collapsed into republican revolution. In the resultant bloodshed, the king was guillotined and the Catholic Church was persecuted. Tens of thousands of people were executed for "crimes against the people" – the first but certainly not the last time in European history that this excuse would be used. Yet out of that brutal chaos there emerged a new liberal philosophy that would change politics forever. Just as Nostradamus predicted, it was "a renovation of the age".

The Wars of 1700 (or 2025)

I.49

> *Beaucoup, beaucoup avant telles menees,*
> *Ceux d'orient pat la vertu lunaire:*
> *L'an mil sept cens feront grands emmenees,*
> *Subjugant presque le coing Aquilonaire.*

Translation:

> Long, long before these happenings,
> The people of the Orient influenced by the Moon:
> In the year 1700 shall carry away great multitudes,
> Subjugating most of the Northern region.

This is one of the more confusing of the quatrains. Although one of the few to give a specific date, it is baffling in that the year 1700 hardly seems a turning point in history. If the figure is actually a Nostradamus riddle, it has yet to be solved.

The second line may refer to the Turks, whose banner was the crescent Moon. The third and fourth lines describe this nation "influenced by the Moon" sweeping away "multitudes" in 1700 and conquering most of *"Aquilonaire"* (from the Latin *aquilonaris*, meaning "northern").

In AD 1700, the Russians under Peter the Great defeated the Ottoman Turks and took the towns of Azov and Kouban. At the same time, Charles XII of Sweden took Iceland and Peter the Great, as a result, declared war on him (this later became known as "the Great

Northern War"). Although these were momentous actions in themselves, they do not indicate the "subjugation" described by the quatrain, nor were the "people of the Orient" the winners. Even the seer's admirers concede that this prediction seems to be a "miss".

However, in *The Complete Prophecies of Nostradamus*, Henry C. Roberts suggests that Nostradamus started his dating not from AD 1, but from the First Council of Nicaea[3] in AD 325. Thus, if 325 is added to 1,700, the result is AD 2025. Roberts goes on to suggest that the quatrain predicts the invasion of Russia by China in the twenty-first century.

A Century of Turmoil: 1702–1802

I.51

> *Chef d'Aries, Jupiter et Saturne,*
> *Dieu eternel quelles mutations!*
> *Puis par long siecle son maling temps retourne*
> *Gaule, et Italie quelles emotions!*

Translation:

> Heads of Aries, Jupiter and Saturn,
> Oh eternal God what changes!
> After a long century evil times return
> France and Italy what turmoil!

As we saw in the chapter on Nostradamus and astrology, his use of astrological imagery in the *Centuries* is apparently aimed at giving a rough dating system.

The first line mentions the planets Jupiter and Saturn and the sign of Aries. Since Jupiter and Saturn are both slow-orbiting planets, they align very rarely. The first alignment of Jupiter and Saturn in the House of Aries following the publication of the

[3]This was the fundamental debate over the future direction of Christianity. Father Arius of Alexandria insisted that Jesus was merely a human being and was therefore only a prophet, like Moses or Abraham. Athanasius (later Saint Athanasius) countered that Jesus was of the same substance as God and therefore was God himself. Athanasius won the argument and denounced Arius as a heretic.

Nostradamus, the grandson of a Jewish convert, may have considered this debate all important because it was there that Christianity finally divorced itself from its Jewish roots.

Centuries took place on 13 December 1702. The quatrain clearly predicts a turbulent century following this date and, indeed, the eighteenth century was an age of new invention, educated enlightenment and bloody revolution.

This interpretation is strengthened by the prediction in the third and fourth lines: that "evil times" will return after a "long century", shaking France and Italy. By 1802, Napoleon Bonaparte had consolidated his dictatorship of France and had conquered northern Italy. Although this was a victory for the French Republic, the other major European powers now became alarmed by Napoleon's expansionist policy and dedicated themselves to his destruction. The next thirteen years[4] were among the bloodiest in Europe's history – arguably an "evil time", even when compared to the upheavals of the previous century.

It should be noted in passing that the next conjunction of Jupiter and Saturn in Aries after 1702 was 2 September 1995. If the above interpretation of *Century I*, quatrain 51, is incorrect, then we ourselves may be facing a changeable century ahead.

French Wars in 1580 and 1703

VI.2

> *En l'an cinq cens octante plus et moins,*
> *On attendra le siecle bien estrange:*
> *En l'an sept cens, et trois (cieux en tesmoings)*
> *Que plusieurs regnesun à cinq feront change.*

Translation:

> In the year five hundred eighty more or less,
> There shall be a strange age:
> In the year seven hundred and three (witness heaven)
> Many kingdoms one to five shall be changed.

Erica Cheetham suggests that this quatrain predicts two periods of war in France. In 1580 (Nostradamus probably left out the thousands on the dates for the sake of scansion), France was in the midst of the so-called "Seventh War": a religious civil war fuelled by the St Bartholomew's Day Massacre of Parisian Protestants in

[4] Culminating with Napoleon's defeat at Waterloo.

1572. In 1703, Louis XIV was obstinately involving France in the Spanish War of Succession (see IV.2 and IV.5 later in this chapter). Cheetham suggests that the phrase "kingdoms one to five" in the last line refers to the lands that the war won for Philip V, Louis's grandson. On his accession to the Spanish throne Philip was, on paper at least, the ruler of Spain, Sicily, Milan, the Netherlands and America.

Henry Roberts, using his own eccentric dating system based on the Council of Nicaea (see I.49 above), adds 325 years to the above years and suggests 1914 (he assumes "580 more or less" equates to 1589) and AD 2028. The first date, the beginning of World War I, was indeed a "strange age". From the second date, Roberts predicts there will be a "complete change in the line-up of nations".

The Spanish War of Succession: 1701–13
IV.2 & IV.5

> *Par mort France prendra voyage à faire,*
> *Classe par mer, marcher monts Pyrenées,*
> *Espaigne en trouble, marcher gent militaire:*
> *Des plus grand Dames en France emmenées.*

Translation:

> By reason of a death France shall undertake a journey,
> Fleet at sea, marching troops over the Pyrenean mountains.
> Spain shall be in trouble, an army marches:
> Some great ladies carried away to France.

A French military intervention into Spain is clearly described here. Most Nostradamus scholars believe the quatrain to be a prediction of the Spanish War of Succession, which took place between 1701 and 1713.

In 1700, Charles II of Spain died, bequeathing his kingdom to Philip, Duke of Anjou. Although Philip was only related to the Spanish royal family through marriage, the issue would probably have passed without controversy had the new Spanish king not also been the grandson of Louis XIV of France. The joining of the two thrones under the ambitious Bourbon family was more than the other powers of Europe could tolerate. In 1701, England, Austria, the Netherlands, Denmark and, later, Portugal formed a coalition to remove Philip V from the Spanish throne. France and Spain naturally opposed them and war was declared.

The death mentioned in line one of the quatrain would thus be that of Charles II, and the "journey" could be that of Philip from Anjou (in France) to be crowned in Madrid. The second and third lines seem self-explanatory: France sends fleets and armies to aid Spain, the latter crossing the Pyrénées Mountains, which form a natural border between the two countries.

Erica Cheetham suggests that line four is a reference to the beginning of the whole affair. Some years before, two Spanish princesses were married into the French branch of the House of Bourbon, guaranteeing trouble if Charles II died without a male heir – as indeed he did.

> *Coix paix, soubz un accompli divin verbe,*
> *L'Espaigne et Gaul seront unis ensemble:*
> *Grand clade proche, et combat tresacerbe,*
> *Coeur si hardi ne sera qui ne tremble.*

Translation:

> Cross peace, under an accomplished divine word,
> Spain and France shall be united:
> A great disaster, and savage fighting,
> No heart so brave that will not tremble.

The peace "under an accomplished divine word", mentioned in the first line, might be Clement XI's papal bull of 1713. Although this bull had nothing to do with the Spanish War of Succession, Clement was an active peace-broker during the conflict and published his *Vineam Unigenitus* in the year that an armistice was finally achieved. The remaining three lines accurately describe the cause of the war (the political joining of the French and Spanish thrones) and the savagery of the fighting.

In 1711, after ten years of war across Europe, France and Spain were close to defeat on all fronts. However, Britain then decided that total victory might make the Austrian Empire too powerful, so the British government unilaterally offered peace to the Bourbon faction. Having lost such an important member, the "Grand Alliance" promptly collapsed. Individual peace treaties were signed by the separate nations over the next two years and, ironically, Philip V was allowed to keep the Spanish throne.

The Reign of Louis XV of France: 1715–74
III.15 & III.14

> *Coeur, rigeur, gloire le regne changera,*
> *De tous points contre ayant son adversaire,*
> *Lors France enfance par mort subjuguera,*
> *Un grand regent sera lors plus contraire.*

Translation:

> Heart, vigour, glory shall change in the kingdom,
> In all points having an adversary opposing,
> Then France will be ruled by a child through a death,
> The great regent will be very contrary.

Louis XIV of France died in 1715 – seventy-seven years old and exhausted from his efforts to win the Spanish War of Succession. His son was immediately crowned Louis XV. However, as Louis was only five at the time, Philippe Duc d'Orleans was made Regent. He was to rule France until 1723, when the king reached the minimum legal age of majority.[5]

Unfortunately, France, which only a few decades before had been one of the strongest powers in Europe, was physically and financially exhausted, thanks to Louis XIV's foreign wars. Thus the Duc d'Orleans did indeed find the regency a "contrary" task, as noted in the last line of the quatrain. On the over-optimistic advice of a Scottish financier called John Law, Philippe printed vast sums of paper money (then a new invention) which caused inflation to go through the roof and, in 1721, bankrupted the whole nation.

---

[5]This was the first time a regent had ruled France since the publication of the *Centuries*.

Par le rameau du vaillant personnage,
De France infime, par le père infelice:
Honneurs, richesses, travail en son vieil age
Pour avoir creu le conseil d'homme nice.

Translation:

By the branch of the valiant person,
Of weak France, through the unhappy father:
Honours, riches, labour in his old age,
For having believed the council of a nice man.

Louis XV, the son (and branch) of the valiant Louis XIV, was only thirteen when he took control of the now benighted nation. The reference to "the unhappy father" in line two might be a comment on the parental failing of Louis XIV: by fighting pointless wars and not producing a son earlier in his life, the old king left his very young heir with a huge task of reconstruction. On the other hand, the word "father" may be another Nostradamus pun. In 1726, Louis XV appointed his old priest and tutor as prime minister. Father Fleury did his best over the next seventeen years and succeeded in partially stabilizing the economy. Unfortunately, in doing so, he imposed draconian taxes on the peasantry and effectively sowed the seeds of later revolution.

Louis XV was a lazy monarch and, for most of his fifty-nine-year reign, left the task of running France to his ministers. The result was gross corruption and mismanagement. Over a few decades the British annexed most of France's overseas holdings, thanks to France's feeble generals. The "bourgeoisie" – the merchant class that had done very well in Louis XIV's prosperous reign – were taxed unmercifully and the French peasants were treated little better than serfs. At the same time, the clergy and nobility were exempted from all state tariffs. By the 1770s, the national situation was one of stagnation, decadence and growing social unrest.

Belatedly, in the last four years of his life, Louis XV realized that reform was urgently needed and took steps to balance matters. He restricted the rights of the nobility – who generally felt themselves to be above the law when dealing with "inferiors" – and imposed taxes on the church and the gentry. Unfortunately, his self-serving court officials blocked him at every possible juncture and the tremendous effort drove him to an early grave. This might be what Nostradamus was referring to in the last two lines of the quatrain. Louis lived a life of honour and riches, then spent his last years labouring to redress the work of Father Fleury (a "nice" but politically short-sighted man – *nice*, oddly enough, is an old French word).

The king's efforts were all wasted. Louis's grandson, crowned Louis XVI, was as lazy and weak-willed as Louis XV had been as a young man. Within only a few years, the bureaucracy and nobility had reversed all Louis XV's reforms and France was on course for bloody revolution.

The Turkish/Persian Armistice: October 1727

III.77

> *Le tiers sous Aries comprins,*
> *L'an mil sept cens vingt et sept en Octobre:*
> *Le Roy de Perse par ceux d'Egypte prins:*
> *Conflit, mort, perte: à la croix grand approbre.*

Translation:

> The third climate comprised under Aries,
> In the year one thousand seven hundred twenty seven in October:
> The King of Persia shall be taken by those of Egypt:
> Conflict, death, loss, to the cross great shame.

This is another of the rare quatrains that contains an apparently precise date. While Henry C. Roberts translates the second line to read, "In the year 2025, the 27th of October",[6] other scholars – like Erica Cheetham and David Ovason – have little doubt that this is an accurate description of Middle-Eastern events in October 1727.

In that month, Shah Ashraf signed a peace treaty with the

[6]He does this by adding 325 (see I.49 above) to 1700 and adding a useful – if not wholly justified – comma to get the date 27 October.

Ottoman Empire, ceding most of western Persia to them. (The word "Egypt" in the quatrain might signify the Turks, as it was then the most significant asset of their empire.) The Ottoman Turks, in return, ceased their invasion plans and formally recognized the validity of Ashraf's dynasty. Although the third line may seem flatly to contradict this interpretation – describing as it does the "taking" of the King of Persia – David Ovason believes that Nostradamus was indirectly describing the ignominious loss of half the Shah's kingdom. Ironically, Shah Ashraf did not live long to enjoy the peace for which he had paid such a tremendous price. He died the following year, in 1728.

The first line of the quatrain may seem rather obscure, but David Ovason points out that it is, in fact, a remarkably precise description of the land areas involved in the peace treaty of 1727. The term "third climate" comes from the work of the Arabic astrologer, Alfraganus. He divided the globe into seven *climata*, or "climates", creating a working, if rather arbitrary, system of latitudes. The "third climate" stretched, approximately, between 28 and 34 degrees north, and included most of Persia, Afghanistan, Iraq and Arabia.

The second part of the line adds "under Aries", and Ovason points out that this is a reference to Ptolemaic astrology. Ptolemy invented a system called "*chorography*", in which each country and land area was assigned to a particular zodiac sign. Persia, in this system, falls under Taurus, but Aries controls Syria, Palestine, Edom and Judea – in fact, the precise area that Shah Ashraf ceded to the Turks. Thus, "the third climate comprised under Aries", may translate as "the Persian Empire, specifically the western provinces".

Despite this remarkable accuracy, the last line describing "conflict, death, loss, to the cross great shame" seems to have nothing to do with the rest of the prophecy. War was avoided and the Christians – who Nostradamus often signified with *la croix* – had nothing to do with the matter. Ovason again offers an explanation: he points out that the modern solidification of Islamic power dates from the treaty of 1727. As we have already seen, Nostradamus seems to have shared his contemporaries' horror of the Ottoman expansion and of Islam in general. Perhaps, says Ovason, the seer was summing up, in eight words, the entire history of mistrust and outright bloodshed between Christians and Moslems since 1727.

Catherine the Great of Russia: 1729–96

VIII.15

> Vers Aquilon grans efforts par hommasse
> Presque l'Europe et l'univers vexer,
> Les deux eclipse mettra en tel chasse,
> Et aux Pannons vie et mort renforcer.

Translation:

> Towards the North great efforts by the masculine woman
> To vex Europe and the universe,
> The two eclipses will be put to flight,
> And will enforce the life and death of the Poles.

Several commentators take this quatrain to be a prediction of the rule of Russia's Catherine II.

Catherine was the wife of Grand Duke Peter of Holstein, the heir to the Russian throne (although he was actually a German). The Grand Duke was crowned Tsar Peter III in 1762, but was so dismissive of his new subjects that he was dethroned by the Imperial Guard within six months. Catherine, on the other hand, had gone out of her way to woo the Russian nobility, so now found herself crowned as ruling Empress. Peter was murdered a few days after he agreed to abdicate.

Catherine was an intelligent, strong-willed woman. A capable commander-in-chief, during her thirty-four-year rule she won several wars, expanded Russia's borders and put down a major Cossack uprising. She was, at the same time, well versed in the liberal attitudes of the Enlightenment, but towards the latter part of her rule became increasingly oppressive and reactionary.

Her affairs were legendary in her own lifetime; she had numerous lovers – ten of whom she made virtual consorts – and, when she died at the age of sixty-seven, the rumour went about that she had been crushed to death while copulating with a stallion.

Although this last scandal was a malicious falsehood,[7] it does give an indication of how much she impressed and worried her

---

[7]Catherine died of a stroke. Her lover, at the time, was a perfectly normal young man, forty years her junior.

contemporaries. In an age when most women were still little better than chattels, Catherine earned her title, "the Great", and frightened Europe in much the same way that Napoleon would a few decades later.

The first line of the quatrain mentions "the North",[8] with a capital letter as if it were a separate country or place. David Ovason also notes that in Latin, *aquila* meant "eagle". He suggests that Nostradamus was employing a double meaning: i.e. a northern country connected with an eagle. Imperial Russia's symbol was the double-headed eagle. Since the time of Nostradamus, Catherine II has been the only female ruler of Russia, and she was certainly a "masculine woman" in her style of leadership, all as described in the quatrain.

The second line describes the vexatious effect of the "hommasse" on Europe and, rather improbably, "the universe". The first certainly fits Catherine, and Ovason offers a rather ingenious explanation of the second. The term *l'univers* may also be rearranged as *luni vers*: Latin for "towards the moon". This may give us the key to line three, which describes two eclipses being put to flight. If, says Ovason, we consider these eclipses to be Earth's shadow on the Moon, we may see a poetic description of Catherine's two successful wars on the Ottoman Empire (whose symbol was the sickle moon).

It is the last line that leads most commentators to agree that Catherine is the subject of the quatrain. Throughout the late eighteenth century, Russia, Prussia (now Northern Germany) and the Austrian Empire teetered on the brink of war. The main bone of contention was the buffer area between them: Poland. In 1772 and 1793, these three super-states sliced off huge sections of Polish territory to be divided amongst themselves: the so-called "Partitions". Finally, in 1795, following a failed attempt at revolt in what was left of Poland, Catherine presided over the total division of Polish lands, removing the hapless nation from the map for 125 years. The Poles became serfs to the greater Russian nation and, in the last year of her life, Catherine was the final arbiter of life and death over most of the Polish people.

[8]"*Aquilon*" derived from the Latin *aquilonius* meaning "northern".

The First Balloon and the Imprisoned Pope: 1783 & 1797

V.57

> *Istra du Mont Gaulfier et Aventin,*
> *Qui par trou avertira l'armeé:*
> *Entre deux rocs sera prins le butin,*
> *De SEXT. mansol faillir le renommee.*

Translation:

> One shall go out from Mount Gaulfier and Aventine,
> Who through a hole shall give notice to the army:
> Between two rocks the prize will be taken,
> Of SEXT. the Sun shall fail in renown.

This is one of Nostradamus' truly stunning predictions. The Montgolfier brothers invented and launched the first hot air balloon in France in 1783. Nostradamus' apparent pun on their name is too precise to be easily dismissed. Even the inventors' nationality is apparently hinted at by the seer: "Gaul" was the Latin name for France.

The balloon was utilized as a scouting device by French generals, aiding the Republican army's victory at the Battle of Flaurus in Belgium eleven years later. This battle consolidated French military power. This, in turn, allowed them to sack Rome in 1797. One of the Seven Hills of Rome is the "Aventine," the last word of line one.

Erica Cheetham suggests that the word "SEXT" in the last line is a shortening of "Sextus", and that "*mansol*" is derived from *manens solus* – "he who is solitary" – a reference, she says, to pontifical chastity. She believes that prediction in this line indicates Pope Pius VI – one of only two popes since Nostradamus' day to be designated "Sextus".

Pope Pius VI was strongly opposed to the French Revolution, but was captured when Napoleon took Rome in 1797. The pontiff was forced to cede large areas of church land to the French – the "rocks", according to Cheetham, upon which the pope's temporal power was based. Pius VI died in captivity in 1799 (see overleaf).

The Beginning of the French Revolution: 1789–92
VI.23, I.53 & V.5

> *D'esprit de regne munismes descriées,*
> *Et soront peuples esmuez contre leur Roi:*
> *Paix, faict nouveau, sainctes loix empirées,*
> *Rapis oncfut en si tres dur arroi.*

Translation:

> Defences undermined by the spirit of the kingdom,
> The people will be stirred up against their King:
> Peace, new made, sacred laws degenerate,
> *Rapis* never was in such great trouble.

By the late 1780s, France was on the edge of social and economic collapse. The lower orders were taxed to the hilt while the tax-exempted nobility wasted money like fools. King Louis XVI was aware of the problem and, over the previous decade, had assigned several reforming ministers to the problem. However, as he invariably failed to support them when they faced the vested interest groups at court and in the Church, these men always failed.

In 1788, Louis was forced to call elections to the Estates-General: a parliament equally composed of nobility, clergy and commoners. (National democracy had been unknown in France since 1614.) The king hoped that a legislative body with lesser powers than his own might win peace with his critics, but the nobility and clergy tried to gang together to suppress the commoners and created even greater tensions. Thus the third line of the above quatrain might be describing this "new made" "peace", undermined by the "sacred laws" and entrenched attitudes of the right-wing factions.

"*Rapis*", mentioned in the last line, is almost certainly an anagram of "Paris" – the seer uses the word in several other quatrains in which he seems to have the French capital in mind. As the tensions within the Estates-General increased, the starving population of Paris became the centre of the growing insurrection and anti-monarchist movements.

Las qu'on verra grand peuple tourmenté,
Et la loi saincte en totale ruine:
Par autres loix toute la Christienté,
Quant d'or d'argent trouve nouvelle mine.

Translation:

Alas how the great people will be tormented,
And the holy laws in total ruin:
By other laws Christianity is troubled,
When new mines of gold and silver are found.

Matters were going rapidly downhill. In June 1789, the commons section of the Estates-General formed their own legislative body – The National Assembly – and voted themselves sole tax-gathering powers. When Louis ineffectually tried to suppress them, they retaliated by vowing to draft a constitution for France (thus threatening Louis with either a constitutional, legally-restricted monarchy or an outright republic). In the face of growing insurrection, Louis capitulated and recognized the National Assembly as the new legislative body.

A few days later, on 14 July, the Parisian mob stormed, captured and demolished the hated Bastille prison on the bank of the Seine. Fearing further escalations of violence, the National Assembly quickly drafted the new constitution and issued 400 million *assignats* – paper money secured on the value of confiscated Church and crown lands. This helped stabilize the economy for a short while, but inevitably sent inflation rocketing.

This issue of paper bills – as opposed to the more normal gold and silver coinage – may be what Nostradamus is referring to in the last line of the quatrain. The other three lines seem to concern the Assembly's disestablishment of the French Catholic Church in 1790. Under the new constitution, priests and bishops were to be created only by the election of the populace, monastic orders were disbanded, Church lands seized and all clergy had to swear allegiance to the state. Nostradamus would have been shocked by this humiliation of the Church, and some scholars hear an echo of his prophetic anger in the following quatrain.

Souz ombre faincte d'oster de servitude,
Peuple et cité l'usurpera lui mesmes:
Pire fera par fraux de jeune pute,
Livré au champ lisant le faux proesme.

Translation:

Under the feigned pretext of removing servitude,
People and city usurp power:
He will do worse because of the trickery of a young whore,
Betrayed in the field delivering a false promise.

Following the storming of the Bastille, the people of Paris exercised great power of fear over the National Assembly, and the more radical and Republican leaders used the threat of the mob to win themselves greater political leverage. This may be what Nostradamus is referring to in the first two lines above.

Louis XVI ruefully accepted his new role as a constitutional monarch, but soon found himself under house arrest in the Palais des Tuileries. Unfortunately, although the king retained the loyalty of many sections of French society, his popularity was undermined by the actions of his wife, the Queen Consort, Marie Antoinette.

Popular history has recorded Marie Antoinette as a rather dim-witted[9] and out-of-touch woman. In fact, she actively connived with the reactionary elements of the National Assembly and openly corresponded with her brother, Emperor Leopold II. This last may seem natural enough, but the Holy Roman Emperor was violently opposed to state reform and was threatening war to topple the French constitutionists. An unpopular foreign national to begin with, Marie Antoinette's virtual acts of treason against France did much to get herself and her husband condemned. Nostradamus, if line three is indeed about the queen, clearly disliked her as much as her Republican enemies.

The last line of the quatrain may refer to the false promise Louis gave to his captors, when he said he would not try to escape – he and his family were originally held captive to protect them from the mob. However, in 1791, the family tried to escape to Austria,

[9]Famously, when told that the poor were rioting because they had no bread, she remarked: "Let them eat cake . . ."

but were captured while still in the French countryside, or "in the field".

Milk and Honey, Blood and Quicklime: 1792 & 1793
IX.20, IV.85, VI.92, I.57 & IX.77

> De nuict viendra par la forest de Reines,
> Deux pars vaultort Herne la pierre blanche,
> La maine noir en gris dedans Varennes
> Esleu cap. cause tempeste feu sang tranche.

Translation:

> By night will come through the forest of Reines,
> Two partners by a roundabout way *Herne* the white stone,
> The black monk in grey at Varennes,
> The elected *cap.* causes tempest fire blood slice.

This is perhaps the most hair-raisingly precise quatrain in the whole of Nostradamus' *Centuries*. If a modern forger decided to fake a prediction after the fact – with the help of a pile of history books – he could hardly give a more accurately detailed version of these events. Yet we know for a fact that Nostradamus published this prophecy over 230 years before the episode took place.

In 1792, tiring of incarceration in the Palais des Tuileries and fearing for the future, Louis XVI and the royal family escaped through a secret door in the queen's apartments, boarded a waiting coach and made towards the eastern border and the Austrian Empire. They were initially heading for the small town of Varennes, but became lost in the dark and went a roundabout route along the route to Reines (although one edition of the *Centuries* prints "forest of Reines" – which does not exist – as "*fores de Reines*", – the "queen's door", through which they escaped from the palace). It was at this point that they were recaptured.

Before his attempted escape, Louis had some hope of survival. Afterwards, he had next to none. Most of his subjects felt that a king who tried to desert his country in time of trouble was no better than a captain who abandons his ship in a storm. Likewise, Nostradamus seems to blame Louis for the "tempest" of fire and blood that followed his execution, but this is unfair. Most historians now agree that Louis XVI was simply an inept ruler, not a tyrant; the mismanagement of his two royal predecessors had all but guaranteed a revolution before he was even born.

The word "Herne" in the second line is probably an anagram of "Rehne" – a medieval spelling of "Reine" ("Queen"). The "white stone" also mentioned is rather obscure but, as the next line accurately describes the shade of the king's clothes when captured – "grey" – this might be a reference to Marie Antoinette's habit of wearing all-white outfits. Louis XVI was of a monkish temperament (this may be also be a comment on his occasional celibacy, the result of bouts of stress-related impotence) although precisely why he should be described as a "black monk" is hard to guess.

The "elected *cap*.", described as causing so much destruction in the last line of the quatrain, is probably Louis himself: "cap." could be a shortening of "*Capet*" – an archaic French word for "King". Louis was the first constitutional (thus "elected") king of France.

The last word of the quatrain is "*tranche*", the French word for "slice". A chilling reminder of the sound of a guillotine – the recently invented execution machine (to whose design the king himself contributed a suggestion)[10] used to behead "enemies of the Republic".

> *Le charbon blanc du noir sera chassé,*
> *Prisonnier faicte mené au tombereau:*
> *More Chameau sus piedz entrelassez,*
> *Lors le puisné sillera l'aubereau.*

Translation:

> The white coal chased out by the black,
> A prisoner carried in a tumbril:

[10]This was one of the greatest moments of black irony in French history. In 1789, a Dr Guillotin was commissioned by Louis XVI to design a humane method of beheading criminals. The weighted, curved blade looked fine on paper but usually failed to sever fully the heads of the test animals. In the Tuilleries, Louis XVI happened to be passing one day and, on hearing Dr Guillotin's problem, suggested the use of a straight, but angled, blade. The suggestion worked perfectly – on the king's own neck as well as on tens of thousands of others.

> Like a camel his feet are tied,
> Then the last born will free the falcon.

In September 1792, the National Convention – the constitution-ally-reformed National Assembly – declared France a republic. Immediately afterwards, the ex-king was tried as a traitor and condemned to death. On 21 January 1793, he was taken in a tumbril (a two-wheeled cart used to transport condemned prisoners) to the Place de la Revolution (now Place de la Concorde). There, bound hand and foot, he was beheaded by the guillotine.

Apart from the keyword "*tombereau*" ("tumbril"), this quatrain is, on the surface, one of the most allegorically obscure of all Nostradamus' predictions. The word "*Charbon*" (or "coal") in the first line may be a rhyme on "Bourbon" – Louis XVI's family name. White was the shade of the Bourbon standard and, as Erica Cheetham points out, Nostradamus often used *noir* as a partial anagram of *rein*, or "king". Although this gives a nonsensical reading to the whole line (i.e. "The white Bourbon flag will be chased out by the king"), it does seem to hint to the identity of the prisoner in the second and third lines.

The word "*chameau*" ("camel") in the third line sounds ridiculous, not least because Louis was not hobbled like a riding beast, but was tightly bound hand and foot. However, in *The Prophesies and Enigmas of Nostradamus*, edited by Liberte E. La Vert (1979), it is suggested that the word *chameau* is actually a misprint of *chamois* – the little French deer that hunters bind tightly around the hooves to allow them to carry them home.

The last line may be a reference to the *Dauphin* – the heir to the French throne. Louis XVI's eight-year-old son – also called Louis – was held in the "protective custody" of the Republican government following his parents' execution. Unfortunately, this did not stop escaped French Royalists declaring him Louis XVII. This made him a threat to the Republic, so few people were surprised when he was reported "dead of tuberculosis" in June 1795. Nevertheless, rumours continued to circulate that he was actually alive. Indeed, over the next few decades, no less than thirty men came forward claiming to be the lost Dauphin (and the rightful king of France).

Young Louis was indeed the "last born" child of Louis XVI and

Marie Antoinette, but we can only speculate on whether the term "free the falcon" refers to his survival.

> *Prince de beauté tant venuste,*
> *Au chef menee, le second faict trahi:*
> *La cité au glaive de poudre face aduste,*
> *Par le trop grand meutre le chef du Roi hai.*

Translation:

> The Prince of such handsome beauty,
> Intrigues against him, the second rank betrayed:
> The city of the sword consumed by the powder that burns,
> By too great a murder the head of the King hated.

Louis XVI was said to have been strikingly handsome as a young prince. Erica Cheetham suggests that the "intrigues" of the second line were the constitutional deliberations that lowered Louis to the "second rank" of constitutional monarch. The "city of the sword" certainly sounds like a description of Paris at this period, and the "powder that burns" might be a reference to quicklime – the caustic substance used to hasten the decomposition of the many executed bodies thrown into mass graves.

As with the death of Charles I in England, the monarchist in Nostradamus seems to consider Louis's regicide "too great a murder". Also like Charles I, Louis XVI's freshly severed head was held up for a mob of former subjects to "hate" and ridicule.

> *Par grand discord la trombe tremblera*
> *Accord rompu dressant la teste au ciel:*
> *Bouche sanglante dans le sang nagera,*
> *Au sol la face ointe de laict et miel.*

Translation:

> By great discord the trumpet trembles
> Agreement broken lifting the head to heaven:
> A bloody mouth swims with blood,
> The face turned to the Sun anointed with milk and honey.

In fact, the death of Louis only brought about a greater level of social unrest in France. Lacking a king to blame for on-going problems, the parties in the National Convention turned on each other. The ballot to execute Louis had scraped through on only 387 votes to 334, and much bad blood had been caused by the near deadlock. Many agreements were broken, as mentioned in the second line, and it was certainly a time of "great discord", as it says in the first.

As noted above, Louis's severed head was held up to the crowd at his execution and, as gruesomely described in the third line, the mouth was wet with blood "vomited" as the blade cut his throat.

Nevertheless, the last line is the reason why many Nostradamus scholars confidently connect this quatrain to the death of Louis XVI: the French coronation ceremony involved the anointing of the new king's head with "milk and honey".

> *Le regne prins le Roi conviera,*
> *La dame prinse à mort jurez à sort,*
> *La vie à Roine fils on desniera,*
> *Et la pellix au sort de la consort.*

Translation:

> The government takes the invited King,
> The captive queen condemned to death by a lottery,
> Life will be denied the Queen's son,
> And the concubine to the strength of a consort.

David Ovason argues that the four lines of this quatrain each predict the death of one of four of the central characters of the French Court. Louis was "invited" to be a constitutional monarch by the government only a few months before he was "taken" and executed on 21 January 1793. Queen Marie Antoinette was tried by a jury from all classes of people, chosen by lot. She went to the guillotine on 16 October 1793. Louis XVII, "the Queen's son", was reported to have died in captivity on 8 June 1795. Whether he died of neglect, or was murdered on the orders of the French government, it would still be accurate to say that his "life [was]

denied". The "concubine" in the last line might be Madame Du
Barry: an ex-courtesan and the influential mistress of the late
Louis XV. She was executed on 7 December 1793.

Ovason adds that each of the above deaths are presented in
chronological order in the quatrain – except for the death of the
Dauphin. He suggests that Nostradamus might have been offering
us a clue that the boy actually died between October and December
1793, but that the matter was covered-up for a year and a half.
However, Ovason himself admits that there is no historical
evidence to back this theory.

The Reign of Terror and the Cult of Reason: July 1793–July 1794
IV.11, VI.57, I.44 & VIII.98

> Celui qu'aura gouvert de la grand cappe,
> Sera induict à quelques cas patrer
> Les douze rouges viendront fouiller la nappe.
> Soubz meutre, meutre se viendra perpetrer.

Translation:

> He that will have covering of the great cloak,
> Shall be led to execute some cases
> The twelve red ones will come to soil the cloth
> Under murder, murder will be committed.

Several Nostradamus scholars believe that this quatrain is some
unspecified or as yet unfulfilled prophecy concerning the papacy –
the term "twelve red ones" being reminiscent of the Cardinal
Bishops in the Vatican College of Cardinals. However, Jean-
Charles de Fontbrune suggests that the seer was actually referring
to the French Revolutionary Committee of Public Safety – the
twelve-man body that ruled over tens of thousands of executions
in the infamous "Reign of Terror".

Although the word "cappe" at the end of the first line of the
quatrain literally translates as "cloak", de Fontbrune suggests that
it is really a deliberate misspelling of "*capet*" ("king") allowing a
rhyme with "*nappe*" ("cloth") at the end of the third line. Thus the
first line might be read: "He that enshrouds the great king." This is
a direct description, de Fontbrune thinks, of Maximilien

Robespierre: a leader of the radical Jacobin Party and the man who virtually forced the execution of Louis XVI on the divided National Convention.

On 13 July 1793, Charlotte Corday – a follower of the comparatively moderate Girondist Party – assassinated a leading Jacobin, Jean Paul Marat, in his bath. The resultant public anger allowed the Jacobins to seize control of the powerful Committee of Public Safety, and Robespierre had himself made chairman. Under the cover of "national security", the twelve-man committee set about persecuting their former opponents ("soiling the cloth" of liberty with their brutal corruption). Although some of the show-trials and automatic executions that followed were of actual rebels against the new Republic, many more were personal murders covered by a show of judicial nicety: "under murder, murder will be committed".

It is a popular misconception that a majority of the victims of the Terror were members of the French aristocracy. In fact, only eight per cent of the 40,000 people executed between July 1793 and July 1794 were aristocrats. A further fourteen per cent were bourgeoisie, and six per cent were members of the clergy. The remaining seventy-two per cent were commoners accused of minor or imaginary crimes. The new regime was already collapsing into paranoia and blood mania.

In some of the quatrains believed to predict the French Revolution, Nostradamus refers to the radical Republicans as "reds" – and this was indeed the colour of their banner. Nevertheless, from the repugnance the seer clearly felt for "*le rouges*", he might also have been thinking of the sea of blood for which they were responsible.

> *Celui qu'estoit bien avant dans le regne,*
> *Ayant chef rouge proche à la hierarchie:*
> *Aspre et cruel, et se fera tant craindre,*
> *Succedera à sacré monarchie.*

Translation:

> He who was a good way to the front of the kingdom,
> Having a red head near the hierarchy:

> Harsh and cruel, and will make himself so feared,
> He succeeds to the sacred monarchy.

By the time Louis XVI came to trial, Robespierre and the Jacobin Party were already the main power within the National Convention. The ferocious Parisian mob gave strong backing to these radical "reds" while, at the same time, the Jacobins' moderate opposition was split into factions and lost popular support. The murder of Marat took place at just the right time to give Robespierre and his cronies the leverage to seize absolute power.

Although still nominally under the direction of the democratic senate, Robespierre and the Committee of Public Safety showed themselves so ruthless and arbitrary that no one dared oppose them. Thus Robespierre "succeeded to the sacred monarchy" as a dictator in all but name.

> *En bref seront de retour sacrifices,*
> *Contrevenans seront mis à martyre:*
> *Plus ne seront moines, abbez, ne novices,*
> *Le miel sera beaucoup plus cher que cire.*

Translation:

> In a short time the return of sacrifices,
> Opposition shall be put to martyrdom:
> There will no longer be monks, abbots, nor novices,
> Honey will be more expensive than wax.

Even before the death of Marat and the rise of the Jacobins, the French Catholic Church was under political siege. Church property was confiscated and the monasteries abolished. On 23 November 1793, the Commune of Paris ordered all churches closed and denounced the local clergy to be enemies of France. These measures quickly spread across the nation, and many churchmen ("monks, abbots [and] novices") were arrested and guillotined.

To replace Christianity, the Republicans instituted the "Cult of Reason": a semi-philosophical, humanist religion, based on the liberal ideas of the Enlightenment. Line one of the above quatrain is argued by Nostradamus scholars to predict the coming of the Cult of Reason as a new form of paganism. "Sacrifices" were not a part of the cult, but Nostradamus may well have seen the executed clergy as sacrifices to a pagan faith.

Before the revolution, the wax from beehives was more valuable than the honey because it was needed in great quantities to make votive candles for the churches. Thus, as the last line of the quatrain suggests, honey became more expensive than wax when the Church was abolished and the demand for candles was greatly reduced.

> *Des gens d'eglise sang fera espandu,*
> *Comme de l'eau eu si grand abondance;*
> *Et d'un long temps ne sera restranche*
> *Ve, ve au cleric ruine et doleance.*

Translation:

> Of the churchmen blood will be spilt,
> As water in such great abundance;
> And for a long time it shall not be restrained,
> Woe, woe for the clergy ruin and grief.

Although there is nothing specific to link this quatrain to the persecution of the Catholic clergy under the Terror, it is an accurate description of their suffering. Since Nostradamus' day, the Catholic Churchmen have only once undergone a similar period of state persecution – in Germany under the Nazis. Let us hope that the above quatrain refers to one of these two periods, and not to some future event.

Thermidor: July 1794

II.42

> *Coq, chiens et chats de sang seront repeus*
> *Et de la playe du tyran trouvé mort.*
> *Au lict d'unautrejambles et bras rompus,*
> *Qui n'avait peur de mourir de cruelle mort.*

Translation:

> Cock, dogs and cats will be replete with blood
> And of the wound the tyrant found dead.
> In the bed of another with arms and legs broken,
> Who was not afraid dies a cruel death.

By spring 1794, the ruling Jacobin party was beginning to experience major rifts. Robespierre and his followers insisted that the bloody slaughter of "enemies of the Republic" must go on, but many previously fervent Republicans had become sickened by the endless executions.

At the end of March, Robespierre acted characteristically to silence his critics: he arrested and guillotined them. However, the zealous ex-lawyer had gone too far this time. His inner core of supporters now saw that any of them might be next, and even the bloodthirsty citizens of Paris were growing tired of the daily butchery.

By June, the Republic's very successes were working against its leaders. The Terror had originally been justified by the danger of invasion by foreign nations, but major victories by the French army in Belgium had all but ended this threat. Robespierre continued to make radical speeches, calling for greater vigilance and more executions, but he was now swimming against the tide of public opinion.

On 26 July (8 Thermidor, under the newly-instituted Republican calendar) Robespierre gave his last speech to the National Convention. He warned that many executions were still necessary, but this time failed to mention any names; the natural result was that everyone in the Convention felt under threat. The next day he was shouted down as he tried to speak, then he and his followers were arrested as they tried to leave. That night Robespierre was rescued by soldiers of the Paris Commune, who took him to the Hôtel de Ville, but Convention troops quickly recaptured him. Robespierre was shot in the jaw during the second arrest, and spent his last night in agony. The next day he and a hundred of his closest followers were guillotined, without even the mock trial they had given so many others. It was 27 July – or the Ninth of Thermidor.

The first line of the quatrain is most reminiscent of the Reign of Terror. The cockerel is the emblem of France and the Parisian mob was certainly animalistic in its thirst for blood.[11] By the beginning of Thermidor, however, even the rabid Commune de Paris was satiated; in the previous month alone, the Committee of Public Safety had executed over 1,500 people.

The second line is reminiscent of the assassination of Jean Paul Marat – found stabbed to death in his bath. Why Nostradamus should hark back to this event, when apparently predicting the fall of Robespierre, is harder to explain.

The third line sounds plain wrong. Although we know that Robespierre was tied to a bed during the agonized writhings of his last night, his legs and arms were not broken. Yet finally – paranoid monster that he certainly was – Robespierre showed bravery in the face of his own execution, echoing the last line of the quatrain.

The Death of Pope Pius VI: 29 August 1799

II.97

> Romain Pontife garde de t'approcher,
> De la cité que deux fleuves arrouse,
> Ton sang viendras aupres de là cracher,
> Toi et les tiens quand fleurira la rose.

Translation:

> Roman Pontiff beware the approach,
> Of the city watered by two rivers,
> You will spit your blood there,
> You and yours when the roses bloom.

When the French Republican army under Napoleon took Rome in 1798, they also captured Pope Pius VI – an ardent enemy of the new Republic. He was subsequently held prisoner at Valence, a city near the joining of the Rhone and Saone rivers at Lyon.

Still under arrest in the summer of 1799, Pope Pius suffered a

[11]Indeed, during the Enlightenment, Parisian crowds would sometimes entertain themselves with cats and dogs – throwing them out of high windows and laughing uproariously when the unfortunate animals burst on the cobblestones below.

severe bout of vomiting. This was so violent that it caused internal bleeding and made him spit blood. Thirty priests were also incarcerated with him, and some may have caught the same malady – thus the use of the phrase "you and yours" in the last line. The pope died on 29 August 1799, as the late roses were coming into bloom.

Chapter 15

Nostradamus and Napoleon

As we have already noted, the *Centuries* are Francocentric; large proportions of the predictions appear to be partially, or exclusively, about the fate of France. The seer dedicated whole series of quatrains to predicting what appear to be fairly insignificant events in French history, but totally failed to mention – for example – the American Revolution. Nostradamus devoted more of his quatrains to the French Revolution than to any other period of history, then dedicated even more to a figure who sounds very like Napoleon Bonaparte.

The quatrains that seem to be about Napoleon's career suggest that the prophet felt rather ambivalent about him. There seems to be evidence of distinct national pride when Nostradamus predicts a great French empire, yet Napoleon himself is described as a destroyer, a butcher and a "fearful thunderbolt". There are several possible reasons for this mixed attitude. To begin with, Napoleon was no friend to religion, and Nostradamus seems usually to have put his Christian faith before his nationalism. Secondly, Nostradamus had a genuine horror of bloodshed – perhaps natural in a medical man – and Napoleon caused some of the bloodiest conflicts in European history. Finally, the seer's predictions suggest a clear knowledge of how short France's "age of empire" would be (he even gives the correct period of "fourteen years" in *Century VII*, quatrain 13).

In the end, perhaps the main difference between Nostradamus and Napoleon was a simple one: it was one of the emperor's policies never to calculate the human cost of his victories, while the seer evidently realized that all the transitory victory parades of history are paid for by the very real suffering of individuals.

The Coming of Napoleon I

I.60 & VIII.1

> *Un Empereur naistra pres d'Italie*
> *Qui a l'Empire sera vendu bien cher:*
> *Diront avec quels gens il se ralie,*
> *Qu'on trouvera moins prince que boucher.*

Translation:

> An Emperor will be born near Italy
> Who will cost the Empire dear:
> They will say when they see his associates,
> That he is less a prince than a butcher.

The future Emperor Napoleon was born in Ajaccio on the island of Corsica in 1769. The above quatrain describes an emperor "born near Italy", and this was both physically and chronologically true of Napoleon. Corsica is equidistant between France and northern Italy and, only a year before Napoleon's birth, the Italian city of Genoa ceded the island to France. (Who knows how history would have differed if Napoleon had been brought up a citizen of Italy rather than of France.)

Line two of the quatrain is equally true of Napoleon, but it is also ironic in that the French would not have had an empire without Napoleon.

The emperor's associates certainly caused gossip, as lines three and four hint. Josephine – his first wife – was a Creole from Martinique in the Caribbean, and was virtually a second-class citizen in the eyes of "home-grown" Frenchmen. Furthermore, Napoleon appointed his brothers as rulers of Spain, Naples, Holland and Westphalia, despite their total lack of training as governors. Aristocratic society across Europe was scandalized that such a low-born family could rise so high. The phrase "less a prince than a butcher" echoes this snobbish indignation, but it might also be a hint to the bloodshed caused by Napoleon's expansionist wars.

Napoleon's father, Carlo Buonaparte, was a successful lawyer and became "Count Carlo" when France took over Corsica in 1768. Although the Buonapartes had never been a military family, Carlo pulled strings to have his second son, Napoleon, sent to the Brienne Military School in Paris. Ironically, it was Louis XVI who paid for the boy's scholarship. Napoleon graduated to a second lieutenancy in the artillery at the age of sixteen. When the revolution broke out, Napoleon joined the Republican side and was made a captain. He won national acclaim in 1793 at the siege of the anti-revolutionary port of Toulon: after his commanding general was wounded, Napoleon's brilliant use of the artillery won the battle. He was promoted to brigadier general at the age of 24.

The butcheries of Robespierre's Reign of Terror left the French army largely unaffected. The Committee of Public Safety avoided accusing military men of treason, just as a woodcutter does not saw at the branch he is sitting on. Thus Napoleon advanced his career and public standing in comparative safety.

In 1795, bread riots broke out in Paris. Following the fall of Robespierre and the Jacobins, the revolutionary government had undergone a political about-turn and was now right wing and reactionary rather than left wing and radical. Their efforts to stabilize the economy hurt the poor so severely that the army was needed to quell the riots. General Napoleon saw to it that the rioters were not only put down, but that he won credit as the "Saviour of the Republic".

> *PAU, NAY, LORON plus feu qu'à sang sera.*
> *Laude nager, fuir grand au surrez.*
> *Les agassas entrée refusera.*
> *Pampon Durance les tiendra enferrez.*

Translation:

> PAU, NAY LORON will be more fire than blood.
> Swimming in praise, the great one will flee to the confluence.
> The magpies are refused entrance.
> Great Bridge Durance will keep them confined.

Pau, Nay and Loron are all small and historically insignificant towns in western France. However, Nostradamus gives the names in capitals – usually a sign that he wants us to find a hidden message. Sure enough, if read as an anagram, the message "NAPAULON ROY" ("Napaulon King") can be constructed from the three words. Even in his own lifetime, Napoleon's name was occasionally written "Napaulon". Alternatively, the misspelling might be a subtle joke; early in his career, Napoleon simplified the spelling of his Corsican surname from "Buonaparte" to the French version "Bonaparte".

Although denigrated by his enemies as the "Monster of Europe", Napoleon was a tyrant only by the most liberal standards. Indeed, he invariably gave the nations he conquered better legal and social systems than they had ever previously enjoyed. On the other hand, his wars spread fire and ruin across the continent. So a retranslation of the first line could read: "Napoleon the King, a rule of military fire, but not of tyrannical bloodthirstiness." The phrase "more fire than blood", might also be a comment on Napoleon's endless zeal. Like Alexander the Great and Julius Caesar, Napoleon seems to have lived for the glory of his military conquests and the acquisition of power. He is quoted as once saying: "Power is my mistress".

Erica Cheetham suggests the remainder of the quatrain concerns Napoleon's imprisonment of Popes Pius VI and VII. She derives this idea from the rather convoluted connections of the word "*agassas*" at the beginning of the third line. *Agassa* is the Provençal[1] name for a magpie. In regular French, the word for magpie is *pie*, which is also the French spelling of the pontifical name "Pius".

In *Nostradamus on Napoleon* (1961), Stewart Robb points out that the Durance River (mentioned in the last line) flows through the south-eastern section of France. It was here, in Valence and Grenoble, respectively, that Pius VI and Pius VII were imprisoned by Napoleon.

Napoleon's Italian Campaign: 1795–8
I.93, III.37 & V.99

> *Terre Italique pres des monts tremblera,*
> *Lyon et coq non trop confederez:*
> *En lieu de peur l'un l'autre s'aidera.*
> *Seul Catulon et Celtes moderez.*

[1]Nostradamus' native province.

Translation:

> Italian lands near the mountains will tremble.
> Lyon and cockerel will not be in agreement:
> In a place of fear they will help one another,
> Only *Catulon* and Celts moderated.

By 1795, the French Republican army was powerful enough to move from defending their own borders to attacking their enemies. In that year, General Bonaparte led his troops across the Alps into northern Italy (then a possession of the Austrian Empire). His campaign was brilliantly successful and, by 1797, the entire peninsula as far as Rome was in French hands.

The second line of the quatrain mentions tension between "*Lyon et coq*". It sounds as though the city of Lyon is the subject, but Nostradamus used the spelling *lyon* for "lion" in other quatrains. Since the cockerel is the traditional emblem of France and the lion that of Britain, it is possible that this is a prediction of the growing enmity between these two nations in the 1790s. Before Napoleon's Italian campaign, Britain saw the new French Republic as detestable, but not as any great threat. However, as Napoleon's "Grand Army" grew in power, the British became increasingly worried about France. War was inevitable.

Later, when Napoleon was forced to abdicate in 1814, Britain became an ally of the reinstated French monarchy. This was partially through a mutual fear of the re-emergence of the French Republicans – as line three seems to hint.

Line four is difficult to fathom. The word "*Catulon*" sounds like Catalonia – a province of Spain – but Erica Cheetham translates it as "freedom", although she gives no explanation why. The word "*Celtes*" is usually translated to indicate the French – a Celtic race in the days of the Roman Empire.

> *Avant l'assult l'oraison prononcee,*
> *Milan prins d'aigle par embushes decevez:*
> *Muraille antique par canons enfoncee,*
> *Par feu et sang à mercy peu receus.*

Translation:

> Before the assault the speech is pronounced,
> Milan taken by the eagle deceived by ambush:
> The ancient walls shattered by cannons,
> In fire and blood few receive mercy.

The northern Italian city of Milan fell on 15 May 1796. Before his assault on the Austrian garrison, Napoleon made a speech to his troops that later became famous across Europe:

> Soldiers, you are starving and half-naked. Our government owes you much but can do nothing for you . . . I will lead you into the most fertile plains in the world . . . There you will find honour, glory and riches . . . Are you wanting in courage?

They were not. In fact the French prepared to attack so threateningly that the Austrians fled without firing a shot. Although this was not a victory "by ambush", as line two predicts, the emblem of the French Republican army was indeed an eagle.

The third and fourth lines of the quatrain could not be about the first capture of Milan – the town fell without bloodshed – but may refer to an event later that year. The citizens of the nearby town of Pavia revolted against the French occupying troops and were joined by the citizens of Milan. The rebellion was suppressed with great brutality.

> *Milan, Ferrare, Turin et Aquillaye,*
> *Capne Brundis vexés par gent Celtique:*
> *Par le Lion et phalange aquilee*
> *Quant Rome aura le chef vieux Britannique.*

Translation:

> Milan, Ferrare, Turin and Aquileia,
> Capua and Brindisi vexed by the Celtic nation:
> By the Lion and eagle phalanx
> When Rome will have the old British chief.

By 1798, Napoleon's army (the "eagle phalanx") had captured all the territories mentioned in the above quatrain, including Rome.

The last line could be a reference to the Cardinal of York – the last direct descendant of the British royal line of Stuart – who died in French-occupied Rome in 1807.

The Egyptian Campaign: 1798–9

II.86

> Naufrage à classe pres d'onde Hadriatique,
> La terre tremble esmeüe sus l'air en terre mis:
> Egypte tremble augment Mahometique.
> L'Heralt soi rendre à crier est commis.

Translation:

> A fleet will be wrecked near the Adriatic,
> The earth trembles pushed into the air and falls to earth:
> Egypt trembles Mohammedan increase.
> The Herald is commanded to cry surrender.

Following his victories in Italy, Napoleon led an expedition against Turkish-held Egypt – through which he hoped to strike at the British in India. Although the French force defeated a much larger army of Mameluke mercenaries at the Battle of the Pyramids, their fleet was destroyed by the British (under Admiral Nelson) at the Battle of Nile. Without naval support, the expedition had to be abandoned.

Whether the Nile can be considered "near the Adriatic", as it states in line one, is a moot point. Erica Cheetham suggests that the second line of the quatrain refers to the explosion of the French flagship during the battle, pieces of which rained down on the nearby shore.

Following this defeat, Napoleon besieged the Turkish held city of Acre (in present-day Israel). When plague broke out among his troops, Napoleon attempted to use trickery to win the city: he sent a herald who demanded Acre's immediate surrender, hoping that the Turkish leaders would lose their nerve. Unfortunately, the Turks knew of the sickness decimating their enemy and refused the demand. The French were forced to withdraw and General Bonaparte returned to France.

Napoleon the Emperor: 1799–1804
VII.13, VIII.57, IV.54 & VIII.53

De la cité marine et tributaire,
La teste raze prendra la satrapie:
Chasser sordide qui puis sera contraire
Par quartorze ans tiendra la tyrannie.

Translation:

Of the city marine and tributary,
The shaved head shall take the satrapy:
Chasing off the sordid who oppose him
For fourteen years he will hold the tyranny.

Napoleon won national fame for his defeat of the port of Toulon in 1793. Toulon is a "marine" city and its rebels were supported and "tributary" – as far as promises were concerned – to Britain. The term "satrapy", used at the end of the second line, is a Persian word for a governor/kingship, and may refer to Napoleon's promotion to brigadier general. However, the phrase that allows many writers to confidently attribute this prediction to Napoleon is *"teste raze"* or "shaven-head". His own soldiers nicknamed Napoleon *"le petit tondu"* – "the little crop-head".

The "sordid" opposition expelled in line three might be the defeated British support fleet at Toulon or, considering Nostradamus' ardent monarchism, it could describe the French Republican government which Napoleon overthrew in 1799.

From 18 Brumaire (9 November) 1799, Napoleon ruled as First Consul then, in 1804, as Emperor. His authoritarian, though not necessarily tyrannical[2], rule lasted until April 1814 – just over fourteen years, as line four of the quatrain states.

De soldat simple parviendra en empire,
De robe courte parviendra à la longue
Valliant aux armes en aglise on plus pire
Vexer les prestres comme l'eau fait l'esponge.

---

[2]Nostradamus may have been using the word "tyranny" in its original Greek meaning. "Tyrant" was first used to describe a usurper rather than despot, and this is certainly a better description of Napoleon, who came to power through a *coup d'état*, but ruled fairly.

Translation:

> From a simple soldier he will attain an empire,
> From a short robe he will attain one that is long
> Valiant in arms much worse towards the church
> He vexes the priests as water soaks a sponge.

The meaning of the first line of the quatrain, although self-evident, might just as easily refer to Adolf Hitler as Napoleon. The second line, on the other hand, neatly describes Napoleon's change from the short ceremonial robe of a First Consul to the flowing coronation robe of the Emperor of France.

Napoleon ended the persecution of the Catholic Church in France by guaranteeing freedom of religion in his new legal code. Unfortunately, Pope Pius VI had died in French captivity two months before the *coup d'état* that raised Napoleon to First Consul. The new incumbent – although naming himself Pius VII in remembrance of his martyred forebear – was reconciled enough to Napoleon to personally crown him Emperor in 1804. However, they fell out shortly thereafter and, in 1809, Napoleon annexed the Papal Estates and imprisoned Pius VII at Grenoble.

The friction between Napoleon's reformist/authoritarian regime and the conservative Church went on throughout his reign – a steady flow of insults and irritations like "water soaking a sponge".

> *Du nom qui onques ne fur au Roy Gaulois,*
> *Jamais ne fut un fouldre si craintif:*
> *Tremblant l'Italie, l'Espaine et les Anglois,*
> *De femme estangiers grandement attentif.*

Translation:

> Of name never held by a French King,
> Never was there such a fearful thunderbolt:
> Tremble Italians, Spanish and English,
> Of female strangers he will be most attentive.

Although an emperor rather than a king, Napoleon was certainly the first French monarch of that name. The description "thunderbolt" in line two also fits Napoleon. His speed of command caused the Duke of Wellington to comment that Bonaparte could handle batteries of cannon as swiftly as another man could handle pistols. Also, Napoleon's Imperial seal had at its centre an eagle gripping crossed thunderbolts. Lord Byron once wrote a poem about the French emperor that contained the line "Never yet was heard such thunder!" – a strikingly close match to the second line of the above quatrain.

Line three contains a distinct hint of national pride, but also states the truth: Italy, Spain and England were all invaded or threatened with invasion by Napoleon's armies.

Like many absolute leaders, Napoleon indulged his sexual passions with many women – French and "foreign" – yet he never allowed his amours to interfere with his work. In fact, quite the opposite is true.

In 1809, Napoleon divorced the Empress Josephine on the grounds that she had not given him an heir, and married Princess Marie-Louise of Austria. The match was primarily to link Napoleon's new dynasty with the ancient ruling house of Habsburg, but the forty-year-old emperor wooed the nineteen-year-old princess with touching and genuine romanticism.

The Failure at the Channel: 1804

VIII.53

> *Dedans Bolongne vouldra laver ses fautes,*
> *Il ne pourra au temple du soleil,*
> *Il volera faisant choses si haultes*
> *En hierarchie n'en fut oncq un pareil.*

Translation:

> Within Boulogne he will want to wash himself of his faults,
> He cannot at the temple of the Sun,
> He shall fly doing things too great
> In the hierarchy he never had an equal.

Napoleon was famously dismissive of the British, calling them a "nation of shopkeepers". For a while he considered invading the islands, and even started preparations at the Channel ports (such as

Boulogne). However, in 1804 he abandoned the project in favour of attacking Austria. If he had invaded Britain, even with only partial success, it is arguable that his defeat at Waterloo would never have happened. So the "faults" mentioned in line one might be Napoleon's basic misjudgment of the danger that Britain posed to France.

The "temple of the Sun", mentioned in line two, sounds like a typical Nostradamus classical allusion. In pre-Roman times, Britain had two famous shrines dedicated to the Sun. The first was Stonehenge, and the second was a temple on the north bank of the Thames – over the ruins of which Westminster Abbey was later built. Failing to invade Britain, Napoleon saw neither of these in his lifetime.

The last two lines are unspecific, but certainly fit Napoleon. In choosing to invade Austria, then Russia, Napoleon could be described as flying to "things too great". As to his being without equal in the hierarchy, as line four describes, many military historians rank Napoleon as the most gifted soldier of the last two centuries.

The Battle of Trafalgar: 21 October 1805

I.77

> *Entre deux mers dressera promontaire,*
> *Que plus mourra par le mords du cheval:*
> *Le sein Neptune pliera voille noire,*
> *Par Calpre et classe aupres de Rocheval.*

Translation:

> Between two seas stands a promontory,
> Who will then die by the bite of a horse:
> The proud Neptune folds black sails,
> Through *Calpre* the fleet nears *Rocheval*.

In October 1805, a French fleet under Admiral Villeneuve was ordered to ship an army from Cadiz in Spain to southern Italy. The thirty-three ships were attacked by twenty-seven ships of the British blockading force at Trafalgar – a point midway between

Cape Roche ("*Rocheval*") and the Rock of Gibraltar (a "promontory" between the "two seas" of the Atlantic and the Mediterranean). The word "*Calpre*" in the last line also sounds very like "*Calpe*" – an old name for Gibraltar.

The British fleet, under Admiral Nelson, split into two halves and attacked the French line of ships from two directions, outflanking and decimating them. Twenty French ships were sunk or taken, and 14,000 Frenchmen were killed or captured. The British lost no ships and only 1,500 men. Among the British dead was Lord Nelson himself. As a sign of mourning, his flagship *Victory* raised black sails as it returned to port – an event apparently predicted in line three. David Ovason further adds that the first three words of the line – "*Le sein Neptune*" – contain a partial anagram of the name "Nelson" (i.e. *Le SiEN NEptune* = NE L S EN).

Pierre Charles de Villeneuve, the French Commanding Admiral, was taken prisoner at Trafalgar. He was allowed to return to France in 1806, but on the way home committed suicide by pushing a long pin into his heart. David Ovason points out that line two may predict this if the word "*cheval*" ("horse") is read as a deliberate misspelling of "*cheville*" ("pin"). He further adds that in Nostradamus' day the term *cheval* also meant a wooden table across which condemned soldiers were tortured. Villeneuve killed himself from tortured guilt over Trafalgar.

The Spanish Peninsula War: 1808–1814

IV.70

> *Bien contigue des grans monts Pyrenées,*
> *Un contr l'aigle grand copie addresser:*
> *Ouvertes veines, forces exterminees,*
> *Comme jusque à Pau le chef viendra chasser.*

Translation:

> Very near the great Pyrenees mountains,
> One will raise a great army against the eagle:
> Opened veins, forces exterminated,
> As far as Pau the chief will chase them.

In 1808, Spain asked France for help in a war with Portugal. Napoleon complied and his generals soon conquered the small state. However, the Spanish were disturbed to note that strong French garrisons were being stationed in Spanish as well as Portuguese strongpoints across the Iberian peninsula. That same year, a palace revolution unseated Charles IV and installed a new Spanish monarch: Ferdinand VII. Napoleon forced Ferdinand to abdicate and crowned Joseph Bonaparte, his own brother, Joseph I of Spain.

The Spanish people rose in revolt against the French occupation force and were joined by their former enemy, Portugal. The British formed an alliance with the rebels and sent an army under Arthur Wellesley (later the Duke of Wellington) to Portugal. This might be what is meant by line two: the "eagle" being the banner of the French army and of Napoleon himself.

Wellesley defeated the French in battle after battle, forcing them back towards, and eventually over, the Pyrenees. Napoleon did what he could from a distance, but was too busy with conquests in the east to take the field against Wellesley himself. The city of Pau – mentioned in line four – is in south-west France on the eastern slopes of the Pyrenees. It was one of the towns the French retreated to following their total ejection from the Spanish peninsula in 1814.

Line three is grimly poetic, but is also accurate. The loss of 300,000 fighting men during the six-year conflict in Spain drained France of strength like a cut vein. Military historians believe that Napoleon's eventual defeat was as much a result of the Iberian war as it was of the retreat from Moscow and the Battle of Waterloo.

The Russian Disaster: 1812–13
IV.82, II.91 & II.99
>Amas s'approche vendant d'Esclavonie,
>L'Olestant vieux cité ruinera,
>Fort desolee verra sa Romanie.
>Puis la grand flamme estaindre ne sçaura.

Translation:

>A mass of men approaches from the land of the Slavs,
>The Destroyer will ruin the city,

He will see his *Romanie* quite desolated.
He will not know how to extinguish the great flame.

Napoleon's rule was aggressively expansionist. He not only saw himself as the founder of a new royal dynasty, but also as the man who would win France an empire to surpass that of Ancient Rome. War with his neighbours was inevitable.

In 1803, Britain declared war on France. Two years later, Russia and Austria joined Britain to form an anti-French coalition. Napoleon reacted with characteristic decisiveness, dropping plans to invade Britain and striking east into the Austrian Empire. He smashed the Austro–Russian forces at the Battle of Austerlitz on 2 December 1805. Then, in 1806, he annexed the Kingdom of Naples and the Republic of Holland, crowning his brothers Joseph and Louis as their new kings. In the same year, Prussia joined the anti-French coalition, but Napoleon destroyed the Prussian armies at the Battles of Jena and Auerstadt. The Russian army was also decisively defeated at the Battle of Freidland and, in 1807, Tsar Alexander I signed a peace treaty with the French. In 1809, Napoleon destroyed what remained of Austria's fighting strength at the Battle of Wagram.

By 1810, the Napoleonic Empire stretched from the Spanish peninsula to the borders of Russia – France was a superpower. Indeed, due to Napoleon's socially reforming rule of the states he had conquered (not to mention the efficiency and size of the French army), there seemed little reason for France not to maintain this powerful position. Then, in 1812, Napoleon's alliance with Tsar Alexander fell apart and the emperor invaded Russia.

Napoleon defeated the Tsar's army at the Battle of Borodino on 26 August and, by 14 September, had taken Moscow. It was at this point, when Napoleon was at the height of his military glory, that the Russian generals hit on the one strategy that could beat such a brilliant tactician – they chose not to fight him.

With the Russian winter fast coming on, Napoleon needed to crush the remainder of the Russian army in one last battle, but the Tsar's troops refused to be baited. Moscow had been evacuated, stripped of provisions, then set on fire, so Napoleon's troops now had to raid the countryside to find food. Army discipline was already eroded when the first snow began to fall in October and, reluctantly, the Emperor ordered a retreat.

Line one of the above quatrain describes a mass of men approaching from "*d'Esclavonie*" "the land of the Slavs". This might describe Napoleon's invasion from the Slavic lands east of Germany, but the term "mass" seems better to reflect the chaotic return journey from Moscow. Staggering through snowdrifts, the troops' discipline soon collapsed and the French army became a straggling disorganized mob.

The city ruined by the "Destroyer" in line two sounds like Moscow – although it was Russian patriots who torched the city, not Napoleon. In fact, he was desperate to extinguish the fires, but could not, as line four seems to suggest.

If the word "*Romanie*" in line three refers to Romania being desolated, it was a stunning piece of precognition by Nostradamus: Romania did not exist before 1861. Although Napoleon's army did retreat just north of what is now Romania – and found it horribly desolate – most Nostradamus scholars think the line is a prediction that the retreat from Russia would eventually cost Napoleon his lands in the Romagna region of northern Italy (along with all his other conquests).

> Soleil levant un grand feu on verra,
> Bruit et clarté vers Aquilon tendants:
> Dedans le rond mort et cris l'on orra,
> Par glaive, feu, faim, mort las attendants.

Translation:

> At sunrise a great fire will be seen,
> A noise and brightness in the direction of *Aquilon*:
> Inside the round death and cries will be heard,
> From sword, fire, famine, death to those who waited.

Radical Russian nationalists set Moscow alight on the night of 16 September 1812. The occupying French did not fully realize what had happened until dawn next day, by which time the blaze was out of control. Line two contains the word "*Aquilon*" (Latin for "northern") which Nostradamus often seems to have used to indicate Russia. Line three describes death and screams from "the round". This fits the burning of Moscow – a roughly circular city

– as 15,000 wounded Russian soldiers were burned to death in the inferno.

The last line may also be a reference to the suffering of these men, but sounds more like a description of the agonies of the retreating French army. All the way back to French-held territory, the Russian army attacked the enemy using hit-and-run tactics. French soldiers who managed to escape the Russian harassment often met a grimmer end in the cold.[3]

> *Terroir Romain qu'interpretoit augure,*
> *Par gent Gauloise par trop sera vexée:*
> *Mais nation Celtique craindra l'heure,*
> *Boreas, classe trop loing l'avoir poussée.*

Translation:

> The Roman land that the auger interprets,
> Will be greatly vexed by the French:
> But the Celtic nation will fear the hour,
> North wind, fleet driven too far.

As we have seen, Napoleon annexed the Papal Estates in 1809, and lines one and two seem to predict this event (Nostradamus often uses the word "auger" to indicate a pope). Lines three and four, in turn, predict a fearful time for France, however, the actual warning is infuriatingly vague. Erica Cheetham argues that the disaster of the Russian campaign is described, because the word "*Boreas*" is Latin for "north wind".

Stewart Robb, in *Nostradamus and Napoleon*, supports Cheetham's interpretation by pointing out that the word "*classe*", in the last line, had a meaning other than "fleet" in the early nineteenth century: the term was also used to describe Napoleon's conscripted troops.

Since this piece of French slang was, naturally, not current in

---

[3] In *War and Peace*, Tolstoy used real accounts of the Russian campaign as a basis for the experiences of his fictional characters. He describes the Russians finding a group of French soldiers sitting round the embers of a huge bonfire. The men had been scorched on their hands and faces from sitting so near the flames, but all were dead – their backs frozen solid.

Nostradamus' time, readers must decide for themselves whether it is either a coincidence or an astoundingly precise prediction. Robb also suggests that Nostradamus was drawing a direct causal link between the theft of the papal lands and the later disastrous retreat from Russia.

Of 600,000 men of the Grand Army that marched into Russia, only 30,000 returned alive. Any possibility of France holding on to her European empire disappeared.

The Escape from Elba: 26 February 1815

II.66

Par grans dangeriers le captif eschapé,
Peu de temps grand a fortune changeé:
Dans le palais le peuple est attrapé,
Par bon augure la cité assiegée.

Translation:

Through great dangers the captive escapes,
In a short time his fortune will change:
In the palace the people are trapped,
By good omen the city besieged.

Napoleon had stripped his empire of troops for the Russian expedition and now most of them were dead. Through 1813 he marshalled what forces he had left, but all of Europe was now allied against him and he could do nothing but retreat to Paris with the enemy hard on his heels. In April 1814, as Cossack troops were watering their horses in the Seine, Napoleon's generals forced him to abdicate.

The Allies agreed to peace with France provided Louis XVIII – Louis XVI's brother – was placed on the throne and Napoleon was condemned to lifelong exile. Bonaparte was sent to the small Mediterranean island of Elba with a ceremonial guard of just under a thousand men. As a final, thinly-veiled insult, the Allies allowed Napoleon to keep the title of emperor, but reduced his empire to Elba alone.

On 26 February 1815, Napoleon and his bodyguard escaped Elba and returned to mainland France. Louis XVIII sent a large army to crush Napoleon's thousand men, but when the forces met, the king's troops immediately joined Napoleon and followed him back to Paris. He was made Emperor of France once more on 20 March.

Although non-specific in detail, line one could describe Napoleon's escape – one of the most important in European history. Line two may be read in one of two ways: that the luck of the "*captif*" will dramatically change for the good or ill. Both were true of Napoleon. He went from exile to reinstated Emperor of France in a matter of weeks. However, although he sued the Allies for peace and even offered to abdicate in favour of his baby son, they pronounced him an "enemy of humanity" and declared war. By the end of June, he was a captive in exile once again.

Line three of the quatrain sounds odd but, as is often the case with Nostradamus, proves accurate when closely examined. Napoleon arrived in Paris on 20 March, and made his way to the palace followed by an ecstatic crowd. As Bonaparte alighted from his coach, the mob lifted him on their shoulders and carried him to the (hurriedly vacated) king's apartments. It was reported that this happy crowd so packed the palace corridors that nobody could get in or out for some hours – greatly impeding urgent state business.

The last line is vague. Paris had already been besieged by the Allies, and was besieged again following Waterloo. What "good omen" may have been connected with these events is unclear.

Waterloo: 18 June 1815

I.23 & IV.75

Au mois troisiesme se levant le soleil
Sanglier, Liepard au champ Mars pour comattre:
Liepard laissé, au ciel extend son oeil,
Un aigle autour du Soleil voit s'esbattre.

Translation:

In the third month at sunrise
Wild Boar, Leopard towards the field of Mars to combat:
The Leopard wearies, lifts his eye to the sky,
An eagle playing about the Sun.

When the former anti-Napoleon Allies heard that he had returned to Paris, they immediately set about preparing a combined army to crush him once and for all. Napoleon, with characteristic swiftness, gathered his own troops and struck at his enemies before they could marshal their forces.

On 15 June 1815, the French army of 123,000 men crossed the Belgian frontier. Facing them were two military forces: an army of 116,000 Prussians and another of 93,000 British troops. These latter were commanded by Napoleon's old nemesis from the Peninsula War – Arthur Wellesley, the Duke of Wellington. Had the Allied armies stayed together, it is doubtful that even Napoleon would have dared such odds, but the Prussians and the British had foolishly separated.

On 16 June, the Prussians, under Field Marshal Blücher, were defeated and forced to retreat. Napoleon sent a third of his force, under General Grouchy, to chase the surviving 70,000 Prussians – hoping to destroy them or, at the very least, stop them reinforcing Wellington.

On the morning of 18 June, Napoleon attacked Wellington's force on a strip of farmland called Waterloo. The British (reinforced by a contingent of Dutch troops, but depleted by earlier fighting) numbered 67,000. The French had 74,000 soldiers and almost double the number of the enemy's cannons. Napoleon had never yet lost a battle with the odds so in his favour.

If the above quatrain is a prediction of Waterloo, it is one of the most strikingly accurate and poetic of all those in the *Centuries*. As stated in the first line, the battle took place exactly three months after Napoleon's return to the French throne. It is also worth noting that the Emperor had regained power in March (the "third month") on the day before the vernal equinox – a date that would have been important to the astrologer in Nostradamus. This may explain the reference to "sunrise" at the end of the line.

The outcome of the Battle of Waterloo hung on whether Blücher's Prussians could evade General Grouchy and reinforce Wellington. Line two seems to hint at this because the emblem of the Prussian army was a wild boar and the British lion might have been rendered as a leopard – Napoleon himself used to describe the heraldic British lion dismissively as "the Leopard of England".

The battle began at 11.30 in the morning. By mid-afternoon the British forces were sagging. The French attacks were being held, but it seemed only a matter of time before the British lines broke. Looking southward across the battle, Wellington would have seen the French Imperial eagle standards "playing about the [sinking] sun", just as lines three and four seem to describe.

> *Prest á combatre fera defection.*
> *Chef adversaire obtiendra la victoire.*
> *L'arriere garde fera defension,*
> *Les deffaillans mort au blanc territoire.*

Translation:

> One ready to fight will desert.
> Chief adversary obtains the victory.
> The rear guard makes the defence,
> Those that fall away die in a white country.

At four o'clock in the afternoon, the army of 70,000 Prussians attacked the French right wing. Since the battle began, Napoleon had sent several messages to General Grouchy – who was still in pursuit of the rear of the Prussian army – ordering him to either engage the Prussian forces or stop following them and rejoin the main army. Grouchy did neither. Although his troops were "ready to fight", as line one states, Grouchy simply pursued Blücher, not even attempting to cut off his march towards Waterloo and Wellington. Although not really a desertion, Grouchy's failure to follow orders lost Napoleon the battle.

Wellington had long been Napoleon's "chief adversary", as line two describes. He had consistently beaten French armies in Spain and Napoleon's generals were afraid of him. Although Waterloo was the first battle in which Wellington and Napoleon had actually fought against each other, their personal enmity for one another was long-standing. The return of Blücher's Prussians to the conflict dashed any hope that the French might win the day so, as line two states, Wellington "obtained the victory".

The Allies lost 22,000 men in the battle, while the French lost 40,000. Certainly more Frenchmen would have died in the rout that followed if the Old Guard (a regiment of fiercely loyal veterans) had not fought a valiant rearguard action – eventually being killed to the last man – an event apparently described by line three.

The meaning of line four is uncertain. It might be an out-of-place reference to the retreat from Moscow: men dying in a country white with snow. On the other hand, it could be a prediction of the return of Louis XVIII to the French throne. Louis's flag was Bourbon white. It was reported that the people of Paris were so anxious to curry favour with the new regime that, on Napoleon's second arrest, the city looked as if it was carpeted in snow because of all the white banners and cockades.

St Helena: 1815–21

I.32

> *Le grand empire sera tost translaté,*
> *En lieu petit, qui bien tost viendra croistre:*
> *Lieu bien infime d'exigue comté,*
> *Ou au milieu viendra poser son sceptre.*

Translation:

> The great empire will soon be translated,
> To a small place, which soon will begin to grow:
> A miserable place of small area,
> In the middle of which he will lay down his sceptre.

Following Waterloo, Napoleon returned to Paris. Although the Parisian populace begged him to fight on, the generals and politicians abandoned his cause. He fled to the port of Rochefort, but there surrendered to the British warship *HMS Bellerophon*. His second and final exile was to the small Atlantic island of St Helena.

Nostradamus uses the word "empire" in the first line of the quatrain, as opposed to "kingdom" or "nation." Napoleon is one of the few leaders, since Nostradamus' day, to have "translated" a great empire for a "small place."

The end of line two may be a reference to Napoleon's hundred-day return to power after escaping Elba, but the rest of the quatrain sounds like a grim description of Napoleon's final site of imprisonment.

Napoleon died of stomach cancer on St Helena on 5 May 1821 (although there is some evidence that he was poisoned). He was fifty-two years old.

Chapter 16

Nostradamus and the Nineteenth Century

It must be admitted that, when we come to the nineteenth century, the prophet's obsession with his own country begins to look like parochialism. He fails to foresee Dalton's atomic theory, Darwin's theory of evolution, the discovery of steam power, the Industrial Revolution, the South Sea Bubble or the American Civil War. Yet there are prophecies that appear to be detailed accounts of French political life over the same period.

The relative significance (or insignificance) of the events does not seem to have been the deciding factor. Nostradamus was apparently quite aware that France would become a secondary world power after the defeat of Napoleon Bonaparte, but he is always, at heart, a Frenchman. Before we condemn him as small-minded, we should perhaps ask if we ourselves – placed in a position of foreseeing the future – would not take more interest in our own culture than those of other countries.

The Fall of Sultan Selim III: 1807

I.52

> Les deux malins de Scorpion conjoinct,
> Le grand seigneur meutri dedans sa salle:
> Peste à l'Eglise le nouveau roy joinct
> L'Europe basse et Septentrionale.

Translation:

> The two evils of Scorpio conjunct,
> The great lord murdered in his hall:
> Plague to the Church by the new king
> Lower Europe and the North.

The first line of this quatrain seems to be another of Nostradamus' astrological dates. The two planets of evil portent are usually accepted to be Mars (representing war) and Saturn (representing old age and decay). These conjoin in the sign of Scorpio around three times every hundred years, giving us fourteen such dates since 1555.

One such conjunction took place in 1807 – the year that Sultan Selim III of the Ottoman Empire was deposed. He was murdered the following year. Erica Cheetham points out that one of Selim's titles was "Seignoir": just as the quatrain says.

The last two lines seem to link the quatrain to events around 1807. By that time the Catholic Church was in direct conflict with Napoleon, although the Pope himself had crowned him emperor ("new king") only three years earlier. Bonaparte had also "plagued" "lower" and "Northern" Europe by that time, defeating the Austrians, Prussians and the Russians in major battles.

The End of Napoleon's Luck: 1809–15
II.44 & I.88

> *L'aigle pousée entour de pavillions,*
> *Par autres oiseaux d'entour sera chassée:*
> *Quand bruit des cymbees, tubes et sonaillons,*
> *Rendront le sens de la dame insensée.*

Translation:

> The eagle flying among the pavilions,
> By other birds shall be driven away:
> When the sound of cymbals, trumpets and bells,
> Restores sense to the lady insane.

Nostradamus scholars generally agree that when the seer mentions an "eagle", he is often referring to the badge of Napoleon Bonaparte. Following the emperor's disastrous retreat from Moscow in 1812–13, his previously cautious European enemies found the courage to attack him. The image of a flock of lesser birds harrying an eagle over military pavilions is reminiscent poetically of these events.

The third and fourth lines depict music returning a lady to her senses. Such a vague outline is, needless to say, difficult to pin down to an actual event. Some Nostradamus scholars believe that the "dame" is France, returned to Bourbon rule under Louis XVIII with military pomp and music. Others suggest the lines may concern the mad jealousy of the Empress Josephine, divorced by Napoleon in 1809.

There is little in the quatrain to back the second interpretation, apart from the link with Napoleon's defeat in the first two lines; it is a traditional French belief that the emperor's luck abandoned him when he abandoned Josephine.

> *Le divin mal surprendra le grand prince,*
> *Un peu devant aura femme espousse.*
> *Son appuy et credit à un coup viendra mince,*
> *Conseil mourra pour la teste rasée.*

Translation:

> The divine malady overtakes the great prince,
> A little while after he marries a woman.
> His support and credit become slender,
> Council will die away for the shaven head.

This quatrain also seems to predict the fall from luck of a "great prince". The "divine malady" mentioned in the first line sounds like another of Nostradamus' classical allusions. In Ancient Greece, the human weakness that was supposed to provoke divine vengeance was hubris (conceit and overweening ambition) – a failing to which Napoleon was rather prone.

The second line connects this fall from grace with an ill-starred marriage. Again, this sounds like Napoleon's change of fortune after divorcing Josephine and marrying into the royal line of Habsburg.

The third line is only accurate of Napoleon after his retreat from Moscow in 1812. Even then, the Emperor's "support and credit" only ran short with his own politicians and generals – the French public were still enamoured of the emperor, even after Waterloo.

The last line is generally true of Napoleon's last years in power. A combination of absolute power, middle age, a crushing workload and chronic stomach ulcers made him less prone to listen to counsels that he did not agree with. The result was that sycophants surrounded him and his good counsellors faded into the background.

The last two words of the quatrain echo quatrain 131 of *Century VII: "teste razé"*, or "shaven-head". Napoleon's troops nicknamed him *"le petit tondu"*, or "the little crop-head".

The Fall of Paris: 3 July 1815

IX.86

> *Du bourg Lareyne ne paviendront droit à Chartres*
> *Et feront pres du pont Anthoni pause,*
> *Sept pour la paix cantelleux comme martres.*
> *Feront entrée d'armee à Paris clause.*

Translation:

> From Bourge-la-Reine they will not come straight to Chartres
> And near the Pont d'Anthony they will pause,
> Seven for peace crafty as martens.
> Armies enter a closed Paris.

Following the French defeat at Waterloo, the allied elements of seven nations' armies entered Paris on 3 July 1815: Britain, Russia, Austria, Prussia, Sweden, Spain and Portugal. The seer is perhaps being insulting to them when he calls them as "crafty as martens",[1] but he also seems to admit that their mission was not one of conquest, but to bring peace (albeit on their own terms).

There was no battle for the French capital and the Allies easily occupied and "closed" Paris because the shattered French army had already left the city. Just as lines one and two describe, the

[1] Small, wily carnivores – closely akin to weasels – native to northern Europe.

remnant of Napoleon's Grand Army made its way to the Loire town of Chartres via Bourge-la-Reine, and even bivouacked a night under the Pont d'Anthony.

The 1815 Occupation of France

I.20

> Tours, Orleans, Blois, Angers, Reims, et Nantes,
> Cités vexées par subit changement:
> Par langues estranges seront tenues tentes,
> Fleuves, dards Rones, terre et mer tremblement.

Translation:

> Tours, Orleans, Blois, Angers, Reims and Nantes,
> Cities vexed by sudden change:
> By strange languages tents shall be pitched,
> Rivers, darts at Rennes, land and sea tremble.

The first three lines of the above quatrain seem to predict a foreign invasion of northern France, where all the cities listed in the first line are situated. Such an event has taken place several times in the last two centuries, but not between 1815 and Nostradamus' day.

The 1815 invasion is the most likely candidate for this prediction (to date) because the anti-Napoleonic Allies were a more mixed group of nationalities ("*langues estranges*") than in any subsequent invasion. The cities mentioned were also "vexed by sudden change" in this period: Napoleon fell in 1814, returned in 1815 to dethrone Louis XVIII, was dethroned himself and exiled 100 days later, and Louis again became king.

The last line is less easy to fathom. Rennes is another northern French town that was briefly occupied in 1815, but no record of an earthquake or similar event is known from this time.

The Assassination of the Duc de Berry: 13 February 1820

III.96 & I.84

> Chef de Fossan aura gorge coupee,
> Par le ducteur du limier et laurier,
> La faict patre par de mont Tarpee,
> Saturne en Leo treziesme de Fevrier.

Translation:

> The Chief of the *Fossan* has his throat cut,
> By the keeper of hunters and greyhounds,
> The act committed by those of the Tarpian Rock,
> Saturn in Leo thirteenth of February.

Louis XVIII lived for nine years after the exile of Napoleon to St Helena. Although he initially persecuted the remaining French Bonapartists and Republicans, Louis was also increasingly attracted to the new liberal doctrines of state and kingship. However, this liberality ceased following the murder of his son and heir, the Duc de Berry, in 1820.

The Duc was stabbed to death while attending the opera on 13 February – the date given in line four of the above quatrain. The term "Saturn in Leo" is astrological: the sign of Aquarius rules Saturn, so when that planet is in the opposing house of Leo, it is said to be in a "malevolent" position.

The murderer was a Republican called Louvel. In the days of the Roman Republic, traitors were executed by being thrown off the Tarpean Rock; thus line three seems to hint at Louvel's political motivations. Line two could also be true of Louvel, who worked in the royal stables and might well have been in charge of hunting horses and greyhounds. Unfortunately, line one throws doubt on this interpretation, because the Duc de Berry did not have his throat cut. On the other hand, Erica Cheetham offers a link (if somewhat tenuous) between de Berry and the phrase "Chief of the *Fossan*" – de Berry's maternal grandfather was King of Fossano in Sardinia.

> *Lune obscurcie aux profondes tenebres,*
> *Son frere passe de couleur ferrugine:*
> *La grand caché long temps soubs les tenebres,*
> *Tiedera fer dans la plaie sanguine.*

Translation:

> The Moon will be obscured by profound darkness,
> Her brother passes the rusty colour:

> The great one hidden a long time in shadow,
> Cools the blade in the bloody wound.

Erica Cheetham also connects this quatrain with the assassination of the Duc de Berry, but has to use some rather circuitous arguments to justify her translation.

She suggests that the first three lines describe poetically the Comte d'Artois – younger brother of Louis XVI and Louis XVIII. D'Artois escaped into exile during the Revolution and remained there, "obscured by profound darkness", for over two decades. Cheetham translates the second line to read: "His brother becomes bright red in colour" taking this to be a reference to the execution of Louis XVI. The third line, she says, is a further comment on d'Artois's long period in the political wilderness. Even following the restoration of the Bourbon monarchy, d'Artois found that his reactionary, ultra-royalist views were out of step with the liberal trends at court.

Whether or not one finds the above argument overstretched, line four does sound a grimly accurate description of de Berry's assassination. As de Berry lay stabbed – the blade of the murder weapon literally cooling in his dying flesh – he is said to have moaned: "I am murdered. I am holding the hilt of the dagger."

Despite the accusatory sound of the last two lines of the quatrain, it is highly unlikely that the Comte d'Artois had anything to do with his nephew's murder. Nevertheless, he did gain by it. First, his elder brother Louis XVIII swung to the ultra-royalist party and ended his liberal reforms. Second, d'Artois became the heir apparent following the murder; on Louis's death in 1824, he was crowned Charles X of France.

Pax Britannica

X.42

> *Le regne humain d'Anglique geniture,*
> *Fera son regne paix union tenir,*
> *Captive guerre demi de sa closture,*
> *Long Temps la paix leur fera maintenir.*

Translation:

> The humane reign of English offspring,
> Shall cause the reign of peace and union,
> Captive war half enclosed,
> A long time the peace maintained by them.

This quatrain delighted British Nostradamus scholars in the nine-teenth- and early twentieth century, as it all but proclaims "Rule Britannia!"

As we have already seen (in the chapter on Nostradamus' predic-tions for the seventeenth century), the seer was apparently quite aware that the English would achieve an ocean-spanning "great empire"[2] – although England was only a third-rate power in Nostradamus' day. This quatrain goes even further by predicting that England would reign in "peace and union". Taking the two quatrains together, Victorians saw a virtual endorsement of the British Empire.

Whether British Imperialists were correct to claim that their empire was so "humane" is a matter for debate – but, ignoring this aspect, the quatrain does contain another striking prediction. In both the famous "British Empire" quatrains, Nostradamus refers to "England" and the "English" ("*Angleterre*" and "*Anglique*"), not to "Great Britain" or the "British". This is hardly surprising; England and Wales were only joined in the seer's own lifetime (in 1543); Scotland remained separate until 1707, and Ireland was treated as little more than a protectorate up to the 1920s. The idea of the "British Nation" was not widespread in the sixteenth century, nor was the possibility of the islands becoming a "United Kingdom". Nevertheless, line two of the quatrain predicts the "English offspring" (perhaps meaning the descendants of the English of the seer's own day) would rule a "union".

The Abandoned Heir: 1820

V.39

> *Du vrai rameau de fleur de lys issue*
> *Mis et logé heretier de Hetrurie:*
> *Son sang antique de long main tissu*
> *Fera Florence florir en l'armoirie.*

[2] *Century X*, quatrain 100.

Translation:

> Out of the branch of the fleur-de-lys issue
> Placed and lodged as heir to Etruria:
> His ancient blood a long woven tissue
> Will make the coat of arms of Florence flourish.

Although the Comte d'Artois was named the heir to Louis XVIII following the murder of the Duc de Berry, there was another claimant to the throne of France. The Duchess de Berry was two months pregnant when her husband was killed. The resulting son was named the Comte de Chambord and, when d'Artois became Charles X, was declared the heir apparent.

However, the child's late birth was the cause of a national controversy. The Duc d'Orleans – himself in line to the throne, although not of pure Bourbon blood – accused the Duchess of trying to foist a bastard on the royal family. In 1830, following the July Revolution, the boy and his mother went into self-imposed exile in Venice. Northern Italy was also the home of the ancient people called Etruscans, their country being called Etruria (see line two above).

The Comte de Chambord was the last of the true French Bourbon line, but never attained his birthright. The Duc d'Orleans took the throne after the abdication of Charles X (as we will see below). Nevertheless, the Comte de Chambord lived a happy and productive life. In 1846, he married the daughter of the Duke of Florence. Both families – who shared the fleur-de-lys on their coats of arms – did well from the union, just as the quatrain seems to predict.

The Murder of Louis Bourbon Condé: 1830

I.39

> *De nuict dans lict le suspresme estrangle,*
> *Par trop avoir sejourné, blond esleu:*
> *Par trois l'empire subrogé exanche,*
> *A mort mettra carte, et pacuet ne leu.*

Translation:

> At night in bed the final one is strangled,
>   For much bribery, blond elect:
> By three substitutes the empire enslaved,
> He is put to death document, and packet unread.

Erica Cheetham thinks this quatrain predicts the death of Louis Bourbon Condé. The last of the Condé line ("the final one"), Louis was found hanged in his bedroom in 1830. Although accepted as suicide, the rumour went about that he had actually been throttled in bed, then hanged from a rafter to disguise the strangulation marks. The public blamed Louis Phillipe, Duc d'Orleans.

If Condé was murdered, it was probably for the support ("bribery") he gave to the cause of the Comte de Chambord – son of the Duc de Berry and heir elect ("*esleu*") to Charles X. The "three substitutes", seen enslaving the "empire" in line three, could therefore be the three regimes that usurped the throne from the Bourbons: Louis Phillipe, the Second Republic, then Napoleon III.

Condé is believed to have left a will favouring the young Comte de Chambord, but this was apparently substituted for an earlier testament, favouring the son of Louis Phillipe, Duc d'Orleans. This may explain the meaning of the last line of the quatrain.

Citizen King: 1830

V.69

> *Plus ne sera le grand en faux sommeil,*
> *L'inquietude viendra prendre repoz:*
> *Dresser phalange d'or, azur, et vermeil,*
> *Subjuger Affrique la ronger jusques oz.*

Translation:

> No more will the great one be in a false sleep,
>   Unease takes the place of repose:
> He shall raise the phalanx of gold, azure and vermilion,
> Subjugating Africa and gnawing it down to the bone.

By 1830, the reactionary, seventy-three-year-old Charles X had pushed France to the edge of another revolution. His overriding of the democratic Chamber of Deputies, his attempts to restrict the voting franchise and his draconian curbs on the free press roused the people of Paris to open rebellion. On 26 July they stormed and took the Hôtel de Ville – the centre of government. After three days of fighting, Charles saw that his troops could not regain control of the streets, so he capitulated to the rebels' demands and was forced to abdicate.

The leaders of the July Revolution called for a return to the Republic, but the liberal bourgeoisie managed to have Louis Phillipe, Duc d'Orleans, crowned as a constitutional and legally restricted monarch. As such, he was nicknamed "Citizen King".

This Louis Phillipe was the same Duc d'Orleans who had questioned the legitimacy of the Bourbon heir, the Comte de Chambord. He was also one of the men implicated in the death of Louis Bourbon Condé, not least because the dead man's estates were suspiciously handed over to d'Orleans's son. He was clearly something of a political schemer, unwilling to risk an open attempt on the throne, but always plotting to that end. The first line of the quatrain, depicting a "great one" ending his pretence of sleep, poetically describes Louis Phillipe's election to the throne after a decade of plotting.

The second line also fits Louis Phillipe. Having achieved his end, he found kingship a very mixed blessing. Over the next eighteen years, he must often have thought ironically of the comparative repose of his days as a schemer compared to the uneasy task of actually ruling a volatile and quickly-changing France.

The third line mentions a "phalanx of gold, azure and vermilion". Louis Phillipe was the first king of France to adopt the revolutionary tricolour flag: three bars ("phalanx") of red ("vermilion"), white ("gold") and blue ("azure").

This year, 1830, was also the year that the French army captured Algiers. Over the next two decades, the French annexed and colonized all of Algeria. In French eyes they were civilizing and bringing modern amenities to the Algerians. To the Arabs, however, the French were arrogant imperialists who treated them as third-class citizens. Troubles continued for the next century, culminating in the 1954 War of Algerian Independence. This bitter conflict continued until the French were forced to give the colony independence in 1962.

Since that time, Algeria has had continuous misfortune. When the general election of 1992 was on the point of being won by an Islamic fundamentalist party, the military cancelled the ballot, seized power and declared a state of emergency. The resulting conflict between the military government and Islamic terror groups was horrifically savage – both sides apparently targeting women and children in wholesale slaughters. French influence, backing the military regime, has been widely rumoured. If so, France can still be accused of "gnawing [Algeria] down to the bone", as Nostradamus seems to suggest in the last line of the quatrain.

Napoleon's Bones: 1840

V.7

> Du Triumvir seront trouvé les os,
> Cherchant profond thresor aenigmatique,
> Ceux d'alentour ne seront en repos.
> Ce concaver marbre et plomb metallique.

Translation:

> The bones of the Triumvir will be found,
> When they search for a deep and enigmatic treasure,
> Those around will not be restful.
> This concavity of marble and metallic lead.

When Napoleon died in 1821, he was buried on his island of exile, St Helena. Louis XVIII or Charles X would have no more wanted the remains of the former emperor brought home than they would have considered building a marble tomb for the regicide Robespierre. King Louis Phillipe, on the other hand, saw Napoleon's bones as a way to make peace with the still-active Bonapartist faction and boost his own flagging popularity. In 1840, he ordered Napoleon's body to be disinterred and brought back to Paris.

The first line of the above quatrain describes the finding of the bones of the "Triumvir".[3] The First Republic – which Napoleon

[3] A Latin term for one of three joint rulers of a state.

took over in the Brumaire coup – was run by a "Directory" of five men. One of Napoleon's first acts on taking power was to reduce this number to three – with himself as ruling First Consul. Thus he could certainly be called a "Triumvir".

The "deep and enigmatic treasure" mentioned in line two could be the secret of Napoleon I's seemingly boundless popularity with the French people – an approval that King Louis Phillipe hoped to find through association with the dead emperor. It is some indication of the king's desperation that he attempted to make friends with the Bonapartists – a group dedicated to putting Napoleon's nephew, Louis Napoleon Bonaparte, on Louis Phillipe's throne.

Despite Louis Phillipe's efforts, the Bonapartists were certainly "not restful", as line three predicts. They had led two revolts against the Citizen King in 1836 and 1840, and were only slightly mollified by the return of "their Emperor" to Paris.

The bones of Napoleon Bonaparte were reinterred with great ceremony and pomp at Les Invalides, on the left bank of the Seine. As line four of the quatrain predicts, the body was placed in a lead coffin in a marble tomb.

The Reign and Fall of the Citizen King: 1830–48
IX.89

> *Sept ans Philip fortune prospere,*
> *Rabaissera des Arabes l'effaict,*
> *Puis son midi perplex rebours affaire*
> *Jeune ognion abismera son fort.*

Translation:

> Seven years Philip's fortune will prosper,
> Cutting down the Arab exertions,
> Then in the middle of a perplexing and contrary affair,
> Young *ognion* shall put down his strength.

The first seven years of Louis Phillipe's reign were troubled but fundamentally successful. Although disappointed Republicans and the starving poor often rioted, the Bourgeois Chamber of Deputies provided solid support for their "Citizen King." Arab attempts to block the French colonization of Algeria were easily frustrated by Louis Phillipe's troops (just as line two predicts) and France began to win back her prestige in international affairs.

Louis Phillipe was unhappy with his limited position during this period, but saw that he would go the way of Charles X if he attempted to increase the political power of the monarchy. This did not stop him establishing his Bourbon-Orleans family as the new French royal dynasty and dispensing honours and government posts to his personal cronies. The result was that by the mid-point of his eighteen-year reign, corruption was rife in the Palace.

The "perplexing and contrary affair", mentioned in line three, could be the so-called "Eastern Question", concerning the decrepitude of the once-feared Ottoman Empire. As the Turks continued to lose their grip on Greece and the Balkans, it was becoming increasingly clear that Russia was growing stronger. Britain and France saw Russian expansion as a threat to the balance of power in Europe and tried various diplomatic measures to curb the Tsar's power. The Eastern Question was still unresolved when Louis Phillipe was toppled from his throne.

By the late 1840s, Louis Phillipe's corrupt regime had forced many of his former backers in the Chamber of Deputies to seriously consider the creation of a new republic. Although not attempting to rule as an absolute monarch, the king used his veto to block the social reforms that France desperately needed to modernize herself. Many, therefore, saw the monarchy itself as an obstacle to progress.

The end came in September 1848, the year of several European revolutions, when the king sent troops to crush a Republican demonstration in central Paris. The resulting riot turned into a full-scale revolution and Louis Phillipe, like Charles X before him, was forced to abdicate and flee into exile. A group of Republican leaders formed the new government and declared the birth of the Second Republic.

Erica Cheetham connects this event with the word "*ognion*" in line four. She suggests that this word should actually read "*Ogmios*" – the Celtic Hercules – and can be seen as an image of resurgent French Republicanism.

The End of the Second Republic and the Birth of the Second French Empire: 1848–52

VIII.42

> Esleu sera Renad ne sonnant mot,
> Faisant le faint public vivant pain d'orge,
> Tyranniser apres tant à un coup,
> Mettant pied des plus grands sur la gorge.

Translation:

> The Fox is elected without saying a word,
> Playing the saint in public while eating barley bread,
> A tyrant after such a coup,
> Putting his feet on the necks of the greatest ones.

The constitution of the new French Republic created the post of President, to act in concert with the elected senate. One of the candidates for the first presidential election in 1859 was Louis Napoleon Bonaparte, the nephew of the Emperor Napoleon. Despite his support from the Bonapartists, the political pundits ignored Louis Napoleon as a rank outsider, thus his landslide victory came as something of a shock to the French political establishment.

Louis Napoleon rode to power on a groundswell of popular support created by his uncle's undying popularity and his own daring escape from imprisonment by King Louis Phillipe in 1856. Nostradamus' description, in line one, of a foxy politician being elected without having to utter a word on his policies is, therefore, true of President Bonaparte.

Unfortunately for Louis Bonaparte, the presidency only ran for four years, and the constitution banned further election of the same person. So for two years, he pretended to be an ardent Republican while secretly plotting to overthrow the state. This situation fits the prediction in line two – a "saint in public" "eating barley bread", (a French equivalent of the British phrase, "feathering one's own nest").

On 2 December 1851, the president of France staged a *coup d'état*. He declared the Second Republic dead and initiated the "Second Empire". He also claimed the right to be called "the Emperor Napoleon", but because the first Napoleon's son had been declared Napoleon II in 1815, Louis Bonaparte had to settle for the title "Napoleon III".

Nostradamus' term "Tyrannizer", at the beginning of line three, is a quite accurate description of the early part of Napoleon III's reign. He forcefully repressed political opposition, exiled his enemies, and his secret police – the *ratapoils* – were simply club-wielding thugs. So Napoleon III certainly put his "feet on the necks" of the "greatest ones" of the banned Republican movement, as line four describes.

The Attempted Assassination of Napoleon III: 14 January 1858
V.9 & V.10

> Jusques au fonds la grand arq demolue,
> Par chef captif, l'ami anticipé:
> Naistra de dame front face chevelue,
> Lor par astuce Duc à mort attrapé.

Translation:

> Below the great fallen arch,
> By the chief captive, the friend anticipated:
> Son born of a woman hairy forehead and faced,
> Then through cunning the Duke escapes death.

The first decade of Napoleon III's rule was dictatorial and repressive. Many Frenchmen must have anticipated or hoped for an attempt on the Emperor's life but, when this eventually happened in 1858, its source proved surprising.

In his younger days, Louis Bonaparte had been something of a political radical and had fervently supported the cause of Italian nationalism. Now, as Napoleon III, he was in a prime position to help his former friends, but (apparently) did nothing. A small group of Italian revolutionaries, led by Count Felice Orsini, decided to make him pay for this betrayal. The conspirators tried to blow the emperor to pieces with a bomb as he left the Paris Opera on 14 January 1858. The explosion damaged the building ("the great fallen arch" mentioned in line one of the quatrain) and killed a number of innocent bystanders, but Napoleon III escaped with only minor wounds.

Line two may be a prediction of the arrest of Pieri – one of the three co-conspirators with Orsini – the night before the assassination attempt. This interpretation, coupled with the use of the word "cunning" in line four, allows Erica Cheetham to argue that Napoleon III escaped death through foreknowledge of the plot, although the history books offer no supporting evidence for this theory.

Line three has no obvious explanation in the context of the assassination attempt. Nostradamus throws in descriptions of strange births throughout the Centuries, possibly because he, like most of his contemporaries, believed such 'monsters' were portents from God. Some Nostradamus scholars suggest he used these descriptions to make allegorical points to illuminate his message. Others believe he mentions them as concurrent events to provide a further method of dating his predictions. If the latter is true, the idea failed: accounts of freak births were often mentioned in Nostradamus' beloved almanacs, but rarely found their way into the history books.

> *Un chef Celtique dans le conflict blessé,*
> *Aupres de cave voyant siens mort abbatre:*
> *De sang et plaies et d'ennemis pressé,*
> *Et secourus par incognus de quatre.*

Translation:

> A French chief wounded in the conflict,
> Near the cellar he sees his people struck dead:
> By blood and wounds and enemies pressed,
> And saved from four unknown people.

If, as Nostradamus himself claimed, his quatrains were deliberately mixed up to disguise their chronological order and relation to each other, V.9 and V.10 may have escaped his attention. Both have been argued to predict the assassination attempt on Napoleon III.

As noted above, the emperor was only slightly wounded in the bombing. His survival was due to the crowd of people between himself and the explosion, so – as line two states – he must have seen a lot of dead citizens as he was led away. The word "*cave*" in this line should be translated as "theatre" according to Erica Cheetham: "*cavea*" being a Latin name for a theatre.

The "four unknown people", mentioned in line four, could therefore be Count Orsini and his three co-conspirators.

With most tyrants in history, an assassination attempt tends to drive them towards evermore draconian policies. Fortunately, Napoleon III was an exception. By 1860, two years after the attempt, he had begun a series of liberal reforms that were to transform France from an absolute monarchy to a modern democracy.

It should be added that the vengeful Orsini was ignorant of the French Emperor's secret dealings with Italian revolutionary groups. The year following the bombing – undeterred by the bloody misunderstanding – Napoleon III launched a war to free Italy from the Austrian Empire.

Napoleon III and the War to Free Italy: 1859
V.20 & X.64

> *Dela les Alpes grand armée passera,*
> *Un peu devant naistre monstre vapin:*
> *Prodigieux et subit tournera,*
> *Le grand Tosquan à son lieu plus propin.*

Translation:

> Beyond the Alps a great army passes,
> A short while before a wretched monster will be born:
> Strange and suddenly,
> The grand Tuscan will return to his native land.

French troops crossed the Alps into Italy in early 1859 and, together with Italian revolutionaries and the Sardinian army, attacked the occupying Austrians. As a commander-in-chief, Napoleon III proved to have an excellent grip of modern warfare. A technically-minded general, he used his new, long-range artillery and scouting balloons to great effect – decisively winning the battles of Magenta and Solferino by the middle of the summer.

The first line of the quatrain describes a "great army" crossing the Alps, but this could equally be about Napoleon I's invasion of northern Italy in 1795. However, lines three and four seem to link the quatrain with Napoleon III's war in Italy.

Early in the campaign, Leopold II, Grand Duke of Tuscany, was driven out of Florence by the pro-independence allies. He returned in disgrace to his native Austria, fulfilling the prediction that the "grand Tuscan will return to his native land".

The second line may be another of Nostradamus' "freak-birth" inclusions (see above). But Erica Cheetham suggests it might be a prediction of the birth, in 1807, of Giuseppe Garibaldi: the great Italian revolutionary.

Garibaldi was born poor ("wretched") but why Nostradamus should describe him as a "monster" is harder to say. Garibaldi's forces assaulted French troops holding the Italian Papal States in 1866, but the seer was usually above such national partisanship and, besides, Garibaldi fought for France in the Franco–Prussian War, four years later.

Of course, it is possible that Nostradamus was using the term "monster" in its ancient meaning: the word derives from the Latin verb "*monere*", meaning "to warn". Even in Nostradamus' day, a "monster" was seen as more than just a freak of nature; such births were also seen as portents. Garibaldi – the forerunner of all twentieth-century, anti-imperialist revolutionaries – could certainly be seen as a portent of future things. However, one must then accept that Nostradamus meant "a short while" (in line two) to mean fifty-odd years.

> *Pleure Milan, pleure Luques, Florance,*
> *Que ton grand Duc sur le charmontera,*
> *Changer le seige pres de Venise s'advance,*
> *Lors que Colomne à Rome changera.*

Translation:

> Weep Milan, weep Lucca, Florence,
> When the grand Duke mounts the chariot,
> Changing the siege of Venice advances,
> When *Colonne* changes at Rome.

Milan, Lucca, Florence and Venice are all cities in northern and central Italy – the region of the 1859 war – large areas of which were abandoned by the Austrians following the precipitate withdrawal of the Grand Duke of Tuscany. The towns mentioned were delighted to be free of the yoke of the Austrian Empire, so perhaps the weeping mentioned in line one of the quatrain signifies tears of joy.

Venice was not freed until the near collapse of the Austrian Empire, which followed the latter's war with Prussia in 1866. Whether this long-term Austrian occupation counts as a "siege", as line three states, is a matter of individual interpretation.

Rome herself did not join the unified Italy until 1870. Both Erica Cheetham and David Ovason suggest that the word "*Colonne*" in the last line may refer to the Colonnas – a great Roman family – but neither can offer an explanation as to what the line is actually meant to predict.

The Return of Savoy to France: 22 March 1860

V.42

> *Mars esleue en son haut befroi,*
> *Fera retaire les Allobrox de France:*
> *La gent Lombarde fera si grand effroi,*
> *A ceux de l'aigle comprins souz la Balance.*

Translation:

> Mars raised to the belfry,
> Will cause *Allobrox* to retire to France:
> The people of Lombardy shall be in such great fear,
> Of those of the eagle included in the Balance.

In late 1859, despite his successes in the war to free Italy, Napoleon III began to worry about his military situation. Austria was loosely allied with Prussia and the southern German states. If these latter decided to take the field on Austria's behalf, France would be in serious trouble. He therefore signed a peace treaty with Austria, leaving his former allies to fend for themselves. The Sardinians and Italians doubtless felt betrayed, but eventually managed to win independence without further French help.

France, nevertheless, demanded a reward for her efforts. On 22

March 1860, the new Italian king, Victor Emmanuel II, ceded the duchy of Savoy to French ownership as a reward.

The rather odd sounding first line of the above quatrain is probably too literal a translation. Perhaps "a warrior [Napoleon III?] achieving the height of success", might be a better paraphrase.

The word "*Allobrox*" in the second line sounds very like the name *Allobroge*: a tribe that once dominated the Savoy region. This interpretation seems to be further confirmed by the mention of Lombardy in the third line (Lombardy is a region of northern Italy; Savoy is sandwiched between Lombardy and France.)

The last two lines apparently describe the northern Italians ("Lombardy") throwing out the Austrians (the sign of imperial Austria was an eagle). Erica Cheetham translated "*la Balance*" as Libra, the scales, and equates this with Italy, presumably because Italy was "liberated".

The Franco-Prussian War: July 1870–February 1871
I.92, VIII.43, IV.100 & X.51

> *Sous un la paix par tout sera clamee,*
> *Mais non long temps pillé et rebellion:*
> *Par refus ville, terre, et mer entamee,*
> *Mors et captifs let tiers d'un million.*

Translation:

> Under one the peace will be proclaimed everywhere,
> But not long after will plundering and rebellion:
> Because of a refusal town, land and sea will be assaulted,
> Dead and captured a third of a million.

The expanding power in late-nineteenth-century Europe was Prussia.[4] The brilliant but ruthless Prussian chancellor, Otto von Bismarck, dreamed of unifying all the Germanic states and saw war as the quickest method of achieving this. He started with a diplomatic campaign to annoy Austria – fully aware of how decadent and brittle the Austrian-ruled Holy Roman Empire had become. The resulting conflict, in 1866, became known as the Seven Weeks' War, which resulted in the swift victory of the Prussian army.

[4] A state situated across what is now northern Germany and Poland.

By 1870, Bismarck was ready to humiliate France as he had Austria. If he could make the French start a conflict, he felt sure he could use the situation to unify the disparate German states under one flag. To his delight, Napoleon III played straight into his hands.

The Prussians had tried to place a member of their own dynasty, the Hohenzollerns, on the recently-vacated throne of Spain. France, seeing that this might leave them with hostile forces on both eastern and western frontiers, demanded the candidate's withdrawal. Bismarck refused and Napoleon III declared war on 19 July 1870.

The French emperor had set in motion important political reforms since 1860, transforming the nation from a totalitarian state to a free democracy headed by a constitutionally-bound monarch. Unfortunately, Napoleon III's zeal for internal reform was not matched by his diplomatic skills in judging foreign situations. The French were quite unprepared for the war. They could only marshal 200,000 men, while the Prussians and their south German allies had 400,000. Only Napoleon III's personal conviction that he was a military genius can explain the appalling folly that led him to declare war against such odds.

The first line of the above quatrain echoes Napoleon III's complacent announcement in the late 1860s: "*L'Empire, c'est la paix*" ("The Empire is at peace"). Chancellor Bismarck had no intention of letting that situation continue.

Line two mentions "looting and rebellion", the first is certainly true of the Prussian invasion force. The second came true when Paris rebelled on hearing the news of the dismal performance of Napoleon III at the Battle of Sedan. Although the Paris Commune continued to fight the Prussians, they now did it in the name of the "New Republic", not the emperor.

Line three describes the ruin of "town, land and sea", because of a "refusal". This might be the flat refusal of Bismarck to withdraw his Hohenzollern candidate's claim to the Spanish throne, thus causing the war.

The last line describes a third of a million "dead and captured". It is estimated that 299,000 were killed or wounded in the Franco–Prussian war – a figure close to the seer's prediction.

> *Par le decide de deux choses bastars,*
> *Neveu du sang occupera le regne,*
> *Dedans lectoyre seront les coups de dars,*
> *Neveu par peur plaire l'enseigne.*

Translation:

> Through the decision of two bastards,
> Nephew of the blood will occupy the throne,
> Within *lectoyre* there will be blows of lances,
> Nephew through fear will fold up his standard.

The Battle of Sedan was the deciding moment of the Franco–Prussian War. The French had already lost four major battles, and had allowed the Prussians to split their forces down the middle. On the morning of 1 September 1870, over half the French army (120,000 men) found itself sandwiched between the Belgian border and a force of 200,000 Prussians. The French fell back on the town of Sedan, where they were surrounded and mercilessly bombarded. The French commander, MacMahon, was badly wounded early in the battle. When, in the late afternoon, Napoleon III himself arrived to take command, he immediately saw that surrender was the only possible course of action.

Seventeen thousand French soldiers were killed in the fighting; 83,000 were taken prisoner, along with Napoleon III himself.

Erica Cheetham suggests that the phrase "*le decide*", in the first line of the quatrain, should be translated not as "the decision", but as "the fall" – from the Latin "*decidere*": to fall. Thus, the seer may have been referring to "the fall" of the "Citizen King", Louis Phillipe, and the subsequent Second Republic. Both might have been seen as "bastards" in the eyes of Nostradamus: an absolute monarchist.

Napoleon III took the French throne, as described in line two, by right of being the nephew of Napoleon I. He was the only nephew of a monarch to attain the crown between Nostradamus' day and the end of the French monarchy.

The word "*lectoyre*", in line three, Erica Cheetham argues, is an anagram of *Le Torcey*. This suburb of Sedan was the scene of some of the bloodiest fighting in the battle.

Line four describes the "nephew" folding his standard through fear: a blunt, but essentially accurate, description of Napoleon III's humiliating surrender.

> *De feu celeste au Royal edifice,*
> *Quant la lumiere de Mars defaillira:*
> *Sept mois grand guerre, mort gent de malefice,*
> *Rouen, Eureux au Roi ne faillira.*

Translation:

> Fire falls from the sky on to the Royal edifice,
> When the light of Mars fails:
> Seven months great war, people dead by evil,
> Rouen and Evreux will not fail the King.

The first line of the above quatrain sounds like the Prussian artillery. Even with odds of two to one against, the French commanders initially believed that they could beat the enemy. From the very beginning, the war was fought on French territory, giving the French army the advantage of fighting from their fortifications. However, this advantage was soon checkmated by the superiority of the Prussian artillery. As reports came in of French garrisons being blown to pieces in their forts, the captured Napoleon III may have bitterly remembered the words of his uncle and namesake: "The army that stays within its fortifications is already beaten."

The "Royal edifice" receiving "fire from the sky" could be the Tuileries Palace, destroyed by Prussian shells during the siege of Paris. The French capital was bombarded from late September 1870 to 19 January 1871. The Parisians fought heroically with crude, home-made weapons, but with the French army destroyed, they had no hope, and surrender was inevitable.

Line two describes "the light of Mars fail[ing]". As we saw in the quatrain on the French annexation of Savoy (V.42 above), Nostradamus may have used the nickname "Mars" for Napoleon III (inappropriate as it may seem in hindsight). The Bonaparte dynasty was emasculated by the Franco–Prussian War, and with their fall, the throne of France ceased to exist forever – a stunning *Götterdammerung* for a French monarchist like Nostradamus.

Line three describes "people dead by evil". This could also be a prediction of the siege of Paris, by the end of which the Parisians were reduced to eating dogs, cats and rats. Thousands died of starvation. As to the war lasting "seven months", the Franco–Prussian war continued from July 1870 to February 1871 – precisely seven months.

Rouen and Evreux, mentioned in line four, are both towns in Normandy. This area remained loyal to Napoleon III, even after he was captured by Bismarck. The rest of France had declared itself a republic in pure disgust.

> *Des lieux plus bas du pays de Lorraine,*
> *Seront des basses Allemaignes unis,*
> *Par ceux du siege Picards, Normons, du Maisne,*
> *Et aux cantons ce seront reunis.*

Translation:

> The lowest places in the county of Lorraine,
> Will be united with lower Germanies,
> By reason of the siege of Picardy, Normandy and Maisne,
> And in cantons they will be reunited.

Following the surrender of Paris, the Prussian army occupied the whole of France ("Picardy, Normandy and Maisne"). Bismarck demanded territorial rights to a large part of Lorraine and, further south ("*plus bas*") the region of Alsace. He also demanded five billion gold francs in war reparations. The French had no choice but to agree. The debt was not paid off until September 1873, and only then did all the German troops leave French territory. France was reunited as a free country, as line four suggests, but why Nostradamus uses the word "*cantons*" (a Swiss term for a county) is hard to fathom. Lorraine remained lost to France until 1919.

Bismarck got the German unity he had gambled for. King William I of Prussia was crowned *Kaiser* (Caesar) of Greater Germany in Versailles in 1871. France has remained a republic since the Franco–Prussian defeat and, considering modern political trends, is highly unlikely to ever be ruled by a monarch again.

Napoleon III lived the rest of his life as an exile in Britain, dying during a routine medical operation in January, 1873.

Louis Pasteur: 1822 to 1895

I.25

> *Perdu trouvé, caché de si long siecle,*
> *Sera Pasteur demi Dieu honoré:*
> *Ains que la lune acheve son grand siecle,*
> *Par autres vents sera deshonoré.*

Translation:

> Lost found again, hidden for a long cycle,
> Pasteur as a demi God is honoured:
> But before the Moon ends her great cycle,
> By ancient ones shall be dishonoured.

This is another of Nostradamus' stunningly-accurate predictions – even giving the name of one of the greatest French scientists of the nineteenth century: Louis Pasteur.

Throughout history, doctors had been unable to discover the fundamental cause of disease. In Nostradamus' day, for example, it was universally believed that "ill humours in the air", such as marsh gas, caused sickness. It was not until Pasteur, through his work on fermentation in wine and milk, hit on the concept of "microbiology" that the modern renaissance in medicine began.

Pasteur argued that microscopic objects called *bacteria* – discovered the previous century – caused the spoiling of liquids like milk. These tiny pieces of matter were alive, he insisted, and their life-cycle produced acids as a by-product, making the milk sour. If the milk were heated then sealed in an antiseptic bottle, it would be less prone to spoil – thus *pasteurisation* was invented.

He went on to argue that many diseases were the result of attacks on the human organism by "germs" – his name for dangerous bacteria. Although he was roundly attacked by traditionalist doctors – who refused to believe that something so tiny could harm much larger creatures, such as human beings – eventually his theory was proved correct. Quite apart from his discovery that anthrax, rabies and other illnesses could be prevented by vaccination, it is arguable that Pasteur's initial idea – that bacilli were a danger that should be tightly controlled – has saved most of us from premature deaths.

As we saw in the chapter on Nostradamus' life, it has been argued that his success against plagues might have been due to precognition of future medical practice, with its emphasis upon cleanliness. This would certainly explain why he singled out Pasteur as one of the most significant figures in history.

Line two describes "Pasteur" being honoured like a "demi God". This is truer today than it was in Pasteur's own lifetime. As line four seems to hint, senior medical men ridiculed the theory of microbes for a long time; many died refusing to accept any of the growing evidence for Pasteur's "germs".

The Pasteur Institute was founded in 1889. This, Erica Cheetham points out, was at the end of a 320-year lunar cycle. The most bitter criticism of Pasteur took place before this date, and therefore "before the moon end[ed] her great cycle", as it says in line three.

The first line of this quatrain is one of the most extraordinary in all the *Centuries*, because it seems to mean that the existence of microbes was known a long time before Pasteur's discoveries, but somehow became "hidden".

In 1990, Robert Schoch, a geologist from Boston University, confirmed the assertion of the Egyptologist John Anthony West that the Great Sphinx of Giza was eroded by rain, not wind-blown sand. Schoch's own estimate of its age was around 7000 BC – 3,000 years older than any known civilization.

Is it possible that a forgotten civilization built the Sphinx? John West believes it is – he calls it "Atlantis", while admitting that this is merely a convenient, if arresting, label. West also believes that the remarkable sophistication of medicine in Ancient Egypt was a legacy of this former civilization, which was destroyed (as Plato described in the *Timaeus*) in a great cataclysm.

Is it conceivable that this is what Nostradamus meant when he said that Pasteur rediscovered knowledge that had been "hidden for a long cycle"?

As to the last line about being dishonoured by "other winds" ("*autres vents*", often translated as "old ones", or "*vieux*"), it might refer to Pasteur's dissenting colleagues, or might suggest a more disturbing possibility. Bearing in mind that, in Nostradamus' day, it was believed that diseases were caused by bad odours on the wind (which is why the wealthy carried handkerchiefs soaked in scent), it sounds as if Nostradamus is saying that Pasteur's discovery will be rendered useless by germs that are not so easily destroyed.

It was only towards the last decades of the twentieth century that this possibility presented itself. That is to say, Pasteur's discoveries can offer little to help us in the face of the more deadly viruses.

These microscopic killers are simply DNA strands surrounded by inanimate protective casings. Unlike bacteria, they are not living organisms, and therefore cannot be killed by antibiotics. On the other hand, they are not wholly inanimate, as they can reproduce – often with fatal repercussions for their host organism.

Viruses are the oldest creatures on the planet ("old ones") and can hibernate for millions of years.[5] A lone batch of a virus might literally hide under a rock for millennia, springing to life the moment a suitable host uncovers it. Thanks to modern jet travel, this infection could then spread across the world in forty-eight hours, just as new types of influenza (another occasionally fatal virus) do on a virtually yearly basis.

Both HIV and Ebola – viruses that kill 99–100 per cent of infected sufferers – may have originated in the jungles of Africa. They had probably been "hidden" there since before the birth of mankind, and only our modern incursions into the once untouched forests released them. Horrible as both these diseases are, they are relatively difficult to catch; the next virus to be "released" may be as lethal as AIDS and might travel on the air ("*autres vents*") like the flu.

Viral biologists refer to such a bug as a "slate-wiper", because it would almost certainly wipe all of mankind off the slate.

---

[5]The phrase of the visionary horror writer, H. P. Lovecraft comes to mind: "That is not dead that can eternal lie . . .". Lovecraft called his hidden monsters – poised to destroy mankind – "the Great Old Ones": a close echo of Nostradamus' phrase.

The Dreyfus Affair: 1893–1906

I.7

> *Tard arrivé l'execution faicte,*
> *Le vent contraire lettres aux chemin prinses:*
> *Les conjurez quatorze d'une secte,*
> *Par le Rousseau semz les enterprinses.*

Translation:

> Arriving too late, the execution is done,
> The wind is contrary, letters intercepted on the way:
> The conspirators fourteen of a sect,
> By the Rousseau the enterprise is undertaken.

The Dreyfus scandal shook the turn-of-the-century French establishment. Alfred Dreyfus was an artillery captain assigned to the general staff in Paris when he was accused, in late 1893, of selling military secrets to the Germans. An anonymous letter to the German Embassy had been intercepted, containing a list of top secret documents. Someone thought the handwriting resembled that of Captain Dreyfus, who, because he was a Jew, was not popular with his superiors. Despite the doubtful supporting evidence, he was convicted and sentenced to life imprisonment on the prison colony called *l'Ile du Diable* (Devil's Island).

Two years later, in 1896, Lieutenant Colonel George Picquart, head of the French intelligence service, found evidence that a Major Esterhazy was actually responsible for the "*bordereau*" ("list" – as the document became known). However, when he presented this evidence to his superiors he was ordered to remain silent and was dismissed from his post. Whether through Picquart, or from their own investigations, Dreyfus's family discovered the same evidence against Esterhazy and published it. In 1898, the embarrassed military authorities were forced to send Esterhazy to trial, but they saw to it that he was acquitted despite the weight of the evidence against him.

Shortly after Esterhazy's trial, Picquart's successor, Lieutenant Colonel Hubert Henry, publicly confessed that he had discovered that the evidence used against Dreyfus had been forged. He was immediately arrested and was later found dead in his cell.

In 1899, Dreyfus was brought back from prison to appeal his case. To the rage of the public, his guilty sentence was upheld, although his prison term was reduced to ten years. Ten days later, the new Prime Minister of France, Pierre Waldeck-Rousseau, ordered Dreyfus pardoned. He was reinstated in the army as a major and, rather ironically, awarded the Legion of Honour – effectively for surviving the anti-Semitic bigotry of his own military superiors. Dreyfus later fought with distinction in the Great War.

Esterhazy fled to England and later confessed to being the author of the "*bordereau*".

Line one of the quatrain may predict the "execution" of Dreyfus's sentence, despite his known innocence by his judges; French justice "arriving too late" to save him from five undeserved years on Devil's Island.

The phrase "*le vent contraire*", at the beginning of line two, is the French equivalent of the English phrase: "the tide is against you". This may reflect the public indignation and anti-Semitic bigotry at the time of Dreyfus's first trial, or it might be a warning to the anti-Dreyfus conspirators that the truth would eventually be revealed. The "letters intercepted" in the second part of the line could be the forged documents that convicted Dreyfus, or the true evidence that Esterhazy was the guilty man.

Whether there were fourteen people, as described in line three, involved in the conspiracy to convict Dreyfus cannot now be verified. The mention of "Rousseau" in the last line may, in fact, be a hint that the Prime Minister who eventually pardoned Dreyfus was actually one of the conspirators. It is known that Rousseau was violently anti-Dreyfus, and it was almost certainly Rousseau who was behind the reconviction at retrial in 1899. He only pardoned Dreyfus when he saw that popular indignation might cost him his own job.

The Dreyfus case had implications far beyond the embarrass-ment of the French government. The image of the military estab-lishment conniving to allow racism to triumph over justice caused a scandal that echoed round the world. The Dreyfus case was a watershed, the first of a series of scandals in which the establishment has been shaken by popular indignation or (worse still) derision.

Chapter 17

Nostradamus and the Twentieth Century

As has already been noted in previous chapters, Nostradamus' quatrains tend to be interpreted by different scholars to reflect their own personal interests. This is equally true of periods of history. Seventeenth-, eighteenth- and nineteenth-century studies of the *Centuries* tend to find interpretations that match their own historical background – only to be reinterpreted in the light of new events that seem to fit the predictions better to the eyes of later generations.

Turning now to the events of the twentieth century, I am quite aware that I too might suffer from such a partisan outlook. Nevertheless, some of the "matches" of twentieth-century events to the seer's riddling quatrains are quite remarkable . . .

I suspect that the only truly unbiased Nostradamus scholar would be one that shared the seer's apparent gift of precognition.

Rasputin and the Empress Alexandra: 1905–16
VI.72

> *Par fureur faincte d'esmotion divine,*
> *Sera la femme du grand fort violée:*
> *Judges voulans damner telle doctrine,*
> *Victime au peuple ignorant imolée.*

Translation:

> By a feigned fury of divine emotion,
> The wife of the great one will be violated:

Judges willing to condemn such a doctrine,
The victim sacrificed to the ignorant people.

Grigory Yefimovich Rasputin was a holy man (*starets*) from the depths of Siberia. Born the son of a peasant in 1869, he spent his first thirty years working the land as an uneducated serf. He abandoned his family and his life as a farm labourer in 1901, taking to the road as a wandering preacher and faith healer. By 1905 he had made something of a name for himself and travelled to St Petersburg (the then Russian Imperial capital). It soon became a fashion among the aristocracy to visit the wild-looking, heavily-bearded holy man – especially among the ladies, who found his powerful personality attractive, and vied for his favours.

The heir to the Russian throne, Crown Prince Alexei, was a haemophiliac – that is, his blood would not clot, so that cuts, or even bruises, could be fatal. One day in 1907 (when the child was three), a fall resulted in high fever. Rasputin (who had already been presented to the royal family) was hastily summoned. The wild-bearded faith healer prayed by the bedside for half an hour, then the boy's temperature suddenly dropped to normal.

From then on, Rasputin was constantly in attendance at the palace, and was unofficially accepted as the Tsarina's chief spiritual adviser. However, it is fairly certain (notwithstanding many rumours and Nostradamus' suggestion of "violation") that the Siberian was never the Tsarina's lover.

Tsar Nicholas II was a kindly but vacillating character, who would have been much happier in private life. He and the Tsarina adored one another and lived in a private cocoon, which (since Russia was seething with revolutionary ferment) was disastrous both for them and the country. By the time World War I broke out Rasputin, through the Tsarina, was a major power in the palace, and became the Tsar's adviser on political appointments – adding to Russia's chaos.

Not surprisingly, in class-obsessed Imperial Russia, many aristocrats hated the former serf (not least because he had many aristocratic mistresses). On the night of 29/30 December 1916, a group of Rasputin's enemies, led by the spoilt Prince Felix Yusupov, invited the holy man to a party, where they laced his sweet wine with enough cyanide to kill an elephant. Rasputin did not appear to notice. Yusupov shot him in the back, and he collapsed, apparently dead – only to stand up and attack Yusupov ten minutes after being pronounced dead. More shots and blows from a steel bar subdued Rasputin, and he was finally dropped into the frozen River Neva through a hole hacked in the ice. Medical examination later revealed that he had managed to untie one of his hands before he drowned.

If the above quatrain is indeed about Rasputin, it is clear that Nostradamus disliked him – the prediction reads like a scandal sheet composed by one of the assassins. Yet there are undoubted similarities between the two men. Both were religious, both apparently had "second sight" and – not least – both were court favourites of powerful queens.

The first two lines describe "feigned" religious passion causing the wife of "the great one" to be "violated". This may be an echo of rumours in St Petersburg that the Tsarina was having an affair with Rasputin – which, as already noted, was probably untrue. Alexandra was too devoutly religious and adored her husband and family too much to have behaved in such a way.

The fact that Nostradamus used the word "*violée*" – a term more indicative of rape than adultery – may suggest that he is condemning Rasputin's violation of the Tsarina's trust (and undoubtedly revelation of Rasputin's lecherous and drunken behaviour would have shocked her deeply).

The last two lines may predict two circumstances in this context; and knowing Nostradamus' love of riddles, he could have intended both meanings. Influential people ("judges") in Russian society certainly condemned Rasputin's "doctrine" – it was generally supposed that he was a member of a sect called the *Khlysty* whose religious ceremonies were believed to end in orgies. Or could the line suggest that it was the Russian people who passed judgment on their self-indulgent aristocracy? Line four – a "victim sacrificed to the ignorant" – may refer to Rasputin, but seems more likely to refer to the Tsar and his family, who were murdered in 1918 by Bolsheviks in Ekaterinburg.

Rasputin told the Tsar that, as the absolute ruler, he must act like a Tsar, not like a half-hearted democrat (a piece of advice that Joseph Stalin seemed later to have taken to heart). If Nicholas had taken this advice, it might have saved Russia from revolution.

There seems little doubt that Rasputin had genuine supernatural gifts. Even his enemies had to admit he could heal apparently terminal cases by the touch of his hands and that his presence, even when drunk, was magnetic. However, what is less well attested is his prophetic power.

In 1916, Rasputin wrote a strange document headed "The Spirit of Grigory Rasputin-Novyhk of the village of Pokrovskoe", which was found among his papers after his murder. It begins by stating that he had foreseen that he would not live beyond 1 January, and that he had a message for the Tsar and the "Russian Mother" (the Tsarina). If "common assassins" killed him, especially peasants, the Tsar had nothing to fear and Russia would remain a monarchy for centuries to come. If, on the other hand, he was murdered by nobles, the Tsar and his immediate family would all die within two years, and all Russian aristocrats would have died or been driven out of the country within twenty-five years (by 1942).

By 1942, Russia was firmly in the tyrannical grip of the Soviet Premier, Joseph Stalin. Any surviving aristocrat in the USSR would have been living in anonymous poverty with his fellow Soviet citizens.

The Great War: 1914–18

III.18, II.1 & IV. 12

> *En Luques sant et laict viendra plouvoir,*
> *En plusieurs lieux de Reims le ciel touché:*
> *O quel conflict de sang pres d'eux s'appreste,*
> *Peres et fils Rois n'oseront approcher.*

Translation:

> After a long rain of milk,
> Several places in Rheims struck from the sky:
> Oh what bloody battle prepared,
> Fathers and sons' Kings dare not approach.

Nostradamus seems peculiarly reticent on the subject of World War I. While he apparently dedicated many quatrains to conflicts such as the Napoleonic wars and the Franco–Prussian War, only a few seem to be specifically linked to the "war to end war" (to use H. G. Wells's phrase).

This may, of course, be our failure to understand certain quatrains, or it could be that Nostradamus was so preoccupied with minutiae that he failed to recognize a conflict on such a massive scale.

Line one mentions a "long rain of milk". Jean-Charles de Fontbrune and Henry C. Roberts feel that this is a poetic description of France's *belle Epoque*: a period of peace and plenty around the turn of the century.

On 28 July 1914, the Austro–Hungarian Empire declared war on the little nation of Serbia after the Serbian nationalist, Gavrilio Princip, shot and killed the heir to the Austrian throne, Archduke Ferdinand, in Sarajevo. On 1 August, Austria's ally Germany declared war on Russia – Serbia's ally – turning a local war into a European conflict. By 4 August, Britain and France had entered the war on the side of Serbia and Russia. Eventually thirty-two nations were drawn into the conflict, creating the planet's first "world war". Over 20 million people were to die in less than five years of conflict; an unprecedented horror perhaps reflected in lines three and four of the quatrain.

Line two describes something falling from the sky on Rheims. This town in north-eastern France was close to several major battles in World War I. By the 1918 Armistice, the Germans had shelled and bombed Rheims to little more than rubble.

> *Vers Aquitaine par insuls Britanniques,*
> *De pars eux mesmes grands incursions,*
> *Pluies gelées feront terroirs uniques,*
> *Port Selin fortes fera invasions.*

Translation:

> Towards Aquitaine by British assaults,
> By them shall be great incursions,
> Rains and frosts make the terrain unsafe,
> Port *Selin* makes strong invasions.

The first line of the quatrain contains the word "Britanniques" which is interesting, since Britain as a nation did not exist in the time of Nostradamus. However, as we saw in the chapter on Nostradamus and the nineteenth century, *Century X*, quatrain 42, seems to show that Nostradamus was aware that the British Isles would one day be unified as a single nation. Here he describes "British" assaults towards Aquitaine (a region of south-west France) and, in the second line, making "great incursions".

Much of the fighting in France took place in the north-east of the country, in and around Belgium on the so-called Western Front. This was a long way from "Aquitaine", but the appalling weather, described in line three, is reminiscent of the conditions that made the trench warfare so grim.

Of course, the latter part of World War II also saw large British (liberating) "incursions" through south-western France, but line four of the quatrain seems to rule out this interpretation.

Francis X. King points out that "Port Selin" means "Port of the Crescent [moon]". This is one of the old names for Istanbul, the Turkish capital. Turkey was neutral throughout the Second World War, but fought on the German side in World War I.

The 1915 major Allied offensive ("strong invasions") in the Dardanelles (in north-west Turkey) was an unmitigated failure. Over half of the 489,000 British, French, Australian and New Zealand troops sent on the invasion were killed, captured or badly wounded.

> *Le camp plus grand de route mis en fuite,*
> *Gauires plus outre ne sera pourchassé:*
> *Ost recampé, et legion reduicte,*
> *Puis hors ses Gaules du tout sera chassé.*

Translation:

> The greatest army is routed and put to flight,
> But shall not be pursued further:
> They re-encamp, and the legion is reduced,
> They will be driven out of France.

The Germans mobilized almost 14 million men throughout the period of the war. Britain, by contrast, fielded only 8.9 million,

France 8.4 million and the USA 4.3 million; only Russia came close to Germany's sheer numbers with 12 million troops. So the Germans could accurately be called "the [single] greatest army" as it says in line one. However, by the beginning of November 1918, this huge army was defeated and was in full retreat from the Western Front.

The end of World War I was not as complete a defeat for the Germans as the end of World War II would be. On 11 November, an armistice was signed. Hostilities ceased immediately and the retreating German army was "not . . . pursued further", as line two says. However, it was completely "driven out of France", as it predicts in line four.

Line three describes "the greatest army" reforming after the rout, but then being reduced. Following the German surrender, the victorious Allies forced them to demobilize their army. The humiliating Treaty of Versailles allowed Germany a standing army of only 100,000 men, demanded enormous war reparations and annexed much of the Germans' most valuable industrial territory (making repayment of the reparations nearly impossible).

It has been argued that these acts of vindictive and greedy revenge by the Allies all but guaranteed another major war with Germany.

The Russian Revolution and the Murder of the Royal Family: 1917–18

VIII.80

> *Des innocens le sang de vefue et vierge.*
> *Tant de maulx faitz par moyen se grand Roge*
> *Saintz simulacres tremper en ardent cierge*
> *De frayeur crainte verra nul que boge.*

Translation:

> The blood of innocents the widow and the virgin.
> Many evils committed by the great Red
> Saints' icons soaked in burning candles
> Of fear none will be seen to move.

Trying to determine which of Nostradamus' predictions refer to the Russian Revolution is complicated by its similarities to the earlier French Revolution. Both rebel factions were called "Reds", both were republican and executed aristocrats, and both were hostile to the Church and committed regicide. Considering the seer's obvious predilection for French history, it is not surprising that many commentators prefer the French interpretation for quatrains that might refer to either. However, the reference to "*simulacres*" (icons – Russian Orthodox paintings of saints), suggests that it is Russia that Nostradamus has in mind here. (The French for statue is "*statue*".)

Following a popular uprising in March 1917, Tsar Nicholas II was forced to abdicate. A democratic provisional government was set up, but in October the Bolsheviks (Reds) seized power. Nicholas and his family were imprisoned by the "Red[s]", who then seemed to be at a loss as to what to do with them. They were initially held at Tobolsk in Siberia, but in the spring of 1918 they were moved to Ekaterinburg. By July it seemed plain that "White Russian", counter-revolutionary forces were going to take the town, so the decision was taken to kill the royal family.

On the night of 16/17 July, the Tsar and Tsarina, their five children, their doctor and three servants were led down into the cellar of the house in which they had been held. The Tsar was given a chair to sit on and their gaoler, Yurovsky, announced: "Nicholas Alexandrovich, your followers have tried to set you free. They failed. Now you are to be shot." "What?" Nicholas demanded. "This . . ." said Yurovsky, and shot him in the chest with a revolver. The others fell to their knees and were shot by the rest of Yurovsky's firing squad. The Tsar's doctor, Botkin, the three servants and even the Tsarina's pet spaniel were killed as well. A week later the Whites took Ekaterinburg, but the bodies had already been partly burned and secretly buried in the forest.

The "great Red", mentioned in line two, is presumably Lenin. Nostradamus seems to have disliked the Bolsheviks as much as he did the French Jacobins, speaking of the "evils" committed by them.

Line three seems to be a prediction of the Communist persecution of the Church, with overturned candles soaking the icons with wax; the Bolshevik government went on to fully abolish the

Russian Orthodox Church, along with all other religions within Soviet territory.

The first and last lines may refer to the deaths of the Russian royal family, although the Tsarina was a "widow" for only the few seconds between her husband's death and her own murder. The children – a son and four daughters – were all "virgin[s]" when they were killed, and the monarchist seer seems to regard the shedding of "the blood of innocents" with indignation.

For many years after the executions, there was a persistent rumour that not all the members of the royal family had been shot. In 1922, a young woman in a German mental hospital told the psychiatrist that she was really the Grand Duchess Anastasia – the youngest of the Tsar's four daughters. She was about the right age and looked very like the Grand Duchess. Indeed, many of Anastasia's relatives were convinced that she was genuine. Now, however, we know that they were wrong. The bones of the Russian royal family were found buried in the Siberian forest in 1991; Anastasia's remains were identified by DNA testing.

Perhaps line four of Nostradamus' quatrain predicts the deaths of all the Tsar's family when it says, "none will be seen to move". Or perhaps he refers to the Stalinist terror that followed, when so many Russians were forced to watch their relatives being unjustly sentenced to execution or forced labour, but themselves dared show no sign of dissent

The 1918 Influenza Pandemic

IX.55

L'horrible guerre qu'en l'occident s'apreste,
L'an ensuivant la pestilence,
Si fort horribles que jeune, vieux, ne beste,
Sang, feu, Mercure, Mars, Jupiter en France.

Translation:

The horrible war is prepared in the west,
The following year will come the plague,
So powerfully horrible that young, old, nor beast,
Blood, fire, Mercury, Mars, Jupiter in France.

The First World War ended on 11 November 1918, having killed over 20 million soldiers and civilians in a four-year period. The great 1918 influenza pandemic (a worldwide epidemic) killed at least that many people again in a single year.

The First World War was certainly "prepared" many years in advance, as line one states. From the end of the Franco–Prussian war, in 1871, two military power blocks had been developing in Europe. On one side were the Germans, the Turkish Ottomans, the Austro–Hungarian Empire and Bulgaria: the so-called Central Powers. On the other were France, Britain, Russia and a number of smaller European states: the Allies. Some statesmen felt that the tremendous military forces built up by both groups would be a natural deterrent to war – the prospect being too catastrophic for anybody to contemplate. In fact, the military jingoism that went hand in hand with the keeping of such large standing armies ultimately made war virtually inevitable.

The year following the Armistice of 1918 saw one of the worst pestilences in modern history: the Great Influenza Epidemic.

The virus had, in fact, killed large numbers in America in the months before the end of the war, but the greatest number of deaths occurred later – one reason being the demobilization of millions of troops. Ships and trains crowded with troops might have been designed to incubate the disease, and thousands arrived home only to infect their families and then die.

The final line of the quatrain – about "blood, fire, Mercury, Mars, Jupiter in France" – seems at first baffling as influenza is not associated with blood or fire. But war is. The solution is obviously that the second line of the quatrain – about the plague – should actually be the last. Then we have:

> The horrible war is prepared in the west,
> Blood, fire, Mercury, Mars, Jupiter in France
> So powerfully horrible that (neither) young, old nor beast
> (shall be spared)
> The following year will come the plague.

This becomes obvious when we reflect that the "*fort horrible*" of line three obviously refers to the horrible war of line one, and that this war took place mainly in France – which does not apply to the 'flu epidemic.

The references to beasts makes the same point: although there is a type of 'flu virus (Influenza A) that can affect birds, pigs and horses, the great 'flu epidemic was not notable for animal deaths.

The League of Nations: 1919–47

I.47

> *Du lac Leman les sermons faschermont,*
> *Les jours seront reduicts par les sepmaines:*
> *Puis mois, puis an, puis tous deffailliront,*
> *Les magistrats damneront leurs loix vaines.*

Translation:

> Of lake *Leman* the sermons become troublesome,
> The days are dragged out into weeks:
> Then months, then years, then all will fail,
> The magistrates will condemn their own inept laws.

The 1918 Treaty of Versailles was a great disappointment to American President Woodrow Wilson. A liberal and a genuine idealist, he had all but begged his principal allies – France and Britain – not to impose humiliating reparation demands on the defeated Germany. His arguments were ignored, but to placate him, his fellow allies agreed to the setting up of a "League of Nations": an international debating chamber, whose main aim was the preservation of world peace.[1]

It was a laudable idea, but was ultimately doomed to failure by the imposition of war reparations aimed at bankrupting Germany. With hindsight, the greedy and vindictive demands made by Britain and France guaranteed another European war, so that the period from 1918 to 1939 (between the Great War and World War II) might be seen as an interlude of peace in a single, major conflict.

The first line mentions a lake called "Leman". This is an old (but still widely used) name for Lake Geneva in Switzerland, a

---

[1] Ironically, America refused to join, much to the sorrow of President Wilson. The US remained outside the League for the whole of its existence, greatly reducing its political, financial and military potency.

traditionally neutral nation and site of the League of Nations' conferences.

Lines one to three describe "sermons" stretching out for weeks, months and years, but ultimately failing. This is exactly what happened – endless sermonizing speeches (about the shortcomings of other nations) and petty, self-serving arguments occupied most of the League's time, but the delegates ultimately failed in their main purpose: the prevention of another world war.

The last line describes "magistrates" condemning their own inept law-giving. Following World War II, the League admitted its failure, blaming bureaucracy and lack of legal "teeth".

Sixty-three countries belonged to the League at one time or another, and it scored certain successes in limiting international prostitution, drug trading and illegal immigration. Unfortunately, it failed utterly in its major task as peacekeeper. The Nazis withdrew Germany from the League in 1933, when they began the process of rearming in violation of the Treaty of Versailles. Japan also withdrew that year, when other League members criticized their savage invasion of Manchuria. When the League condemned the Italian invasion of Ethiopia in 1935, Mussolini simply ignored them. Finally, the League was powerless to stop the onset of World War II. When world peace was again restored in 1945, the League of Nations voted for its own dissolution, to be replaced by the stronger (US- and Soviet-backed) United Nations organization.

The Abdication of Edward VIII: 11 December 1936

X.22

> Pour ne vouloir consentir à divorce,
> Qui puis apres sera cogneu indigne,
> Le Roi des Ilse sera chassé par force
> Mis à son lieu que de roi n'aura signe.

Translation:

> For not consenting to a divorce,
> Which afterwards will be recognized as unworthy,
> The King of the Isles shall be chased by force
> Another substituted who had no sign of kingship.

Edward – known to his family as David – was the oldest son of George V of Great Britain, and succeeded his father in the first month of 1936, at the age of 41. A liberal with inclinations towards socialism (and an admiration for Hitler), Edward VIII was naturally at odds with his Conservative Prime Minister, Stanley Baldwin. This political difference would certainly have been glossed over, had the king not also been an incorrigible playboy, who enjoyed seducing other men's wives, and who, as monarch, believed that a king ought to rule, rather than be a rubber stamp for Parliament.

He was naturally casual and careless – for example, he tended to leave top-secret documents lying around Buckingham Palace for the servants to pick up (and read, if they happened to have friends in the German or Russian espionage services). It was indicative of Edward's work and lifestyle that he often gave such documents back to Baldwin half-read and covered with wine stains and cigar ash.

Finally, Baldwin started to withhold the more secret documents from Edward, as a matter of national security. However, the king's sex life was a matter he could not deal with so easily. Edward had been having an affair with a respectable (but middle-class) English widow for some years. This, in itself, was hardly likely to cause raised eyebrows, particularly since he had no intention of marrying the lady.

The political problems arose when he threw over this mistress for a married American woman called Wallis Warfield Simpson. Even this might have been controllable, since the British press had no intention of exposing the affair; then Edward told Baldwin that Mrs Simpson had obtained a divorce, and that he intended to marry her as soon as possible. Baldwin replied that, as official head of the Church of England, the king could not marry a divorcee. Unfortunately, Edward was so accustomed to getting his own way that this made no impression. The American press soon broke the story, and the more discreet British press – this was 1936 – had no alternative but to follow suit.

The general public was scandalized, particularly since Mrs Simpson was an American, and the idea of an American queen seemed as unthinkable as having W. C. Fields as king. Yet Edward would not be swayed. Finally, under considerable pressure, he announced his abdication. It was 11 December 1936. His younger brother was crowned George VI.

Line four describes a successor to the throne who lacks the "sign of kingship". This description certainly fits George VI, who was shy and had a bad stammer – although historians now classify him as one of the most successful monarchs in modern British history.

In due course George VI was a major factor in boosting British morale during the Second World War – while his deposed older brother, under the nagging insistence of the former Mrs Simpson, connived ineptly with Nazi agents.

General Franco and the Spanish Civil War: 1936–39
III.54 & IX.16

> *L'un des plus grands fuira aux Espaignes,*
> *Qu'en longue playe apres viendra saigner:*
> *Passant copies par les hautes montaignes,*
> *Devastant tout et puis en paix regner.*

Translation:

> One of the great men will fly to Spain,
> That will cause a wound that will bleed for a long time:
> Leading troops over high mountains,
> Devastating all and afterwards reigns in peace.

Politically, Spain was falling apart in the early 1930s. The world-wide economic depression had the effect of deepening the hatred between the left- and right-wing factions, and partisan terror gangs stalked the streets at night.

On 18 July 1936, a fascist military coup d'état attempted to overthrow the government of the Second Republic. Much of the population in the countryside (which always tends to be conservative) backed the coup, but it failed in most of the major cities. Thus two factions split the nation: the besieged, leftist government – the Loyalists – and the right-wing rebels – the Nationalists. A bloody civil war began.

One of the chief ("great") men of the Nationalist side was Major General Francisco Franco. A career military man, his attitudes had been brutalized in Spain's grim war to crush Moroccan independence in the 1920s. When the coup took place, Franco was commanding the colonial army in Morocco. Since the pro-Loyalist Spanish navy held the Straits of Gibraltar, Franco made a deal with the German Nazi government to lend his troops the necessary transport planes. Thus, as it says in line one, he literally "flew" back to Spain.

On his arrival, Franco swiftly deployed his troops and marched on Loyalist-held Madrid. The calculated brutality of his troops cowed the Loyalist enemy and impressed the Nationalists. Madrid eventually fell and Franco was made head of the Nationalist faction.

General Franco fought an all-out war – using ruthlessness and cruelty as strategic weapons. This made him a very effective commander, but meant that the Spanish Civil War was a "wound" in the nation's psyche that would "bleed" for generations – just as line two describes.

Troops certainly "passed over high mountains" (the Pyrenees) to aid both sides in the civil war, as line three describes. Military aid was sent from fascist Italy and Germany to the Nationalists, and similar aid came from the USSR for the Loyalists – as well as thousands of young political activists from all over Europe, who hurried to fight in what they considered a war of ideology.

Franco, despite or perhaps because of his brutal methods, won the war – as line four seems to predict. He then kept his exhausted country out of the Second World War, and ruled in semi-tyrannical "peace" until his death, at the age of eighty-three, in 1975.

> *De castel Franco sortira l'assemblee,*
> *L'ambassadeur non plaisant fera scisme:*
> *Ceux de Ribiere seront en la meslee,*
> *Et au grand goulphre desnier ont l'entrée.*

Translation:

> From *castel* Franco comes the assembly,
> The ambassadors not pleased create a schism:
> Those of *Ribiere* will be in the melée,
> And the entry is denied to the great gulf.

This is a remarkable quatrain, since it names Franco and connects his name with Spain (the word "castel" is usually translated by Nostradamus scholars as "Castille": a town in Spain).

Francis X. King, in *Nostradamus* (1995), suggests that the "assembly", mentioned in the first line, and the contention of "ambassadors", mentioned in the second, are both predictions of the disagreement between Spain and Germany in 1940. As we have already noted, General Franco kept Spain neutral in the Second World War, but was still willing to support his fellow fascists unobtrusively. Hitler asked Franco help him take Gibraltar from the British, thus breaking their stranglehold on entry into the Mediterranean "gulf". Franco saw that this would violate his neutrality and flatly refused. At the time it was a political gamble to annoy a powerful neighbour like Hitler, but in maintaining his neutrality, Franco guaranteed his political survival when the Allies won the war.

The word "*Ribiere*" in line three is generally assumed to be a misspelling of "Rivera". General Miguel Primo de Rivera ruled a military dictatorship in Spain from 1923 to 1930. He went into exile when his government fell. His son José entered politics to clear his father's name and founded the Spanish fascist party, Falange, in 1933. As such, any "melée" involving Franco's fascists might have been said to contain "those of Rivera".

José Rivera may have either supported Franco's push for power or fought to head the Nationalist side himself, but we will never know because the Loyalists shot him in 1936.

Adolf Hitler: 1889–45

II.24, III.35, IX.90 & III.58

> *Bestes farouhes de faim fleuves tranner,*
> *Plus part du champ encontre Hister sera,*
> *En caige de fer le grand fera treisner,*
> *Quand Rin enfant de Germain observa.*

Translation:

> Beasts wild with hunger swim rivers,
> The greater part of the field will be against *Hister*,
> In a cage of iron the great one is drawn,
> When the child of Germany sees the Rhine.

We know that Hitler himself read this quatrain as a prediction of his own future. Nazi propaganda made much of Nostradamus, claiming that the *Centuries* clearly predicted that Germany would conquer Europe and rule a thousand-year empire. It would, no doubt, have gratified Nostradamus, who delighted in ambiguities and ironies, that the Allies also used his work for propaganda purposes, as proof of their own inevitable victory. By now, the reader will have seen how easy it is to read varied and often contradictory meanings into the same quatrain.

The word "*Hister*" in line two is plainly a name, because Nostradamus gives it a capital letter. Hitler, we know, believed this to be a reference to himself. He pointed out to acquaintances that the River Danube used to be called the "*Ister*" by the Ancient Romans. Hitler was born in the Austrian town of Braunau am Inn, which is on the banks of the River Danube. To Hitler, Nostradamus' word "Hister" was a combination of Ister and Hitler – a play on words and a confirmation that it was he who was intended in the prediction.

It is not known if he came to this rather tenuous conclusion before or after he changed his name to Hitler from his original surname: Schicklegruber.

The first line mentions ravening "beasts" crossing rivers. Hitler saw this as a prediction that his own troops[2] would conquer to gain the *lebensraum* ("living-space") that his people needed. (With the benefit of hindsight, we could also interpret it as the ferocious drive of the Allies, hungry for revenge against the Nazis.)

Line two can be read as predicting that most of Europe would eventually be "against" Hitler and Nazi Germany. Likewise, the "iron cage" of line three could be a description of the steel and concrete bunker in which Hitler confined himself during his last days, and in which he took his own life.

As a matter of passing interest, almost the exact phrase was used of an earlier dictator; in 1815, Marshal Ney was sent with a large French army to capture Napoleon (who had just escaped from Elba). Ney told Louis XVIII that he would "drag [Napoleon] back to Paris in an iron cage". In fact, as we saw in an earlier chapter, the whole army deserted to join Napoleon . . . including Marshal Ney.

[2]Nazi troopers liked to be described as "blond beasts".

The last line seems baffling, until we recall the transposed lines of the quatrain about the 'flu epidemic of 1919. If we transpose lines three and four, then the quatrain states that the rest of Europe will be against Hitler when he crosses the Rhine and attacks France.

> *Du plus profond de l'Occident d'Europe,*
> *De pauvres gens un jeune enfant naistra:*
> *Qui par sa langue seduira grande troupe,*
> *Son bruit au regne d'Orient plus croistra.*

Translation:

> In the deepest part of Western Europe,
> Of poor people a young infant will be born:
> Who with his tongue will seduce many people,
> His reputation will increase in the eastern kingdom.

The above quatrain matches the lives of both Hitler and Napoleon, but the reference to western Europe tends favour Hitler – Napoleon was born in Corsica.

Hitler's father, Alois Schicklegruber, was a badly-paid border official. Napoleon's father was a lawyer and a count, but could not afford to send his son to military school and had to petition a scholarship from Louis XVI.

Line three describes this "infant" seducing many people with his tongue. Hitler made his political career as an orator; we now tend to think of him as a ranting demagogue, but contemporaries like Albert Speer noted that Hitler could "seduce" just about any audience by matching his tone to their sensibilities. Napoleon, of course, was primarily a general, but he had a famous ability to inspire his troops with his speeches before battles.

Finally, line four describes the leader in question increasing his reputation in the "eastern kingdom" (presumably meaning Eastern Europe). We might assume that Nostradamus was being ironic here. Both Hitler and Napoleon dreamed of crowning their military achievements by conquering Russia, and both lost their reputations for infallibility in their Russian campaigns.

Un capitaine de la grand Germanie,
Se viendra rendre par simulé secours,
Un roi des rois aide de Pannonie,
Que sa revolte fera de sang grand cours.

Translation:

A captain of greater Germany,
Will come to deliver simulated help,
A king of kings to support *Pannonie*,
Whose revolt will cause great bloodshed.

In Nostradamus' day, "Germany" consisted of a number of independent principalities. Yet the term "captain of greater Germany" suggests that the seer knew that the country would one day come under the domination of a single ruler. This would have then been considered as unlikely as England forming a union with Wales, Scotland and Ireland – an event that Nostradamus also foresaw.

There is a single, complex meaning contained in these four lines, not two, three or four sub-predictions as the quatrains usually contain. The seer predicts that the "captain of greater Germany" will offer "simulated help" to "*Pannonie*" ("*Panonia*" was the classical name for Hungary). This will make him a "king of kings", but the resultant bloodshed will be very great.

The quatrain fits Hitler perfectly. He was indeed the sole "*Fuhrer*" ("leader") of "greater Germany"; in fact the Third Reich was often referred to by the Nazis as "*Grossendeutschland*" ("greater Germany"). The Hungarians sided with the Germans in World War II, but following terrible losses on the Russian front, they secretly sued to the Allies for peace. Hitler invaded his wavering ally and set up a puppet government. He described this invasion as "help" for the people of Hungary, but his troops then arrested and murdered hundreds of thousands of Hungarians.

Hitler's invasions certainly made him a "king of kings" for a while, but the war he started shed the lifeblood of an estimated 80 million people – 55 million of whom were civilians.

Aupres du Rhin des Montaignes Norique,
Naistra un grand de gens trop tard venu.
Qui defendra Saurome et Pannoniques,
Quon ne sçaura qu'il sera devenu.

Translation:

Near the Rhine from the mountains of Noricum,
Will be born a great man of the people but he comes too late.
Who will defend Poland and Hungary,
It will not be known what became of him.

The word "*Norique*" in the first line sounds like "Noricum", the Ancient Roman name for Austria. Hitler was an Austrian who led the Germans – a people whose national river is the Rhine. He was "too late" because land war to build an empire had become, by 1939, a thing of the past. Hitler and his slavery-based Third Reich were a throwback to a more savage, bygone age.

Line three might be read as a question: "Who will defend Poland and Hungary?" On the other hand, German troops certainly did defend these countries, not least from the Poles and the Hungarians. Again we may catch a whiff of prophetic irony from the seer.

The last line states that it would not be known what happened to this "great man of the people". This is also true of Hitler. Although official sources insisted that Hitler killed himself in the Berlin bunker, the fact that his body was never recovered fed rumours that he had survived and escaped to live out the rest of his life in hiding in South America. Given the lack of evidence, it is possible that this belief may never be fully disproved.

The Nazi Swastika

VI.49

De la partie de Mammer grand Pontife,
Subjugera les confins du Danube:
Chasser les croix par fer raffe ne riffe,
Captifz, or, bagues plus de cent mille rubes.

Translation:

> The Pontiff of the party of *Mammer*,
> Subjugating the borders of the Danube:
> Chasing the iron cross by hook or by crook,
> Captives, gold, jewels more than a hundred thousand rubies.

The first line of the quatrain describes the "Pontiff of the party of *Mammer*". This could be a neat description of Hitler with the added twist of a typical Nostradamus double meaning . . .

"Mamers" was the Sabine name for the god Mars, but by adding another "m", the seer gives a second indication: that of "Mammon", the demon of money and greed. The Nazis certainly had a near-religious respect for war and militarism, and coupled this with an undisguised love of wealth.

In fact, a third meaning may also be extracted from this single word, provided the reader is willing to extrapolate on an extrapolation. The Sabines were a tribe in central Italy – the same country to form the first "fascist" party, which the Germans copied and called the National Socialist (or Nazi) Party.

The Nazis certainly subjugated the "borders of the Danube", as line two predicts, and their bravest soldiers "chased" hopes of winning the medal known as the Iron Cross ("*croix par fer*") as it says in line three.

Many Nostradamus translators have also read a prediction of the Nazi swastika in this line. "*Raffe ne riffe*" is a French version of "by hook or by crook". Some scholars simply translate the line into: "chasing the crooked iron cross" – the swastika.

We can take line four, with its gold, jewels and rubies, as Nostradamus' shorthand for the vast amount of wealth the Nazis' plundered from banks, museums and chateaux in the territories they overran, although "rubies" could also be a poetic image of all the blood shed during the war.

World War II: 1939–45
II.38, II.39 & II.40

These next three quatrains are commonly thought to describe the run up to an early part of the Second World War. The fact that they follow one another in sequence in *Centuries II* might mean that

Nostradamus meant us to read them together. Certainly, as we will see, the last two are meant to be read in this way.

> *Des condamnez sera fait un grand nombre,*
> *Quant les monarques seront conciliez:*
> *Mais l'un deux viendra si malencombre,*
> *Que guere ensemble ne seront reliez.*

Translation:

> There shall be a great number condemned,
> When the monarchs shall be reconciled:
> One will come to such a bad encumbrance,
> That their reconciliation will not last long.

The first quatrain sets the tone for all three World War II predictions in its first line, describing "great numbers condemned". With over 80 million dead and millions more maimed and dispossessed, this description certainly fits World War II.

One could also accept Erica Cheetham's interpretation that it is a prophecy about the Nuremburg War Crime Trials that followed the downfall of the Nazis. Over 120 Nazi war criminals were eventually "condemned" to death.

The quatrain's link to the Second World War is seen in the remaining three lines, which echo the events of the Hitler–Stalin Pact. In August 1939, Joseph Stalin and Adolf Hitler shocked the world (and their own nations of Russia and Germany) by announcing a non-aggression treaty ("the monarchs shall be reconciled"). These previously mortal enemies even cemented their friendship by jointly invading and partitioning Poland the following month.

Informed and understandably cynical political commentators saw, however, that the alliance was simply a ruse by both parties. Hitler's army was still too small to defeat the massive Soviet armed forces. Stalin, on the other hand, could not launch an attack on Germany because he had – unfortunately – shot almost his entire officer corps in the previous decade of purges. Until these weaknesses could be repaired, both leaders had good reason to delay their otherwise inevitable conflict.

Line three goes on to predict that one of these "monarchs" would meet a "bad encumbrance" that would lead to a crumbling of their reconciliation (in line four). Hitler successfully invaded France in spring 1940, but found his attack on Britain barred by the English Channel and the Royal Air Force. Thus "encumbered", he decided to simply contain the British, and turned his attention and resources to preparing to stab his Soviet "ally" in the back. He beat Stalin in the treachery stakes – invading the USSR in June 1941.

Other commentators have speculated that the alliance between Hitler and Mussolini ("the brutal friendship") might be meant – certainly, Mussolini had become an "encumbrance" to his ally long before the end of the war . . .

> *Un an devant le conflict Italique,*
> *Germaines, Gaulois, Hespaignols pour le fort:*
> *Cherra l'escolle maison de republique,*
> *Ou, hors mis peu, seront suffoque mors.*

Translation:

> A year before the Italian conflict,
> Germans, French, Spanish for the strong:
> The school house of the republic will fall,
> Where, except for a few, they suffocate to death.

In 1939, the Italian dictator, Benito Mussolini, told Hitler that Italy would not be ready to support the Germans in the war until 1942 at the earliest – the Italian army was simply too small and badly trained.

However, in 1940, Mussolini was overcome by his own greed. He saw how easily France had fallen and calculated that Britain and Russia might also fall before 1942. This would obviously leave little of value for him to conquer for his own empire. So Italy entered the war with an under-trained army which, as a result, lost virtually every battle it fought.

If we take this quatrain to be a prediction of the Second World War, then "a year before the Italian [entry into the] conflict", would be 1939. The second line of the quatrain supports this interpretation, because it matches the political affiliations of Western

Europe in that year. Fascist Spain was friendly towards Nazi Germany – as were a significant section of France's ("*Gaulois*") right-wing politicians, those that later formed the heart of the quisling Vichy Government after the German invasion.

Hitler's *blitzkrieg* invasion took France by surprise in the spring of 1940, and seems to be predicted in line three. France was the first modern European republic and, as we saw in previous chapters, disseminated her political philosophy both by argument and force. To call France the "school house" of modern republicanism would be far from inaccurate. Certainly, the Nazi invasion caused the "fall" and flight of the French Republican Government.

France, although unable to field troops for most of the war, lost an estimated 675,000 of her citizens – many of whom might be said to have "suffocate[d]" under the crushing Nazi rule.

> *Un pres apres non point longue intervalle,*
> *Par mer et terre sera faict grand tumulte:*
> *Beaucoup plus grande sera pugne navalle,*
> *Feux, animaux, qui feront plus d'insulte.*

Translation:

> Shortly afterwards not a long interval,
> By sea and land there is made a great tumult:
> Greater than ever will be naval battles,
> Fires, animals, which will make great affront.

This quatrain is clearly supposed to be a continuation of the previous prediction (or predictions) as line one refers back to it.

The European war did not become a "world war" until Japan entered on the Axis side in December 1941. The Japanese stayed nominally neutral during the fall of France and the collapse of the Nazi–Soviet pact (apparently predicted in the previous two quatrains). Then came the Japanese attack on Pearl Harbour. The major land and sea battles of the war ("great tumult[s]") did not occur until after this event, just as line two seems to predict.

The major sea battles in the Atlantic – predicted by British and German military planners at the start of the war – never took place. Apart from the hunting and destruction of the German pocket battleships, the main battle in this area was a cat-and-mouse conflict to crush the U-boat menace (see below).

However, the American–Japanese war in the Pacific turned on several major sea battles (Coral Sea, Midway, Leyte Gulf and the Marianas "Turkey Shoot"[3]). These "naval battles" were certainly "greater than ever" (i.e. greater than those that went before them) because of the new giant aircraft carriers deployed by both sides.

Line four is puzzling, with its fire and animals. Erica Cheetham suggests that it is a comment on "animals" who can "fire", describing riflemen, or perhaps tanks and submarines. However, the word "*insulte*"("insult" or "affront") at the end of the line may suggest another meaning. The Nazis slaughtered millions like "animals" in concentration camps, "fire[ing]" the bodies in huge incinerators. This, it is now universally agreed, was an "affront" to humanity.

The Battle of the Atlantic and the Holocaust
IV.15 & III.71

> *D'où pensera faire venir famine,*
> *De là viendra le rassasiement:*
> *L'oeil de la mer par avare canine,*
> *Pour de l'un l'autre dorna huile, froment.*

Translation:

> From the place famine will be thought to come,
> From there will come plenitude:
> The eye of the sea like a covetous dog,
> One gives oil and wheat to the other.

Hitler relied on his U-boats (submarines) to reduce Britain to starvation. He knew that the UK had too high a population-to-land ratio to be self-sufficient in food, so believed that cutting the supply route from America, across the North Atlantic, would eventually starve the besieged nation into surrender. So the U-boat "wolfpacks" ceaselessly hunted the cargo ships making their way to and from America. Hundreds of vessels were torpedoed and one out of four Allied merchant seamen did not live to see 1945.

---

[3]So called because the once-fearsome Japanese "Zero" fighters were so heavily out-gunned by the new American fighters.

Fortunately, the U-boat fleet was always kept under-strength for the task allotted them because Hitler ordered his limited number of armament factories to build tanks rather than submarines. As a result, Allied technology had enough time to counter the U-boat threat, and the new sonar and radar equipment, and improved naval tactics, had turned the Battle of the Atlantic against the Germans by the mid-point of the war.

Three out of four U-boat crewmen were killed during the war; going to the bottom of the ocean as their "iron coffins"[4] were depth-charged or shelled by Allied destroyers. This was the worst casualty rate of any service on either side of the conflict.

The first two lines of the quatrain seem to suggest an overall historical view of the Battle of the Atlantic. Hitler and Churchill both knew that the Atlantic seaways were the key to winning the war in Europe. If America could be physically barred from intervening, Russia would stand alone, except for a starving, weaponless Britain. Nevertheless, thanks to the bravery of the British, American and Canadian merchant fleets and their Navy escorts, vital supplies and, later, troops made it across the Atlantic in a continuous stream throughout the war.

The third line is one of Nostradamus' most poetically striking. Up to the end of the nineteenth century, this description ("the eye of the sea like a covetous dog") was simply a puzzle. Yet the invention of the "submersible torpedo boat" in 1906 could have provided a clue to any contemporary Nostradamus scholar with an interest in military inventions. The new German *U-boot* could fire a torpedo while under water by aiming with a telescopic periscope: "the eye of the sea [hunting] like a covetous dog".

The fourth line is connected with the second – an apparent prediction that the U-boats would fail to inflict starvation on Britain. However, the inclusion of the word "*huile*" ("oil") is striking. In Nostradamus' day, oil was used as a condiment in cooking, a cheap substitute (in lamps) for candles and something you used to grease cart axles: in other words, useful but non-vital. During World War II, however, crude oil was as vital as food to Britain, because it could be refined into petrol.

---

[4]The bitter nickname U-boatmen gave to their submarines.

> *Ceux dans les isles de longtemps assiegez,*
> *Prendront vigeur force contre ennemis:*
> *Ceux par dehors mors de faim profligez,*
> *En plus grand faim que jamais seront mis.*

Translation:

> Those of the islands that have long been besieged,
> Shall use vigorous force against their enemies:
> Those overcome outside will die of hunger,
> As great a famine as has ever been known before.

The first two lines seem to echo the prediction given above: Britain besieged, but fighting back and ultimately winning against Hitler.

The last two lines, on the other hand, seem to predict something much darker. There was, in fact, great starvation in German-occupied countries ("those overcome") during the war, but this was not a historically-unprecedented famine, as line four seems to predict. On the other hand, if we take the line to mean a man-made famine, we might see a prediction of the deliberate starvation of millions in Nazi concentration camps: the first time in history that so many people were murdered in this cruel way.

Pearl Harbor: 7 December 1941

IX.100

> *Navalle pugne nuit sera superee,*
> *Le feu naves à l'Occident ruine:*
> *Rubriche neufue la grand nef coloeree,*
> *Ire à vaincu, et victoire en bruine.*

Translation:

> Naval battle night is overcome,
> The fire in the ruined ships of the West:
> A new coding the great coloured ship,
> Anger to the vanquished, victory in a fog.

Just after dawn ("night is overcome") on 7 December 1941, the Japanese navy launched a massive air attack from its carrier ships, secretly anchored off the Hawaiian coast. The target was the US Pacific Fleet docked in Pearl Harbour. (The war vessels were painted camouflage style – and this might be what Nostradamus means by "great coloured ship[s]" in line three.) Japanese bombers and fighters sank eighteen ships, including eight battleships, destroyed almost 200 aircraft (most of which did not have time to get off the ground) and killed nearly 3,000 people.

The Japanese government had actually issued a declaration of war a few hours before the attack, but because of American bureaucratic bungling, the fleet at Pearl Harbour had not been informed that they were at war and so were taken by complete surprise. In fact, it is rumoured that the Americans intercepted and translated the Japanese-coded orders to attack Pearl Harbour some days before. However, US President Franklin D. Roosevelt ordered the information to be suppressed, so America could enter the war as an ally of Britain: an attack by Germany's Japanese ally would have given him the necessary leverage to budge his solidly anti-war Congress. Whether that is true is still a matter of some debate. However, line three, with its mention of a "new coding" might suggest the interception of the Japanese signal.

The last line speaks of "anger to the vanquished". This might be a reference to the rage of the American people over the Japanese "sneak attack". Overnight the country went from being largely pacifist to being fervently militaristic.

The words "victory in a fog" are harder to understand in this context, but they may refer to the fact that the Japanese attack failed to sink the US carrier ships, which were out on exercises at the time. Missing these ships "in the fog of battle" was a major disappointment to the Japanese. Their survival gave the Americans just enough foothold in the Pacific to launch a counter offensive. Arguably these American carriers were the main reason Japan lost control of the sea and, ultimately, the war.

The Bomb: 8 AM, 6 August 1945

II.6

> *Aupres des portes et dedans deux cités,*
> *Seront deux fléaux et oncques n'apperceu un tel:*
> *Faim, dedans peste, de fer hors gens boutés,*
> *Crier secours au grand Dieu immortel.*

Translation:

> Near the gates and within two cities,
> There will be two scourges the like of which have
> never been seen before:
> Famine within plague, people thrust out by the sword,
> Crying for succour to the grand God immortal.

The Allies' atomic fission bomb project was originally aimed at destroying Berlin, but Germany collapsed before the weapon could be made ready. However, mainland Japan was still holding out, and American military planners were certain that tens of thousands of US servicemen would die in the upcoming invasion. Therefore Harry Truman – the new American president since Roosevelt had worked himself to death – gave orders to drop single atom bombs on the coastal ports of Hiroshima and Nagasaki, in the hope of shocking the Japanese into surrender.

The first bomb exploded over Hiroshima at just after 8 a.m., on 6 August 1945: 129,558 people were killed. The second bomb was dropped on Nagasaki three days later: 66,000 people were reported killed or severely injured.

By Second World War standards, these casualty figures were comparatively light. For example, six months previously, 135,000 people had been killed in one night in the German town of Dresden by a "conventional" air-raid. Nevertheless, Japan surrendered.

Erica Cheetham translates the word "*portes*" in the first line as "harbours" rather than "gates". Given Nostradamus' penchant for deliberate, riddling misspellings, it is not unreasonable to suspect that he added an "e" to the French word "*port*" ("harbour") to make "*porte*" ("gate"). Both Hiroshima and Nagasaki are harbour towns.

The second line speaks for itself. The atom bombs were

unquestionably "scourges". And certainly, such weapons had "never [been] seen before", in the history of warfare.

Line three sounds like a description of acute radiation sickness. Victims first suffer total loss of appetite or extreme nausea. Deterioration of the body's cell structure follows, appearing as "radiation burns" on the skin. In such extreme cases, death is usually inevitable. Nostradamus – a veteran of numerous plague outbreaks in his own time – may well have described these symptoms as "famine within a plague".

The last line may be a prediction of the despairing prayers of the bomb victims, but it also seems to carry an undertone of the prophet's own horror.

The Founding of Israel: 1947

III.97

> *Nouvelle loi terre neufve occuper,*
> *Vers la Syrie, Judee et Palestine:*
> *Le grand empire barbare corruer,*
> *Avant que Phoebus son siecle determine.*

Translation:

> A new law will occupy a new country,
> Towards Syria, Judea and Palestine:
> The great barbarian empire crumbles,
> Before the cycle of the Sun is determined.

The British army captured Palestine – the former Jewish homeland up to the dispersal of Jewish Judea in the second century AD – from the Turks in the First World War. They promised the Palestinian Arabs independence in exchange for their support, but they had also promised the Jews (whose help they also needed) a homeland in Palestine. After the war, the British continued to occupy Palestine, and prevaricated when asked to fulfil their (mutually-exclusive) promises. Thirty years of revolt and terrorism followed.

After the Second World War, exhausted and sick to death of the "Palestine Problem", the British announced (in 1947) that they would pull out by mid-1948. The newly-formed United Nations was left to sort out the mess and they, partly out of guilt over the

Nazi Holocaust, supported the Jewish demands: over fifty per cent of Palestine was to be given over to Jewish rule. The Palestinians were naturally outraged, and the neighbouring Arab states of Syria, Egypt, Lebanon, Jordan and Iraq supported them.

After a year of war, the Jews – or rather the Israelis – had beaten off their attackers and subdued their own Arab population. Israel was back on the map for the first time in almost 2,000 years.

Being of Jewish stock himself, one might guess that Nostradamus would have had a special interest in the rebuilding of the State of Israel. Although the above quatrain gives no indication as to who would rule this "new land", the position the seer gives in line two is exactly correct. The third and fourth lines describe the crumbling of a "great barbarian empire . . . before the cycle of the Sun is determined". From a late-twentieth-century perspective, it is hard not to see this as an accurate prediction that Soviet rule in Russia would collapse before the end of the second millennium (AD 2000).

The Crushing of the Hungarian Revolution: 1956

II.90

> Par vie et mort changé regne d'Ongrie,
> La loi sera plus aspre que service:
> Leur grand cité d'hulements plaincts et crie,
> Castor et Pollux ennemis dans la lice.

Translation:

> By life and death the kingdom of Hungary will be changed,
> The law will become more bitter than service:
> Their great city will howl lament and cry,
> Castor and Pollux are enemies in the field.

As noted above, Hungary fought on the German side during the first half of the Second World War, but was then invaded and brutally occupied by their former ally. The Soviet Army was therefore welcomed as a liberating force by most Hungarians. Sadly, by the mid-1950s the rejoicing was over. Stalin's rule was little better than the Nazi occupation, and many Hungarians dreamed of a return to democracy.

In 1956, student demonstrations in Budapest – calling for an end to compulsory Russian language courses – quickly spread the unrest to the whole country. The communist puppet regime was ousted and multiparty democracy was reinstated. The new Hungarian leaders – egged on by promises of aid and military assistance from the West – declared Hungary a "neutral nation". Stalin sent in the tanks.

Desperate pleas for help were sent out from the last free radio station in Budapest ("[the] great city will howl lament and cry"), but the western governments ignored them for fear of starting another world war. The free Hungarians fought back with the few weapons they had, but had no chance against the massive Soviet invasion force.

The last line of the quatrain describes "Castor and Pollux" as "enemies in the field". Castor and Pollux were Greek heroes who had been born as twins. In 1956, communist Hungarians joined the advancing Russians and fought to suppress their brother Hungarians.

The Soviets shot hundreds of "counter-revolutionaries" and imprisoned thousands more. The Communist regime was reinstated as an absolute state, where even whispered dissent could lead to the death sentence; so, in line two, the "law [became] more bitter than service" – or perhaps we might translate the word "service" as "slavery".

Fidel Castro in the USA: 1959

VIII.74

En terre neufue bien avant Roi entré,
Pendant subges lui viendront faire acueil,
Sa perfidie aura tel recontré
Qu'aux citadind lieu de feste et receuil.

Translation:

Into the new land the King advances far,
While the subjects come to bid him welcome,
His perfidious action shall have the result
That to the citizens it is a reception rather than a feast.

As the English called America "the New World", the French of Nostradamus' day called the newly-discovered continent "*le Terre Neuve*". It is hard to believe that Nostradamus could have used this phrase, in line one of the above quatrain, without realizing that it would make his readers think of the Americas.

Although the rest of the quatrain is too vague to offer an obvious historical incident, it does seem to echo Fidel Castro's ill-fated diplomatic trip to the USA in spring 1959.

Cuba was a thoroughly corrupt right-wing dictatorship, but, in 1956, the young political exile Fidel Castro and his brother Raoul sailed back to the country with eighty fellow revolutionaries. Seventy were killed on the beach by a government ambush, but the Castros escaped. They launched a popular revolution and, by December 1958, had taken Havana and driven out the former dictator, Fulgencio Batista, into exile.

The USA viewed the Cuban revolution without enthusiasm. The American government had backed the corrupt Batista regime, and now Castro started to talk of "land reform" and nationalization of the (largely American-owned) oil and sugar industries: a socialist plan, bordering on communism.

In the spring of 1959, Castro flew to Washington to try to win American support. He was rudely denied a meeting with President Eisenhower, and instead met with Vice-President Richard Nixon. According to Castro's version of events, Nixon was cold towards him. The Cuban revolutionary explained that he was not a communist, but merely wanted to help his country's transition into the twentieth century. He added that he could not do this without the help of one or other of the two rival superpowers – the USA or the USSR. Nixon reported to Eisenhower that Castro was a communist and should not be helped in any way. So Cuba sided with the Soviet bloc.

The language of the last three lines of the quatrain is subtle, but Castro *was* seen as "perfidious" in the rather paranoid eyes of post-McCarthy America, so his welcome was chilly: a forced "reception rather than a [welcoming] feast".

It is interesting to wonder how the world would look today if Nixon had been diplomatic and friendly to Castro; it is possible that Cuba might have joined the western powers and, at the very least, the world might have been saved the emotional trauma of the Cuban missile crisis.

The Kennedy Assassinations: 22 November 1963 and 5 June 1968
IX.36

> *Un grand Roi prins entre les mains d'un Joine,*
> *Non loing de Pasque confusion coup coultre:*
> *Perpet. Captifs temps que fouldre en la husne,*
> *Lorsque trois frères se blesseront et meutre.*

Translation:

> A great King taken into the hands of the Young,
>   Not far from Easter confusion knife state:
> Permanent captives times when lightning is above,
>   When three brothers are wounded and murdered.

President John F. Kennedy was killed (almost certainly by multiple snipers) as his motorcade passed through downtown Dallas on 22 November 1963. His younger brother, Senator Bobby Kennedy, was shot dead when walking through the kitchen of the Ambassador Hotel moments after winning the Californian nomination for the Democratic leadership on 5 June 1968.

Both assassinations caused widespread shock, so it is not surprising that subsequent Nostradamus scholars should have searched the quatrains for predictions of these murders. Of course, bearing in mind that Nostradamus' interests never strayed too far from France and Europe, it is perhaps not surprising that there seem to be few "hits". It is true that about half a dozen quatrains have been linked to the Kennedy assassinations, but all rely on rather remote connections – so that, for example, any mention of "brothers" and death in the same quatrain has been seized upon.

Another example, *Century II*, quatrain 57, describes the "fall" of "the great one to death, death too sudden and bewailed". True, the snipers' bullets that killed Jack Kennedy struck "too sudden", and his loss was certainly "bewailed", but the link is hardly convincing.

The above is one of the most quoted "Kennedy quatrains". I offer it here in order to allow the reader to judge the material for themselves. Also, if it is indeed about the Kennedys, it seems to predict that Senator Edward Kennedy will follow his two older brothers in being assaulted.

Line one may be a description of John F. Kennedy winning the presidency (the youngest man ever to do so) after the retirement of President Eisenhower.

Line three describes "lightning from above", and this has been linked to the overhead sniper shot that burst Kennedy's skull.

Line four describes "three brothers wounded and murdered". Whether the remaining Kennedy brother of that ill-fated generation, Edward, needs to be cautious of knives around Easter, as it suggests in line two, is a matter for conjecture.

Space Exploration: 4 October 1957 to the present day
IX.65

> *Dedans le coing de luna viendra rendre,*
> *Ou sera prins et mis en terre estrange,*
> *Les fruitz immeurs seront à la grand esclandre,*
> *Grand vitupere à l'un grande loiange.*

Translation:

> He will be taken to the corner of the moon,
> Where he will be placed in a strange land,
> The unripe fruit will cause a great scandal,
> Great shame, to the other great praise.

The Space Age began on 4 October 1957, when the Soviets launched the world's first orbital satellite: Sputnik 1. The USA, caught napping, hurried to catch up in what became known as the "Space Race". However, the Russians beat them again, sending the first manned rocket into orbit on 12 April 1961. However, in 1969, the Americans at last won the initiative when, on 20 July, they were the first nation to put a man on the Moon.

The first line sounds odd – but close examination shows that it is an accurate description of the Apollo 11 "Moonshot". The astronauts did not, strictly speaking, "fly" to the Moon. Their rocket was fired on a predetermined trajectory in much the same way that the circus performer called a "human cannonball" is shot into a distant net. Since they had minimal control over the space-flight, it would therefore be accurate to say that the astronauts were "taken" to the Moon.

It certainly sounds paradoxical to speak of a "corner" of a spherical object – until we remember that, to Nostradamus' contemporaries, the Moon was a flat plate. We now know that although it is a ball that revolves round the Earth, the Moon does not rotate on its own axis, so it always presents the observer with the same "face". The Sea of Tranquillity, where Apollo 11 landed, is in the upper left-hand corner of that face.

The "strange land" of line two is certainly an apt description of the barren lunar surface on which the astronauts touched down (or in Nostradamus' words, were "placed").

Various writers have connected lines three and four with the Challenger shuttle disaster. On 28 January 1986, seventy-three seconds after take-off, the space shuttle exploded, killing the six NASA crewmen and a young teacher called Christa McAuliffe – the first civilian to be invited on a NASA space mission. Francis X. King suggests that the "unripe fruit" mentioned in the third line is a reference to the faulty shuttle design that led to the disaster. He also concludes that the "great shame", mentioned in line four, was the public anger (and a cut in funding to NASA) over the incident. The "great praise", he suggests, was the public enthusiasm for Neil Armstrong and his fellow Moon-walkers.

Conspiracy theorists have added another interpretation to the words about "great shame" – in fact, two. The first is the suggestion that the Moon missions never actually took place. Discovering that the mission was not technically possible with their under-developed ("unripe") technology, NASA, they claim, faked all the landings at a secret movie set in the Nevada desert.

The other theory involves the so-called "Face on Mars". In 1976, NASA scientists studying the Viking Mars-Orbiter photographs found what they thought looked like a mile-long construction on the Martian surface. This object appeared to be a giant sculpture of a human face looking directly upwards. Ever since then, the "Faceists" (as they call themselves) have argued that there is a cover up of evidence of alien artefacts found by NASA and the (now former) Soviet Space Agency.

They suggest that the governments involved do not believe that the mass of the human race is psychologically mature enough to face the vast implications of the finding of the remains of extra-terrestrial civilizations – one might say that they think we are all the "unripe fruit" Nostradamus speaks of.

If either of these theories were true, it would certainly involve "great shame" for the governments involved. In which case, presumably the conspiracy theorists who eventually unmask the hoax will reap "great praise".

The Iran–Iraq War: 1980–88

V.25

> Le prince Arabe Mars, Sol, Venus, Lyon,
> Regne d'Eglise par mer succombera:
> Devers la Perse bien pres d'un million,
> Bisance, Egypte, ver. serp. invadera.

Translation:

> The Arab prince Mars, Sun, Venus, Leo,
> The Kingdoms of the Church overcome from the sea:
> Towards Persia very near a million,
> Turkey, Egypt ver. serp. invades.

This quatrain seems to be one of the most chillingly accurate in the *Centuries*. In September 1980, Iraq invaded its giant neighbour Iran. The Iraqi president Saddam Hussein ("the Arab prince") was prompted by greed for land, by the belief that Iran (having just suffered bloody Islamic revolution) would be militarily weak, and by a fear that their Islamic fundamentalism would be exported to his own repressed population.

Initially Iraq – a nation between Iran and the seas of the Mediterranean and the Persian Gulf – did well. As it says in line two, "the Kingdoms of the Church" (Islamic, Imam-led Iran) were "overcome from [the direction of] the sea". However, the Iranians rallied their nation and, by 1982, had driven the Iraqi troops out of Iran.

The war continued because Iran wanted to punish Iraq. This led to more than five years of brutal fighting, much of it from First-World-War-style trenches, with both sides employing poison gas.

The directions Nostradamus gives are quite correct in the context of this conflict. The Iraqis attacked towards "Persia", the old name for Iran, beyond which (to the north-north-west) lay "Turkey". The Iranians, on the other hand, directed their attacks towards Baghdad – beyond which (to the south-west) lay "Egypt". Although both Turkey and Egypt were not directly involved in the Iran–Iraq War, it is possible that the seer is indicating the sweeping directions of attack. (It should also be noted that neither Iran nor Iraq existed in Nostradamus' day, so he would presumably have been vague about their precise boundaries.)

The first line gives one of Nostradamus' astrological combinations, which David Ovason suggests are a complex method of dating the predictions. This conjunction of Mars, the Sun and Venus in the House of Leo is rare. The last such event was 20 August 1987.

The Iran–Iraq War actually lasted into 1988, but United Nations peace resolution 598 – whose acceptance by Iran signalled the end of the conflict – was passed on 20 July 1987.

Erica Cheetham suggests that "*ver. serp.*" may be short for "*vera serpens*" (Latin for "true serpent") – perhaps an unflattering description of Saddam Hussein.

Exact casualty figures in the eight-year conflict could not be ascertained by either side; Nostradamus' figure, "near a million", is as close as the Iranians and Iraqis can come themselves.

The Fall of Soviet Communism: 1989
V.81, IV.32 & II. 89

> *L'oiseau royal sur la cité solaire,*
> *Sept mois devant fera nocturne augure:*
> *Mur d'Orient cherra tonnerre esclaire,*
> *Sept jours aux portes les ennemis à l'heure.*

Translation:

> The royal bird over the city of the Sun,
> Seven months together gives nightly warnings:
> The Eastern wall will fall and lightning shines,
> Seven days the enemies shall be at the gate.

Growing unrest in the Soviet Bloc countries in the 1980s led Russian president Mikhail Gorbachev to introduce sweeping political and economic reforms. One by one the former Soviet client states followed suit. Revivified opposition parties then swiftly – and usually bloodlessly – toppled one absolute communist government after another.

The Berlin Wall had been a symbol of repression and anti-western paranoia since it was erected in a single night on 13 August 1961. Berlin, although deep within communist East Germany, had been split down the middle in the post-war agreement between Stalin, Churchill and Truman. The prosperous, capitalist, western-ruled half of the city was a permanent temptation to East Berliners. The wall, with its watchtowers and machine-gun nests, was erected down the thirty-mile, east–west city boundary by the East German government to prevent East Berlin from becoming totally deserted. Between 1961 and 1989, at least seventy people were killed trying to cross the wall.

In 1989, Hungary suspended its border agreement with East Germany, and allowed thousands of East German citizens to cross into Austria and thence West Germany. This exodus drastically undermined the authority of the East German government, and they were finally forced into holding free elections which, of course, they lost. The Berlin Wall was immediately torn down by joyous Berliners – often aided by the Soviet border guards.

The first line could be a description of the Brandenburg Gate, a triumphal arch in the middle of Berlin, closed by the building of the wall in 1961, and the "royal bird" the statue of a winged Angel of Victory that stands on top of the gate. For Nostradamus, "the city of the Sun" would be an accurate description of Berlin, the capital of North Germany, whose astrological ruler is Leo – the principal sun sign.

Seven months "of warnings" is also a fairly accurate estimate of the period of demonstrations and minor riots, on both sides of the Berlin Wall, before it came down.

Es lieux et temps chair un poisson donra lieu,
La loi commune sera faicte au contraire:

Vieux tiendra fort plus osté du millieu,
Le Pánta chiona philòn mis fort arriere.

Translation:

In places and times when meat is replaced by fish,
The common law will be against it:
The old stands fast then is removed,
The Things held in common among friends is set aside.

Soviet communism fell because its internal infrastructure was corrupt and rotten. As stated in line one, the Soviet population often had to eat fish because the state shops could not provide meat.

The "common law", of line two sounds like Nostradamus' way of speaking of common public opinion. As line three states, the old order stood fast up to the moment it was removed.[5]

"*Pánta, chiona philòn*" in line four is a Greek phrase that literally translates as "things shared in common among friends", an apt characterization of the ideal of communism.

Un jour seront demis les deux grands maistres,
Leur grand pouvoir se verra augmenté:
La terre neufue sera en ses hauts estres,
Au sanguinaire le nombre racompté.

Translation:

One day the two great masters will be friends,
Their great powers will be increased:
The new land shall be at the height of its power,
To the man of blood the number is reported.

American president Ronald Reagan naturally welcomed the liberalization of Russia – a country he had described, only a few

---

[5]For three days in August 1991, the world looked on gloomily as Soviet military hardliners attempted a coup d'état to return Russia to absolute communist rule. Fortunately, political reformers, led by the future Russian president Boris Yeltsin, with the aid of the citizens of Moscow, peacefully disarmed the generals and went on with the dismantling of the communist, one-party government.

years earlier, as "the Evil Empire". There was a warm friendship between Reagan and Mikhail Gorbachev ("the two great masters will be friends").

Economically speaking, both the West and the East gained by the cessation of the cold war – military budgets were cut, allowing urgently needed funds to be siphoned elsewhere.

We have already encountered the term "new land" in Nostradamus (see *Century VIII*, quatrain 74, above). Here, in line three, it also seems to indicate the United States, which became the world's most powerful country after the downfall of Soviet communism. In calling this zenith "the height of its power", on the other hand, Nostradamus may be hinting that the USA too might be on the verge of sliding downhill.

The "man of blood" of line four sounds like Mikhail Gorbachev, who had a large "port-wine" birthmark on his forehead. When Russia and America agreed to nuclear disarmament, observation teams from both sides checked that the missiles were genuinely destroyed, then reported the figures to their respective leaders.

1990s Political Environmentalism

III.76

> *En Germanie naistront diverses sectes,*
> *S'approcant fort de l'heureux paganisme,*
> *Le coeur captif et petites receptes,*
> *Feront retour à payer le vrai disme.*

Translation:

> In Germany diverse sects are born,
> Approaching very near to happy paganism,
> The heart captive and small receivings,
> They will return to pay the true tithe.

Although this quatrain has been linked to the creation of Protestant sects in the sixteenth century (Cheetham) and the rise of German fascism in the 1930s (de Fontbrune), I am personally inclined to see it as a reference to the growth of political environmentalism in the last two decades of the twentieth century.

Most of the political parties of Europe and America have embraced certain environmental policies, although they are often aimed simply at netting the "tree-hugger" vote.

The first green-specific politician to win office in a national parliament was the Swiss, Daniel Brelaz, in 1979. In 1981, four "greens" were elected to the Belgian parliament. However, it was not until 1983, when Petra Kelly and twenty-seven other environmentalists were elected to the German Bundestag, that politicians realized to what extent environmentalism could be a vote winner. (This seems to be indicated by the reference to Germany in line one.) Since then, the environment has figured as widely in political debate as unemployment or defence spending.

As to "happy paganism", in line two, environmentalism is often associated – much to its annoyance – with nature worship, paganism and even Wicca (white witchcraft).

Lines three and four seem to suggest the gradual disillusionment experienced by greens faced with "small receivings" from uninterested or cynical governments. The result described in the last line – "they will return to pay the true tithe" – sounds like a reference to the immense cost of repairing the natural environment if the warning is unheeded.

The King of Terror: 11–17 August 1999

X.72

> *L'an mil neuf cens nonante neuf sept mois,*
> *Du ciel viendra un grand Roi deffraieur.*
> *Resusciter le grand Roi d'Angolmois.*
> *Avant que Mars regner par bonheur.*

Translation:

> In the year nineteen-ninety-nine and seven months,
> From the sky will come a great King of terror.
> Resurrecting the great King of *Angolmois*.
> Before and after Mars will reign happily.

For a long time, this quatrain was one of the most debated in all the *Centuries* – largely because it contains a hint of Doomsday and, most strikingly, a precise date.

In the run up to July (the seventh month) 1999 there was much press excitement over this supposed "end of the world" prediction. As one of the pundits questioned over what it might mean, I had to admit I had no idea – apart from suggesting a connection with the upcoming eclipse of the Sun across northern Europe in early August 1999.

Obviously, the end of the world did not take place that summer, but now with the luxury of hindsight I think I can offer a set of events that may fit the prediction. First, though, let's consider the quatrain itself . . .

The first line is strikingly straightforward for Nostradamus – a simple statement of a date. The only question was whether he meant the seventh month (July) or the month after seven months of the year had been completed (August).

Line two is obviously a crucial one – who precisely was the great "King of terror", and why is he described as coming from the sky?

In the nineteenth century, the Second Coming or the advent of the Antichrist was feared. Following the publication of H. G. Wells' *War of the Worlds* in 1898, an attack by Martians became a popular alternative. The Cold War raised the spectre of a pre-emptive nuclear strike, but when this ended, it was replaced by fears of terrorist germ warfare, meteorite strikes and, in an echo of the turn of the century, extraterrestrial invasion.

The word "*Angolmois*" in the third line could have been a reference to Angoumois, a province in southwestern France, but since this area has never had a "King" of any note, the accepted view was that the word was a partial anagram of the French word "*Mongolois*": "Mongols".

The only "King of the Mongols" Nostradamus would have been likely to have heard about was Genghis Khan. This thirteenth-century warlord, with his wild horsemen from the steppes, conquered China, then turned his attention westward. His generals led a huge army across Persia and northern Turkey, and on into Europe as far as Hungary. Only a succession problem back in Mongolia stopped the total conquest of Europe. The

Mongol army, after beating the cream of Europe's Teutonic knights, simply turned around and returned the way they had so brutally come.

Even in Nostradamus' time, three centuries later, the memory of Genghis Khan still made Europeans shudder. More specifically, Genghis Khan was probably the only person that Nostradamus would have known to be directly responsible for the slaughter of hundreds of thousands of people. A terrifying spectre to be "resurrected".

Line four will come as no surprise to any student of modern history. "Mars", the god of war, certainly had a "happy" reign in the late twentieth century. Yet Nostradamus said that this bloody rule would continue after 1999 – therefore this quatrain did not predict the end of the world . . .

The eclipse of the Sun across northern Europe came on 11 August 1999. Nostradamus might well have known this, considering his expertise in astronomy as well as prediction. Solar eclipses have long been thought of as harbingers of fear – or "King[s] of terror" – and Nostradamus may have meant line two to be a reference to this event.

Less than a week later, on 17 August, a terrible earthquake struck northern Turkey. Its destruction radius stretched from the outskirts of Istanbul to the city of Adapazari, north-east of the Sea of Marmara. The industrial city of Izmit and the naval base of Golcuk were devastated. The death toll was over 15,000 and more than 40,000 people were badly injured. Some 244,000 homes and workplaces were destroyed or seriously damaged and an estimated 600,000 people were made homeless.

As noted above, this was the very area ravaged by the Mongol Army when they broke from Asia into Europe in 1242. To give an example of their treatment of the Turkish inhabitants: as the Mongols approached a town, they would demand immediate surrender. If there was even a hint of defiance or resistance they would move on, leaving smoking ruins and three stinking piles – the severed heads of all the men, women and children found in the town.

The horrific Izmit earthquake might indeed be likened to the resurrection of the "King of the Mongols". It might also be noted that the 11 August total solar eclipse was visible in the northern part of Turkey – including the area hit by the earthquake.

Chapter 18

Edgar Cayce – the Sleeping Prophet

On 11 October 1923, the celebrated "psychic healer" Edgar Cayce was in a trance. In this condition, he was able accurately to diagnose illnesses and, despite a lack of any medical training, prescribe medical treatment for patients he had never even seen. Cayce, by this stage, had been "practising" for some years in his native US and had a national following, including many doctors who had checked his diagnoses and found them exactly correct. On this occasion, however, something else emerged from the "Sleeping Doctor's" trance state. Cayce dictated to the stenographer the words: "Third appearance on this plane. He was once a monk."

Cayce never remembered what he had said during his trances when he woke up, and so was shocked to read this remark. It clearly implied reincarnation and he, as a devout Christian, believed reincarnation was a pagan superstition.

Nevertheless, from that day onward, Cayce often made similar remarks while in his trance state – sometimes going as far as explaining the problems of a patient in terms of the traumatic events in a past life.

For example, one woman who was suffering from many disabilities, including angina and pernicious anaemia, was told by Cayce that in a past life she had been a boon companion of the Emperor Nero and had actively persecuted Christians. However, Cayce went on to say that the woman had made remarkable spiritual progress in past lives, and so was ready to stop paying penance for her past-life iniquities.

This "Nero diagnosis" made sense to the patient for a rather odd reason. She had recently learned to play the piano, although so badly that she was the despair of her piano teacher. However, she inexplicably played one tune much better than any other: she could play the music from the chariot race from the Cecil B. DeMille movie, *Ben Hur*, perfectly, over and over again, with tremendous gusto. The reason was, the patient said, because the picture on the front of the music – of a Roman horse-drawn chariot – seemed to become real as she looked at it, so she felt herself to be actually in the Roman Coliseum as she played. On Cayce's advice, she applied herself determinedly to conquering her disabilities until, as she later said: "Now I am almost the picture of health."

Another patient to whom Cayce gave a "life reading", this time in 1936, is of particular interest in the context of our earlier study of religious prophets. The female patient, Cayce said, had been a "sister superior" or officer in the religious sect called the Essenes in first-century Judea. As such, she had often seen Jesus in the flesh and had been trained in the same "school of prophets".

This reference to the Essenes aroused little attention in 1936, when not much was known of them; but in 1947, the Dead Sea Scrolls were found, shedding much light on this monastic and secretive community. Jesus, as we saw in chapter 6, may have been a prominent member of the Essene community. What is further implied by Cayce's life reading is that there was actually a school where Essenes were trained in prophecy – much as the Pythia women at Delphi were apparently trained in casting oracles by the priests of Apollo.

In another life reading, in 1939, Cayce spoke of the patient being present, in a previous life, at the raising of Lazarus from the dead by Jesus. In passing, Cayce also mentioned a group of "holy women" being present at Lazarus' resurrection. These included known Jesus followers, like Martha and Mary, but also one with the ill-starred name of Salome. The only New Testament Salome was the lascivious temptress of Herod Antipas, who got John the Baptist executed – an unlikely disciple of Jesus, but perhaps the name was common in first-century Judea.

In 1960, Dr Morton Smith of Columbia University found a long-lost letter written by an early Christian leader, Clement of Alexandria (AD 150–215) which mentioned the raising of Lazarus and stated that a woman named Salome had been present.

Edgar Cayce (pronounced "Casey") was born on a farm in Christian County, Kentucky, on 18 March 1877. His father, Leslie Cayce, was a Justice of the Peace, and was addressed as "Squire". He was not a particularly affectionate father, and Edgar had a difficult upbringing, partially because he was clumsy and always getting into trouble. As one biographer, Joseph Millard, put it: "It seemed to his distracted parents that every time they took their eyes off him, there would be a crash and a yell to signify another disaster." The Cayce family even hired an eleven-year-old to keep the younger boy out of trouble.

Edgar was a daydreamer at school, and never seemed to be able to remember anything. His teacher had to rap him on the knuckles again and again for not paying attention and despaired of him ever learning even the basic lessons.

Cayce's maternal grandfather was an excellent dowser, and was always being asked by neighbours where they should sink their wells. Cayce may have derived his odd powers from this side of the family. Unfortunately, his grandfather was killed in an accident when Edgar was only four – his horse panicked when he rode it into a pond to drink, and he was thrown into the water. Trying to get up, he was brained by the horse's flying hooves. Shortly after his grandfather's death, Edgar saw him in the family tobacco barn, and the old man talked to him at length. Edgar told his mother and grandmother about the visit, but never mentioned it to his no-nonsense father.

Despite his lack of academic promise, and perhaps because of his otherworldliness, the young Edgar conceived a burning enthusiasm for the Bible, and read it from beginning to end continuously. He decided he wanted to be a minister and travel all over the world, "saving heathens".

The boy also prayed for the power to heal the sick. He later told how, at the age of ten, he woke up one night and saw a woman standing at the foot of the bed, emanating a strange light that filled the room. Edgar ran to tell his mother about it, and she soothed him and told him to go back to bed. Once again in his room, he saw the woman, who told him: "Your prayers are answered; you will have the power to heal the sick."

Despite this, Edgar was still so bad at his school lessons that his father once forced him to stay awake one night, threatening that he would beat him unless he had learned a set amount by the morning. Cayce claimed that a voice told him that if he went to sleep, he would learn more than by staying awake. When his father found him asleep over his books he prepared to thrash him, but Edgar knew his lessons perfectly. Unfortunately his father, far from congratulating his son, decided that this was proof that Edgar had been pretending to be stupid to stay at school as long as possible, to avoid having to start work on the farm. So Edgar received yet another beating. From then on, he claimed, he was able to go to sleep with a book under his pillow and wake up knowing its contents.

It was soon after this that he revealed his ability to prescribe medicine. A baseball had struck him on the spine, and he suddenly became noisy and uncontrollable. Finally, forced into bed by his father, he seemed to fall asleep. Then, although apparently unconscious, he began to speak, explaining that he had had a shock from the baseball and that his mother should make a poultice from certain local herbs that were to be mixed with chopped onions. This was done and the next morning, he was normal again.

In spite of his new scholastic abilities, Edgar continued to be a daydreamer, so his father forced him to leave school at the age of fifteen to work on the farm. He was in his early twenties when the family gave up farming and moved to the nearby town of Hopkinsville. There Edgar got a part-time job in a bookstore and continued his biblical studies. He also fell in love with a girl named Gertrude Evans, the daughter of a prominent local architect. Although he had very few savings and no support from his father, he and Gertrude were married.

Edgar soon miserably realized, however, that despite his strange ability to learn while asleep, it would take him several years to learn enough to become a minister, and could thus be in a position to support Gertrude. So he abandoned his dreams of the church and took a better-paid, full-time job in a shoe store. Then, realizing that this was still not going to be enough to support a wife, he became first a salesman for a stationery firm, then an insurance salesman.

Over the New Year of 1900, aged twenty-three, Cayce suddenly lost his voice. Three months later, he could barely whisper. Cayce himself later realized that his illness was purely psychosomatic – a salesman cannot sell without a voice, and his unconscious mind was telling him that he had better things to do than sell insurance. At that time, a hypnotist named Hart was performing at the local theatre (stage hypnotists had been a popular vaudeville act since the 1880s) and was told about Cayce's strange illness. He offered to restore Cayce's voice for $200.

Hart was a famous and successful hypnotist – known as the Laugh King – and his act consisted of placing people under hypnosis on stage and then making them do absurd things, such as believing they were a hen laying an egg or that they were carrying an imaginary person up an imaginary ladder. Cayce's friends were impressed enough with Hart's reputation to offer to finance the cure. Unfortunately, under hypnosis Edgar's voice came back but, as soon as the hypnotist awakened him, his voice vanished again.

Another hypnotist, called Dr Quackenboss, also tried to cure Cayce, but only succeeded in alarming everyone by putting him to sleep for more than twenty-four hours.

Finally, Edgar met a man called Al Layne, whose wife ran a millinery shop while he studied hypnotism. On 31 March 1901, Layne put Cayce into a state of deep hypnosis, and then told him that his unconscious mind could cure his problem. Cayce immediately replied:

The trouble is partial paralysis of the vocal cords, due to nerve strain. To remove the condition, it is necessary only to suggest that the body increase the circulation to the affected area.

Layne leaned over him and told him to increase the circulation to the affected area. Cayce's throat immediately turned a deep red colour. Then suddenly, Cayce said: "The condition is cured. Suggest the circulation returns to normal, then wake me up." A few moments later, Cayce was shouting triumphantly: "I can talk! I can talk!" When Cayce's explosion of sheer joy had subsided,

Layne remarked: "You know, you sounded just like a doctor when you were in your trance. If you can look inside closed books when you fall asleep, maybe you can do the same thing with somebody who's sick." Cayce thought about this and decided to give it a go.

The next day, Layne placed Cayce in a trance, then said: "I want you to check over my body and find out what's wrong with me." "Yes, I can see your body clearly," Cayce replied immediately, and then began to talk as if he had had a lifetime of medical training. Layne was amazed. He wrote down what Cayce said, including parts of the body with Latin names, prescriptions and all kinds of detailed instructions. When Cayce awoke, he looked at Layne's notes and shook his head in bafflement. "I've never heard of most of these things." Nevertheless, Layne followed the instructions precisely and was soon enjoying much better health. Cayce, however, remained sceptical of something he could not understand.

Layne explained that it was a case of clairvoyance: the curious ability possessed by some people to know things that they simply should not know – for example, what is happening in other places, or what somebody they have never met looks like. The mind, Layne said, obviously has all kinds of powers that we do not even begin to understand.

Layne was so delighted with the successful experiments that he decided to set up his own office, above his wife's millinery shop, to treat people by suggestion. To do this, he needed Cayce to be placed in a trance and then to answer questions about the customer's ailments. Cayce agreed, on condition that he was not told the identity of the other person.

Their first patient/customer duly arrived and when Cayce woke up a few minutes after being put in a trance, Layne told him that his diagnosis had agreed exactly with what a doctor had told the patient – but that the doctor had been unable to prescribe a remedy. Cayce had just prescribed one.

Cayce began to help Layne regularly, but always refused to take any money. All that the unconscious Cayce needed to know was exactly where the patient was at the moment he was asked about them – they did not need to be in the same room, and might even be sitting in Layne's outer office. Yet he could always describe their ailment and prescribe something for it.

On one occasion, a mother came to see him, frantic with worry – her child was very slowly choking to death, but an X-ray taken at the local hospital had shown nothing wrong. Cayce was hastily put into a trance by Layne, and said that the problem was a celluloid shirt button that the child had swallowed – celluloid, having a similar density to flesh, is hard to see on an X-ray. The child was rushed back to hospital, and the shirt button found exactly where Cayce said it would be.

Cayce soon became so good at it that he could put himself into a trance and treat the sick without even coming into contact with them – a postal address and name were sufficient. The only thing that reconciled him to this strange ability – which, because he could not understand it, made him nervous – was that he felt he was doing God's work, which had been his ambition ever since he was a child.

For religious reasons, Cayce continued to refuse to take money for his cures. Fortunately, he had discovered that he was a talented photographer, and thus made enough to keep Gertrude and his growing family.

Cayce's list of historically verifiable successes remains one of the most impressive on record.

When his son was eight, he lit some of the magnesium used for flashlight photographs, and lost the sight in one eye. An oculist recommended an operation, but Cayce went into a trance and ordered that a bandage soaked in tannic acid should be placed over the eye. The boy's sight came back within two weeks.

There is some evidence, despite his own near-scepticism, that Cayce displayed some psychic powers while conscious. On one occasion, a Kentucky businessman he was talking to over the telephone admitted his scepticism; Cayce promptly – and without going into a trance – described him precisely, then told him the route he had taken from his home to the office that morning. The man was convinced.

One day, in his trance, he recommended a drug called Codiron to a patient, and gave the address of the supplier in Chicago. Over the telephone, the drug manufacturer admitted to being baffled – Codiron was a new product, and they had only decided on its name two hours before Cayce had given the consultation.

In 1906, Edgar Cayce solved a murder in Canada. A woman

had been found shot. Cayce stated that her sister had killed her because both were in love with the same man. He said that the woman had pushed the weapon down a drain, and gave its serial number. When the police recovered it, the sister admitted her guilt.

On another occasion, he gave one of his clients a stock-market forecast that helped them to make a vast sum of money. Offered a share, Cayce refused, saying that after waking from that particular trance, he found that he had such a bad headache he swore never to get involved in financial matters again.

Of course, Cayce also had his failures. When the baby of Charles Lindbergh, the famous aviator, was kidnapped in 1932, Cayce was totally unable to suggest the identity of the kidnapper, or how to save the toddler. It later turned out that the kidnapper had strangled the baby almost immediately after stealing him from his bedroom.

But on another occasion, consulted about a railway accident, Cayce declared that the blame should be placed on a trusted employee, and said that there would be another fatal accident unless he was dismissed. The vice-president of the company refused to dismiss the employee, then was himself killed in the fatal accident that Cayce had prophesied.

It was in 1910 that Cayce finally began charging a small fee for his help. This was because Dr Wesley Ketchum, a homoeopath who practised in Hopkinsville, wrote an enthusiastic article about his successes, and sent it to the American Society of Clinical Research in Boston. When the article was reprinted in the *New York Times*, Cayce became famous overnight and was overwhelmed with requests for help. Even so, the fees he accepted only just paid for his time, and he remained a poor man who kept his head above water with a small photography business.

In the 1920s, as we saw at the beginning of this chapter, Cayce began to develop a new speciality – what he called "life readings". In one of his trances, for example, he said that he had seen himself in a previous life on a raft on the Ohio River, fleeing from marauding Indians, who finally killed everyone in the party. The conscious Cayce, however, remained deeply sceptical and conservatively Christian.

(In 1923, a Dayton printer named Arthur Hammers asked Cayce

about past lives. When Cayce said that he didn't believe in reincarnation, because the Bible said nothing about it, Lammers replied that in the New Testament, the Jews who did not believe in Jesus asked whether he was Elias returned from death, which seemed to indicate that they believed in reincarnation. Cayce, however, remained sceptical.)

Soon, under hypnosis, he was telling his subjects about their past lives – sometimes in India, China, Persia or Egypt. According to his biographer, Jess Stearn, in *The Sleeping Prophet*: "Cayce outlined how past life experience had influenced the present, and what the individual must overcome to fulfil this [present] life." Stearn goes on to add:

> As he got deeper into life readings, he frequently spoke alien languages in trance, chiefly the familiar Romance tongues. Yet, once asked to speak Greek by a Greek scholar, he broke into Homeric Greek as though living in that period.

We have already seen that Cayce was able to prophesy that a fatal railway accident would occur unless an inefficient employee was replaced, and how he was able to advise a businessman who questioned him about the stock market while he was in trance. He was clearly capable, therefore, of foretelling future events as well as reading past lives and diagnosing present illnesses.

In March 1929, Cayce warned a man not to invest in stocks and shares. When, that afternoon, a stockbroker described a dream that had worried him, Cayce said that it meant there would be a downward movement of long duration in the market, and advised him to sell his entire portfolio. On 6 April 1929, Cayce told another financier: "There must surely come a break when there will be a panic in the money centres, not only on Wall Street, but a closing of the banks in many centres."

The following 24 October – known as Black Thursday – saw the rampant overspeculation of the 1920s come home to roost. Stock prices tumbled as share dealers panicked. Men who had woken up complacent millionaires that morning were suicidal bankrupts by nightfall. The Great Wall Street Crash caused the US stock market to collapse completely within a week, followed shortly thereafter by similar crashes in money markets around the globe. Banks closed their doors to customers when it was realized that panic withdrawals might bankrupt the banks themselves – all as Cayce, an ill-educated Southern States photographer, had predicted over six months before.

Before the outbreak of the First World War, one of Cayce's readings stated that a war would spread across the world and involve America. Twice during the First World War, Cayce was summoned to Washington – exactly what happened is still unknown. In another reading, he predicted the breaking up of the Western Front in Europe, the end of the war, and the Russian Revolution of 1917. Yet during this same reading, Cayce stated: "On the religious development of Russia will depend the hope of the world." By 2003 – the time of this writing – it still seems as meaningless as it did at the time.

In December 1918, a new influence entered Cayce's life. The editor of a newspaper in Cleburne, Texas, wrote to ask his advice on business matters, and Cayce wrote back saying that he did not use his powers for financial gain – either his own or other people's. They began to correspond, and the editor told him that he believed in astrology. He asked Cayce's exact date and time of birth and, although Cayce thought that astrology was nonsense, he sent them. When the horoscope came back, he was staggered at its accuracy. Moreover, horoscopes continued to come in from all over the world – at the request of the Texan editor – and what impressed Cayce was that they agreed so closely.

These horoscopes told Cayce, without exception, that a conjunction of planets on 19 March 1919, between 8.30 and 11 p.m., would be a good time for him to ask important questions. Accordingly, Cayce went into a trance at that time, and his wife Gertrude asked the questions. When she asked: "Do the planets have anything to do with the destiny of man?" the reply was, "They do".

The unconscious Cayce went on to say:

The inclination of man is ruled by the planets under which he is born. In this way, the destiny of man lies within the sphere of the scope of the planets. With the given position of the solar system at the time of the birth of the individual, it can be worked out – that is the inclinations and actions, without the willpower taken into consideration.[1]

Cayce, in his trance-state, then sent a message to his conscious self: his natural and supernatural inclinations meant that he should live by the sea and should always have done so. Following the suggestion, the Cayce family eventually moved to Virginia Beach, a small seaside village in Virginia.

Many of Cayce's prophetic successes were remarkable, but not all were direct hits. He prophesied, for example, the defeat of Hitler and India's independence. He also stated that two twentieth century American presidents would die in office, as Roosevelt and Kennedy did. But, asked in 1938 if there would be a war that would involve the United States between 1942 and 1944, he missed a golden opportunity by answering that this depended on whether there was a "desire for peace".

In fact this was not wholly inaccurate, as it was the "America First" peace party that kept the US out of the war in Europe, despite President Roosevelt's desire to come in on the side of the Allies. What Cayce might have mentioned was that the Japanese attack on Pearl Harbour, in December 1942, combined with Hitler's subsequent ill-judged declaration of war on the US, would mean that no "desire for peace" could keep America out of the war indefinitely.

Asked what would be the cause of a second world war, Cayce replied: "selfishness" – an oversimplification of Hitler's reasons for going to war, but not inaccurate.

Some of Cayce's predictions, however, are apparently just plain wrong. In 1934, for example, he declared that there would be born

---

[1]This may sound like nonsensical gibberish to non-astrologers, but it should be noted that Cayce's sleeping self referred to *planets* influencing human "inclinations", not *stars*. This is in contradiction to mainstream astrology, which considers both to be determining factors in a person's destiny and personality.

Within our solar system we live in an invisible network of gravitational and magnetic forces. The influence of both gravity and magnetism on the human mind and body is still little understood, but it seems increasingly likely that we are sensitive to such forces in ways we scarcely comprehend in our conscious lives. Thus the effect of a distant planet's position at the time of birth could conceivably be an influence on a person's personality and inclinations. On the other hand, the gravitational and magnetic effect of stars – unimaginable distances from Earth – is all but non-existent.

in America, in 1936, a baby named John Penniel, "who would be beloved of all men in all places when the universality of God in the earth has been proclaimed." Penniel would "come as a messenger not a forerunner", and bring to the earth's "a new order of things". When this was about to happen, "the sun will be darkened and the earth shall be broken in several places". At the time of this writing – by which time Penniel would be sixty-seven – there has still been no sign of this world saviour.

During this same reading, Cayce's "sleeping" form also made some very ominous predictions:

> The greater portion of Japan must go into the sea. The upper portion of Europe will be changed as in the twinkling of an eye. Land will appear off the east coast of America. There will be upheaval in the Arctic and in the Antarctic that will make for the eruptions of volcanoes in the torrid areas, and there will be the shifting then of the poles.

When that happens, he said, "frigid or sub-tropical" climates will become tropical. All this, he went on to state unequivocally, would occur *before* 1998. This is obviously another miss. Global volcanic activity increased in the 1990s, but not by the degree described by Cayce.

In 1941, a businessman asked Cayce whether it would be a good idea to move out of New York, in case Hitler or the Japanese bombed the city. Cayce advised the man to move out of New York, not because of the threat of war, but because he had foreseen that, within the next two generations, seismic catastrophes would devastate the US Eastern Seaboard: "Watch New York, Connecticut and the like. Many portions of the east coast will be disturbed . . . New York City itself will, in the main, disappear." Since more than two generations have passed since 1941, it would be natural to discount this prediction as a total miss. However, recent discoveries on the eastern side of the Atlantic may point to Cayce being only incorrect in his timing of the predicted catastrophe.

In the year 2000, Dr Simon Day, of the Benfield Greig Hazard Research Centre at University College, London, discovered that one flank of the Cumbre Vieja volcano on the island of La Palma, in the Canaries archipelago, is unstable and could soon plunge into the westward ocean. This may sound like a minor problem for the US, until one realizes that the so-called "ripple-effect" from the resulting splash could wipe out much of the US Eastern Seaboard with a huge tidal wave.

The volcanic landslide, estimated to consist of up to half a trillion tons of rock, would quite probably fall into the water all at once. In this worst-case scenario, a wave 2,130 feet high would spread out and travel across the Atlantic at speeds up to 450 miles per hour. (Fortunately for West Africa and Western Europe, the blocking effect of the remaining eastern side of the Cumbre Vieja volcano would stop a similar wave heading eastward.)

The wall of water would weaken as it crossed the ocean, but would still be 130–160 feet high by the time it hit the US mainland. The surge would create havoc and terrible destruction as much as twelve miles inland.

Needless to say, this disaster would fulfil Cayce's prediction that New York and Connecticut "and the like" would be "disturbed". A 150-foot high tidal wave, tearing up to twelve miles inland, could make New York City effectively "disappear".

Fortunately, the scientists say that, although the Cumbre Vieja volcano *might* collapse at any moment, it is still unlikely to do so in the next ten to twenty years, giving us some time to avert the disaster.

At the same time that he was giving "life readings" that involved the past lives of clients in ancient civilizations, Cayce also began to talk about Atlantis. What is of particular interest here is that Cayce declared that Atlantis began to disintegrate in 10,700 BC, and finally disappeared a thousand years later. The Ancient Greek philosopher Plato – the original and only (known) source on Atlantis – gave the date of the destruction of Atlantis (in the book *Timaeus*) as about 9,500 BC: he, in fact, says about 9,000 years before the date of his writing. But a Belgian engineer named Robert Bauval has recently – in his book *The Orion Mystery* – pointed out some interesting evidence to back Cayce's date.

In the Cairo Museum, Bauval saw a photograph of the three Giza pyramids taken from the air, and was struck by their rather odd arrangement on the ground. The first two pyramids – the Great Pyramid of the Pharaoh Cheops and the pyramid of Cheops' son,

Chefren – were neatly arranged so a straight line could be drawn from the upper-left-hand corner of the Great Pyramid, diagonally through to the opposite corner, then on through the same two corners of the smaller Chefren Pyramid.

It might be expected – given the Ancient Egyptians' mastery of construction and design – that this line should continue on through the two corners of the last and smallest of the three pyramids, that of the Pharaoh Menkaura. So why, wondered Bauval, was the third pyramid completely out of alignment? And why was it so small compared to the other two? Menkaura was as powerful a pharaoh as his father and grandfather; so why did he settle for a pyramid that, in comparison to Cheops' Great Pyramid, looked like a scale model?

The answer came to Bauval when he was in the Egyptian desert one night, and noted the three stars of Orion's Belt – the constellation of Orion looks like two overlapping triangles placed point to point, with the three stars of the "belt" running across the intersection. These three stars were arranged exactly like the three pyramids of the Giza Plateau – two "larger" stars in line, with the third, "smaller", star slightly out of alignment.

Moreover, the Milky Way, stretching across the sky beside them, looked very like the Nile running north past the pyramids on Giza. Bauval knew that the Ancient Egyptians regarded their land as a reflection of heaven. Did they mean that quite literally, he wondered? Did they build the pyramids to "reflect" on the ground the belt of the constellation of Orion which, to the Ancient Egyptians, represented the great god Osiris?

However, Bauval noticed that, if the pyramids were meant as a representation of the stars of Orion's Belt, they were not quite an exact reflection. Due to a phenomenon called the "precession of the equinoxes", the positions of the constellations move up and down the sky over a period of almost 26,000 years. As the constellations do so, they also twist slightly – imagine that the double triangle of Orion's Belt is impaled on the end of the minute hand of a clock. You can see that as it moves from twelve o'clock to half past twelve, it will turn completely upside down. Actually, precession causes the constellation to move only to about ten past twelve then back again, but it still changes its angle.

Bauval realized that the last time Orion actually "reflected" the pyramids of Giza – as if reflected in a vast mirror – was about 10,500 BC. He felt that this date must have had some deep significance for the Ancient Egyptians – in fact, that it was what their holy scriptures referred to as *zep tepi*, "the first time", meaning the beginning of Egyptian history.

(It should be noted here that Robert Bauval does not mention Atlantis or Cayce in his book, but his date of 10,500 BC is just 200 years after Cayce's date when the continent of Atlantis was supposed to have started its thousand-year collapse into the sea.)

The twentieth-century philosopher Gurdjieff mentions, in a chapter on Atlantis in *Beelzebub's Tales to his Grandson*, that there is an occult tradition that many of the inhabitants of Atlantis migrated to Egypt when Atlantis was destroyed, and that they built the Sphinx there.

An early twentieth-century Egyptologist, Schwaller de Lubicz, has also referred to this tradition that survivors of Atlantis moved to Egypt and built the Sphinx. If the Atlantis catastrophe started in 10,700 BC, as Cayce said, then 10,500 BC would certainly be a reasonable date for the building of the Sphinx as one of the escaping Atlanteans' first creations in the Nile Valley.

Robert Bauval indirectly supports this conjecture. The Sphinx is now known, thanks to geological study, to be one of the oldest known Ancient Egyptian constructions.[2] What was more probable, Bauval suggests, than that the Sphinx was built during that "first time" – the founding of Egyptian civilization – around 10,500 BC?

There are hundreds of references to Atlantis in Cayce's work, and – as his son Edgar Evans Cayce has pointed out – they have an impressive internal consistency. Edgar Cayce states that the island of Atlantis began to suffer catastrophes in around 10,700 BC. Within a few hundred years, many Atlanteans had been driven to migrate to safer parts of the globe, like the Nile Valley. By

[2]Mainstream Egyptology still insists, on the basis of a single, badly-damaged inscription, that the Great Sphinx was built at the same time as the Giza Pyramids. These latter, we know through carbon dating, to date from around 2500 BC. However, geological studies of the Sphinx show it to have been extensively damaged by water precipitation – i.e. rain. This would suggest that the Sphinx dates from before the desertification of the area. As the Giza Plateau has not known heavy rain in over 10,000 years, a construction date of around 10,500 BC would fit the facts better than the Egyptologists' 2500 BC.

9,700 BC, these Atlantean "colonies" were all that was left of that prehistoric civilization, because the island of Atlantis had been completely destroyed. As we have seen above, these statements parallel Robert Bauval's theory.

In another striking reading involving Atlantean Egypt, Cayce declared that the Nile had once flowed in a westerly direction. Ridiculous as this may sound, it has since been proved to be true – the Nile once flowed into Lake Chad, halfway between the present Nile Valley and the Atlantic Ocean.

Cayce also stated that the civilization of Atlantis had dated back to 50,000 BC, and that the Atlanteans had possessed some kind of "crystal stone" for trapping the rays of the Sun, as well as steam power, gas and electricity.

Cayce also forecast that Atlantis would begin to rise again in the area of the Caribbean island of Bimini, between 1968 and 1969. Indeed, underwater artefacts that appeared to be the remains of ancient sunken roads were found near Bimini in 1968. However, many archaeologists have disputed that these are ancient ruins at all, insisting instead that they are natural, if very odd, seabed formations. Whatever the case, there has so far been no further sign of "Atlantis rising".

During the Second World War, Cayce's health began to fail. Floods of requests kept him busy, and he occasionally spent several hours of the day in a trance, giving readings. In autumn 1944, he had a complete breakdown. In a reading, his unconscious self advised him to go to a particular nursing home near Roanoke. During the next session he had his wife ask how long he should stay. The answer came back: "Until you are well, or until you are dead."

Cayce went into the nursing home, but disliked the inactivity. He worried about the people he could be helping and that made his health worse. Eventually he had a stroke that left one side of his body paralysed.

Shortly after Thanksgiving 1944, he came home to Virginia Beach and on New Year's Day 1945, he told a visitor: "I am to be healed on Friday, the fifth of January".

On the evening of 3 January, Cayce died, aged just sixty-seven. Three months later, on Easter Sunday, his wife Gertrude also died. His sons, Hugh, Lynn and Edgar, continued the Edgar Cayce

Foundation, as well as the Association For Research and Enlightenment, and the Edgar Cayce Publishing Company. The interest in his life and work has continued unabated – dozens of books about him have appeared since his death.

It is difficult to neatly summarize Edgar Cayce's life as a psychic and as a prophet. His accuracy was at times incredible – especially as a "psychic doctor" – but it is unfortunately untrue, as Jess Steam has stated, that "his batting average on predictions was incredibly high, close to one hundred per cent".

He does represent one striking fact, however – the power and even the partially separate identity of the subconscious mind. Awake, Edgar Cayce was an unremarkable, if very charitable man from a poor and all but uneducated background. In a trance, on the other hand, he became an almost superhuman creature – knowledgeable and capable of extraordinary mental feats. It is tempting to wonder if all minds contain such potentialities, kept from us by the indefinable barrier between the conscious and the subconscious.

Chapter 19

Wolf Messing – Stalin's Seer

Wolf Messing, who worked mainly behind the Iron Curtain, has every right to be regarded as one of the greatest psychics and seers of the twentieth century. When Hitler made a pact with Stalin, Messing – who would become Stalin's favourite psychic – nevertheless reported: "Soviet tanks will within a few years enter Berlin." The Germans heard about this and made official protests to the Kremlin.

Addressing a wartime audience in the Opera House in Novosibirsk, in Siberia, Messing declared: "The war will end victoriously for Russia in May 1945, and most likely in its first week."

The West first learned about Messing in 1970, in a remarkable book called *PSI: Psychic Discoveries Behind the Iron Curtain,* by Sheila Ostrander and Lynn Schroeder, which startled everyone who was interested in parapsychology. Most people had assumed that the Soviet Union was rigidly materialistic in its outlook, and that it would not tolerate anything that looked like occultism or mysticism. Yet this was to overlook the natural mysticism of the Russian temperament, embodied in writers like Dostoevsky, Solovyev and even Tolstoy.

The account of Messing's life had been published in the Soviet Union in 1965. His autobiography, *About Myself*, began serialization in the journal *Science and Religion*, numbers 7 and 83. However, as far as can be ascertained, it has never been published in full.

Messing also related the story of his life to a friend, Tatiana

Lungin, who would write it all down in her book *Wolf Messing: The True Story of Russia's Greatest Psychic,* edited by D. Scott Rogo. (Published by Paragon House, 1989, with whose kind permission I quote it.)

Messing began his interview with Tatiana Lungin:

I was born on 10 September 1899, in Russia, to be precise.

I was born on the eve of the new century – September 10,1899, in the small town of Gora-Kalewaria, near Warsaw. At that time we were part of the Russian Empire. The life of the Jews living in that tiny town was hard, as it was, however, for many others. It was a monotonous existence, filled with fear, superstition, and struggle for pieces of bread, for a tiny place under the sun.

I left home at an early age, and so I cannot relate everything about the life of our family. My father worked in a garden that did not belong to us, and he nursed fruit trees and raspberry and currant bushes. Even now I can clearly see the tender eyes of my mother, and my brothers with their gay and quarrelsome games. The visit of the famous writer Sholom Aleichem, then already an important figure in Jewish literature, was very memorable – how could it have been otherwise!

He hadn't come to make a special visit to our remote little town. He was only passing through. But fate granted me a personal meeting with him. He possessed a small beard, luxuriant moustache, and, most importantly, a kind, attentive gaze that emanated from underneath his eyeglasses. He patted me gently on the cheek, and, for some reason, declared that I would have a shining future. This, of course, was not the prediction of a prophet. Sholom Aleichem simply wanted to see a future celebrity in every Jewish boy. I never again had occasion to meet this amazing man, but, from that point in my childhood, I came to love him with all my heart for the great humanity of his books.

Our family was religiously orthodox, at times to the point of fanaticism. Thoughts of God permeated not only the consciousness of my parents, but every insignificant step and action in their lives. They looked upon God as a demanding but just master of the destinies of men. Unlike my mother, my father did not spoil us with affection. He had a heavy hand that he was quick to raise. God forbid one of us went to him with a complaint! He did not like grumblers and whiners and could flog us mercilessly just because someone else had offended us already. He tried to raise us as tough and hardy little beasts, capable of standing up for ourselves in the hard and pitiless world.

I unfortunately have no photographs in my possession – either of my father, my mother, or of any of my brothers. I lived in difficult times. My mother died of a heart attack with my name on her lips, and my father and brothers died violent deaths in the Majdanek concentration camp and the Warsaw ghetto.

At the age of six, Wolf went to a Jewish school. The main subject in the curriculum was the Talmud, which had to be learned by heart. Wolf had a good memory and managed this quite easily. His teachers even held him as an example to the lazier pupils.

As a child he did not doubt the existence of God. Any other view seemed blasphemous and criminally foolhardy. The rabbi, noticing his early piety, decided to send him to the *yeshiva* (Jewish Orthodox seminary college) to prepare for religious services and devotion. His parents were pleased; they considered this a great honour.

But I have to admit that I wasn't very pleased by such a turn of events. Why? I don't know . . . perhaps I was tired of cramming, or maybe it was something else, but I began to resolutely protest the destiny being prepared for me. They entreated me persistently, and when that didn't work, they beat me. But I persisted too, and finally they left me alone.

One evening, his father sent Wolf to the store for matches. It was dark by the time he returned home. On the steps of the porch a gigantic white-robed figure appeared before him, and spoke with a deep bass voice: "My son! I am sent to you from above to determine your future. Become a yeshiva student! Your prayers will please Heaven!"

Wolf fainted, naturally enough, and when he came to, he saw the faces of his parents over him, praying in ecstasy. He told them what had happened, and his father roared delightedly: "So He wishes!"

Wolf decided to do as they, and apparently Yahweh, wanted. He left his father's house and began a life of prayers and the Talmud. Everything took place within the boundaries of the prayer house where he lived and studied.

Unfortunately Wolf soon noticed that one of the itinerant tramps who often took shelter in the school was the "messenger from Heaven" who had announced his calling: a man of enormous height and unusual voice, but otherwise fairly unremarkable and, more importantly, he wasn't Jewish.

Wolf's parents had tricked him into joining the yeshiva. The realization shattered the young man's faith. How, he wondered, could the all-powerful God that he had been taught to have believed in have permitted this heathen to speak in His name? "From that moment," he told Tatiana Lungin, "I have been an atheist."

Rather disinclined to return to his father's house, Wolf set off to roam the world. At the local station he climbed on to the first train passing through, which, as it turned out, was headed for Berlin. There were only a few people in the coach, and so the chance of being caught without a ticket was great, so Wolf climbed beneath the compartment seat and slept.

While sleeping, he stretched so that his legs stuck out, and the first inspector passing by spied them. He asked Wolf for his ticket. He feverishly tried to think of a way out of the unpleasant situation. He picked up the first piece of paper on the floor and handed it to the inspector. "Our gazes crossed. How I wanted him to accept that dirty scrap of paper for a ticket!" Wolf mentally suggested to him: "It is a ticket . . . a ticket . . . a ticket . . .". Handing the "ticket" back to him and smiling benevolently, the inspector asked Wolf what he was doing sleeping under the seat when he had a valid ticket. "That was the first time my power of suggestion manifested itself."

He had heard that in Berlin poor Jews stayed at Dragonerstrasse, and he searched out this street, and found the home for newcomers. There he became an errand boy, and did other menial jobs. He washed dishes, shone shoes and scrubbed floors. Despite working as hard as he could, however, he was still earning too little to avoid slow starvation. These, he later felt, were the most difficult days of his life.

Berlin overwhelmed the twelve-year-old Wolf with its population and enormous size – and the multitude of temptations requiring money that he did not possess.

One day Wolf was sent to the suburbs to deliver a parcel, but the long walk and the effects of chronic malnutrition caused him to collapse in a faint. He was taken to the hospital, without a pulse or any other sign of life, and was put in the morgue. He would have been buried in a communal paupers' grave if a medical student hadn't noticed that he still had a faint heartbeat. He was brought back to consciousness on the third day after his collapse by Professor Abel, a neuropathologist. It was he who would eventually discover Wolf's powers.

The boy regained consciousness but was lying with his eyes closed. Suddenly, someone's words sounded in his head: "This must be reported to the police, and then a shelter must be found for the boy." Wolf opened his eyes, and saw a kindly looking man dressed in a white gown, who was sitting on the edge of the bed feeling his pulse. Thinking that the doctor had spoken aloud, Wolf said: "Please don't call the police, and don't send me to a shelter." The man, Professor Abel, looked astonished: "But did I say that?" "I don't know," Wolf replied hazily, "but you were thinking it."

Dr Abel invited a colleague, a psychiatrist named Schmidt, to examine the patient. He experimented by giving Wolf mental commands – open your mouth, close your eyes, raise your arms, and so on. The next day they conducted more complicated experiments.

Abel spent a short period working with Wolf, testing for telepathic abilities, but soon realized that the boy needed to work, as there was no funding to keep him living in the hospital indefinitely. Guessing just how much money someone of his talents could make on the stage, Professor Abel introduced Wolf to his first manager.

Zellmeister was a heavy-set man; cunning, ruthless and intense. Ensnaring Wolf in a labyrinth of contractual arrangements, he kept him firmly under his thumb, while pretending to be a benefactor concerned only with his wellbeing. It wasn't long before Zellmeister hired Wolf to a freak show: the Berlin Panoptikum.

On the programme at the Panoptikum was a fat woman with an enormous beard who exhibited herself naked to the waist. The spectators were even allowed to pull on her beard in order to convince themselves it was real. Siamese twins comprised another exhibit; they were sisters joined at the side. They exchanged jokes, some quite bawdy, with the young people gaping at them. An armless man also entertained the gaping crowd. He would shuffle a pack of cards with his feet, then would roll a cigarette, strike a match and light up.

The fourth act, appearing three days a week, was the "boy-wonder": Wolf Messing. Before the opening of the show, he would crawl into a crystal coffin and place himself in a cataleptic trance. His entire act was to lie in the sealed box, defying suffocation.

In the almost six months I was there, I spent half of my time lying in that cold, transparent coffin. They paid me all of five marks a day. This seemed like a fabulously large sum to a young boy accustomed to starvation and privation, but my dandified manager received thirty marks each day for me."

The schedule gave Wolf four free days a week, and he tried to make the maximum use of them by devoting all his time to psychic exercises. Every day he went down to the Berlin market district and tried to penetrate the thoughts of the crowd – to hear their innermost secrets. Household worries, the intrigues of neighbours and the sexual fantasies of unattached bachelors.

He wanted not only to hear their thoughts, but to verify the accuracy of his perceptions. He walked up to the market tables, looked intently into a person's eyes, and said things like: "Don't worry, dear Gretchen. Don't think about it. Everything will be all right, trust in fate . . . Hans will return to you." Cries of astonishment or embarrassed silences convinced him that he was right. He spent more than a year training himself like this.

Then his manager sold him to the variety show at Berlin's Wintergarten. This was a major stepping-stone in his career: instead of playing the role of a living corpse, he could at least be himself. He appeared before the audience in two different capacities. In the first, he portrayed an Eastern fakir, who had his chest pierced with needles and swords run through his arms and legs.

At the end of the show, an actor appeared on stage portraying a rich idler—a fashionable dandy dressed like an aristocratic millionaire. He wore a tailcoat and top hat, and his fingers were covered with diamonds. Suddenly "robbers" would burst on to the stage and "kill" him, after first stripping him of his jewels. After this, they became the kindest of philanthropists, distributing amethysts, sapphires and diamonds to the spectators, and suggesting that they hid them wherever they liked without leaving the auditorium. Then a brilliant young detective appeared – Wolf Messing. He walked about among the spectators, passing from one dining table to the next, asking the ladies and gentlemen to return this or that jewel, hidden in such and such a place. This trick was invariably successful, and the public poured in to see the presentation. But still Wolf was paid the same pitiful five marks a day.

When he turned fourteen, Wolf again became an exchangeable commodity. This time he was sold to the Busch Circus – a show famous throughout Europe. Fortunately, Messing had already grown accustomed to this buying and selling process.

He travelled throughout Europe with the circus. His employers, concerned only with his popularity on stage, instilled in him the idea that show business success was the key to all good things in life, but he still managed to find time to educate himself, and the greater part of his salary often went on tutorial fees.

Wolf's celebrity continued to rise and his success soon relieved his manager, although not himself, of all financial worries. In 1913, Zellmeister booked him into the Vienna Prater Amusement Park, one of the premier showplaces of Europe, where the boy became the hit of the season.

His growing fame and evident abilities won the teenager some interesting new friends. For example, it was at this time that Wolf became acquainted with a young Swiss mathematician called Albert Einstein. Einstein had arrived in Vienna from Zurich in November 1913, after receiving an invitation to report on his recent findings to a convention of mathematicians and physicists.

Wolf claimed that he met Einstein by accident at the apartment of a mutual acquaintance – the psychiatrist, Sigmund Freud.

Freud's apartment amazed the education-starved Messing with its abundance of books. It seemed incomprehensible to Wolf that one man could even lightly skim through such a sea of volumes in a single lifetime. Of course, Sigmund Freud's research was closer in spirit to Wolf's work than Einstein's calculations and formulae. On the other hand, it is likely that Wolf would have had a better time talking to the famously fun-loving physicist than to the rather humourless psychiatrist.

Freud was a confirmed sceptic on matters of the paranormal, but he was open to the idea that the human mind was capable of much more than we are usually aware of. Later, after becoming better acquainted with psychoanalytic theory, Wolf decided that Freud was mistaken when he tried to apply his findings – based largely on his work with hysterics – to everyone. He also disagreed with Freud's emphasis on the libido as the central aspect of human consciousness.

Freud had heard reports of Messing's powers and proposed that they should conduct some experiments immediately. He assumed the role of the message sender, and mentally ordered Messing to go to the dressing table, pick up a pair of tweezers, walk over to Einstein and pull out three hairs from his luxuriant moustache:

> You can imagine my reaction. What could I do? I walked up to Einstein and explained apologetically what his friend wanted me to do. Einstein smiled and submissively presented his cheek to me. Freud was pleased with the result, but did not try to interpret it psychoanalytically.

After two years in Vienna, Zellmeister told Messing that he had organized an extensive worldwide tour. The itinerary extended over four years and encompassed such countries as Japan, Brazil, Argentina and Mexico. It was thus that Messing escaped the Great War.

Finally cutting himself loose from the exploitative Zellmeister, Wolf returned to Warsaw in 1921. Much had changed in Eastern Europe during his absence. The revolution had hit Russia like a hurricane, and Poland had achieved its independence. The little town where Messing had been born now belonged within Polish borders.

Messing had, by this stage, turned twenty-two and was forced to enter the Polish army, but his service was strictly symbolic. He wore a soldier's uniform during his term of service, but never once saw a firearm, nor did he have to go through basic training. By the next year he was a civilian again.

Messing, deciding to restart his show business career, didn't have to look for a new manager; his fame had them banging on his door. The man who eventually won the contract was called Kobak – a totally different personality from the ruthless Zellmeister. Kobak was a handsome man, who was always gentle and smiling. He was full of energy but didn't go running about booking tours. Instead, a modern-minded manager, he handled the major portion of the negotiations over the telephone.

Once again, Wolf began to travel through Europe, visiting Paris, London, Rome, Stockholm, Geneva and Riga. On this tour he tried to widen his repertoire. In Riga, for example, he drove an automobile through the streets while blindfolded by a large black scarf. He had no experience of driving – his hands held the steering wheel, and his feet worked the pedals, while a professional chauffeur seated beside him gave him mental instructions. Many thousands of people, who formed a solid wall along the pavements and roads, witnessed this experiment.

Wolf and Kobak also travelled to the other continents – to Australia, South America and several Asian countries. In India he became acquainted with yogis, and envied their capacity for entering a state of deep catalepsy for longer periods of time than he could – sometimes several weeks. Wolf's personal record was only three days. He also claims, while in India, to have met Mohandas Gandhi.

When back in Poland, people would often come to Messing with requests to use his powers on their behalf, like a sort of psychic Sherlock Holmes:

You can't imagine what I was forced to listen to! I never pandered to anyone's petty desires or idle curiosity. I always governed my life by two principles. First, my help had to be truly essential. Second, the situation had to be of some personal interest to me.

On occasion, however, Messing's ability to read the minds of his importunate guests saved him from graver consequences. For example, he recounts how, during the 1920s, a beautiful young woman visited him unannounced in his hotel room. She was strikingly attractive with ash-blonde hair down to her shoulders, sky-blue eyes and a slim and attractive body encased in a fashionable red, knee-length dress.

Messing never claimed to be a saint – his wandering lifestyle kept him from finding a wife, but his fame meant that he was rarely short of female company. However, one glance at this visitor and alarm bells went off in the young psychic's head.

"Sit down, madam," he said politely before she could introduce herself. "Make yourself at home and excuse me for one moment while I order some refreshments." Closing the door behind him, Wolf then rushed off to Kobak's room.

"Run to the police, bring several men and come back right away. Don't burst into my room, but spy through the glass over the door. Hurry!" he shouted at his flabbergasted manager before rushing back to his own suite.

Back in his room, he began to shower compliments upon the beautiful woman in the traditional Polish manner – but also to stall for time. "Her dirty plan was as clear as day to me," he later told Tatiana Lungin.

"You perform such miracles. Amazing things. But do you know what I'm thinking right now?" the woman asked him coquettishly.

Wolf was perfectly aware of what she expected him to think, as well as her actual plan, but replied politely: "Forgive me, madam, but offstage I avoid using my powers. However, I'm absolutely certain that in such a charming little head there could only be charming thoughts."

"Can't you tell?" she replied hotly, "I want to be your lover, right now, this instant!" She then proceeded to rip open her dress but, instead of hurling herself into Wolf's arms, she rushed to the window and shouted with all her might: "Help! Rape!"

Messing then gave the signal to his manager that the unscheduled show was over, the door was flung open, and the police entered the room and arrested the woman for exposing herself from a public window and causing a breach of the peace. In custody, she confessed that she had been paid to ruin Messing's reputation by some of his jealous rivals – although did not say whether their rivalry was professional, or the result of his more successful amorous encounters.

In 1937, during an appearance at a Warsaw theatre, Messing predicted that any German attack on the East would end in the eventual destruction of Germany. He made this prediction before an audience of a thousand, very appreciative people – Poland was then living in constant fear of Nazi expansionism. An accurate prophecy in the long run, this statement was to cost Wolf dearly. When the Nazis conquered Poland in 1939, they placed a price of 200,000 Reichsmarks on Messing's head.

Messing initially sought shelter in his father's home in the village of Gora-Kalewaria near Warsaw. Later, when he sensed that things had cooled down a little, he moved to Warsaw, meaning to get out of Poland. However, just when he was being especially alert and careful, he was caught. Walking along a street in Warsaw, he was stopped by a Gestapo officer.

The Nazi had evidently been sent to find Messing, as he had a photograph of him, by which he was quickly identified. Wolf soon ceased to resemble the picture, however, because the Gestapo man – furious that a Polish Jew had predicted the downfall of Germany – punched out most of Wolf's teeth there in the street.

Messing was taken to the local police station and thrown into a cell, but without first being searched. While sitting there bleeding heavily, Wolf realized that he had to escape or die. Once more, he called upon the powers of his mind:

Focusing my will, I hypnotically compelled the police guards outside the building to join their colleagues inside. Then I compelled all the police on the premises to gather in my cell, telepathically suggesting to them that they were entering an empty cell. I can't say exactly how many there were – at least nine or ten. They talked about me, but paid absolutely no attention to me. I hypnotized each guard, compelling them to stay in the cell, and told them to wake up in half an hour.

I breathed a sigh of relief only when the bolt on the iron-bound door fell into place behind me, and I no longer had to fear an immediate chase. I can imagine the commotion that took place half an hour later!

Covering up his heavily bruised lower face, Wolf made his way to a suburb where he knew a trusted friend lived – a kind-hearted Hungarian circus clown named Janos. There he sheltered and recovered for two days.

Messing realized he had to make his way to the USSR. Escape to the West was now impossible, but the Soviets (still allied to the Nazis) maintained a passable border. Before dawn on the third day, a peasant cart filled with hay stopped in front of Janos's house, and a friendly peasant took Messing out of Warsaw.

Within a week, the largely recovered Messing reached the Western Bug River, which he crossed by night. Navigating by the stars, he steered east, avoiding any border posts. He was unfamiliar with the area and with the customs of this new country, and had to blend in with the stream of refugees. He was forced to spend his first night in the USSR in a synagogue – still an uncomfortable place for him after his disillusioning childhood experiences. The next morning he went to talk to the Soviet authorities.

The Cultural Affairs Department eventually agreed to include Messing in an official troupe of entertainers touring the region to put on shows for the troop build up along the Fascist–Soviet border. Things were looking up, but Wolf was often in trouble because his Russian was poor and, like most Polish refugees, he was suspected of being a spy.

Perhaps to escape this life-threatening stigma, Wolf quickly and volubly dedicated himself to the communist cause. He marched in the ranks of the intelligentsia in a May Day demonstration in 1940, one year before the USSR entered the war, and was even allowed to carry a poster of Joseph Stalin, "Father of the People".

This enthusiasm – and his amazing talents – were duly noted and he was soon after transferred to Minsk, capital of Byelorussia, where his performances attracted the interest of the highest authorities. Wolf was presented to the secretary of the republic's Central Committee, Panteleymon Kondratyevich Ponomarenko, and it was this man who drew Stalin's attention to Messing.

Later, when Messing was performing in a club in Gomel, two

KGB officers entered the hall. They unceremoniously interrupted the act, apologized to the spectators, and escorted him away. The officers did not explain where they were taking him, but he could sense tension and secretiveness in their behaviour. Reading their minds as best he could, Wolf felt that even they were not sure what awaited him. They pushed him into an expensive Party limousine and drove him to Moscow. There he was driven to an enormous mansion, where he was escorted to the second floor, then led into a spacious, luxuriantly furnished living room.

After a wait, a man sporting red cheeks and a fat nose above a well-tailored suit entered. Only several years later did Messing discover through newspaper photographs that this was Alexander Poskrebychev, the all-powerful assistant and personal secretary to Joseph Stalin. Poskrebychev asked: "Are you carrying any weapons?" Wolf replied that he was not, but Poskrebychev frisked him anyway.

After another short wait on his own, Wolf heard the door open softly and he found himself gazing at Joseph Stalin. The dictator greeted him but did not offer a hand to shake. Messing answered politely, but then "the devil took hold of me," and he said: "I carried you in my arms just recently." Messing expected him to be dumbfounded, but Stalin possessed a legendary inscrutability – he merely looked questioning. Messing explained that he had carried his huge portrait during a demonstration. "It seems you're a humorist as well," Stalin said in his strong Georgian accent. A mass-murderer on a scale that dwarfed even Hitler, Stalin had men shot on the slightest pretext, but Messing felt no sense of threat.

Stalin then began to ask questions, all of a political nature. Never during that conversation did he inquire about Messing's telepathic abilities. He questioned him about the situation in Poland, and about his pre-war meeting with Pilsudski and other Polish leaders. This was the first of several meetings with Stalin. It was after the second one that Stalin gave the KGB orders to check Messing's psychic abilities.

Messing was asked to withdraw 100,000 roubles from a branch of the state bank. He handed the bank clerk a blank sheet of paper and mentally suggested that he was giving him a cheque – the same trick he had accidentally used on the Polish ticket inspector as a boy. The crux of the experiment lay in the sheer enormity of the sum: the clerk would only be able to issue the funds after thoroughly checking the "document", and he would be extremely careful with such a transaction.

The bank clerk, a middle-aged man with a thin grey moustache, took the paper, which was a sheet torn from an ordinary school notebook. He studied it intently and for a long time, shifting his eyes between Messing and the document. Then he opened the safe and began to count out the money.

When the cash had been handed over, three official witnesses, dressed in civilian clothes, signed a document testifying to the experiment's success, and even counted the money Messing had placed in a briefcase: it was all there.

Next Messing returned to the cashier's window and handed him the same piece of paper. This time, mentally commanding him to see it as it actually was: the only thing on the otherwise blank sheet was a stamp and his own signature. The man cast a glance at the paper, looked back at Messing in horror, then collapsed back into his chair.

Abetting a bank robbery – like many other things in Stalin's Russia – was a capital offence. Unfortunately, the appalling shock had given the bank clerk a heart attack before the true situation could be explained. The man survived, but Messing always felt guilty that he had not handled the matter more diplomatically.

Another experiment consisted of Messing walking past three sets of security guards at a military establishment. All the guards were given a detailed description of Messing and the time of his anticipated exit, and had been strictly ordered not to let him pass. Yet Messing strolled past them, apparently invisible.

On another occasion, Stalin asked Messing to try to enter his presence without the necessary authorizations. Messing must have guessed that this was a dangerous task – the guards might shoot him if he failed and the paranoid Stalin might have him shot if he succeeded. Yet his ability to read Stalin's mind seems to have convinced him that hiding his light under a bushel, so to speak, was the more dangerous course of action.

At the time, Stalin was working in his country *dacha* (villa) and Messing was billeted in a guesthouse in the grounds. Wolf left his room and walked directly past a dozen guard posts and knocked on Stalin's study door. The flabbergasted dictator asked how he did it and Messing replied that he had simply projected a mental image of Lavrenti Beria – Stalin's much-feared hatchet man. Since Beria had the run of Stalin's home, Wolf guessed that no guard would dare to stop him.

Despite the strict control of classified information in wartime USSR, rumours about the Messing experiments soon spread to the general public, although in a greatly exaggerated form. It was likely, in fact, that the KGB – masters of scaremongering and disinformation – deliberately publicized Messing's abilities. It was soon put about that Wolf took part in the interrogations of prisoners in the cells of the notorious Lubyanka Prison; the idea that the KGB had an interrogator who could read thoughts must have frightened anyone with something to hide.

Fortunately, this story was pure invention. "Papa" Stalin, convinced by the experiments, insisted that Messing's powers were made available to only him – Wolf became a twentieth-century court magician in all but name.

Frustratingly, Messing only hints at what his actual duties were for Stalin. It should be remembered that he gave his interview to Tatiana Lungin during the Cold War, and doubtless felt that many of his wartime activities came under the heading of "state secrets". However, it is fairly plain that he rendered Stalin enough useful service to be considered a valuable asset.

Unfortunately, although Stalin trusted Messing (as far as that ruthless paranoid trusted anyone), he refused to believe any of Wolf's predictions that he did not want to hear . . .

Stalin had entered the non-aggression pact with Hitler in August 1939 (just a month before the German invasion of Poland) because the Soviet army was then in no condition to fight the Nazis. During the 1930s, Stalin's purges had killed off virtually every experienced Soviet military officer above the rank of lieutenant, and the new officers were both inept and, not surprisingly, too nervous to exercise any individual initiative.

Stalin, who was perfectly aware that the Nazis hated him as much as he hated them, had been told that army reforms and retraining would take until the summer of 1941 at the very earliest. He was quite aware that, left to themselves, the Germans would eventually break the pact and attack the USSR, but gambled that he had time – while the Germans conquered France and attacked

Britain – to complete his army reforms so he could stab the Nazis in the back before they could do it to him.

Unfortunately, Stalin soon convinced himself that this risky gamble was actually a sure thing . . . despite a large amount of highly detailed espionage information that proved the Germans were about to make the first move.

Messing also warned Stalin that the Nazis would soon invade, and even gave him the date: 22 June 1941. Stalin ignored the warning. Undeterred, Wolf tried again and again to get someone in authority to listen to his premonition of Germany's imminent attack, but he always received the reply that he would be notified when his advice was needed.

Perhaps it was his insistence on playing Cassandra that led to Wolf being put back on the entertainment circuit. Even *listening* to a man whose opinions contradicted Stalin might be seen as high treason – and since Stalin had also ruled that Messing was too valuable to be shot or sent to a labour camp, the only alternative was to get the dangerous psychic out of Moscow. Throughout the spring of 1941, Messing appeared before his first large Soviet audiences in tours through Odessa and Kharkov in the Ukraine, and then in Tbilisi.

It was in Tblisi, on 22 June, that Wolf heard the "news" that the Germans were invading Soviet territory. He was both unsurprised and depressed that all his warnings had not deflected the great disaster. The Russian armies on the Western Front had been taken totally by surprise and were being thrown back in enormous confusion. Stalin's reaction to the news was characteristic: he had the commander of the Western Army and his entire staff arrested and shot – further adding to the confusion.

Messing hurriedly returned to Moscow enshrouded in gloomy thoughts. The passenger train stopped at all the stations, sometimes for long periods of time. During every stop he walked about the platform, but never attempted to penetrate the thoughts of the anxious people storming the ticket offices. He could see that their thoughts were all the same: to escape the oncoming Nazis.

Wolf was detained several times by military patrols as his long hair and foreign accent invariably aroused suspicion. Even after his arrival in Moscow, he was arrested and spent several hours in a military command post while his identity was checked. To disguise his poor Russian, he tried to avoid conversation.

Moscow was in an uproar and nobody had time for a court magician, so Wolf was sent to western Siberia and the city of Novosibirsk to entertain troops and factory workers. This might also have been to keep him safe: until the Russian winter and elite Russian snow troops hurled them back in late 1941, it looked very likely that Moscow itself might fall to the Germans.

In Siberia, Messing saw first-hand the strange contradiction of the 1940s Soviets – they would remain as meek as sheep under their Party overseers, but were as fearless as wolves in the face of the Nazi invasion:

> The Russian soul is an enigmatic one. It can both lift a person up and crush him, leaving him crying and laughing at the same time. The audience of soldiers couldn't help but know that many of them would never return from battle, but during my performances a feeling of healthy optimism prevailed.

It was during his many performances in Novosibirsk that Messing began regularly to predict that the war would end in May 1945, with the total defeat of Germany and with Russian troops marching through the rubble of Berlin. At the time it doubtless sounded like simple propaganda talk – in 1941 it seemed to many that Russia would be lucky to simply survive unconquered. Yet Messing was actually slightly pessimistic in his prediction: he suggested that the European war would end in early May, when Hitler's death actually ended the conflict on 30 April.

In 1944, after an appearance in Novosibirsk, a young woman called Aida approached Messing backstage. She was a little overweight, wore her hair short, and spoke softly. Yet she was no shy fan. She flatly told Messing that his act needed a better introduction and offered to write one for him. Soon she was introducing and assisting him herself, dressed in a plain dark suit. Under Aida's influence, the act lost much of its show-business glitter and Messing was able to utilize his powers with a more scientific air.

Shortly after this fruitful meeting, Wolf and Aida were married. However, their happiness was not to last long. Aida was diagnosed with a malignant breast tumour. The doctors agreed that, as a young fit woman, she might pull through, but Messing furiously refused to be comforted:

> Listen, I'm not a child! I'm *Messing*. Don't try and tell me nonsense. She is not going to recover. She is going to die. She will die on the second of August at seven o'clock in the evening.

As Messing foretold, Aida died on 2 August at seven in the evening.

Wolf Messing met Tatiana Lungin, his future biographer, during the war when she came to him with a request: she had heard nothing from her husband, who was in the army – was he dead?

Messing held her wrist, then told her to envisage walking into her apartment in Leningrad. Apparently reading her mind, he was able to follow her, step by step, speaking aloud as if she were actually leading him through the flat. Tatiana later wrote his words down verbatim:

> Go slowly to the left, the door to someone else's room – the hallway, to the right. Your room, walk in. NO, the piano is not by the wall next to the door, but right by the window. The glass is broken, the top is open, and there is snow on the ground. Well, why did you stop? Go further. The second room is almost empty: no chairs or table either, no shelves – the books are lying in a heap on the floor in the middle of the room.

Needless to say, he described her apartment's layout accurately, despite never having seen it before.

Messing then suddenly let go of her wrist and told her: "Your husband is alive. He is ill, very ill. You will see him. He will come here on 5 July at ten o'clock in the morning."

July the fifth eventually came, but there was still no word from Tatiana's husband. Ten in the morning came and went with no sign of him and, as the hours dragged by, Tatiana decided she no longer believed in Messing's powers. She could not bring herself to leave the flat that day, however. At seven in the evening there was a tap at the door. It was her husband. When she told him she had been expecting him since ten that morning, he explained that his train had arrived at ten, but that he had been queuing all day for bread.

Shortly thereafter, when Tatiana and her husband returned to their flat in Leningrad, it was exactly as Messing had described it – the piano with the open lid, the broken window and the pile of mouldering books on the floor: Tatiana's neighbours had burned the chairs and bookshelves for fuel during the siege of the city.

Wolf Messing died in Russia in 1974. Before this, despite the strictures of the Cold War, he confidently told his old friend Tatiana that she and her son would leave Russia in 1978, and would eventually to settle in the United States. She was not, therefore, surprised when an unlikely sequence of events allowed her to do just that.

What we can gather from Wolf Messing's story is by no means certain. We can be reasonably sure that he was not an invention of Tatiana Lungin, and that he indeed visited India in the early decades of the twentieth century – Messing is mentioned as a powerful western mystic/psychic in several Indian spiritual publications (for example, *Shirdi to Puttaparthi* by Dr R. T. Kakade and *Sathya Sai Speaks*, Volume XIV, by Dr Veerabadhra Rao and Guru Sathya Sai Baba).

On the other hand, we only have his word that most of his fantastic adventures actually took place. (I have yet to hear of any Messing-related material being made available by the Russian archives). He *might* have been a twentieth-century Baron Münchhausen – a dreamer addicted to spinning self-aggrandizing lies. Yet, if we cautiously accept his story, Messing offers some interesting possible insights into precognitive prophecy . . .

Wolf Messing's actual predictions – although accurate – were relatively few. He stands out as a singularly powerful psychic rather than as a new Nostradamus. Yet Tatiana Lungin's description of his "tour" of her apartment in Leningrad, just before he accurately predicted when her husband would return, suggests that part of Messing's mental power was the key to his ability to precisely foretell the future.

Remember, Messing did not describe Tatiana's apartment as she remembered or imagined it, but as it actually *was* in bombed-out Leningrad – something that neither of them, in far off Novosibirsk, could have known by any ordinary means. This suggests that

Messing was doing something that psychics call *psychometry*, or "remote seeing".

A psychometrist claims that they can psychically "read" events connected to an object, person or place by simply touching them. A hammer might reveal an image of the person who owns it, for example, or a crime scene might reveal the image of the criminal.[1]

Messing seems to have gone a step further – projecting his mind to a place that he knew would have a psychic residue of Tatiana's missing husband. Having thus made psychometric contact, he could trace the man's psychic trail and divine his future as if he was holding *his* hand, not Tatiana's. Where prophets like the Brahan seer seem to have had predictions more or less forced upon them, Messing was apparently able to utilize his considerable mental powers to "force" the future to reveal itself.

People like the Brahan seer and Mother Shipton seem to have been born with a natural talent for prophecy, which they generally took for granted. Rare cases like Messing (and possibly the deliberately self-obfuscating Nostradamus) suggest that rigorous training and mental control might also be a way to gain visions of the future.

---

[1] It is the latent "psychometric" ability in apparent non-psychics that some paranormal investigators, like the late Tom Lethbridge, believe are the origin of ghost sightings. A ghostly nun, regularly seen walking down the aisle of a "haunted" chapel, for example, might actually be what Lethbridge called a "psychic recording" of a long-forgotten event.

Chapter 20

Jeane Dixon – the White House Seer

On Friday 22 November 1963, three women met for lunch in the Mayflower Hotel in Washington DC. They were: Mrs Harley Cope, widow of a rear admiral, Mrs Rebecca Kaufmann, a Washington hostess, and the psychic – and real estate agent – Jeane Dixon. But while the other two began to eat, Jeane Dixon simply sat staring at her plate. "Why aren't you eating?" asked Mrs Kaufmann.

Jeane Dixon replied: "I just can't. I'm too upset. Something dreadful is going to happen to the President today."

For several weeks, Jeane Dixon had been foreseeing a tragedy for President Kennedy. At that moment, the orchestra stopped, and the conductor, passing their table, said: "Someone has just tried to take a shot at the President." Jeane Dixon simply commented: "The President is dead."

"No," said the orchestra leader, "he may not even be hit. Somebody has just taken a shot at him."

"He is dead," Dixon replied flatly.

In fact, President Kennedy, driving in the motorcade through Dealy Plaza in downtown Dallas, had been struck by at least two bullets. One, a head shot that passed through his brain, had killed him instantly. Dixon was quite right.

Indeed, Jeane might have actually saved Kennedy if her predictions had been better trusted in government circles. A few weeks before, Jeane Dixon had gone to the house of Kay Halle, another Washington hostess, in order to tell her husband: "The President has just made a decision to go some place in the

South, and it will be fatal to him. Please get the word not to make that trip."

Eleven years before, in 1952, Jeane Dixon – who was a Catholic – had entered St Matthew's Cathedral for her morning meditation. Before she knelt in prayer in front of a statue of the Virgin, however, she suddenly saw the White House – the residence and workplace of the US president – glowing in radiant brilliance. She also saw the date 1960 above it and a young man standing in front of it. And she suddenly knew that whoever was elected in 1960 would die in office.

Four years later, she told two reporters from *Parade* magazine: "A blue-eyed Democratic president elected in 1960 will be assassinated." Her prediction appeared in the issue of 11 March 1956.

In the summer of 1963, the president's three-day-old son Patrick died, and someone asked Jeane whether this could be the "cloud" that she felt was hovering over the White House. She answered no, because she could see a large coffin being carried into the White House.

In October 1963, dining with F. Regis Riesenman at Duke Zeibert's restaurant, she told him that she had had a vision in which she saw Lyndon B. Johnson's name being removed from the vice-presidential door. She said she had glimpsed the name of the man who had caused this to happen and that although it had faded rapidly, she noticed that it was a two-syllable word containing five or six letters. She felt that the second letter was an S.

Jeane Dixon had already told this prediction to journalist Ruth Montgomery the day before. She said that the name of the man who was causing the plaque to be removed had a name that began with an O and the second letter was S.

Jeane Dixon told many others of her premonition that Kennedy would be assassinated and on the morning of the 22nd, Jeane Dixon told a friend Mr Bentor: "This is the day it will happen."

Within three months of the death of President Kennedy, Jeane Dixon told three friends, including Ruth Montgomery: "The tragedies in the Kennedy family are not yet ended. I see another one soon for another male member of the family."

On 19 June 1964, she told her friend Mrs Walter Stork that Teddy Kennedy must be warned to stay out of private planes for the next two weeks. The next morning, the newspapers had a headline saying that Senator Edward Kennedy had been gravely injured in the crash of the chartered plane in which his closest assistant and the pilot were both killed.

Jeane Dixon was born Jeane Pinckert, the daughter of German parents. Her father, Frank Pinckert, came to America just before the First World War – on his honeymoon – and had decided to apply for American citizenship while there. Jeane was born in Wisconsin, on 5 January 1918, and a few years later her father moved out to California. He was a friend of the famous horticulturalist Luther Burbank, and when one day he heard that a gypsy woman was camped on Burbank's property, he suggested that his wife should take Jeane to see her.

"The gypsy lady had a covered wagon with a stovepipe jutting out of the canvas roof," Jeane remembered. "Chickens poked their heads out of the wagon door, and the horse that was tied to a tree kicked and bounced wildly while we were there. The gypsy lived mostly out of doors but she kept the ground spotlessly clean by sweeping it with a broom and I remember she pared her fingernails with a pocket knife."

The gypsy was telling someone's fortune with cards as Mrs Pinckert and eight-year-old Jeane arrived. As soon as the gypsy looked at her palm she said:

This little girl is going to be very famous. She will be able to foresee worldwide changes, because she is blessed with a gift for prophesy. Never have I seen such palm lines.

Here is a Star of David, and with this double headline leading from it, she will need no other symbol in order to have the gift of prophesy. But look at this! She has another star on the Mount of Jupiter, [The name for the hump at the base of the index finger], and in her right palm is this tremendous star that reaches in all directions. I've never seen such a headline, it completely crosses the palm and wraps around the hand with a half-moon on its outer cuff!

The gypsy went on to say: "The lines of the left hand are the blueprint of one's dreams and potential. Those in the right hand signify what you do with what God has given you. She is already developing fast."

The gypsy then gave Jeane a crystal ball. "You will be able to meditate on this and see wonderful things in it for the markings on your hand are those of a mystic."

When Jeane peered into the ball, pictures began to form in it. It was as if, she said, she was looking at a TV screen. She seemed to see the gypsy in a distant landscape of her own home. Suddenly, she exclaimed that the gypsy must be careful not to scald herself. The next time we returned for a visit, her hands were bandaged – she said they were deeply burned from scalding water.

Jeane's ability to see the future also told her that black-bordered letters would be arriving from Germany with the news that her grandfather was dead. And a year later, while her father was on a business trip to Chicago, Jeane told her mother that he would bring back a big black-and-white dog – and when he returned with a black-and-white collie, Jeane said that she had "seen" her father buying it. She also foresaw – correctly – that her brother Erny was going to become a famous footballer.

When the family moved to Los Angeles they met an apparently washed-up actress named Marie Dressler – a former co-star of Charlie Chaplin, but now forgotten by the studios and the public alike. She told the Pinckerts that she intended to open a boarding house, because she saw no future for herself in the movie business. Jeane told her that, on the contrary, she would become a great star and earn lots of money.

In 1927, the arrival of "talkie" sound pictures unexpectedly revived Marie Dressler's career. Her skill as a verbal comedienne and as a character actress (of course wasted in silent films) made her a fortune acting in numerous comedies. She won the Oscar for best actress in 1931 and, of course, never needed to think of opening a boarding house again.

In her mid-teens, Jeane developed a crush on a businessman named James L. Dixon, and was mortified when he married someone else. She turned to show business to try to forget her heartbreak and, having a lovely mezzo-soprano voice, started to take auditions.

In 1939, she played Mary Magdalene in *A Life of Christ* at the Hollywood Bowl. Immediately afterwards, at the race track, she bumped into Jim Dixon, who was now divorced. He was dazzled by her beauty, and within five weeks they were married. This was hard for Jeane because she was a devout Catholic and Jim was not only a Methodist but a divorcé.

During World War II, Jeane was in a beauty salon in Los Angeles when the actress Carole Lombard – wife of Clark Gable – strolled in. As they were shaking hands, Jeane told her: "Oh Miss Lombard, you must not go anywhere by plane for the next six weeks." Carole Lombard replied that she was leaving immediately on tour to promote war bonds, to which Jeane replied she must only travel by car or train. A few days later, Carole Lombard disregarded the advice and died in a plane crash.

While her husband went east to work on defence projects for the war, Jeane continued living in Los Angeles, and became acquainted with Henry Ford. When she told Ford that he would outlive his only son Edsel, Ford was sceptical – and he was even more so when she told him that there would be a seven year gap in Ford's assembly line production of cars. Within a week, Jeane was proved right as the Ford plant was turned over entirely to war production.

When her husband was about to set out for a flight to Chicago, Jeane told him that she had had a vision of a plane crashing, and advised him to take the train. When he hesitated, she stamped her foot angrily. He finally took her advice – and the plane on which he had a ticket crashed near Chicago killing all the passengers.

Jim Dixon was assigned to work in Washington to handle real estate acquisitions; this is how Jeane eventually came to the nation's capital. Unable to work for the hospital because she was too sensitive to the sufferings of the patients, she joined a Home Hospitality Committee to provide recreation for servicemen. There she gave readings to the servicemen, and was immensely popular. At this time she devised a patriotic catchphrase that she would tell the young men while reading their futures: "It's not what your country can do for you – it's what you can do for your country," which later became the rallying cry in President Kennedy's inaugural address.

It was at about this time that Jeane Dixon shook hands with Vice-President Harry S. Truman and prophesied: "You will become president through an act of God." Truman, of course, would replace Franklin D. Roosevelt after his sudden death in office in 1945.

Eric Johnston, former President of the National Chamber of Commerce, asked Jeane Dixon whether he would receive the appointment as Republican presidential contender. She replied that the answer was no, but that he would accept another high post to do with the motion picture industry. Johnston laughed out loud, but a few months later was offered the presidency of the Motion Picture Association of America, which he held for eighteen years until his death in 1963.

In November 1944, Jeane Dixon was asked to go to the White House to meet President Roosevelt. When Roosevelt asked her how long he had to finish his work, she answered: "Six months or less". Roosevelt then asked her about Russia. She replied that she had been seeing in visions that America, France, England and Germany must be allies before we would have real world peace – Germany needed to be on our side helping to conquer Russia instead of the other way round.

"Shall we remain allies with Russia?" asked the president. Jeane Dixon shook her head: "The visions show otherwise, but we will become allies again later on, against Red China."

"'Red China?" the president asked, amazed. "But China isn't Red!"

Looking at her crystal ball, Jeane Dixon said: "China will go Communist and become our biggest trouble; Africa will be our next biggest."

When Roosevelt again asked her how many years he had to live, she corrected him gently: "Not years – months. Less than six months."

Two months later, she was asked to provide the president with another reading. When she arrived at the White House, Jeane noted that Roosevelt looked thin and haggard. After warning him again that China would become Communist, she told him that America would have bloodshed over the question of racism. "The racial situation will not be solved before 1980," she told him. It was then that Jeane Dixon warned him not to give Russia "half of anything that isn't ours to give". In fact, at the Yalta conference the following February, he gave Russia dominion over half of

Germany. On 12 April 1945, Roosevelt died of a cerebral haemorrhage at Warm Springs, Georgia.

Jeane Dixon repeated her prophecy that China would go Red in October 1946, at a party in the Hillstapus Estate which served as the Chinese Embassy in Washington. The wife of one State Department official said with astonishment: "Why China isn't Red, and with its rich cultural heritage would never go for an alien ideology like Communism." Jeane Dixon repeated flatly: "China will go Communist."

Someone who was present later remarked: "No one believed her that day," and with good reason. China, although savagely attacked and partially conquered by the Japanese in the 1930s and 40s, remained one of the most culturally inward-looking and conservative nations on the planet. The idea that Karl Marx could have an influence in the nation of Confucius seemed ridiculous to outside observers in 1946.

It happened, of course, on 21 September 1949, when Mao proclaimed a Communist People's Republic, and General Chiang Kai-shek withdrew to the island of Formosa (now called Taiwan).

Again, in 1945, at a reception given by Sir Girja Shankar Bajpai, Jeane Dixon shocked everybody by announcing that there would be a partition of India within two years. "No, no," was the reply, "there will never be a partition of India." On 20 February 1947, Colonel Sher Ali sent her a telegram pointing out that she had been mistaken about Indian partition on that date. But, as she had prophesied, the division of India was announced before the end of that day.

On another occasion a friend of Jeane's learned that a Cadillac was to be raffled off, and jokingly suggested that she should use her psychic powers to win it. Accordingly, she selected a ticket and wrote her name on the back. It won, at odds of 14,000 to 1.

Ruth Montgomery's book on Jeane Dixon contains hundreds of anecdotes of her powers, but one thing seemed to happen repeatedly: her glimpses of the future would often occur when she was either thinking about something else, or was talking to someone else about their own future. In mid-1947, for example, she was listening to a management consultant who was talking to her husband about his forthcoming trip to the Far East, when quite suddenly she said: "Mahatma Gandhi will be assassinated." As they had talked about India, she had seen a vision of Gandhi being assassinated. She gave the date as within six months, and on 3 January 1948, Gandhi was killed by a Hindu fanatic who disapproved of his multi-cultural views.

In 1961, she was talking to a friend about a woman who had threatened to commit suicide when Jeane Dixon said suddenly: "She never will, but Marilyn Monroe will." At that time, just after Marilyn Monroe had sung happy birthday to President Kennedy, nothing seemed less likely. Yet the suicide came about nine months after Jeane Dixon's prediction.

It was while discussing a plane trip abroad with another friend that Jeane Dixon remarked: "It's all right so long as you don't fly in the same plane with Dag Hammarskjold in mid-September. His plane will crash, and he will be killed." When Hammarskjold's death came about, Jeane Dixon added that she had considered the possibility of warning him, but had already known in advance that he would take no notice.

Jeane Dixon laid her reputation on the line when it came to the question of whether Harry Truman would be re-elected. The general feeling in Washington was that he would not be. It was while Jeane Dixon was doing a reading for the wife of a Washington attorney that she told her to make a wish, then added: "Your wish was not a personal one, but it will be granted."

The wish had been that Harry Truman should be re-elected. All the political commentators felt that the odds were heavily against it, and one friend even urged her to change her forecast "because you'll be making yourself ridiculous". But although the odds seemed to be heavily on Thomas E. Dewey, Truman's contender, a few weeks later, to everyone's amazement, Truman won the 1948 election.

Four years later, Jeane Dixon was invited, along with her crystal ball, to a garden party shortly before the Democratic Party nominating convention in 1952. She told two of the candidates that they would not receive the Democratic nomination because it would go to someone whose name began with S. In fact, it went to Adlai Stevenson.

However, Dixon also told Stevenson that he would have an illness that would prevent him from winning. Just as she had predicted, Stevenson was rushed to hospital for an operation, and

Eisenhower won the presidency for the Republicans. Again, more accurate than any modern pollster, Jeane Dixon had correctly forecast an Eisenhower landslide.

On 14 May 1953, Jeane Dixon appeared on television with an expert on the Russians, Joseph E. Davies, a former ambassador to Moscow. When he asked her how long Malenkov would be Soviet premier, she replied that she saw Malenkov being replaced by another man with an oval-shaped head, wavy grey hair, a little goatee, and greenish eyes, and that this would happen in less than two years. The ambassador declared that Russian premiers were not so easily replaced – they either died or were shot. Moreover, Russians did not usually have oval-shaped heads. Nevertheless, Jeane went on to say that shortly after this event, "a silver ball" will go into outer space and then circle the Earth.

The ambassador rather patronizingly assured Jeane that neither event was likely to happen in the near future, because that was simply not the way that things were done in Russia. Political and scientific breakthroughs were always heralded by events that experts, like himself, could easily interpret. He advised her to read his book *Mission to Moscow*, and learn a little more about Russian affairs.

Nevertheless, two years later, Malenkov was replaced as Soviet premier in a bloodless coup by Marshall Bulganin who – incidentally – corresponded precisely to Jeane's description.

Also in 1957, the Sputnik space satellite was launched. The first man-made object to orbit the planet, the small tin ball – containing nothing but a radio bleeper – panicked the complacent western powers. The Soviet space programme and its comparatively advanced state of development had been kept totally secret . . . from everyone, that is, but Jeane Dixon.

When an official of the American Federation of Labour was talking to her, Jeane Dixon saw "a vision of a gold wedding ring descending over his union and its chief rival, the CIO (Congress of Industrial Organisations)." It seemed a completely unlikely forecast, tantamount to announcing the merger of Coca-Cola and Pepsi-Cola. Nevertheless, it happened two years later.

When she was about to appear on a television programme with comedian Bob Hope, she was introduced to him as a psychic. Hope commented: "Well, Mrs Dixon, I've been playing golf with

Ike this afternoon. If you're so good tell me what my golf score was." Looking into her crystal ball she replied: "Your score was 92 and the president's was 96." Hope looked as if he was about to have apoplexy, and later told his manager: "This Dixon woman has ruined me. The president will never believe I didn't tell her I won!"

Sometimes her forecasts were unwelcome. When she told Sir Winston Churchill in 1945 that he would be turned out of office by the British electorate if he called an early election, he grunted: "England will never let me down." Nevertheless it did – the British badly needed a change after five years of war, and Churchill and his Conservatives were replaced by Clement Attlee and a Labour government. She also foretold that Churchill's death would come at the end of 1964 – in fact, he died in early 1965.

When she foretold that President Eisenhower would be re-elected, she added: "Senator Estes Kefauver will fail in his dream of the presidency, but is the likeliest winner of the second place nomination on the Democratic ticket." Kefauver lost the nomination, but won second place in a contest against a young senator called John F. Kennedy.

In fact sometime earlier, when a friend of hers was invited by Kefauver to become part of a committee that would attempt to make him president, Jeane Dixon told her friend: "Senator Kefauver is not going to be president."

When, shortly after that, Jeane Dixon met Kefauver, she told him the reason why – his timing was wrong: "You should have waited to make your bid until 1960 when the Democrats will win." They did, of course – but the new Democratic president was the young Senator Kennedy.

Ruth Montgomery notes that, from her own point of view, Jeane Dixon's most astonishing prophecy was when she asked her about John Foster Dulles. The reply was that Dulles would not be the secretary of state in Eisenhower's cabinet. And when Ruth Montgomery commented that Eisenhower would never discharge him, Jeane Dixon replied that that would not happen either – Dulles would be dead within six months.

Ruth Montgomery decided to soften the prophecy in her newspaper column, and simply said that Jeane Dixon had foretold that Dulles would retire from the cabinet. Yet she told editor Milton

Kaplan that Jeane Dixon had actually foreseen his death. Kaplan was thus able to confirm the prediction when Dulles died of cancer in May 1959, less than six months after Jeane's forecast.

Ruth Montgomery also reveals that Jeane Dixon could have made a good "psychic detective" like Gerard Croiset, Robert Cracknell or Peter Hurkos. On 11 January 1959, the Jackson family, consisting of Carroll Jackson, his wife Mildred and their two daughters – Susan aged four and Janet aged eighteen months – were driving to their home in Virginia when they were driven off the road by another car. Police found the wrecked vehicle, but the Jackson family had apparently been abducted.

It was more than a month later that the dead bodies of Carroll Jackson and his eighteen-month-old daughter were found in the ditch near Fredericksburg. When Mildred and Susan Jackson's bodies were discovered dumped shortly thereafterwards, both showed evidence of having been sexually abused before they were murdered.

Dr F. Riesenman, a Washington psychiatrist, decided to bring over to America the Dutch psychic Peter Hurkos to try to solve the murders. Hurkos led the police to a trash collector, who was committed for observation. But Jeane Dixon insisted that he was the wrong man. She said: "The murderer is a musician. He's tall and has dark bushy hair."

Not long after that, the police received an anonymous letter stating that the killer was a dark-haired jazz pianist named Melvin Rees. Rees was arrested in Memphis, Arkansas, and a search of his parents' home turned up a journal in which he gloated over the abduction and murder of the Jacksons. The journal also admitted to the killing and posthumous rape of a woman called Margaret Harold – more than enough evidence to send him to the electric chair and to confirm Jeane Dixon's prediction.

In November 1964, Peter Hurkos was asked about the disappearance of an attractive girl from her apartment in Washington the previous August. Hurkos was only able to state that the girl was still alive, so Dr Reisman asked Jeane Dixon for a psychic reading. When she was handed a photograph of the girl, she was able to say: "She is alive. Her physical condition is satisfactory but she is very sick emotionally. She is living under an assumed name in New York." When the girl finally returned home of her own accord, she verified that Jeane Dixon had been right.

Jeane Dixon was also correct when she forecast the American race riots of 1963 and 1964. In contrast, however, the American magician James Randi has pointed out that Jeane Dixon's record is not the non-stop string of successes recounted by her friend, Ruth Montgomery. In *The Supernatural A–Z*, Randi writes:

> In the 11 March, 1956 issue, *Parade* Magazine reported that Jeane said, concerning the 1960 Presidential Election: "Mrs Dixon thinks it will be dominated by Labor and won by a Democrat. He will be assassinated or die in office, though not necessarily in his first term.
>
> The election was not "dominated by Labor". She was correct on the winner's party, and the death prediction was in line with the Presidential Curse [which states that, beginning in 1840 with William Henry Harrison, and at twenty-year intervals up to 1960, each president elected or re-elected in those years died in office], since Kennedy fell into that pattern. Yet when 1960 arrived and the election was closer Mrs Dixon declared that Richard Nixon would win the Presidency.
>
> The endless chain of Dixon's major failed predictions (Tom Dewey as "assistant President", the fall of India's Nehru that never happened, Richard Nixon's return to Office, germ warfare in 1958 with China, a monster comet striking the Earth, the election of a female US President and the dissolution of the Roman Catholic before 1990) establishes that her actual written record is hardly impressive.

In his book *Prophecy and Prediction in the 20th Century*, Charles Neilson Gattey has "A Chapter for Cynics", in which he points out some other modern prophetic failures. For example, although seventeen major earthquakes took place between January and August 1970, the forecasters in *The American Astrology* magazine missed every one.

> Of the sixteen earthquakes predicted by them, they were right for only three minor upsets and failed to give any advance

warning of the worst disaster of the century to strike Peru on 21 May, when some 30,000 people perished.

In 1971, many psychics predicted that California would be destroyed by an earthquake and tidal wave in April:

"Members of the spiritualist churches in Los Angeles and elsewhere were urged by their ministers to take refuge in the hills of Georgia and Tennessee, and many obeyed. Andrew Widrovsky of Santa Barbara even described to reporters his awesome pre-vision of "two titanic earth convulsions, followed by five tidal waves and a deluge of radio-active ash that will cover the entire south-western part of the state." [Widrovsky also announced that he had invented an "anti-radiation belt" which if worn, would save people's lives. These could be purchased direct from him.]

There was some confusion as to the date of the expected disaster. When the news broke that California's then Governor Ronald Reagan would be going away to Arizona on 4 April, the rumours spread that he had received a confidential warning from a friendly top psychic, yet nothing untoward had occurred that day, and the favourite date then became 18 April – the date of the terrible earthquake of 1906 that almost destroyed San Francisco.

Enterprising shop keepers urged customers to buy protective helmets and fire-proof clothing, while one store put on a "how to be the Best Dressed for the Earthquake" fashion show.

The event was expected by most astrologers to begin at 3.15 p.m., and at 5 a.m., Joseph Alioto, San Francisco's mayor, gave a great Earthquake Party in its Civic Center Plaza. Undeterred by having to rise so early, over 7,000 gathered to await the predicted havoc with song, dance and drink, and were entertained with earthquake scenes shown on a giant screen from the MGM movie *San Francisco*. Yet the elements did not rage that afternoon, neither did they the next day at 8.19 a.m., the time chosen by a group of mystics supported by the hippies Haight-Ashbury.

On a similar note, one of Jeane Dixon's notable "misses" was her statement:

> Towards the middle of the 1980s, the Earth will be struck by a comet. Earthquakes and tidal waves will be the result of this tremendous collision which will take place in one of the great oceans. It will be one of the worst disasters of the 20th century. Although the approximate point of impact has already been revealed to me, I believe that I shall not reveal it yet, but at a future date I will give more detailed information."

Reading the final two chapters of Ruth Montgomery's biography of Dixon, published in 1965, the modern reader becomes aware of many other "misses". But these do not invalidate her numerous "hits".

It has been commented that the study of psychic phenomena is not like research in the more regular scientific fields. Indeed, one wag has pointed out that "psychic events are, like the male erection, difficult to reproduce under laboratory conditions. Yet we don't hear scientists debunking the existence of the male erection."

Ruth Montgomery talks of four "momentous visions" Jeane Dixon experienced in the 1950s. Shortly after midnight on 14 July 1952, Jeane had a strange dream in which a green snake twined itself round her body as she lay in bed and looked into her eyes so that she felt the "all-knowing wisdom of the ages". When the snake looked towards the east, she felt that she was also being told that she must look towards the east. She came to believe that the purpose of this vision was to prepare her for the three subsequent ones.

The second occurred one morning in 1958 in St Matthew's Cathedral. About to burn candles, she felt her hand entangled in the mass of purple and gold balls. One of them floated upwards and gradually merged into a massive purple disc edged in gold, and then circled the statue of the Virgin Mary until it encircled her head like a halo. Then the face of the statue came alive and sunshine flooded down from the dome of the church. Although it had been almost empty, it was now suddenly full of peasants, kings and queens in royal garments, and rich and poor of every nationality and creed. This she interpreted as being knowledge that a Council of the Church would soon bring together in Rome the religions and nationalities of all the world. She later told her secretary that the pope was about to call a great council of all the faiths and creeds. Less than four years after this vision, Pope John XXIII summoned an Ecumenical Council of the Church in Rome – the modernizing Second Vatican Council – to which twenty-eight non-Catholic dignitaries were also invited.

This, Jeane Dixon believed, was another step in her awakening knowledge of the future of religion. The next came when she was kneeling in prayer in the cathedral holding her crystal ball in her hands. Suddenly she once again saw the Virgin surrounded by golden white rays and above her head she was able to read the word "Fatima". She saw the throne of the pope, but it was empty. She also saw a pope with blood running down his face and dripping over his shoulder. She interpreted this to mean that a pope would be bodily harmed sometime in the late twentieth century.

Fatima, of course, was the wilderness spot in Portugal where, on 13 May 1917, three children – Lucia dos Santos and her cousins Francisco and Jacinta Marto – had a vision of "the Lady of the Rosary". In subsequent visitations she gave the children a number of prophecies, principally concerning two world wars and the future of Russia. By October – on the day predicted to bring the sixth appearance of the Lady of the Rosary, accompanied by a miracle – 70,000 people travelled in a downpour to reach Fatima.

At noon the rain stopped, the sun burst through, and one of the children, Lucia, cried out that "the Lady" had come. Then a celestial display stunned a large proportion of the crowd – the sun was seen to spin about in the sky three times, suddenly plunge downwards, but then gradually resume its proper place in the heavens. It should be noted, however, that no such solar twirling was seen anywhere else at that time and, perhaps more importantly, not all the crowd at Fatima saw the Sun do anything unusual. Some researchers have put the apparent solar event at Fatima down as a textbook case of mass hysteria and mass hallucination.

As usual, the children claimed to have been given a message by the Lady of the Rosary that nobody else could see or hear. This time, however, they insisted that the Lady of the Rosary would appear no more at Fatima. Francisco and Jacinta Marto died shortly afterwards, but Lucia de Santos survived to give evidence to several Church enquiries over subsequent decades. Her experience was eventually accepted as a genuine miracle – the Lady of the Rosary was declared to have been the Virgin Mary – and Lucia entered a Carmelite convent in 1948.

In her evidence to one of the Church enquiries, Lucia claimed that Christ had also appeared to her during the last Fatima event, and had given her a special prediction that was not to be revealed until 1960. Her transcript of the prediction was sealed in an envelope and taken to the pope in Rome.

Jeane Dixon believed that the vision she saw in 1958 was the same as the "secret" Fatima prophecy, and foretold the close of the papal reign of the Church within the twentieth century – an event, needless to say, that did not happen.

For some reason, however, the content of the "secret Fatima" envelope was not revealed in 1960. In fact the Vatican did not publish the text of the last Fatima prediction until June 2000.

It turned out to be an apparently symbolic vision in which the pope and other churchmen make a pilgrimage up a despoiled mountain towards a great cross. The prediction ends by saying:

> . . . the Holy Father passed through a big city half in ruins and half trembling with halting step, afflicted with pain and sorrow, he prayed for the souls of the corpses he met on his way.
>
> Having reached the top of the mountain, on his knees at the foot of the big cross he was killed by a group of soldiers who fired bullets and arrows at him, and in the same way there died one after another the bishops, priests, religious men and women, and various lay people of different ranks and positions.
>
> Beneath the two arms of the cross there were two angels each with a crystal aspersorium in his hand, in which they gathered up the blood of the martyrs and with it sprinkled the souls that were making their way to God.

Giving a distinct impression of whistling in the dark, the Vatican announced that the last Fatima prediction was actually a fore-sight of the attempted assassination of Pope John Paul II by a

Turkish extremist, Ali Agca, in 1981. Given the prediction's specific description of some, or perhaps all the Catholic hierarchy and lay membership being brutally executed, this seems an overly optimistic appraisal. Others have suggested that it is a prediction of the bloody destruction of the Catholic Church – coupled with the possible destruction of Rome – sometime in the future.

Jeane Dixon regarded her supreme vision as one that occurred on 5 February 1962. This was a day of a rare conjunction of the planets, although she was apparently unaware of this.

On three successive evenings, the light in her room dimmed, causing her to assume that a fuse was giving way. Yet, on closer inspection, she saw tiny balls of light inside the darkened bulbs in her crystal chandelier. Unable to divine any meaning from these lights, she went to bed.

On the third morning, after a night of these odd visions, her clock told her she had overslept. Yet when she got up and walked towards the bay window that faced east, she saw it was still before sunrise. Instead of the city outside, she saw a bright blue sky above a barren desert with a bright Sun glowing like a golden ball. Stepping from its rays, hand in hand, were a Pharaoh and Queen Nefertiti. The queen was cradling a baby on her arm, with ragged soiled clothing. Jeane also saw a pyramid to one side of Nefertiti. In the ball of the Sun, Jeane saw Joseph, Jesus' stepfather, guiding the tableau like a puppeteer. As the queen paused beside a large brown water jug, she was stabbed in the back by a dagger. Jeane heard her death scream.

The baby had now grown to manhood, and a cross above him began to expand until it dripped all over the earth. People of every colour were lifting arms in worshipful adoration, and Jeane believed she had been shown the answer to the vision:

A child, born somewhere in the Middle East shortly after 7 a.m. on February 5, 1962, will revolutionise the world. Before the close of the century he will bring together all mankind in one embracing faith. This will be the foundation of a new Christianity, with every sect and creed united through this man who will walk among the people to spread the wisdom of his Almighty Power. This man although humble of peasant origin, is a descendant of Queen Nefertiti and her husband.

Clearly, this is another prophecy that has not been fulfilled.

The last chapter of Ruth Montgomery's biography is devoted to prophecies of the future: "The role of war drums will be silenced. Peace will return to the earth in the year 1999, but not before a world holocaust has shocked mankind into spiritual renewal."

Another of Jeane Dixon's long-range predictions is as follows:

Red China will cause great strife among African and Asian nations and will provoke a world war in the decade of the 1980s. Vietnam and Korea will lead us into this inevitable war with Red China. America will align itself with Russia in the war against Red China.

Russia, Dixon also prophesied incorrectly, would be the first nation to put a man on the Moon.

She believed that America would have three presidents in the eight-year period between 1961 and 1969. This was correct – John F. Kennedy, Lyndon B. Johnson and Richard M. Nixon – but is also a remarkable prediction in that it is rare to see so many presidents elected in the same decade. A US presidential term is for four years, and the majority of presidents are elected to a second term.

Dixon predicted that "great honours would be showered on [Senator] Barry Goldwater, in spite of his defeat by Kennedy, he will come to be venerated to an even greater degree than was the late [President] Herbert Hoover." This is a miss: Goldwater was beaten by Lyndon B. Johnson in the 1964 presidential election. (If he had not been assassinated, Kennedy would almost certainly have faced Goldwater in that election instead of Johnson.) Barry Goldwater remained an important statesman until his death in 1998, but was never exactly "venerated".

Dixon also predicted that within a decade of 1968, the two-party system "as we have known it" will vanish from the American scene. Arguably another miss: the Republican/Democrat hold on power remains as strong as ever, although, since the late 1960s, unelected pressure groups (like the environmental movement) and vested interest groups (like the tobacco industry) have grown greatly in political influence.

And so, unfortunately, Ruth Montgomery's book ends with many false predictions. Yet Jeane Dixon's many "hits" remain on record. The "Seer of Washington DC" was either gifted with precognition or was a political genius.

Chapter 21

Nostradamus and the Future

There is an important question we have yet to address: did Nostradamus offer us any clues as to *how* he actually foresaw the future?

In *Nostradamus: Prophecies for Present Times?* (1985), David Pitt Francis offers one of the most systematic analyses of the *Centuries* so far. He splits the predictions into two sets – long-term and short-term – and examines them, virtually word by word, with a statistician's eye. For example, he assembles the magical and astrological references, and shows that – contrary to popular belief – the predictions contain a comparatively small proportion of such mystical material.

He also argues that many of the quatrains containing political, geographic and ecclesiastical information can be interpreted as short-term predictions concerning Nostradamus' own period, not sweeping predictions of far-distant future events.

Francis then sets out to show that Nostradamus was a penetrating and well-informed commentator on contemporary history who, out of caution, disguised his political, social and religious opinions as opaque predictions of future events. The result was the Rorschach ink-blot effect we discussed in an earlier chapter: the process that might be said to have led every commentator to read his own period of history (and his personal opinions) into the quatrains. Francis goes on to argue that individuals like Napoleon and Hitler deliberately set out to fulfil their personal interpretations of Nostradamus' predictions in the hopes of personal glorification.

Nostradamus: Prophecies for Present Times? sounds like the rationalist's answer to the Nostradamus enigma – except that Francis feels obliged to admit that some of the quatrains undeniably foretell specific future events that happened centuries after Nostradamus' native period. Francis seeks to explain this by suggesting that Nostradamus copied these prophetic "hits" from biblical predictions – which, oddly enough, Francis unquestioningly accepts to be genuinely precognitive. This view may or may not be correct – we have already looked at the historical validity of many biblical prophecies in earlier chapters – but it is hardly logical to try to demonstrate one unproven assertion by depending on another.

So, unfortunately, it has to be acknowledged that Francis's apparently scientific approach to Nostradamus' work is actually doing what every other writer on the Seer of Salon has done – finding evidence only for what he personally wishes to believe. Apart from reiterating the suggestion that Nostradamus was a highly intelligent man with a wide knowledge of contemporary politics – which was already self-evident – Francis has shed little light on just how the Seer of Salon accurately foretold the future.

The obvious place to seek further enlightenment is Nostradamus' own writings. The very first two quatrains of the first book of the *Centuries* seem to be a guide to how he saw into the future. *Century I*, quatrain 1, reads:

> *Estant assis de nuit secret estude,*
> *Seul reposé sur la selle d'aerain:*
> *Flambe exiguë sortant de solitude,*
> *Fait prosper qui n'est à croire vain.*

Translation:

> Sitting at night in secret study,
> Alone reposing over the brass tripod:
> A slender flame emerges from the solitude,
> Making prosper that which is not in vain.

The meaning of the first line seems self-evident, and we know from other sources that Nostradamus always conducted his studies at night in the secluded tower room of his house in Salon. Line two may remind readers of the Delphic oracle. The pythia, we may recall, sat on a bronze tripod above the sacred fissure in the ground, from which emerged mystical (possibly petrochemical) vapours. Any classically educated contemporary of Nostradamus would have recognized the mention of a brass tripod as an allusion to the Delphic Oracle.

The last two lines are harder to interpret. Line three might suggest the arrival of a precognitive vision in the gloom or, more mundanely, that the seer is lighting a brazier – perhaps, it has even been suggested, containing hallucinogenic herbs. The last line is usually taken to mean that Nostradamus knew that the Centuries would "prosper" and that his predictions would not, ultimately be "in vain".

Century I, quatrain 2:

> *La verge en main mise au milieu des BRANCHES,*
> *De l'onde il moulle et le limbe et le pied:*
> *Un peur et voix fremissant par les manches:*
> *Splendeur divine. Le divin pres s'assied.*

Translation:

> The wand in hand is placed in the middle of the BRANCHES,
> He moistens with water his foot and garment hem:
> A fear and voice makes him tremble in his sleeves:
> Splendour divine. The divine sits near.

The penultimate line is probably a poetic description of the terrifying, but euphoric, effect of Nostradamus' predictive practices on his senses, while the religious aspect of the last line is unmistakeable.

The last word of the first line seems to be another of the seer's historical allusions – "BRANCHES" in capitals, underlining the hint. *Branchus* was a demigod in Ancient Greek mythology. He possessed the gift of prophecy and could bestow it upon his followers. The fourth-century chronicler Iamblichus of Chalcis gives the following description of the prophetic rite of the Branchus worshippers:

The prophetess of Branchus either sits upon a pillar, or holds in her hand a rod bestowed by some deity, or moistens her feet or hem of her garment with water . . . by these means . . . she prophesies. By those practices she adapts herself to the god, whom she receives from without.

The similarity between lines one and two of the above quatrain and the quote from Iamblichus is so obvious that one can only assume that Nostradamus had read the ancient scholar. Whether he is actually suggesting that he received inspiration from Branchus is an open question, which in turn leads us to the subject of Nostradamus' religious beliefs . . .

Nowhere in his work can we confidently infer Nostradamus' personal convictions. Various commentators have seen in his writings evidence of faiths as diverse as Catholicism, Protestantism, Judaism and Paganism – some have even accused him of intercourse with powers of darkness.

This latter theory points to *Century* I, quatrain 42, as evidence:

> *Le dix Kalende d'Avril de faict Gothique,*
> *Resuscité encor par gens malins:*
> *Le feu estainct assemblé diabolique,*
> *Cherchant les os du d'Amant et Pselin.*

Translation:

> The tenth of the Calends of April calculated Gothic,
> Resuscitated by the wicked people:
> The fire put out, a diabolical assembly,
> Seek for bones of the demon of *Pselin*.

We have already considered the meaning of the first line in an earlier chapter (Nostradamus seemed to have foreseen Pope Gregory XIII's calendar reformation that was implemented decades after the seer's death.) This quatrain also seems to offer another hint as to Nostradamus' predictive methods. The last line almost certainly refers to the Byzantine philosopher Michael Psellus, who wrote *De Operatione Daemonum* (also known as *De Daemonibus*). In spite of its apparently lurid title (it actually translates as "the operation of spirits" not "demons") this tome was in fact a treatise on the history of Near Eastern magic. The passage Nostradamus had in mind could be the following, from Psellus' section on the history of prophecy:

> There is a type of predictive power in the use of the basin, known and practised by the Assyrians . . . Those about to prophesy take a basin of water, which attracts the spirits of the depths. The basin then seems to breathe as with sound . . . Now, this water [in] the basin . . . excels a power imparted to it by the charms which have rendered it capable of being imbued with the energies of the spirits of prophecy... a thin voice begins to utter predictions. A spirit of this sort journeys where it wills, and always speaks in a low voice.

From other hints the seer dropped, it seems likely that he used a bowl of water much as a fortune-teller might use a crystal ball. This practice, known as *scrying*, was a common method of predicting future events.

As we noted in the second chapter, gazing fixedly into a reflective surface – a crystal ball, a bowl of water or a freshly removed liver – can induce a state of trance (or perhaps self-hypnosis) in a trained or gifted seer. In this state, they claim to be able to see visions in the reflections. (The wicked queen in the Grimm fairytale *Snow White and the Seven Dwarfs* uses her "magic mirror" to scry whether Snow White is alive or dead, for instance.)

Psellus' *De Daemonibus* was, unsurprisingly, on the Catholic Church's blacklist in the sixteenth century: even admitting to have read it could have led Nostradamus to a charge of heresy. So it is possible that the "wicked people" referred to in the second line are those from whom he had to disguise the reference. Which, in turn, might mean that the Catholic Church was the "diabolical assembly" who sought to extinguish the "fire" of knowledge. Again, we are reduced to guessing, probably just as Nostradamus meant us to be.

Yet there is one quatrain – *Century II*, quatrain 13 – that seems to be a direct (if still obscure) statement of Nostradamus' religious beliefs:

Le corps sans ame plus n'estre en sacrifice.
Jour de la mort mis en nativité:
L'esprit divin fera l'ame felice,
Voyant le verbe en son eternité.

Translation:

The corpse without soul no longer at the sacrifice.
At the day of death it is brought to birth:
The spirit divine makes the soul rejoice,
Seeing in the word eternity.

The first line may be seen as a direct rejection of Catholic belief. On the Day of Judgment, the souls *and* bodies of the dead will, according to *The Revelation of St John the Divine*, rise from the grave (see chapter 7). Apart, possibly, from a few unfortunates who may already have been sent to Hell, everyone, faithful and sinner alike, must remain in the grave until the Final Judgment. Dead bodies, according to Revelation, still contain the souls of the departed, and will continue to do so until God calls them to be judged.

This is why strict Christians long opposed medical autopsies on anyone but executed criminals. There was even a Christian protest movement against the Victorian reinvention of the pagan tradition of cremating corpses – might not the trapped soul feel the flames?

For Nostradamus to speak of a corpse without an attached soul might have been regarded as heresy, if line one had been stated in a more direct fashion.

Line two has been seen by some as a statement of Nostradamus' actual faith: reincarnationism. Specifically, he seems to say that the soul of a dead person is "brought to [re]birth" on the day of his death.

If this is so, then line three can be interpreted as an echo of the Buddhist belief in the "Great Soul": that universal entity with which all lesser souls struggle to blend through gradual purification over numerous lives. So the last line sounds like a depiction of the Nirvanic state – in which the universe and eternity can be viewed as one by the purified soul.

On the other hand, a Catholic could choose the opposite interpretation. The first line means that the dead can no longer attend mass ("the sacrifice"). Lines two and three offer hope, showing the departed soul "rejoice[ing]" through "[re]birth" to the "divine spirit". Line four is an echo of the first words of the Gospel of John: "In the beginning was the word . . .". Thus Nostradamus may be saying that the soul attains "eternity" through the word of God.

Typically, Nostradamus manages to create fertile ground for argument, but does not leave enough clues to allow anyone to reach definite conclusions.

The magic practices Nostradamus describes are straight out of antiquity, but leave us none the wiser about how precognition might be attained. Perhaps, where Nostradamus was concerned, it was not "attained", but came naturally.

In his epistle to Henri II, Nostradamus says: "I will confess, Sire, that I believe myself capable of presage [precognition] from the natural instincts of my ancestors . . ." Perhaps, like Mother Shipton and the Brahan Seer, Nostradamus was a "natural" prophet. Any ceremonies he conducted simply helped to focus his inborn talents.

This would suggest that genuine prophets are not made, but can only be born.

Disasters (natural and artificial)

The following are some of the many Nostradamus predictions that seem to deal with natural – or possibly man-made – disasters. As with the other quatrains examined in this chapter, none have a specific date or historical detail to tie them to a past event, so I am listing them as "yet to come to pass".

Floods and Droughts

I.17, III.12, IV.67 & IX.31

Global warming might reduce some areas of the globe to deserts while, at the same time, melting the polar icecaps and flooding lowland areas.

> Par quarante ans l'Iris n'apparoistra,
> Par quarante ans tous les jours sera veu:
> La terre aride en siccité croistra,
> Et grans deluges quand sera aperceu.

Translation:

> For forty years the rainbow will not appear,
> For forty years it will appear every day:
> The dry earth will grow more parched,
> And there will be great floods when it is seen.

The biblical reference to God's rainbow, which signalled the end of the Great Flood, is plain. Whether the seer was also using the figure "forty years" as a poetic echo of the Bible's "forty days and forty nights", or is literally predicting four decades of flooding and drought, is a matter of opinion.

> *Par la tumeur de Heb, Po, Tag, Timbre et Rosne,*
> *Et par l'estang Leman et Arentin,*
> *Les deux grands chefs et citez de Garonne,*
> *Prins mors noyez. Partir humain butin.*

Translation:

> By the swelling of the Ebro, Po, Tagus, Tiber and Rhône,
> And the lakes of Geneva and Arezzo,
> The two chief cities of the Garonne,
> Taken, dead, drowned. Human booty divided.

The Ebro and Tagus rivers are in Portugal, the Po and Tiber in Italy and the Rhône in France. Geneva is in Switzerland and Arezzo in central Italy. The two chief towns of the Garonne region (with such grim futures) are Bordeaux and Toulouse.

This quatrain, therefore, is possibly a prediction of Europe-wide flooding.

> *L'an que Saturne et Mars esaux combuste,*
> *L'air fort seiché longue trajection:*
> *Par feux secrets, d'ardeur grand lieu adust,*
> *Peu pluie, vent chault, guerres, incursions.*

Translation:

In the year that Saturn and Mars are equally fiery,
The air is very dry long meteor:
From hidden fires a great place burns with heat,
Little rain, hot winds, wars, invasions.

The astrological configuration in the first line is a relatively common one, so specific dating of the prediction is not possible. Drought and wars at the time of a meteor or comet are foretold.

Les tremblement de terre à Montara,
Cassich saint George à demi perfondrez,
Par assoupie, la guerre esveillera,
Dans temple à Pasques abismes enfondrez.

Translation:

The trembling of the earth at *Montara*,
Cassich saint George shall be half sunk,
Drowsy with peace, war arises,
At Easter abysses open in the temple.

"*Cassich*" in line two could be a reference to the Ancient Greek *Cassiterides*, or "Isles of Tin": their name for the county of Cornwall in Britain (the island of "saint George"). "*Montara*", where the earthquake originates that will leave the English southwest "half sunk", is hard to place. There is nowhere in Cornwall with this name, but it is worth noting that there is an inactive earth fault line that runs along the south Cornish coast.

Local legend holds that as recently as the tenth century AD, a major earthquake drowned a whole region of south-west Cornwall, called Lyonesse, beneath the Atlantic.

Famine

I.67 & III.42

La grand famine que je sens approcher,
Souvent tourner, puis estre universelle:
Si grand et long qu'un viendra arracher,
Du bois racine et l'enfant de mamelle.

Translation:

> The great famine I see drawing near,
> Turns one way then another, then becomes universal:
> So great and long that they pluck,
> The root from the tree and the child from the breast.

Unlike many of his often egotistical profession, Nostradamus was a seer who rarely used the personal pronoun. His use of it in this quatrain seems to make it all the more chilling.

> *L'enfant naistra à deux dents en la gorge,*
> *Pierres en Tuscie par pluie tomberont:*
> *Peu d'ans apres ne sera bled ni orge,*
> *Pour saouler ceux qui de faim failliront.*

Translation:

> A child will be born with two teeth in his mouth,
> It will rain stones in Tuscany:
> A few years after there will be neither wheat nor barley,
> To feed those that are weak with hunger.

Once again, Nostradamus seems to be dating this prediction by a freak birth. It is not unknown for children to be born with a few teeth – Louis XIV was, for example. Of course, the word "gorge" can be translated as "throat" as well as "mouth" – this would suggest an altogether more unpleasant birth abnormality, reminiscent of radioactive mutation or chemically induced malformation.

A Nuclear Meltdown in the Mediterranean?
II.3 & II.4

> *Pour la chaleur solaire sus la mer,*
> *De Negrepont les poissons demi cuits:*
> *Les habitans les viendront entamer,*
> *Quand Rhod, et Gannes leur faudra le biscuit.*

Translation:

> By heat like the Sun upon the sea,
> Around *Negrepont* the fish are half broiled:
> The inhabitants will cut them up,
> When Rhodes, and Genoa are in want of biscuits.

According to Erica Cheetham, "*Negrepont*" is the Italian name for the island of Ruboea. What form of "heat like the Sun" is involved is not clear, but it would take a vast amount of energy to half cook fish in open water. The possibility of the meltdown and explosion of a nuclear engine, like those that power nuclear submarines, naturally leaps to mind. Alternatives – such as impacts of meteors or comets with the Earth – are equally alarming.

The second two lines seem to hint at starvation caused by the disaster. "Entamer" literally means "to cut up" – perhaps this is a description of the animal autopsies that would be part of the clean up operation.

> *Depuis Monarch jusque aupres de Sicile,*
> *Toute la plage demourra desolée:*
> *Il n'y aura fauxbourg, cité ne ville,*
> *Que par Barbares pillé soit et volée.*

Translation:

> From Monaco as far as Sicily,
> All the sea coast will be left desolate:
> There shall be no suburbs, cities nor towns,
> Which will not be pillaged and violated by Barbarians.

There is no specific reason to link this prediction with the disaster of the preceding quatrain, other than that it follows directly in *Century II* and deals with roughly the same area of the world. If the predictions are connected, the last line may undermine the "nuclear meltdown" theory – looters would hardly risk stealing from an area affected by radiation.

Economic Collapse

VIII.28, IV.50 & X.81

Several of the quatrains seem to point to major international economic problems. Whether they refer to several such periods in history, or to one major economic crisis, is unclear.

> *Les simulacres d'or et argent enflez,*
> *Qu'apres le rapt au lac furent gettez,*
> *Au desouvert estaincts tous et troublez.*
> *Au marbre script prescript intergetez.*

Translation:

> The copies of gold and silver inflated,
> Which after the theft are thrown in the lake,
> Being discovered that all is destroyed by debt.
> All bond and scrip will be cancelled.

Paper money – "copies of gold and silver" – was undreamed of in Nostradamus' day, as was inflation, yet the seer seems to have foreseen these economic commonplaces of the future.

This prediction may already have happened. Lines three and four are reminiscent of the Third World debt crisis of the 1980s.

Throughout the 1970s, the world banks lent vast amounts of money to impoverished nations then increased the interest payments to an impossible extent. Finally, when Mexico threatened to default, it was realized that the whole world economy could collapse as a result. (The banks relied on the regularity of the debt payments to secure their own borrowings – if the Third World nations had refused to pay en masse, the banks would have collapsed, taking every currency in the world with them.)

Partial debt cancellation was hurriedly organized with the aid of the major governments (and their taxpayers' money) and the disaster was narrowly averted. As of this writing (2003), however, the world banks and national governments still insist on holding impoverished nations to crippling debts originally run up (and paid for, bar the vast interest) decades before.

Libra verra regner les Hesperies,
De ciel et terre tenir la monarchie:
D'Asie forces nul ne verra paries,
Que sept ne tiennent par rang le hierarchie.

Translation:

Libra will be seen to reign over the West,
Holding the rule over heaven and earth:
No one will see the strength of Asia fail,
Until seven have held the hierarchy.

Libra is an astrological sign of wealth and prosperity. "Hesperies" literally means "the West", but also seems to be one of Nostradamus' codenames for the USA.

This quatrain may describe the 1997–8 collapse of the Asian "Tiger" economies. For many years, the forum of the world's seven most industrialized capitalist nations (Canada, France, Germany, Great Britain, Italy, Japan and the USA) was called "G-7" (for "Group 7"). In 1997, Russia applied to join the group and the title was changed to "G-8". This may be the end of the "hierarchy" of seven, mentioned by Nostradamus in the last line. Shortly afterwards, the previously bullish Asian-Pacific economies unexpectedly collapsed through bad investment and massive state incompetence and corruption.

Mis tresor temple citadins Hesperiques,
Dans icelui retiré en secret lieu,
Le temple ouvrir les liens familiques,
Reprens ravis proie horrible au milieu.

Translation:

A treasure placed in a temple by Western citizens,
Withdrawn within to a secret hiding place,
The hungry serfs will throw the temple open,
Recaptured and ravished a horrible prey in the middle.

Some commentators have suggested that this quatrain predicts a major economic crisis, which will prompt impoverished Americans to literally raid the Federal Gold Reserve at Fort Knox. Given that, in an economy that has totally collapsed, food would be more valuable than gold, I have my doubts about this interpretation.

Computer Viruses

I.22

> *Ce que vivra et n'ayant ancien sens,*
> *Viendra leser à mort son artifice:*
> *Austun, Chalan, Langres et les deux Sens,*
> *La gresle et glace fera grand malefice.*

Translation:

> That which lives but has no senses,
> Will cause its own death through artifice:
> Autun, Chalan, Langres and the two Sens,
> Hail and ice cause great damage.

Francis X. King makes the suggestion that this description of something that lives without senses could be Nostradamus' attempt to describe a computer. He further suggests that the "death through artifice" in the second line could be a reference to computer viruses – the "artifice" being the efforts of hackers to vandalize the information stored in other people's systems.

Future War

As the reader will have noticed, most of Nostradamus' quatrains are given over to predicting conflicts of one sort or another. Many writers since the Second World War, have found clues in the *Centuries* pointing to a catastrophic, possibly terminal, third world war, sometime in the near future. I personally see no evidence to back this conclusion. Certainly Nostradamus often predicted horrendous battles and great loss of life, but he never suggested that these quatrains should be linked to form a picture of a single, humanity-destroying Armageddon. On the contrary, he seems to suggest that mankind still has, at the very least, a few thousand years ahead of it.

I suggest that the *Centuries* suffer from the same problem as military history books: no matter how well written, a history consisting solely of one war after another will give the reader the impression that mankind is constantly in a state of conflict. While it is true that there is usually a war going on somewhere on the globe at any one time, concentrating on this aspect of history misses the fact that most people down the ages have lived peaceful lives.

The following are some of the seer's many non-specific military and war-like predictions. I include them in this chapter because all seem to have some modern or futuristic aspect.

War Towards the End of a Century

I.16

> *Faulx à l'estang joint vers le Sagitaire,*
> *En son hault auge de l'exaltation,*
> *Peste, famine, mort de main militaire,*
> *La siecle approche de renouvation.*

Translation:

> A scythe joined with a pond in Sagittarius,
> At the high of its ascendancy,
> Plague, famine, death from military hands,
> The century approaches its renewal.

The "scythe" is the sign of Saturn, and the "pond" (or lake) may be Aquarius. The quatrain seems to say that when Saturn is in Aquarius with Sagittarius at the noon position towards the end of a century, a terrible war will take place. Unfortunately, this astrological event is too common to give us a specific date.

Missiles or Submarines?

I.29

> *Quand la poisson terrestre et aquatique,*
> *Par fort vague au gravier sera mis:*
> *Sa forme estrange sauve et horrifique,*
> *Par mer aux mure bien tost les ennemis.*

Translation:

> When a fish that is both terrestrial and aquatic,
> By a great wave is thrown upon the shore:
> With its strange, smooth and horrible shape,
> From the sea the enemies soon reach the walls.

This quatrain has reminded modern commentators of sea-launched, intercontinental ballistic missiles or cruise missiles ("fish" that can travel over water and land). The second line suggests, on the other hand, a beached submarine.

Less alarmingly, Henry Roberts suggests that this is a prediction of the landing craft hitting the beaches during the D-Day landings in Normandy in World War II.

Peace Followed by War
Les fleurs passés diminue le monde,
Long temps la paix terres inhabitées:
Seur marchera par ciel, serre, mer et onde,
Puis de Nouveau les guerres suscitées.

Translation:

> The plagues pass away the world grows smaller,
> For a long time the lands are inhabited peacefully:
> All will travel safely through the sky, the land and the sea,
> Then wars will begin again.

This is a remarkable quatrain as it matter-of-factly predicts the defeat of major diseases (an impossible dream in Nostradamus' day) and the advent of air travel. Line one even seems to quote the modern cliché that, as travel methods become faster, the world seems to be getting smaller.

A long period of peace, when "plagues" are eradicated and all travel is totally safe, has yet to materialize. Unfortunately – as the seer predicts – when it does, it won't last.

Air War

I.64

De nuit soleil penseront avoir veu,
Quand le pourceu demi-homme on verra:
Bruict, chant, bataille, au ciel battre aperceu:
Et bestes brutes à parler lon orra.

Translation:

At night they will think they have seen the Sun,
When the pig half-man is seen:
Noise, chants, battles seen fought in the sky:
And brute beasts will be heard to speak.

This quatrain sounds like modern science fiction. Seeing the "Sun" at night suggests a giant, possibly nuclear, explosion or fire. A pig-like half-man could be a colourful description of a man in breathing gear – perhaps a pilot in an oxygen mask or a soldier in a gas mask. The third line may be a prediction of air battles, or it could be a portent of visionary sky battles, like that reported over the First World War Battle of Mons.

The last line is very odd, but it could be a prediction of vehicles with computerized voices or even a description of genetically enhanced animals.

Destruction in New York

I.87

Ennosigee feu du centre de terre,
Fera trembler au tour de cité neufue:
Deux grands rochiers long temps feront la guerre,
Puis Arethuse rougira nouveau fleuve.

Translation:

Ennosigee fire from the centre of the Earth,
Will cause the new city to tremble:
Two great rocks will war on each other for a long time,
Then *Arethuse* will redden a new river.

"*Ennosigee*" in the first line is probably a distortion of the Greek word "*ennosigaeus*": meaning "earth-shaker". Modern commentators generally translate the Nostradamus phrase "*cite neufue*" as "New York", although, of course, any newly-built city could be meant.

"*Arethuse*" sounds like *Arethusa*, the Greek nymph who was transformed into a stream. Erica Cheetham, on the other hand, suggests it might be a cross between the word "Aries" (the Greek god of war) and the letters "USA".

War in the West
I.91

> *Les dieux feront aux humains apparence,*
> *Ce qu'il seront auteurs de grand conflict:*
> *Avant ciel veu serin espee et lance,*
> *Que vers main gauche sera plus grand afflict.*

Translation:

> The gods will make it appear to mankind,
> That they are the authors of a great conflict:
> The once serene sky will show sword and lance,
> The left will be the most afflicted.

"Sword and lance" in the sky, in line three, could be an exchange of missiles and/or the vapour trails of war planes. The political concept of "left" and "right" was unknown in Nostradamus' day, but on European-made maps, the "left" is the western hemisphere, so several Nostradamus scholars have linked this quatrain with a war that damages America more than its co-combatant.

A Slaughter of Fugitives

III.7

> *Les fugitifs, feu du ciel sus les piques.*
> *Conflict prochain des corbeaux s'esbatans,*
> *De terre on crie aide secours celiques,*
> *Quand pres des murs seront les combatans.*

Translation:

> The fugitives, fire from heaven on their pikes.
> The next conflict will be that of the crows,
> They cry from the Earth for heavenly aid,
> The soldiers draw near the walls.

The first three lines seem to paint a grim picture of fugitive troops[1] being fired on from above, leaving only crows to fight over their dead bodies.

On 16 January 1991, a coalition of allies led by the USA waged the Gulf War to eject invading Iraqi troops from the small Arab state of Kuwait. By late February, the Iraqi army was in full retreat and the Kuwait–Iraq highway was gridlocked for hundreds of miles by Iraqi soldiers seeking to escape in any vehicle they could commandeer.

Despite the fact that many of these troops were unarmed and therefore, under the Geneva Convention, refugees, the Allies killed thousands of the soldiers trapped on the highway with airstrikes.

Germ Warfare

III.75

> *Pau, Verone, Vicence, Sarragousse,*
> *De glaives loings terroirs de sang humides.*
> *Peste si grance à la grand gousse,*
> *Proche secours, et bien loing les remedes.*

Translation:

> Pau, Verona, Vicenza, Saragossa,
> Foreign swords wet the land with blood.
> Plague will come in a shell,
> Though relief is near, the remedy is still far off.

Three of the places mentioned in the first line are in Italy, a country with a history of foreign invasions and plague outbreaks. The same applies to Spain, where Saragossa is located.

The most disturbing aspect of this quatrain is the word *"gousse"*

[1]"Pikes" might be translated as any long weapon, such as rifles for example.

in line three. This translates as "husk" or "shell". The implication – that the "plague" will come from a sealed container (possibly an artillery shell, missile or test tube) – causes germ warfare to spring to mind.

The last line seems to predict that although there will be medical facilities for the afflicted, an actual cure for the plague will take a long time to find.

A Brutal Airborne Invasion of France

III.82

> *Friens, Antibor, villes autour de Nice,*
> *Seront vastees fort par mer et terre,*
> *Les saturelles terre et mer vent propice,*
> *Prins, morts, troussez, pillés, sans loi de guerre.*

Translation:

> Fréjus, Antibes, the towns around Nice,
> Will be greatly devastated from sea and land,
> Locusts with favourable wind by land and sea,
> Captured, dead, trussed-up, plundered, without law of war.

The towns in the first line are in the south of France. There has only been one invasion of France from this direction since Nostradamus' day: the Allies' second French front in 1944. Unlike the Normandy landings, this assault went largely unopposed by the retreating Germans – indeed, since the Allied troops encountered so little resistance, they dubbed the front the "Champaign Campaign". The savagery – described in lines two to four – seems to rule out this easy invasion, so we must assume that this quatrain refers to the future.

The word "locusts", in line three, may be a poetic description of a modern piece of technology; given the context, airborne troop-carriers or paratroops seems a reasonable assumption.

The ignored "*loi de guerre*" ("laws of war") may be the Geneva Convention – a dire prediction for France.

Holy War in the Skies

IV.43

> *Seront ouis au ciel les armes battre:*
> *Celui an mesme les divins ennemis:*
> *Voudrant loix sainctes injustement debatre,*
> *Par foutre et guerre bien croyans à mort mis.*

Translation:

> Weapons will be heard fighting in the sky:
> In the same year the divines will become enemies:
> They will unjustly debate the holy laws,
> Through thunder and war the true believers will die.

Here Nostradamus seems to predict the advent of aerial warfare, almost as a subtext to a quatrain about a religious conflict. As already noted, it is difficult to pinpoint the seer's exact religious leanings, but here he plainly foresees "true believers" being bested and slaughtered in a modern war.

American War?

IV.95

> *La regne à deux laissé peu tiendront,*
> *Trois ans sept mois passée feront la guerre.*
> *Les deux vestales contre eux rebelleront,*
> *Victor puis nay en Armorique terre.*

Translation:

> The reign left to two they shall not hold it long,
> Three years seven months pass and they go to war.
> The two vestals rebel against them,
> The victor will be born on *Armorique* soil.

This quatrain seems to foretell a falling out between two great powers. Given the context, it is reasonable to suspect the word "vestals" in line three is actually a corruption of the word "vassals", and refers to two rebelling vassal nations or peoples.

The key word in this quatrain is *"Armorique"* in line four.

Armorica was the Ancient Roman name for Brittany. Yet most modern interpreters translate "*Armorique*" as "American". If they are correct, this is certainly a striking prediction.

The word "America" was only coined by the mapmaker and bogus explorer Amerigo Vespucci around 1512 (we now know he barely set foot across the Atlantic). The name did not come into common usage until at least 100 years later, so it would be remarkable if Nostradamus indeed mentioned it in this quatrain.[2]

Understanding of the quatrain will probably only be possible after the event – just as the seer meant it to be.

Rocket Attacks on the West?

IV.99

> *L'aisné vaillant de la fille du Roy,*
> *Repoussera si profond les Celtiques:*
> *Qu'il mettra foudres, combien en tel arroi,*
> *Peu et loing puis és Hesperiques.*

Translation:

> The valiant eldest son of the King's daughter,
> Will drive the Celts back very far:
> He will use thunderbolts, so many in such an array,
> Few and distant then deep into the West.

The grandson of a leader will press the "Celts" very far, according to the first two lines. "*Celtiques*" is apparently used elsewhere in the *Centuries* to indicate the French.

Line three describes this man using arrays of "thunderbolts"; since line four describes them reaching "deep into the West", Erica Cheetham believes that this is a description of ballistic missiles or battlefield rockets.

The word "*Hesperiques*" is given a capital letter, indicating that it is a specific place. Henry Roberts suggests it is Spain – the far west of Europe – but most other Nostradamus commentators translate the word to mean America.

---

[2]In fact, he certainly seems to have done so in a late quatrain (see X.66 below).

Chemical War in Greece

V.90

> Dans les Cyclades, en Corinthe et Larisse,
> Dedans Sparte tout le Pelloponnesse:
> Si grand famine, peste par faux connisse,
> Neuf mois tiendra et tout le chevronesse.

Translation:

> In the Cyclades, in Corinth and Larissa,
> In Sparta and all the Peloponnese:
> Shall be great famine, plague through false *connisse*,
> Nine months throughout the whole peninsula.

The places described in this quatrain are all in southern Greece. A catastrophe is plainly predicted, but its cause is harder to guess; the words "false *connisse*" are clearly the key to the mystery. "*Connisse*" could mean "exertion" (from the Latin *connissus*) or "dust" (from the Greek *konis*). Given the context, the latter seems more likely.

"False dust", Erica Cheetham suggests, might indicate a man-made plague and famine – i.e. chemical or biological warfare. However, it is worth noting that Nostradamus also uses the image of a plague combined with a famine in *Century II*, quatrain 6 (see the chapter on Nostradamus and the twentieth century). There, apparently predicting the destruction of Hiroshima and Nagasaki by the atom bomb, he describes "famine within plague". If we are right to see this as a prediction of the effects of radiation poisoning, we might be justified in seeing "false dust" as nuclear fallout.

The ill-maintained, former Soviet nuclear power stations in the Balkans spring to mind.

Aerial Bombing

VI.34

> Du feu volant la machination,
> Viendra troubler au grand chef assiegez:
> Dedans sera telle sedition,
> Qu'en desespoir seront les profligez.

Translation:

> The machine of flying fire,
> Will trouble the besieged great chief:
> Within there will be so much sedition,
> That those abandoned will be in despair.

The "machine of flying fire" in line one is reminiscent of twentieth-century bomber aircraft. Unfortunately, there is no indication as to which conflict the quatrain might refer to.

The London blitz in World War II is one possibility; thus making Prime Minister Winston Churchill the "besieged great chief", in line two. However, the Nazi attempts to break British morale by mass bombing raids failed – in contradiction to the prediction of lines three and four.

Another candidate for this quatrain is the mass bombing of Baghdad during the 1991 Persian Gulf War (this time with President Saddam Hussein as the "great chief") but, again, the morale of the Iraqi civilians held, despite the devastation.

The Poisoning of New York

X.49

> *Jardin du monde au pres du cité neufue,*
> *Dans le chemin des montaignes cavees,*
> *Sera saisi et plongé dan la Cuve,*
> *Beuvant par force eaux soulfre envenimees.*

Translation:

> Garden of the world near the new city,
> In the road of the hollow mountains,
> It will be seized and plunged into the Tank,
> Forced to drink water poisoned with sulphur.

The phrase "new city", in line one, has convinced many people that this quatrain describes the poisoning of New York (the phrase also occurs in I.87 and VI.97 above) but, of course, any newly-built metropolis might be referred to.

Nevertheless, Francis King points out that New York's neigh-

bour, New Jersey, has dubbed itself "the Garden State" i.
years ("Garden of the world near the new city"). Also, the
"road of the hollow mountains", in line two, certainly sounds
a description of New York's wide streets running beneath
towering skyscrapers.

The last two lines seem to be a prediction that somebody will
poison the city's water supply with "sulphur" (just as hippies
threatened to pour a pint of pure LSD into Chicago's city reservoir
in 1968).

Famine and Chaos from Space

VI.5

> *Si grand Famine par unde pestifere.*
> *Par pluie Longue le long du pole arctique,*
> *Samarobrin cent lieux de l'hemisphere,*
> *Vivront sans loi exempt de pollitique.*

Translation:

> The great Famine by a pestilent wave.
> Through long rain will come the length of the arctic pole,
> *Samarobrin* a hundred league from the hemisphere,
> Living without laws exempt from politics.

We have seen the description of famine linked with pestilence
twice before in the *Centuries*: both times sounding ominously
like radiation sickness. The second line seems to describe the
cause of the famine falling in a "long rain" over the Northern
hemisphere.

The source of this pestilence is perhaps indicated in line three.
"*Samarobrin*" (possibly another of Nostradamus' riddled – or
anagrammed names) is described as being "a hundred leagues
from the hemisphere". Any object that high above the Earth
would be in orbit; in other words, an orbital satellite or space
station.

Another possibility is that Nostradamus is describing the
detonation of a comet in Earth's upper atmosphere. The eminent
astrophysicist Sir Fred Hoyle suggested in the 1970s that complex
amino acids (the basic building blocks of proteins) might exist in

the interstellar clouds out in space; although controversial at the time, his theory has since been proved correct. Hoyle went on to suggest that apparently spontaneous outbreaks of plagues like the Black Death might be the result of comets (basically balls of frozen cosmic debris) plunging through our atmosphere and depositing new viruses on those below.

The last line seems to suggest social chaos following the disaster. It should be noted that in the sixteenth century, people living "exempt from politics" would not mean a utopian ideal, as some might see it today. "Politics" in Nostradamus' day simply meant "good sense".

The Shaking of the Vatican

The Irish Saint Malachy is said to have made a pilgrimage to Rome in 1139. On cresting the last hill and looking down on the Holy City, Malachy is said to have had a vision of the 111 popes from Celestine II (who reigned for less than a year in 1124) to the end of the papacy. His short, poetically descriptive Latin motto for each future pontiff was carefully noted and the document was given to the incumbent pope, Innocent II.

That, at least, is the legend attached to the "Malachy Prophecies". Many scholars now doubt that Saint Malachy was responsible for the predictions at all – a forgery around 1590 being generally suspected. Nevertheless, even if we accept this later date, the predictions after 1590 have still proved disturbingly accurate.

For example, the papacy of Benedict XV (1914–22) was predicted with the epithet "*Religio Depopulata*" ("Religion Depopulated"). Benedict's reign covered the period of the Great War and the 1918 influenza pandemic, during which millions of Catholics – as well as those of other religions – died.

John XXIII (1958–63) had been the Patriarch of the port city of Venice before his election. The motto given by Malachy was "*Pastor et Nauta*" ("Pastor and Sailor").

John Paul I (1978) was given the motto, "*De Medietate Lunae*" ("The Middle of the Moon"). John Paul I died – or was secretly assassinated – less than a month after his election. The date was 28 September: exactly in the middle of the lunar cycle.

The present pope (as of this writing in 2003) is John Paul II. His Malachy motto is "*De Labore Solis*" ("The Labour of the Sun").

John Paul II is, of course, Polish – the first pope from Eastern Europe which, from Rome, is the direction of the rising Sun.

Despite his age and failing health, John Paul II has insisted that he will not retire and will "die in harness" – "labour[ing]" for the Church to his last breath. He was born on 18 May 1920, a date which was marked by a total eclipse of the Sun in the northern hemisphere.

The Malachy Prophecies list only two more popes to come. After John Paul II will be "*Gloria Olivae*" ("Glory of the Olive"). John Hogue suggests, in *The Millennium Book of Prophecy* (1994), that this pope might broker reconciliation (the "olive-branch" of peace) between the Arabs and Israelis as a non-partisan third force.

The last pope of the prophecy is referred to in these lines:

> During the last persecution of the Holy Roman Church, there shall sit Petrus Romanus [Peter of Rome], who will feed the sheep amid great tribulations, and when these have passed, the City of the Seven Hills [Rome] shall be utterly destroyed, and the dreadful Judge will judge the people.

The "dreadful Judge" is usually seen as the God of the Last Judgment, but the prophecy might also be a prediction of a more "mundane" disaster for the city of Rome,[3] or might simply be a poetic description of the collapse of Roman Catholicism as an organized faith.

Nostradamus seems to have partially supported this latter possibility in the *Centuries*. Several of his quatrains hint at major disruptions at the Vatican and a fundamental reorganization of religious practice and belief in the future.

---

[3]The third Fatima prophecy, publised by the Vatican in June 2000, seems to support the idea of a violent overthrow of the Catholic Church sometime during the twenty-first century.

See the chapter on Jeane Dixon in this volume for further details on the Fatima prophecies.

A Controversial Pope

III.65 & V.56

> *Quand le sepulcre du grand Romain trouvé,*
> *Le jour apres sera esleu Pontife:*
> *Du Senat gueres il ne sera prouvé,*
> *Empoisonné son sang au sacré scyphe.*

Translation:

> When the sepulchre of the great Roman is found,
> The next day a Pope is elected:
> The Senate will not approve of him,
> His poison blood in the sacred chalice.

The last two lines of the quatrain sound like a prediction of the death – suspected as murder – of Pope John Paul I in 1978. At this time, much of Italian public life was being manipulated by a secret Masonic group called the P2. Leading politicians, judges, military men and (so it is rumoured) Catholic cardinals were members of P2, forming a web of corruption that spread across the whole nation.

Pope John Paul I was certainly not one of these tainted men and, on his election in August 1978, announced that he would personally study the books of the Vatican Bank to weed out illegal transactions and punish those responsible. He was found dead in his bed a month later – only a few days before he was to announce his findings. The Vatican (which is literally a state unto itself) blocked moves to hold an autopsy. Subsequent rumours declared that John Paul I was given poison in his bedside bottle of stomach medicine.

As the quatrain says, the "Senate" – or the corrupt powers ruling Italy – did not approve of a reformer being elected pope. The last line mentions poison.

On the other hand, the first two lines of the quatrain do not fit this interpretation. As far as I can ascertain, there was no archaeological discovery in Rome the day before the election of John Paul I. Therefore this quatrain could also be a prediction of a future, unpopular pontiff, whose "poison blood" would stain the "sacred chalice", although whether literally or metaphorically is presently impossible to judge.

> *Par les trespas du tres vieillart pontif,*
> *Sera esleu Romain de bon age:*
> *Qu'il sera dict que le seige debisse,*
> *Et long tiendra et de picquant ouvrage.*

Translation:

> By the death of the very old pope,
> Shall be elected a Roman of good age:
> It will be said that he weakens the seat,
> And he shall live long through stinging labour.

There have certainly been many "very old" popes since Nostradamus' day, but few "of good [presumably 'young'] age". None of even relatively youthful age has, since the mid-sixteenth century, lived to reign a long time. It is therefore likely that that this unpopular pontiff, who will "weaken the seat [of the Papacy]" has yet to be elected.

The Breaking of the Old Religion
I.15, I.96 & II.8

> *Mars nous menace par la force bellique,*
> *Septante fois fera le sang espandre:*
> *Auge et ruine de l'Ecclesiastique,*
> *Et plus ceux qui d'eux rien voudront entendre.*

Translation:

> Mars threatens us with war-like force,
> Seventy times this will cause the spilling of blood:
> The clergy will be exalted and reviled,
> And more from those who wish to learn nothing from them.

Mars was the Roman god of war, and is here predicted to cause seventy conflicts – when, how and of what scale is unclear. The first two lines are a typical Nostradamus warning: chilling, but too obscure to be precise. The only difference in this case is the use of the word "us" in line one – suggesting Nostradamus' personal interest in this quatrain.

As we have seen, Nostradamus was a devoutly religious man (even if we cannot guess his denomination). The second two lines of the quatrain may suggest that the cause of the seventy episodes of bloodshed will be religious or, alternatively, that after a long period of war, religion itself will be attacked.

The third line suggests a confused debate, with the clergy alternately "exalted and reviled". The last line may hint that the cause of the friction will not be religious differences, but pure lack of interest in the clergy's teachings "from those who wish to learn nothing from them".

The diminishing congregations in modern churches may be indicated.

> *Celui qu'aura la change de destruire,*
> *Templus, et sects, changez par fantasie:*
> *Plus aux rochiers qu'aux vivans viendra nuire,*
> *Par langue ornee d'oreilles ressasie.*

Translation:

> He who is charged with destruction,
> Temples, and sects, changed by fantasy:
> He will harm the rocks more than the living,
> By ornate language ears filled.

An influential religious reformer is "charged" (i.e. given the task) of destroying "temples, and sects, changed by fantasy". Perhaps this indicates an attack on "cults" or, alternatively, a move away from the religious traditionalism, which many people now feel has undermined the "true" meaning of religion.

This predicted reformer humanely concentrates on changing the material of the faith, or faiths ("the rocks"), rather than persecute their believers ("the living"). Perhaps the last line indicates that he uses persuasion to defeat dogmatism: filling the ears of his audience with "ornate language".

Temples sacrez prime facon Romaine,
Rejecteront les goffres fondements,
Prenant leurs loix premieres et humaines,
Chassant, non tout, des saincts les cultements

Translation:

Temples consecrated in the early Roman fashion,
Rejecting the tottering foundations,
Sticking to their first humane laws,
Expelling, not all, the cults of the saints.

Unlike the two quatrains above, this prediction seems to solely concern the Christian Church. A return to simple practices of the early Church fathers and a following of more "humane" laws is indicated. The "tottering foundations" of the previous religious practices are rejected.

Erica Cheetham suggests that this might not have been a prediction, but an endorsement of sixteenth-century Protestantism. Catholicm might be described as a "cult of the saints", and Protestantism rejects this (while still rejecting "not all" saints). We have earlier noted James Randi's assertion that Nostradamus was actually a secret Protestant.

Taken together, these three quatrains seem to point to a fundamental reform of Christianity. Considering that Nostradamus seems to claim that his predictions cover a period of several thousand years, such a notion is highly plausible.

We might, on the other hand, see these three predictions as quite separate and unconnected events.

The Antichrist

It is a popular misconception that one of the pivotal figures in the Bible is the Antichrist. In fact, as we saw in chapter 7, this being is only passingly referred to in the New Testament (2 Thessalonians and 1 John) where he is simply a false prophet and a denier of Jesus' divinity. The "beast" in Revelation is generally assumed to be one and the same as the Antichrist, but there is no direct biblical source to back this supposition.

The Antichrist/beast was predicted by the early Church to

appear shortly before the end of the world. His role as the great villain (second only to Satan) was largely the creation of theologians from the late Byzantine period and early Middle Ages, who felt the need for a balancing "enemy" for Jesus.

By Nostradamus' day, the label "antichrist" was used for a wicked person as well as Christ's predicted adversary – just as today one might call someone a "devil" without actually meaning to suggest that they have horns and live in Hell.

Nostradamus mentions no less than three "Antichrists" in the introductions to the *Centuries*. The first two have been linked by commentators to Napoleon and Hitler. The last, and most terrible, is thought to be yet to come.

In fact, the main body of the *Centuries* only contains two direct mentions of an "Antichrist": X.66 and VIII.77.

> *Le chef de Londres par regne l'Americh,*
> *L'isle de l'Escosse tempiera par gellee:*
> *Roi Reb auront un si faux antechrist,*
> *Que les mettra trestous dans la meslee.*

Translation:

> The chief of London by the rule of the Americas,
>   The isle of Scotland suffers frost:
>   King Reb will have a false antichrist,
>   Who will bring them into discord.

We can almost certainly discount this quatrain in the present context, because Nostradamus himself admits that he is predicting a *faux* ("false") antichrist; in other words a wicked man, but not the "true" Antichrist.

Nevertheless, this quatrain is still very interesting. It has a word at the end of line one that is almost certainly "America", a name that was barely in circulation in the mid-sixteenth century. Either Nostradamus obtained this name through precognition, or he had a surprisingly up-to-date knowledge of what was going on in the highly specialized science of cartography.

The name "*Roi Reb*", at the beginning of line three, could mean "King *Reb*", or it might be a prediction of the Highland bandit and rebel called Rob Roy. This was the nickname (meaning Robert the Red) of Robert MacGregor (1671–1734): a freebooter and brigand immortalized and romanticized by Sir Walter Scott in the novel *Rob Roy* in 1817. The link with Scotland in the second line may tend to support this interpretation. Also, during the period of Robert MacGregor's life, the British fought a series of wars with France over the ownership of the North American territories, beginning with the King William's War of 1689–97. Twenty-nine years after MacGregor's death, in 1763, Britain won the French and Indian War, confirming London's brief but uncontested "rule of the Americas".

> *L'Antechrist trois bien tost anniehielez,*
> *Vingt et sept ans sang durera sa guerre.*
> *Les heritiques mortz, captifs, exhilez.*
> *Sang corps humain eua rougi gresler terre.*

Translation:

> The Antichrist three very soon annihilates,
> Twenty-seven bloody years his war will last.
> The heretics dead, captive, exiled.
> Blood human corpses water red hail cover the earth.

The first line may predict that the "Antichrist" will annihilate three persons or groups of persons. Commentators have suggested that the three Cold War superpowers (Russia, America and China) might be indicated, or that three continents will be devastated by the war of line two. Alternatively, line one could mean that Nostradamus' "Third Antichrist" ("*Antechrist trois*") will simply be universally destructive.

The twenty-seven-year war predicted in line two rather undermines those interpreters that see this quatrain as a prediction of a total nuclear holocaust: even using only smaller "battlefield" nuclear weapons, such a war would be unsustainable for such a period. A twenty-seven-year "conventional" war (although, quite possibly, still using limited numbers of weapons of mass destruction) seems more likely from the point of view of military logistics.

The religious aspect of the "Antichrist War" is reinforced by the description of the unpleasant fate of "heretics" in line three.

The grotesque description of the result of the war in line four is as lurid as any in the *Centuries*. Different writers on Nostradamus have seen in it evidence of nuclear fallout, chemical and biological weapons, genocide and the extinction of the human race. Yet all these interpretations are essentially the expressions of the fears of individual commentators; a non-presumptive reader could only say that a savage destruction of human life is predicted.

Nostradamus commentators have linked other quatrains to the "Third Antichrist". The following are some of the most often quoted of these predictions:

I.50

> *De l'aquatique triplicité naistra.*
> *D'un qui fera le jeudi pour sa feste:*
> *Son bruit, loz, regne, sa puissance croistra,*
> *Par terre et mer aux Oriens tempeste.*

Translation:

> Born from the three water signs.
> One who makes Thursday his holiday:
> His fame, praise, reign, and power will grow,
> By land and sea to the Oriental tempest.

The three water signs are Cancer, Scorpio and Pisces. Since an individual can have only one Sun sign (i.e. the sign under which he is born) we must assume that Nostradamus means us to see that two of the signs are prominent elsewhere in the horoscope of the "one" predicted.

Concerning line two, Thursday is not a weekly holiday in any major religion, but it may be worth noting that the American celebration of Thanksgiving always falls on this day.

II.29

> *L'Oriental sortira de son siege,*
> *Passer les monts Apennins voir la Gaule:*
> *Transpercera le ciel les eaux et neige,*
> *Et un chacun frappera de sa gaule.*

Translation:

> The Oriental will come out of his sea[
> Crossing the Apennine Mountains seeing Fr[
> Transported through the sky the waters and sn[
> And shall strike everyone with his rod.

The middle two lines strongly hint at aerial, perhaps even orbital travel. The "rod" of the last line may be a beam weapon, such as a laser.

II.62

> *Mabus puis tost, alors mourra viendra,*
> *De gens et bestes une horrible defaite:*
> *Puis tout à coup la vengence on verra,*
> *Cent, main, soif, faim, quand courra la comete.*

Translation:

> *Mabus* will come, and soon after dies,
> Of people and beasts there will be horrible destruction:
> Then suddenly vengeance will be seen,
> One hundred, hand, thirst, famine, when the comet passes.

"*Mabus*" seems to be a name; perhaps of the Third Antichrist, perhaps not . . .

V.54

> *Du pont Euxine, et la grand Tartarie,*
> *Un roi sera qui viendra voir la Gaule,*
> *Transpercera Alane et l'Armenie,*
> *Et dans Bisance lairra sanglante gaule.*

Translation:

> From the Black Sea and Central Asia,
> A king will come to see France,
> He will pass through Alania and Albania,
> And in Istanbul will leave his bloody pole.

rtary was the medieval name for what we now call Central Asia, but some Nostradamus translators prefer China (in Nostradamus' time the word could mean either). Alania is a region of southern Russia.

The quatrain is so reminiscent of II.29 above, that one might be tempted to believe they both predict the same event (i.e. "bloody pole" might also be a poetic description of some sort of beam weapon).

VI.33

> *Sa main derniere par Alus sanguine,*
> *Ne se pourra par la mer guarantir:*
> *Entre deux fleuves craindre main militaire,*
> *Le noir l'ireux le fera repentir.*

Translation:

> His hand finally through bloody *Alus*,
> He cannot guarantee his safety by sea:
> Between two rivers he will fear the military hand,
> The black angry one will make him repent it.

Erica Cheetham suggests that "*Alus*" could be the name (or an anagram of the name) of the Third Antichrist. Henry Roberts, on the other hand, suggests it is a partial anagram of the English words "all US".

VI.80

> *De Fez le regne parviendra à ceux d'Europe,*
> *Feu leur cité, et lame trenchera:*
> *Le grand d'Asie terre et mer à grand troupe,*
> *Que bleux, pers, croix, à mort dechassera.*

Translation:

> From Fez the kingdom stretches out across Europe,
> The city burns, and sword slices:
> The great one of Asia land and sea a great army,
> That blue, Persia, cross, driven to death.

Fez is a town in Morocco. As we have
to be Nostradamus' shorthand for Christia

The Last Judgment – 2007–8

X.74

> *An revolu du grand nombre septiesh*
> *Apparoistra au temps Jeux d'Hecatomb*
> *Non esloigné milliesme,*
> *Que les entre sortiront de leur tombe.*

Translation:

> The year of the revolution of the great seventh number,
> It will appear at the Games of *Hecatombe*,
> Not far from the great millennium,
> When the dead will leave their graves.

The millennium mentioned in line three could, obviously, be the year 2000: the next millennium date following the publication of the *Centuries*. If this is so, then line one would seem to point to the "revolution" (or end) of the "seventh" year before or after the new millennium. Since 1997 passed without fulfilling the prediction, 2007 is the next in line.

"*Hecatomb*" is a Greek word for a sacrifice of 100 sacred animals. Such massive sacrifices took place only at great public events – such as the Olympic Games ("Games of the Hecatomb").

The Christian Emperor Theodosius discontinued the ancient Olympics at the end of the fourth century AD, so they were only a distant memory in Nostradamus' day. However, in 1896, the Olympic Games were started again. The year 2008 resulting from the "revolution" of 2007 – is an Olympic year.

The last line of the quatrain presumably refers to the Last Judgment, when the dead will rise from their graves. Indeed, if we add *Century X*, quatrain 72 (discussed in the chapter on Nostradamus and the twentieth century) – with its description of a "King of terror" descending from the sky, we may note a close match with fundamentalist Christian beliefs. There the great "Antichrist War" is followed by the Second Coming of Jesus Christ, who rules the Earth in perfect peace for a time. Then comes

all material things, with the dead rising from the grave
e Last Trump.

The trouble with this interpretation is that Nostradamus clearly says elsewhere that his predictions for mankind run much further into the future. In his introductory letter to *Century I*, Nostradamus described the contents as "prophecies from today [1 March 1555] to the year 3797". Later, in *Century I*, quatrain 48, he seems to add to this figure by hinting at a predictive limit of 7,000 years (see chapter 14). How can Nostradamus predict the events leading to the Last Judgment starting in 1999, if the human race has at least 3798 years of history to run?

David Ovason suggests that Nostradamus' "religious" quatrains were added to appease the ever-watchful Church. The protection of Queen Catherine de' Medici was enough to save Nostradamus from charges of witchcraft, but Catherine herself might have faced excommunication if she shielded a man who published shameless heresies.

In effect, Nostradamus may have had to include predictions that the world would end around the second millennium, because that is what the Church insisted was going to happen. He may therefore have left uncommented the fact that he continued to predict for events after the "Apocalypse", as a contradiction that spoke for itself, but could not lead to heresy charges.

Part 3

Disaster Prophecy

Introduction

Nostradamus gives the reason for his deliberate obscurities in his "Preface to my Son", in the first volume of the *Centuries*. He writes that he initially feared that:

> [If I] were to relate what will happen in the future, governors, secretaries, and ecclesiastics would find it so ill-accordant with their auricular fancy[1] that they would go near to condemn what future ages will know and perceive to be true.
>
> This it is which has led me to withhold my tongue from the vulgar, and my pen from paper. But later on, I thought I would enlarge a little, and declare in dark abstruse sayings . . . the most urgent of future causes, as perceived by me, be the revolutionary changes what they may, so only not to scandalize the auricular frigidity of my hearers, and write all down under a cloudy figure . . .

His use of the phrase "auricular frigidity" is cautiously diplomatic – he almost certainly meant "dogmatic preconceptions". This may explain why Nostradamus made his predictions so obscure, but why did he not make more practical use of his gift?

The death of his patron, King Henri II, is a case in point. Nostradamus met the king years before the jousting tournament that would end his life so painfully. Even allowing for the king's lack of interest in the *Centuries* (or, indeed, in books in general), Nostradamus should have been able to find some way to impress upon the boisterous monarch that he should avoid jousting on 10 July 1559.

Nostradamus' general statements about his gift of precognition

[1] The world as they hear and perceive it.

offer a plain, but grim, answer to the mystery. The seer believed that the future was immutable, that the events he foresaw were preordained and could not be changed. It was not that Nostradamus chose not to save Henri, but that he believed the king was destined to die and that nothing could change the fact.

So, rather than an all-knowing magus, perhaps it would be nearer to the truth to see Nostradamus as an agonized and impotent observer – much like a war correspondent who witnesses atrocities, but can only report them. (The reader may remember the Scottish *taibhsears*, discussed in Chapter 12, who preferred to be solitary hermits rather than meet people whose inescapable misfortunes they might suddenly foresee.)

Yet is this all that prophecy can tell us – that our fate is immutable and cannot be changed? According to some Christians sects and, as we have already seen, the Moslem Koran, the future is preordained by God and is therefore immutable.

A strong influence on the western doctrine of predestination was the work of the pagan philosopher Boethius (AD 480–524). He argued that the whole history of the universe, from beginning to end, is already formed and that the gods are actually "outside" its process. So even if the gods are all-knowing, they are also powerless to interfere.

A modern cosmologist might also point out that the whole universe can actually be defined as an unimaginably vast and complex mathematical equation. Since there is no such thing as random chance in mathematics (two plus two always equals four, for example, whatever the local circumstances), then our past, present and future were all preordained from the moment of the Big Bang.

However, mathematics is not all we need to unravel the mysteries of space and time. In the quantum world inside the atom – that of subatomic physics – the law of cause and effect does not operate as it does in our everyday world. Indeed, Wheeler's Parallel Universe theory suggests that a new universe is created every time our universe faces a choice of alternative possibilities, however small. Every time you flip a coin, according to Wheeler, at least three almost identical universes have just been created: one in which the coin landed on heads, one in which the result was tails, and one in which the coin landed on its edge. "You" are in only one of those universes, but that does not mean that the other two "yous" in the other two universes are any less real or self-aware.

Quantum theory is beyond the scope of the present work,[2] but we can see that it suggests an alternative to Nostradamus' depressingly deterministic view of the world. In the non-deterministic world of the quantum, consciousness travels through time down a road of near-infinitely branching possibilities. And it becomes conceivable that, through conscious or, perhaps, subconscious decision, a person might navigate chosen paths of destiny rather than living mechanically.

It is depressing to think that the disasters in the following section might have been averted if, indeed, the quantum world allowed us to "guide" reality. However, just think how many disasters may thus have been avoided, and are being avoided every second, by the human use of free will . . .

---

[2]The interested reader looking for a simple approach to quantum physics is recommended to try Fritjof Capra's *The Tao of Physics* and John Gribbin's *In Search of Schroedinger's Cat*.

Chapter 22

Titanic

Morgan Robertson was a haunted man. A highly productive author of two novels and more than 200 short stories, his own life reads like a Victorian horror story.

Born in Oswego, New York, in 1861, Morgan Andrew Robertson was the son of a pilot on Lake Erie, and in due course he went to sea as a cabin boy. He was in the merchant service for twenty-five years, leaving in 1886.

He then became a jeweller, but his eyes suffered from the close work, and he took up writing sea stories. His stories were better than average, but although they were published in both English and American magazines, he was poorly paid, and never achieved the success of fellow sea veterans like Herman Melville and Joseph Conrad.

Robertson was also dogged by bad luck. A periscope he invented could not be patented because a description of a similar device had appeared in a French fantasy story. His wife was an invalid, and poverty and discouragement led him to drink excessively. But another reason for his alcoholism was a strange obsession that inhibited him from taking up a more profitable trade. Robertson believed that he was possessed.

According to H. W. Francis – a journalist acquaintance – Robertson "implicitly believed that some discarnate soul, some spirit entity with literary ability, denied physical expression, had commandeered his body and brain." He was, in effect, "a mere amanuensis, the tool of the 'real writer'". Robertson himself spoke of his "astral writing partner". He may have been correct – such things are not unknown.

In January 1907, a goldsmith named Frederic Thompson called on Professor James Hyslop, president of the American Society for Psychical Research, to explain that he believed he was possessed by the spirit of a landscape painter named Robert Swain Gifford. Thompson had actually met him once or twice and, after Gifford died on 15 January 1905, Thompson began to hear the artist's voice urging him to paint. Although he had no artistic training, he began producing work of considerable merit in the style of Gifford.

Hyslop heard from a number of mediums who claimed to be receiving messages from a spirit that identified itself as Gifford, and which mentioned that it was trying to influence Thompson. When Hyslop saw some of Gifford's final sketches, made just before his death (and never seen by Thompson), he was amazed to discover their similarity to some of Thompson's sketches – sketches of New England swamps and coastal islands that Gifford knew well and Thompson had never visited. That finally convinced Hyslop that Thompson was genuinely being inspired by the spirit of Gifford. Thompson went on to become a fairly successful painter in New York, and later in Florida; his remarkable story is told by D. Scott Rogo in *The Infinite Boundary*.

So Morgan Robertson's claim to be under metaphysical remote control may well have had some basis in fact. However, he seems to have been less fortunate than Frederic Thompson, whose possessing spirit made sure he never ran short of inspiration.

"For months at a time" writes his friend Francis, "although mentally alert, he would be incapable of writing a single sentence." The "entity" would totally abandon him at these times and he, believing he had no imaginative skill of his own, was left to starve.

Before he could write a word, Robertson would have to lie for some time in a semi-sleeping, hypnogogic state. In this condition the "entity" (when it deigned to be available) could dictate stories to him using dream-like images. These Robertson later formed into a solid block of narrative. The periods of "communication" often lasted many hours, according to another friend, J. O'Neill. Afterwards, Robertson would "sit at the typewriter and pound out his story in a steady stream of words until he had finished what had been communicated in his somnolent state." Then he would be obliged to pause for the next section, which sometimes was not communicated for days or even weeks.

O'Neill explained that:

> [Robertson's] ideas would marshal themselves into a consecutive, coherent narrative up to a certain point, and then they would stop, whether he liked it or not, and that stopping, sometimes in the middle of an exciting situation, was the plague of his literary existence.

It must have been tempting for his acquaintances to dismiss Morgan Robertson's odd working practices as the delusions of an alcoholic who lacked real talent. Certainly his volume of short stories entitled *Futility*, published in 1898, struck many of his readers as the product of whisky-sodden pessimism. At a time when Jules Verne-style optimism about technology and the future was solidly in fashion, Robertson (or his erratic muse) chose to write depressing tales of shipwreck and marine disaster: little wonder it was another flop.

The subject of one of *Futility*'s stories came to Robertson, as usual, in one of his semi-trances. He saw, in his mind's eye, an ocean liner ploughing through a foggy Atlantic night. Initially he was both amazed and delighted by the vision. The ship was truly vast – at least 1,000 feet long – and his sailor's eye was entranced by its beautiful yet sturdy design. He was also amazed to see that the vessel was driven forward by three huge propellers, bigger than any he had ever encountered. But here he noted ominously that the ship must be making at least twenty-three knots, which was too fast for the mid-Atlantic with poor visibility.

In his mind's eye he saw many people moving about on deck, and suddenly knew that the ship carried over 2,000 passengers and crew. Here again, the sheer scale of the vessel stunned him – no other passenger ship had ever carried that many people, including the *Great Eastern*, the 692-foot leviathan built by Isambard Kingdom Brunel. (The *Great Eastern*'s run of non-stop bad luck – which some described as a "curse" – ended in the Liverpool wreckers' yard in 1889; inside its double hull the wreckers found the skeletons of the riveter and his boy apprentice, who had vanished while it was being built in 1856.)

With a growing sense of foreboding, Robertson turned his attention to the lifeboats. There were only twenty-four – an absurdly small number that would not accommodate a quarter of the passengers. As he realized the unsettling implications of this fact, he seemed to hear a ringing voice uttering the word "unsinkable". Then he saw a mountain of ice loom before the ship and knew they were going to strike. As the vision faded, he saw the ship's name. It was the *Titan*.

Robertson hurried to his typewriter. The first line he hammered out was: "She was the largest craft afloat and the greatest of the works of man . . ."

In *The Wreck of the Titan*, Robertson described a ship that was a kind of floating palace. The luxury cabins were as big as city apartments, the decks as wide as promenades, and the passengers felt as safe from drowning as they would on dry land. Nineteen watertight compartments in the bows "would close automatically in the presence of water . . . [Even] with some compartments flooded, the ship would still float." The self-satisfied designers stressed that "no known accident of the sea could possibly fill so many". So the *Titan* was described by its builders as effectively unsinkable.

But on her third voyage – in the month of April – travelling from New York to England, the 75,000-ton liner struck an iceberg in a fog bank. A long gash was torn below the waterline, and too many of the nineteen bow compartments were flooded for the vessel to stay afloat. As the ship sank, the cold night air echoed with "nearly three thousand voices, raised in agonised screams."

Fourteen years later, on the evening of 14 April 1912, the White Star liner *SS Titanic* – which, together with her sister ship the *SS Olympia*, was one of the largest ships ever built – was steaming at 22 knots (roughly 22 miles an hour) on the final leg of her maiden voyage from Southampton to New York. The sea was very calm, and there seemed no reason to anticipate danger. It was true that the recent winter had been the mildest in years, and many icebergs had broken off the northern polar cap and had floated down the Labrador current into the Atlantic, but the Titanic had charted a southerly course, and the nearest iceberg was reported 250 miles away. There was no moonlight, but the stars were so bright that visibility was good.

At 9:40 p.m., the *Titanic* received a message from the *Mesaba*, which was sailing ahead of her. It reported that there were icebergs about and an entire "ice field" of "growlers" (submerged sheets of ice that "growl" as the movement of the sea rubs them together). But the wireless officer, John Phillips, did not pay the dispatch proper attention. He had received several messages about more distant icebergs that day and, at the same time, he was being overwhelmed with messages that wealthy passengers wanted him to send to New York.

At about 11.30 p.m. the seaman in the crow's nest saw an iceberg straight ahead of the *Titanic*, about a quarter of a mile away. He telephoned the bridge and First Officer Murdock yelled to the helmsman: "Hard to starboard!"

It looked as if they would miss the iceberg easily; the *Titanic*, although travelling fast, still had about two and a half minutes to change course. However, to be on the safe side, Murdock ordered the engine room to reverse the propellers. This was a mistake, because reversing the engines on a ship of that size did not slow her momentum significantly, but it did prevent her turn from being fully effective. If the engines had not been reversed, the *Titanic* would not have struck. With only the slightest of judders, the iceberg brushed past them.

As far as those in the bridge were concerned, collision had been avoided. What no one guessed was that under the surface an enormous spur of ice had sliced along the side of the ship like a tin opener. The 330-foot gash cut into three holds and two boiler rooms.

As soon as someone told Thomas Andrews, one of the ship's two designers, that there had been a noise like tearing calico as the iceberg passed by, he rushed below to inspect the damage. He was relieved to find that the doors of the damaged holds had closed automatically. Unfortunately, this was because they were full of water . . . and they were huge. Inevitably, the vessel began to list forward and to starboard, and Andrews belatedly grasped the fatal flaw in her design.

Unlike the fictional *Titan*'s completely sealed compartments, the *Titanic*'s bow compartments had a gap between the top of the wall and the ceiling. As water in a flooding compartment topped the rim, it would gush into its previously dry neighbour. At first, Captain Edward J. Smith and J. Bruce Ismay (the other designer) believed that the ship could survive even this appalling damage, but Andrews knew better. He saw that the flooding process could not be arrested: the *Titanic* was going down in a sea as calm as a village duckpond.

Although the news spread quickly, there was none of the mass panic described by Robertson in *The Wreck of the Titan*. As people crowded on to the decks, asking why the ship had stopped, the stewards told them cheerfully that it was only a minor problem, and the ship would be on its way in a couple of hours. Yet the captain and the ship's designers recognized that no amount of organization or level-headedness could save 2,220 passengers when there were only twenty lifeboats. At the most they could save 1,200 people.

SOS signals were radioed and emergency rockets fired. Unfortunately, Stanley T. Lord, the captain of the *California*, the only ship close enough to have saved them – which had stopped for the night at the edge of the ice field – thought the exploding flares were signs of a party on board the *Titanic*. He complacently went to bed, as did the *California*'s sole radio operator.

Fortunately, the battered old Cunard liner the *Carpathia* picked up the SOS signals and turned about, making full speed, but she was over an hour away, and the Titanic did not have an hour. Below decks, 325 men continued working in the holds and boiler rooms. The ship's band played jazz, including the popular number *Poor Butterfly*. The fifty officers helped the passengers into boats – women and children first. Ismay, the designer – and a White Star director – panicked as he saw the last boat being lowered, and jumped in, pushing ahead of women. He was branded a coward for the rest of his life, just as Captain Lord of the *California* would forever be vilified as the man who went to sleep and let the *Titanic* passengers drown.

If the *Carpathia* had arrived earlier, nearly all passengers and crew could have been saved – as it was the ship saved 711 people – but before it arrived, the *Titanic*'s boilers exploded and hurtled like rockets along the ship. The *Titanic* up-ended and went down like a stone, killing 1,503 people, including her captain, Edward J. Smith, who had been due to retire at the end of the voyage.

Morgan Robertson's *Futility*, which had been a flop in 1898, now achieved belated fame as the incredible similarities between the real and fictional tragedies were noted. *The Wreck of the Titan* was serialized in newspapers across the United States.

Unfortunately, even this stroke of unbelievable, if also lamentable, good fortune was not enough to save Morgan Robertson's career. After publishing fourteen volumes with titles like *Shipmates* and *Down to the Sea*, his "astral writing partner" finally deserted him.

In 1914, the humorist and actor Irvin S. Cobb found him living in poverty with his wife in a Harlem slum tenement. Horrified, Cobb raised enough money to set Robertson on his feet again. He even bought Robertson a fur coat and gold-headed cane, which the ageing sailor confessed he had always wanted. Yet Robertson was still unable to write.

In March 1915, Robertson was found dead of heart failure, in a hotel in Atlantic City. He was sitting, wearing his fur coat with his gold-headed cane across his knees, and was staring out to sea.

Whether Morgan Robertson had seen the future through his own innate psychic faculty, or had somehow received the information from his astral writing partner, it seems that he had accurately foreseen an event that had not yet taken place.

Inevitably, many disagree with this assessment – even those who accept the possibility of precognition. Writing in 1960, Dr Ian Stevenson, Professor of Psychiatry at the University of Virginia, published a paper called: *A Review and Analysis of Paranormal Experiences Connected with the Sinking of the* Titanic. Although he could hardly be described as a sceptic – having been the President of the American Parapsychological Association – he nevertheless took a negative view of Robertson's apparent vision of the sinking of the *Titanic*:

A writer of the 1890s, familiar with man's repeated hubris might reasonably infer that he would overreach himself in the construction of ocean liners which then . . . were man's greatest engineering marvels . . . A large ship would probably have great power and speed; the name Titan has connoted power and security for several thousand years; recklessness would race the ship through the areas of the Atlantic icebergs; these drift south in the spring, making April a likely month for a collision . . . Having reached the general conclusion of the probability of such a disaster, inferences, such as those I have suggested, might fill in details to provide correspondences which would have an appearance of precognition, but which we should, I believe, consider only successful inferences.

Stevenson might also have believed this of a poem called *The Tryst*, published in 1874 by the American poetess Celia Thaxter. This is cited in a book called *Titanic: Triumph and Tragedy*, by John P. Eaton and Charles A. Haas, as a work of literature that seemed to presage the *Titanic* disaster. *The Tryst* describes an iceberg drifting "from out the desolation of the North" to the "warm airs of the sweet South", where a ship full of "brave men, sweet women, little children bright" is sailing. The inevitable "tryst" occurs, and "dully through wind and sea, one awful crash/Sounded, with none to mark."

Certainly, *The Tryst* captures that disturbing sense of inevitability that seems to mark the tragedy of the *Titanic*, but can a poem about a sailing ship really be regarded as a kind of premonition about a massive engine-driven liner?

On the other hand, it is possible to make an altogether stronger case for the striking predictions of the campaigning newspaper editor W. T. Stead, who in March 1886 wrote an article entitled *How the Mail Steamer Went Down in Mid-Atlantic, by a Survivor*, published in the *Pall Mall Gazette*. It describes an unnamed steamer sinking after colliding with another vessel, and how hundreds of passengers are lost because there are not enough lifeboats for them all. Stead concluded the article: "This is exactly what might take place and what will take place if liners are sent to sea short of boats – Editor."

W. T. Stead, as well as being fascinated by nautical matters, was a convinced spiritualist and an active medium. Through a "spirit guide" called Julia he obtained many "messages from the other side" in automatic writing (a practice in which the medium's hand appears to be controlled by an unknown entity). We do not know if Stead received the same sort of supernatural inspiration as

Robertson, but there can be no doubt that he remained obsessed by the threat of an ocean liner disaster to – literally – the end of his life.

In 1893, seven years after his first tale of maritime disaster, he wrote a fictional account of a collision between an Atlantic iceberg and a passenger liner for the Christmas issue of *The Review of Reviews* (which he also edited). What makes *From the Old World to the New* so remarkable is the fact that the captain of the White Star liner *Majestic* – a real ship which Stead describes rescuing the survivors of the doomed vessel – was, at the time of publication, Edward J. Smith, the man who captained the *Titanic* on its last voyage. It is likely, therefore, that Smith might have read Stead's story.

Stead's interests in the paranormal and oceanic safety sometimes intermixed. In *From the Old World to the New*, for example, the survivors are rescued because a clairvoyant passenger has a precognitive vision of the disaster. Ten years later, in 1903, Stead was involved in a séance that convinced him still further that "spirits" boasted the power of precognition.

On 20 March a Bradford medium named Mrs Burchell was dining with Stead and a group of fellow spiritualists in Gatti's restaurant. As an experiment, Stead asked her to hold an envelope he had obtained from the Serbian ambassador. Mrs Burchell had no idea of its contents, but inside was, in fact, the signature of King Alexander of Serbia.

The moment the envelope was put into her hand, Mrs Burchell immediately said: "Royalty! He is a king." Then she gave an accurate description of King Alexander and, with increasing agitation, described how he would be murdered in his palace, together with his queen. While this was happening, another medium in the room fell into a trance and added the detail that the assassins were wearing what looked to her like Russian uniforms. Stead wrote an account of this séance and sent it to the unpopular King Alexander – and his even-less-popular wife, Queen Draga. Alexander, however, was a rationalist, and ignored the warning. Four months later, on 16 June 1903, the king and queen were murdered in their palace in Belgrade by a group of Serbian army officers (whose uniforms resembled Russian military dress).

In 1909, Stead had again showed a flash of something that, in retrospect, looked like clairvoyance. Speaking before the members of the Cosmos Club, he criticized what he felt to be the excessive rigour demanded by the Society for Psychical Research regarding what it considered sound evidence. By way of illustration, Stead conjured up a picture of himself drowning in the sea after a shipwreck. Suppose, he said, that rescuers, instead of throwing him a rope, asked "What is your name?" and when he replied "W. T. Stead," they shouted back: "How do we know you are Stead? Where were you born? Tell us the name of your grandmother!"

"It is quite astonishing," remarks Leslie A. Shephard in the *Encyclopedia of Occultism and Parapsychology*, "how often the picture of a sinking ocean liner with its attendant horrors recurred in Stead's writings."

On 21 April 1912, Stead was due in New York to appear in Carnegie Hall, where he had been invited by President Taft to speak on the subject of world peace.[1] He booked a passage for the *Titanic*'s maiden voyage. In a letter to his secretary, written just before his departure, he wrote: "I feel as if something was going to happen, somewhere or somehow." Whether this was a foreboding of his fate may be questioned in view of his next comment: "And that it will be for good." W. T. Stead was one of those who died on the *Titanic*.

Stead's reservations about sea travel had been thoroughly reinforced by other spiritualists in the months before his death. For example Cheiro, the most famous palmist of his time, sent Stead a warning almost a year before the *Titanic* set sail. Stead had gone to consult Cheiro because he was worried that his crusading zeal (he had once gone to prison for writing a series of articles exposing London's child prostitution) might lead to an attempt on his life. Cheiro studied Stead's horoscope as well as his palm, and noted:

> . . . any danger of violent death to you must be by water and nothing else. Very critical and dangerous for you should be April, 1912, especially about the middle of the month. So don't travel by water then if you can help it. If you do, you will be liable to meet with such danger to your life that the very worst may happen. I know I am not wrong about this

[1] By then, statesmen were well aware of the danger of a potentially catastrophic war in Europe.

"water" danger; I only hope I am, or at least that you won't be travelling somewhere about that period.

Stead received Cheiro's warning in June 1911. The following winter he consulted the clairvoyant W. de Kerlor, whose speciality was crystal-ball gazing. The psychic claimed to see Stead travelling to America "on a huge black ship, but I can only see half of the ship – when one will be able to see it in its whole length, it is perhaps then that you will go on your journey." The *Titanic* was, in fact, completed in the Harland and Wolff shipyard in Belfast by then, but it may also be noted that the ship broke in half as she sank – a fact that was not discovered until the wreck was found, 13,000 feet down, in 1985.

Archdeacon Thomas Colley, who would later write a pamphlet titled *The Foreordained Wreck of the* Titanic, actually sent Stead a warning of the disaster before he sailed. Stead replied that he was sincerely grateful for what he hoped was a groundless warning, but that he felt it was his duty to speak against Europe's growing militancy. Stead added that he hoped to see Colley when he returned from America.

Two days after the sinking of the *Titanic*, before the news of its loss had been made public, a Detroit medium named Etta Wriedt (who had intended to return to England with her friend Stead), went into a trance. She stated that Stead had been killed and also mentioned the names of several other prominent people who had been drowned. The following evening, an entity purporting to be Stead himself spoke through her, describing his death on the *Titanic*.

There are many other stories of psychic premonitions of the disaster. Mrs Esther Hart, wife of Benjamin Hart, was horrified when she heard that the ship was described as unsinkable. She felt sure this was tempting fate. The family, including their seven-year-old daughter Eva, were emigrating to Canada, and could ill afford to waste the tickets (priced at £26.5 shillings each – a reasonably large sum in 1912). Yet Esther begged her husband to choose another ship; even as they were climbing the gangplank, she pressed him to change his mind. He told her that if she was so worried, she should return home with Eva, and come over when he had arrived safely. Understandably, she refused, but each night, after eating in the ship's dining room, she would change out of her dinner dress into warm woollen clothes, then sit up all night, knitting or sewing.

Thus, on the night of 14 April, she was awake in her cabin when the iceberg holed the *Titanic*; the bump was so slight that it did not even cause her glass of orange juice to slop over on the table top. Yet she knew immediately that this was what she had been expecting. She woke her husband and sent him up to the boat deck. When he returned he simply said: "You'd better put my thick coat on. I'll wear another."

Years later, Mrs Hart's daughter – who like her mother, had been rescued – asked her why she had not asked her father what had happened. She said: "There was nothing to ask him." She already knew that the impending disaster had happened. Benjamin Hart, like most of the men on the *Titanic*, was drowned.

An engineer called Colin MacDonald turned down a lucrative offer to become second engineer on the *Titanic* because he had a hunch that it would sink.

Many others cancelled their reservations, including the steel magnate Henry Clay Frick, the multimillionaire George W. Vanderbilt (whose mother-in-law felt that maiden voyages were unlucky) and the banker J. Pierpont Morgan, whose mercantile combine owned the White Star line.

Ten days before the *Titanic* was due to sail, a London businessman named J. Connon Middleton, who had booked a week earlier, had a dream of the *Titanic* floating keel upward, her passengers swimming in the sea. The next night he had the same dream. Yet, although worried, he was too practical minded to cancel his passage. Fortunately, a week before sailing, he received a telegram from business associates saying that the conference had been postponed for a week and asking him to delay his trip for a few days. Middleton mentioned his premonition to many people before the ship sailed, so was able to call on them for corroboration later.

As the ship passed the Isle of Wight on its way out of Southampton, the family of a man named Jack Marshall stood on their roof and waved their handkerchiefs. Suddenly, Mrs Marshall – the mother of novelist Joan Grant – grabbed her husband by the arm and screamed: "It's going to sink, it's going to sink before it reaches America." She was so certain that she refused to be soothed, shouting: "Do something, you fools – I see hundreds of people struggling in the icy water!" In her autobiography *Far Memory*, Joan Grant tells how the whole family was in such a state of tension for the following five days that it was almost a relief to hear that the *Titanic* had sunk.

At Queenstown, in Ireland, a young fireman had a premonition of disaster, and deserted the ship.

On the *Titanic*'s last evening, the Rev. E. C. Carter held a service in the second-class dining room – and included among the hymns the rather ironic choice *For Those in Peril on the Sea*. In Winnipeg, Canada, the Rev. Charles Morgan, of the Rosedale Methodist Church, had already chosen the hymns for that evening's service when he drifted into a doze on the sofa, and heard the words "For those in peril on the sea". He did not know the hymn, but nevertheless went and looked out the music, and took it to church. At the same time the Rev. Carter's congregation were singing the hymn on the *Titanic*, the Rev. Morgan's congregation were singing it in their church.

In his paper for the American Society for Psychical Research, already mentioned, Dr Ian Stevenson (best known for his studies of reincarnation) lists no less than nineteen cases of premonitions of the sinking of the *Titanic*, from England, America and Brazil.

On the day the *Titanic* sailed, a psychic named V. N. Turvey had a sudden intuition that the ship would be lost, and wrote a letter to this effect to Madame I. de Steiger. The letter actually arrived on 15 April, by which time the *Titanic* had sunk; Turvey's letter was published in the magazine *Light* on 29 June 1912.

There is an interesting postscript to this tale of disaster. Precisely twenty-three years later, in April 1935, a young seaman named William Reeves was standing watch on the deck of a tramp steamer called the *Titanium*, carrying coal from the Tyne to Canada. Reeves knew all about the *Titanic* – the story of the great liner fascinated him. His watch was due to end at midnight – the time the *Titanic* struck the iceberg – and he knew that they were in roughly the same spot where this had happened. A sudden intuition of danger filled him with alarm, but he could see nothing ahead. Then, as he recalled that the *Titanic* had sunk on the day he was born, the intuition turned to certainty. He shouted a danger warning. The *Titanium*'s engines reversed, and the ship came to a halt just before it struck an iceberg.

The story of the *Titanic* disaster not only suggests that precognition of the future can occur, but that it may occur more often than we might assume. Of course, this outrages common sense, which takes the view that what has not yet happened cannot possibly be known – unless it happens to be predictable, like the movements of heavenly bodies.

But suppose our view of space and time is badly wrong, and the future can be known? This is not as absurd as it sounds. Although this world that surrounds us looks solid and real and unproblematic, we only have to ask ourselves when time began, or when it will end, to see that things are less simple than they seem.

Cosmologists assure us that in the beginning was the Big Bang, and that the "background hiss" of interstellar space is evidence for it – having said which, they sit back as if to say "Next question please." And we cannot help feeling much like the ancient Hindus when they were told that the world is supported on the back of an elephant, which is supported on the back of a camel, and so on. It is quite obvious that what we call science cannot embrace certain problems because they cannot be reduced to a kind of symbolic logic. The problem of time is one of these.

So, for example, the problem of the future has been tackled in hypnotic regression. In an issue of *Science* in 1954, Robert Rubinstein and Richard Newman describe how, working with a group of hypnotic subjects, they told a medical student that it was now October 1963 (ten years ahead) and asked him what he was doing. He went on to describe his day in detail – an operation on an emergency case, complete with symptoms and diagnosis. When asked if he felt pleased, he mentioned that he had dealt with a similar case in 1958 – five years after the date of the hypnotic session.

Another of the subjects described her anguish in 1963 at the death of her three-month-old son.

The authors go on: "We believe that each of our subjects, to please the hypnotist, fantasised of future." It seems a pity that they did not try asking their subjects about some time closer to the present, and then checking on whether their reports were accurate.

However, a similar experiment was carried out in the early

1970s by an American academic, Charles H. Hapgood, who began experimenting in hypnotism with his students at Keene State University in New Hampshire. One student was a youth named Jay, and on a Sunday evening he was told that it was the following Wednesday, and was asked what he was doing. He said he had been to Keene Airport, and had met a pilot who was able to give him details of an accident at Montpelier in which he was deeply interested. When the hypnotism session ended, Jay was told to forget what he had said, and awoke with no conscious memory of what had happened.

On the following Wednesday evening, Hapgood asked Jay what he had been doing all day, and Jay replied that he had been to Keene Airport, and had met a pilot who was able to tell him about the cause of the Montpelier crash. A comparison of the details of the whole day showed that they corresponded exactly to what Jay had said three days earlier.

Another student named Henry was told under hypnosis that it was the following Thursday, and asked what he intended doing that day. He said he meant to borrow a friend's car, and to drive to Brattleboro to "have a good time". Progressed a few hours by the hypnotist, he explained that he was in a bar drinking beer with two women, who were saying critical things about their husbands and making improper suggestions, which Henry declined to repeat. Taken forward a few hours, he described getting back to Keene slightly the worse for wear, and waking up the dogs when he went home. He too, was then made to forget what he had said.

The following Friday, Hapgood saw Henry, and said: "Henry, I know where you were last night." "I bet you don't," replied Henry. "You went to Brattleboro in *m*'s car, and went to a diner and had a lot of beer." When Hapgood came to the women, Henry looked worried and said: "But you don't know what they said, do you?" Hapgood replied diplomatically: "No Henry, you refused to tell us."

Hapgood goes on:

> Now where does all this leave us? There appears to be good evidence that the human psyche is not bound by the limitations of time and space. Our bodies exist in this physical world, where the laws of time, space, mass and energy

operate in a finite way; but they are only the peaks of icebergs that jut above the sea, leaving nine-tenths of their mass out of sight below sea level. All the phenomena I have mentioned here can be easily duplicated. All that is necessary to demonstrate them is a good hypnotist and a few good subjects.

All this may seem to suggest a negative view of the human capacity for freedom – that we are living lives that have been scripted in advance. Indeed, there is a certain amount of evidence that this is so. Dr Michael Shallis, an Oxford science don, describes in his book *On Time* how he often had a sudden feeling of *déjà vu* in which he knew what would be happening in the immediate future.

As a child of twelve he asked his mother what they were to have for dinner and knew suddenly that she was going to answer: salad. He also describes how, giving a tutorial on radioactivity, he had the same *déjà vu* feeling, and knew that the next thing that had to happen was that he would suggest that he needed a certain book from his office, and would go and get it. He decided to resist this impulse, just to break the pattern – then heard his voice saying "I will pop down to my office to get a book . . ."

But it would surely be a mistake to assume we have no free will. What about the young fireman who decided to get off the *Titanic* at Queenstown harbour because of his premonition of the sinking? Was that preordained too, like the sinking? And if the answer to that might seem to be "Yes", then how about a case described by J. B. Priestley in *Man and Time*, borrowed from the paranormal researcher Louisa Rhine. A mother described a dream in which she was camping with some friends on the shores of a creek. She went down to the creek with her baby to wash some clothes, then realized she had forgotten the soap. She put down her baby while she went back to the tent, and when she returned, found the baby face down in the creek obviously drowned.

Months later she went camping with some friends on the bank of a creek. She took the baby with her to wash some clothes, realized she had forgotten the soap, and started back for it. The baby began throwing stones in the water, when she suddenly remembered her dream. So she picked up the baby and took him back to the tent with her.

This seems to suggest that the future is not predetermined – at least, not rigidly so. Since most self-observant persons are aware how far their lives are largely mechanical,[2] then we might conclude that we exercise free will only in rare moments of "non-mechanicalness".

It might seem to follow that where large masses of people are concerned, there is less chance of an individual exercise of free will making any difference. History itself can be argued to obey mechanical laws – a point of view Tolstoy argues in *War and Peace*. If so, then we may well feel that the sinking of the *Titanic* was somehow predestined.

This argument – between free will and determinism, or free will and compulsion – lies at the essence of religious prophecy. As we saw earlier in this book, the religious, and especially the monotheistic "Prophets of God", occasionally make predictions of future events, but usually prophesy "what God wills". Anyone who believes their God(s) to be omnipotent, must also consider the possibility that free will may be an illusion, as we are all imprisoned by the deity's unassailable plan. Indeed, a large section of western theology has been given over to the question of how free will is possible under an omnipotent, omnipresent God.

This is, perhaps, the place to raise another important point: whether the phrase "written in the stars" can mean anything to any rational, scientifically minded person.

In their book *Astrology, the Divine Science*, Marcia Moore and Mark Douglas point out that the transit of the planet Neptune (called after the sea god) through "watery Cancer" was marked by the sinking of the *Titanic*. In *Prophecy and Prediction in the 20th Century*, Charles Neilson Gattey quotes the astrologer Dennis Elwell, who pointed out that in April 1912, two major planets, Neptune and Jupiter, became stationary in the sky (that is, of course, they looked as if they were stationary from the point of view of the Earth).

The planets were in what astrologers call a "biquintile", an angle

---

[2]For example, if your ear itches, you do not have to think about how to scratch it, your hand does it automatically, often without your being consciously aware of the action.

of 144°. (A quintile is an angle of 72°, signifying strain, so a double (bi)quintile would indicate a double strain.) Jupiter, as the planet of the ruler of the gods, signifies mastery, while Neptune, the planet of the sea, is associated with ships. Elwell sees this as a strain between man's craving for mastery over nature – as in the declaration that the *Titanic* was unsinkable – and the immense forces he was challenging. Moreover, says Elwell, the sinking took place between two eclipses: one of the Moon (on 1 April) and one of the Sun (on 17 April), and eclipses are believed to magnify astrological effects. This may sound like the kind of nonsense with which newspaper astrologers mystify the public, but Elwell goes on to offer supporting evidence.

Early in 1987, he noticed that the same two planets, Jupiter and Neptune, would soon be coming into an aspect that astrologers call a square, which is when there is an angle of 90° between two planets and the centre of the zodiac. A square indicates conflict. Furthermore, there was an eclipse of the sun on the Jupiter arm of the square, increasing the possibility of conflict.

Recalling the *Titanic*, Elwell wrote letters to the P&O and Cunard lines – not so much to warn them of some unspecified disaster, as to place his prediction on record. Elwell also offered to try to pinpoint the danger. He stressed in his letters that it was the first time in forty years as an astrologer that he had felt the need to give such warnings. Both companies replied that their safety procedures were quite adequate.

In fact, the *Queen Elizabeth II* was making her way to New York when Elwell wrote these letters in February, and one was passed on to the commodore of the fleet, who was on board. The voyage was beset with disaster – failed air conditioning, flooded cabins that caused the ship to list 15° so the passengers had to eat their meals at an angle, and various other problems. Perhaps as a precaution, the ship made a 250-mile detour to avoid the place where the *Titanic* sank.

Cunard may have suffered their disaster, but P&O, the owners of the ferry company Townsend Thoreson, still had theirs to come. And if Elwell had known that P&O owned Townsend Thoreson, he might have had more success in pinpointing their disaster. For one of that company's ferries was called *The Herald of Free Enterprise*. The sign Aries is associated with pioneers and precursors – hence with heralds. And Jupiter has been traditionally associated with the idea of freedom. So a time when Jupiter was in Aries, with an associated eclipse, could have spelled danger for a vessel with such a name.

The Herald of Free Enterprise disaster had been waiting to happen, for, as the enquiry later revealed, the car ferry often sailed with her bow doors still open, which was strictly against the rules. In Zeebrugge, on 6 March 1987, with Jupiter in Aries on the horizon, *The Herald of Free Enterprise* left harbour with her bow car-loading doors yet again wide open. A high sea caused water to flood the central car deck and the ferry began to list. Fortunately, she did not sink, but the excess water made her wallow and eventually capsize. Before rescuers could evacuate the ship, 188 people were killed.

Gattey notes that a number of marine disasters also occurred during that period of Jupiter in Aries in 1987. On 24 April, a ship called the *Hengist* collided with a French trawler, which capsized; on 1 May, two ferries collided in the fog; and two days later, there was a collision between a Townsend Thoreson ferry and another vessel in Calais harbour.

Elwell also pointed out that the *Olympic*, the *Titanic*'s sister ship, had not escaped that heavenly warning of disaster; seven weeks after the *Titanic* went down, an extraordinary steering error brought the *Olympic* close to running aground off Land's End. The incident was hushed up, to avoid alarming the public, and was finally revealed, ironically a few weeks after *The Herald of Free Enterprise* disaster.

Chapter 23

The Mothman and the Silver Bridge

During late 1966 and the whole of 1967, something extraordinary took place in the Ohio River Valley – most notably around the West Virginia town of Point Pleasant. Regular-as-clockwork UFO sightings, cattle mutilations, threatening "Men in Black", poltergeist hauntings and, perhaps most striking of all, the terrifying "Mothman". Describing this strange series of otherworldly happenings in his book *The Mothman Prophecies*, investigator John A. Keel noted that "the events of 1966–7 had fractured [the Point Pleasanters'] sense of credulity. Almost anything now seemed possible."

Reading his account of these bizarre events, the reader is tempted to regard Keel's book as a work of fiction. Yet many of these sightings and events were fully documented by local newspapers at the time, and their aftermath, as we will see, was horribly real.[1]

The prophets we have so far looked at – both religious and precognitive – have tended to be surprisingly pragmatic in their

[1]Those readers who have seen the the 2002 movie version of John Keel's book (also titled *The Mothman Prophecies*) may have come away with a false impression of the events around Point Pleasant. As is all too typical of Hollywood when dealing with non-fiction, the movie's plot was thoroughly fictionalized and – in what can only be regarded as questionable taste, considering they were dealing with a real-life disaster – all the events were moved from 1966/7 to 2001.

The main character of the movie version, a political reporter called John Klein, barely resembles paranormal investigator John Keel, and most of the events that happen to Klein in the film are, at best, distorted reflections of what Keel actually reported in his book. The interested reader is strongly recommended to obtain a copy of the book, rather than rely on the movie version.

outlook. Most of the biblical prophets, for example, warned of impending threats or called for much-needed reforms; while seers like Nostradamus, Mother Shipton and Edgar Cayce – although not above a little self-created, self-serving mystery – generally lived lives of admirable common sense. None could be accurately described as "airy-fairy" (as TV and movie oracles and clairvoyants are often portrayed), yet it is what might be called the "fairy prophets" that we will now consider.

If we take the events of the Bible and the Koran to be "Gospel true", visitations by non-humans were relatively common in biblical times and even for some centuries thereafter. Jewish prophets like Lot, Moses and Daniel received visitations and messages from the apparently spiritual creatures they called angels (although Lot ate a meal with the pair that visited him). Even Jesus met the former angel, Satan, during his forty days in the wilderness and, as we have already seen, Muhammad's prophetic contact with Allah was signalled by a visitation from the Archangel Gabriel.

The polytheistic pagans of the Ancient Mediterranean were even more nonchalant over the matter of non-human visitors – regarding it as perfectly possible, if rare, for women to be impregnated by philandering demons, nature spirits or gods like Zeus and Pan; a concept that did not penetrate monotheism until the advent of Christianity.

Depending on one's own religious standpoint, some, or perhaps all, such descriptions of non-human entities might be discounted as primitive superstition. Yet similarly strange visitations are reported regularly – almost daily – in our modern age: some people claim to have met alien travellers in "flying saucers", others see ghosts or strange phantoms and, in the US Bible-Belt especially, angel visitations and demonic possessions are still frequently reported.

A sceptic would list these modern "fairies" as delusions or hoaxes inspired by superstition and over-excited imaginations, but when such "visitors" are said to pass on accurate predictions of future events, further investigation is surely merited . . .

Point Pleasant, West Virginia, was, in 1966, a small industrial town populated mainly by people who worked in factories further up the Ohio River. Point Pleasanters were hardly city sophisticates, but most were well educated and certainly could not be described as superstitious hill-billies; those who wrote off the events of 1966/7 as hysteria among a town of backward rustics were wide of the mark.

The Point Pleasant area, and West Virginia in general, has something of a reputation for mystery. Unlike the grim, over-mined area to the east of the state, this part of the Ohio River Valley remains heavily wooded and, in some people's eyes, has a "haunted" atmosphere.

This feeling may also stem from knowledge of an odd blank in West Virginia's history: before white settlement, the whole area was quite unpopulated. Between 500 BC and AD 100, a mysterious people called the Mound Builders had lived in the region. These people, unlike most North American natives, built large earthwork structures, their use of which we have yet to fully understand. Another mysterious tribe, now known only as the Fort Ancient People, replaced the Mound Builders, but were in turn exterminated by the Iroquois Confederacy around 1650.

Why the Iroquois Confederacy wiped out the Fort Ancient People is now hard to judge, but they did not do it to take their lands – following the extermination, the tribes of the Confederacy left the territory quite alone. This was despite the fact that Native American tribes had occupied every other part of the Eastern Seaboard – to the point that they were constantly fighting each other for land even before the Europeans arrived. Nevertheless, the lush, game-filled forests of West Virginia lay totally uninhabited for over 100 years; then white settlers arrived and took possession.

Any hope of finding out why the Native Americans avoided West Virginia for so long is now, unfortunately, lost. The local tribes that lived in areas bordering West Virginia – the Shawnee, Cherokee, Monacan, Erie and Conestoga – were devastated by European diseases and European weapons. By the time the whites thought of asking why the original locals had so assiduously avoided West Virginia, the tribes' elders and much of their verbal histories and lore were dead and buried.

The weird events around Point Pleasant started in early November 1966. A number of UFO sightings took place in the area around this time – although most were not reported until later, largely because witnesses feared being called crazy.

Two elderly electricians even reported a so-called "close encounter" – a meeting with a passenger from a UFO. They told the local paper – *The Messenger* – that they had seen an "elongated object" flying low through the sky near Interstate 77 on the evening of 2 November. It landed on the road in front of their truck and an apparently normal man got out.

The UFO-naut was wearing an ordinary black coat and trousers, but kept his arms tightly folded with his hands crammed into his armpits, as if he were cold or he was hiding them from view. He walked up to the pair in the truck, grinning in a sickly fashion, and asked a series of inane questions: Who were they? Where were they from? Where were they going? What time was it? He then said farewell, got back into his UFO and it flew away into the darkening sky.

The pair of electricians were badly shaken by the encounter, despite its odd blandness. They kept quiet about the event for two weeks, then both were visited by a "scientist". This man apparently knew all about their encounter, and advised them not to tell anyone about it.

This mysterious "scientist" is possibly the first case of a so-called "MIB" – Man (or Men) in Black – in the Point Pleasant series of events. These threatening characters – usually dressed in black suits – are sometimes reported to have visited witnesses of odd events like UFO sightings. MIBs usually claim to be from some official agency, like the FBI or the CIA, and warn witnesses to keep silent about what they have seen. Later checking of their credentials invariably proves fruitless, as no official agency has ever admitted to employing them.

The popular idea about Men in Black (underlined by the hit movie of the same name) is that they are from some secret government agency, aware of alien visits to the Earth, and assigned to cover them up.

However, as John Keel points out, MIB are very bad at their job. They ask odd questions in odd accents, behave generally strangely (such as arriving and driving away in the dark in a car with the headlights turned off) and often show ignorance of everyday things: one, for example, when offered a bowl of Jell-O (jelly to UK readers) tried at first to drink it, then wrapped a sample in his hanky "for analysis".

This strangely ridiculous behaviour has led some to believe that MIB are actually aliens trying to cover their own tracks, but Keel questions even this. He points out that telling people to keep quiet usually has the opposite effect. He suggests that MIB – whoever or whatever they are – might actually be using reverse psychology to spread the news of paranormal events.

Certainly this was what happened in the case of the Point Pleasant electricians who met a UFO-naut. They were determined to keep their mouths shut *until* the "scientist" told them to keep quiet.

The first recorded sighting of what came to be called "the Mothman" happened on the night of 14 November 1966, on the other side of West Virginia, near the town of Salem. A farmer called Newell Partridge gave the following account:

> It was about 10.30 that night, and suddenly the TV blanked out. A real fine herringbone pattern appeared on the tube, and at the same time the set started a loud whining noise. It sounded like a generator winding up . . . It reminded me of a hand field generator for portable radio transmission.
>
> The dog was sitting on the end of the porch, howling down toward the hay barn. I shined the light in that direction, and it picked up two red circles, or eyes, which looked like bicycle reflectors . . . I certainly know what animal eyes look like – such as [rac]coon, dog and cat eyes in the dark. These were much larger for one thing. It's a good length of a football field to that hay barn. Probably 150 yards; still those eyes showed up huge for that distance.

Bandit, Farmer Partridge's Alsatian dog, charged into the dark after the eyes . . . and did not come back. Partridge was too shaken to follow after his dog and slept that night with a shotgun by his bed. The next morning he went to the spot where the eyes had been hovering. He found Bandit's tracks:

> Those tracks were going in a circle, as if the dog had been chasing his tail, though he never did that. And that was that . . . There were no other tracks of any kind.

Bandit, a dog who was not prone to wandering off, never came home.

The outskirts of Point Pleasant housed a major military chemical stockpile area during the Second World War, the remains of which still mark the landscape. Hollow concrete "hills" were built to store high explosives, but as the camouflaging turf was left to erode after the war, these hundred-odd greyish humps now stand starkly out against the surrounding woods. This area is known simply as "TNT" by the locals, after the explosive that was once stored there, and it was on or near the TNT that many of the strange sightings of 1966/7 took place.

On the night of 15 November, twenty-four hours after the disappearance of Partridge's dog, two young married couples – the Scarberrys and the Mallettes – drove out to the TNT in the same car to see if any friends were hanging out there; the TNT was a notorious "make-out" spot for couples with access to vehicles.

Driving past the abandoned generator building, Linda Scarberry gasped and pointed to two glowing red circles apparently hovering in the dark, about two inches in diameter and separated by about six inches. As the couples stared, they made out that the "eyes" belonged to a large, shadowy figure:

> It was shaped like a man, but bigger. Maybe six and a half or seven feet tall. And it had big wings folded against its back. But it was those eyes that got us. It had two big eyes like automobile reflectors. They were hypnotic. For a minute, we could only stare at it. I couldn't take my eyes off it.

The thing turned slowly and shuffled towards the empty generator building on thick-set, man-like legs. Naturally, the Scarberrys and the Mallettes decided to get out of there as fast as possible. They sped through the TNT's gates and down the road towards Point Pleasant. As they went, they saw the creature, or another like it, standing ahead of them on a small hillock near the road. They hurtled past it and the couple in the back of the car yelled that it was flying after them.

> We were doing a hundred miles an hour, and that bird kept right up with us. It wasn't even flapping its wings.
> It followed us right up to city limits . . . Funny thing, we

noticed a dead dog by the side of the road there. But when we came back a few minutes later, the dog was gone.

Presumably, the couples had noted this dead dog on their more relaxed drive out to the TNT – it seems hard to believe that they spotted such a detail driving at a hundred miles an hour at night with a monster chasing them. Still, we can be sure that, if they were inventing the whole story, they were not doing so on the basis of Newell Partridge's experience the night before – he had not reported it yet.

Of course, if we accept the Scarberrys' and the Mallettes' story, it might be possible that they were the last people to see the mortal remains of Newell Partridge's dog, Bandit. The Partridge farm was over a hundred miles from Point Pleasant but, from their account, the Mothman could have covered that distance in just over an hour . . .

The Mothman (so named as a newspaper subeditor's pun on the camp TV series *Batman*) was seen at least half-a-dozen times before the end of November 1966. Each witness reported roughly the same: a tall, bulky, fairly humanoid figure – grey in shade – with large, but strangely immobile wings on its back, no visible arms and no visible head. The glowing or highly reflective red eyes appeared to be in the creature's upper chest. The Mothman sometimes chased people, but never seemed intent on actually catching them. Nobody claimed to have been physically molested or even touched by the Mothman.

The Point Pleasant police soon started to take these sightings seriously – the witnesses were mostly steady, family types with no previous history of hysteria or hoaxing. However, investigation of the maze-like TNT complex showed no evidence of Mothman habitation – whatever that would look like.

As more Mothman and UFO sightings took place as the winter progressed, sometimes quite a distance from the TNT, the local media and finally the national media picked up the story. Arriving reporters asked what the odds were of seeing a UFO if they stayed up all night – and were told to make their way out to an area called Camp Conley Road before 8 p.m.

Sure enough, whizzing and spiralling coloured lights appeared in the sky over Camp Conley Road every night, at 8 o'clock sharp, for almost a year. Locals joked that you could set your watch by the start of the generally hour-long UFO display.

Of course, UFO-seekers also flooded into the area. Far from people avoiding the fearsome TNT area, it was crowded with hopeful sky-watchers every night. Among this stream of journalists, craziness and sensation-seekers, a few seasoned paranormal investigators also arrived at Point Pleasant, including the author John Keel.

These latter quietly set about interviewing witnesses and comparing notes, but they soon found that the witnesses were becoming less and less willing to come forward, and certainly did not want their names and addresses published. One reason for this reluctance was a number of visits by the creepy Men in Black around the Point Pleasant area – giving their usual warnings about not telling anyone about whatever had been witnessed.

However, Keel makes it plain that it was not the "MIB conspiracy" that deterred witnesses so much as the likelihood that anyone who went public with an odd experience risked being rung or visited by rabid UFO nuts at any time of the day or night. Of course, this did not make matters any easier for more professional investigators, like Keel, but this turned out to be the least of his problems.

While driving down the Ohio side of the Ohio River, Keel decided, on an impulse, to turn into a farm gate and ask the owner if he had seen anything unusual of late. The grim-faced farmer opened his door to reveal that he was holding a shotgun. Keel tried to show his credentials, but the man cut him off, saying: "I know who you are. We don't want anything to do with you. Get out of here!"

Shocked by this reception, Keel left hurriedly. He told local reporter Mary Hyre what had happened and she insisted they go back together to get to the bottom of the matter. However, when they arrived at the farm the next day, they received a very different reception. The farmer was fulsomely apologetic, saying:

You're not going to believe this, but ten minutes before you arrived here yesterday, I got a phone call. It sounded like a neighbour of mine and he said he was calling to warn me of a crazy man . . .

The voice that sounded like the neighbour then described Keel exactly and said that he was driving around threatening people. After the farmer had seen Keel off his property he had called his neighbour back, only to be told by the man's wife that there had been no visit from a "crazy man" and that her husband could not have made any telephone calls, having visibly been working out in the fields all day.

The strangest thing about this incident was that whoever had made the call had done it almost ten minutes *before* Keel had made the quite random decision to turn up at one of many farm entrances – how could the mystery hoaxer have known which farm to call?

This was certainly not the last time such an unnerving trick was played on Keel. Later in 1967 he pulled into a motel when he was too tired to drive any further. Despite the fact he had chosen the motel quite randomly, the desk clerk told him: "We've got a lot of messages for you, Mr Keel."

The messages all turned out to be meaningful-sounding gibberish, but Keel guessed that their real purpose was to impress on him that someone could track even his most randomly determined movements. Since that person had been sending messages to that motel all that day, hours before Keel decided to stop there, they presumably had some way of foretelling the future.

Over the course of 1967, there were many more weird events around Point Pleasant. Odd shapes and lights became so common in the sky that few people bothered to report them. The Mothman, on the other hand, was invariably reported whenever "he" was seen, largely because he had a deeply frightening effect on witnesses. Some said it felt as if he carried an aura of fear around with him.[2]

The disappearance and possible killing of the dog, Bandit, also proved to be a precursor of more ugly events. Ohio Valley folk began to find their family cats and dogs were being killed, and farmers discovered dead cattle in the fields. These animals had been slaughtered and mutilated in a strangely surgical fashion, with apparently random organs having been carefully removed from the bodies. If the Mothman was doing this killing, he must have been trained in butchery.

[2]The Mothman was presumably a lone beast, as witnesses never saw more than one at a time.

Some witnesses of such odd or unpleasant events not only had to put up with subsequent visits by strange Men in Black, but also with poltergeists – invisible forces – smashing crockery, moving heavy furniture about and, apparently, playing with the telephone system.

Even those witnesses who, up to that time, had kept their experience secret were bothered by endless "crank" telephone calls. Sometimes these would involve a voice speaking an unknown language, at other times there would just be a series of electronic beeps or heavy breathing noises. The telephone company claimed to be unaware of any faults in the system, but the weird calls continued.

John Keel also suffered strange telephone calls during 1967, but his were even more disturbing.

Having become known as a sober and reliable person to talk to – as opposed to a UFO nut – he had found himself at the centre of a group of "contactees". These were people, across the country, who believed themselves to be in contact with alien beings. All had met strange humanoid creatures and many claimed to have ridden in UFOs and even to have been taken to other planets.

Certainly some of these people were attention-seeking crazies, but Keel believed that most were normal, sane people who genuinely believed, for whatever reason, that they were in contact with aliens. It might have been easier to discount even these as suffering from hallucinations if it had not been for the prophecies.

One contactee – who Keel calls "Jane" – said that she had been approached by a man called "Apol" (pronounced Apple). This being had casually told Jane several things that happened in her childhood that she had never mentioned to anyone. He also told her to avoid iodine in her diet – only Jane and her doctor knew that she had a minor health problem that demanded she avoid iodine.

Apol then, having revealed himself to be an alien from another world, gave Jane a message to pass on to John Keel – of whom she had never heard. The New York telephone number Apol gave for Keel proved to be correct, however. The message was:

Things will become more serious in the Middle East. The pope will go there soon on a peace mission. He will be martyred there in a horrible way . . . knifed to death in a bloody manner. Then the Antichrist will rise up out of Israel.

As if to confirm his prophetic credentials, Apol also gave a list of plane crashes that were to happen in the next few months. Unfortunately, Keel gives no details in his book about Apol's plane crash predictions – an unforgivable failing for a paranormal investigator to make, as it prevents cross-checking – but he assures the reader that enough of these crashes took place as predicted to convince him that Apol was capable of either telling the future or causing plane accidents (worldwide air travel in the 1960s was still hampered by almost monthly crashes).

Keel admits that he never met Apol in the flesh, but talked with him at length over the telephone. In fact Keel knew that he was actually talking to Jane, who went into a trance to "channel" her alien visitor. Whether Apol was using psychic powers, spiritual possession or was simply Jane's alternate personality, "he" quickly convinced Keel that "he" had amazing powers. Keel tested Apol by asking test questions – things that only Keel could know about, and things that even he did not know: for example, the location of lost objects. Apol passed such tests with flying colours. It even got to the point that Keel would simply *think* of a question to ask Apol and a telephone call would immediately come in from Jane/Apol providing the answer.

Nevertheless, Apol also proved an oddly facetious personality – as keen to gossip or talk about dull trivia as he was to discuss his alien world or predictions of future events. In this he echoed many people's description of conversations with Men in Black. Jane's description of Apol's physical appearance even matched that of a typical MIB: dark but not black-skinned, straight black hair, high cheekbones and a pointed nose, giving an impression of a cross between an Oriental and a Native American.

As time went by, however, Apol improved on his papal assassination prediction: adding that it would come on 26 July 1967, and that it would be preceded by a terrible earthquake.

On 20 July, Pope Paul IV announced that he was going to make a trip to Turkey within the month. Many Turks resented the proposed visit, regarding it as a blatant attempt to proselytize good Moslems into the Catholic Church. An attempt at assassination was feared.

On 22 July, a violent earthquake, south-east of Istanbul, killed almost a thousand people.

By this stage, Keel was wondering just how he could convince the Vatican to call off a state visit because an "alien" had told him that the pope would be murdered. He might have saved himself the grief: the pope landed at Istanbul airport, and was met by an enthusiastic crowd. No assassination attempt occurred.

On his next conversation with Apol/Jane, Keel angrily demanded why he had been tricked in this way, but Apol remained unapologetic. "He" explained that he and his fellow aliens[3] were not native to time the way human beings are. Keel said of Apol:

I felt sorry for him. It became apparent that he really did not know who or what he was. He was a prisoner of our time frame. He often confused the past with the future.

Three years later, on 27 November 1970, a Bolivian painter, called Benjamin Mendoza, attempted to stab Pope Paul VI at Manila Airport in the Philippines. Witnesses claimed Mendoza, who was stopped before he could hurt anyone, was glassy-eyed and appeared to be in a trance. The rumour later went about that he was a practitioner of black magic.

This, Keel generously implies, was perhaps the "assassination" that Apol actually meant in his prediction.

Apol also made other near-miss predictions in 1967 that could suggest he was a creature that had difficulty translating his mind to human cause-and-effect chronology.

For example, Apol warned that presidential hopeful Robert Kennedy was in grave danger and should avoid hotels. (He also added, in passing, that Bobby Kennedy and Marilyn Monroe had had an affair – a fact that had not, at that time, become public knowledge.)

Robert Kennedy won the California state primary on 5 June 1968. His celebration party was held in Los Angeles' Ambassador Hotel and his victory speech was greeted enthusiastically by the Democrat Party faithful, especially his jubilant exhortation: "On to

[3]By this stage Jane said she had met half-a-dozen of Apol's compatriots – some who had cheekily identified themselves with names taken from characters in Keel's largely unsuccessful works of fiction.

Chicago! Let's win there!" – a reference to the party's presidential nomination.

To avoid the crowds – and an endless round of hand shaking – Kennedy was led off the podium through the hotel kitchens. There were no federal security men present (as they were not then considered necessary for presidential nominees). On top of this, Bobby Kennedy had no police protection – an astounding fact that the Los Angeles Police Department later blamed on Kennedy himself, although they have never been able to offer any proof that he asked their officers to stand down.

Halfway across a pantry crowded with well-wishers, a dark-skinned young man called Sirhan Bashira Sirhan jumped in front of the senator and screamed, "Kennedy, you son of a bitch!" Several people saw Sirhan raising a .22 pistol and leap at Kennedy. As he was dragged to the ground, a series of shots rang out; among those hit was Robert Kennedy, a bullet entering his cranium from behind his right ear. A day later, he was dead.

Sirhan Sirhan could not possibly have been the actual killer – Kennedy's wound had powder-burns around it, suggesting that the killing weapon was within six inches of his head when fired; Sirhan was never within six feet of Kennedy. Nevertheless, it is perhaps of note that during his subsequent trial – and conviction – Sirhan was said by witnesses to have been in a glassy-eyed, trance-like state during and immediately after the attack on Kennedy. Sirhan, now over thirty years into a life sentence, claims to have no memory of attacking Kennedy and to have had no previous reason or wish to do so.

In another striking "near-miss" prediction, Apol told Keel that civil rights hero, Martin Luther King, would be murdered on 4 February 1968. He would be standing on a balcony in Memphis, Tennessee, when a sniper's bullet would strike him in the throat.

Keel was impressed enough by the detail of this prediction to try to telephone King to pass on the warning. Given the kookiness of his story, he was unsurprised when nobody would give him a contact number. The specified date came and went with no assassination, but Keel had only a few months to enjoy Apol's apparent failure.

At 6 a.m. on 4 April 1968, Martin Luther King was enjoying the bright sunshine on the balcony at the Lorraine Hotel in Memphis,

Tennessee, when a high-velocity bullet struck him in the right side of the face, passing through his shirt collar as it did so.[4] The result was a fist-sized wound to his head, yet Dr King survived another thirteen hours, dying at St Joseph's Hospital at 7:05 p.m.

Apol, undeterred by the failure of the pope to be assassinated on 26 July, immediately began to insist on a new pair of disaster predictions: he said some kind of industrial disaster would take place on the Ohio River on 3 November 1967, and that at 5 p.m. on the following 15 December, an "electromagnetic effect" would cause an electricity blackout down a significant part of the US Eastern Seaboard, causing chaos and many deaths.

Keel knew that such "EM blackouts" were a side effect of nuclear explosions – and an electricity blackout of the entire east coast might suggest total nuclear war. However, the infuriating Apol refused to give any specific reasons for the disaster. He simply said that the electricity blackout would occur when the president threw the switch to light up the White House Christmas tree – an event that was televised live as part of the run up to Christmas.

Keel was worried enough by these predictions to contact Mary Hyre – the reporter for *The Messenger* newspaper in Point Pleasant. She told him that she herself had recently had a dream that seemed to predict a catastrophe, but that it had nothing to do with either an industrial disaster or an electricity blackout.

She had dreamed, she said, of Christmas packages floating on river water. She could not explain why, but she felt sure that this somehow indicated a very sad event.

The third of November came and went without any sort of disaster on the Ohio River, but Keel, sitting in his New York apartment, could not help but feel very nervous as he watched the televised Christmas tree ceremony on the White House lawn on 15 December. The switch was thrown and Keel breathed a sigh of relief when the power did not go off.

A short while later, however, a newsflash came up on the television screen. The Silver Bridge – a 700-foot suspension bridge

[4]This act alone seems to prove that the official verdict on MLK's murder was incorrect. James Earl Ray was supposed to have fired the shot from a boarding house bathroom some distance away and slightly *above* King. A bullet track that passed through his collar before it hit his face would suggest a sniper close to and *below* King.

that crossed the Ohio River from Point Pleasant – had collapsed at 5 p.m., killing an unknown number of people.

It later turned out that a traffic light at one end of the bridge had stuck on red, stranding a solid line of rush-hour traffic on the bridge. The weight had apparently proved too much and the entire bridge had suddenly collapsed. Forty-six people, many returning from Christmas shopping in Point Pleasant, were crushed or drowned in their cars. Among the debris, wrapped Christmas parcels were seen floating on the river surface.

The Silver Bridge collapse was blamed on poor maintenance of the connections between the support cables and the bridge towers, but some have questioned this (rather hurriedly supplied) explanation. Suspension bridges are designed specifically to prevent such a disaster – *all* the support cables on such a bridge giving way at once was totally unheard of before the Silver Bridge collapse. Also, nobody addressed the claim, made by at least one witness, that two men dressed in black trousers and checked coats had been seen climbing on the bridge a few hours before the disaster.

The strange sightings and paranormal events around Point Pleasant did not stop immediately after the Silver Bridge collapse, but they tailed off to nothing within a couple of months. John Keel suggests that for the exact thirteen months between the first and last Mothman sightings (14/15 November 1966 to 15 December 1967), Point Pleasant was a "window" for paranormal forces, and that the bridge disaster closed that window.

As for Apol and the other "aliens" – they too slowly ceased to call. Keel does not, however, believe them to have been men from another planet, as they claimed. He refers to them as *ultraterrestrials* rather than *extraterrestrials* because, he says, they are as native to the Earth as you or me. They are the source down the centuries, he suggests, of demonic and angelic visitations, fairy sightings, bizarre monsters that disappear without trace (like the Mothman) and UFO and "alien" encounters.

He suggests that ultraterrestrials are a non-corporeal form of life that, under certain "window" circumstances, can manifest themselves either as an influence on the human senses and/or mind or – in the case of poltergeist activity – as short-term physical forces.

Here he is in agreement with the respected "Nessie-hunter" Ted

Holiday. After seeing the Loch Ness Monster many times, Holiday noted that it would often stay in view for a long period, but would dive out of sight the moment he decided to try to take a photograph. Clearly, he thought, the "creature" was somehow aware of his mental processes.

Holiday suggested in his book, *The Goblin Universe*, that the Loch Ness Monster was a "ghost" – a being or projection from another dimension. He even went so far as to suggest that it had been called up by Aleister Crowley, the infamous black magician and self-publicist.

Shortly before the rush of Nessie sightings in the 1920s, Holiday points out, Crowley had attempted to perform a complex magical ritual in a cottage by Loch Ness. Crowley later claimed to have become bored and left the secret ceremony unfinished, but shortly after he left, locals found a strange tapestry hidden in the church graveyard. Embroidered on this obviously newly-made object were a number of black, slug-like creatures with long trunks or necks.

Evasive as he found Apol and his fellow "aliens", John Keel managed to glean a picture of what their existence was like:

> I gathered that [Apol] and his fellow entities found themselves transported backward and forward in time involuntarily, playing out their little games because they were programmed to do so, living – or existing – only so long as they could feed off the energy and minds of mediums and contactees.

Here again, Keel agrees with the findings of another paranormal investigator, Joe Fisher. Fisher investigated the "channelling" phenomena of the 1980s and 1990s, and published his findings in a fascinating book, *The Siren Call of Hungry Ghosts*.

Channelling is the modern-day equivalent of nineteenth-century, table-tapping mediums – a person goes into a trance, and "dead people" possess them and can speak through their mouths.

Fisher was initially sceptical when he started to investigate a channeller in Canada, but was quickly convinced by the wealth of detail the "ghosts" were able to give about their past lives. One claimed to have been a nineteenth-century Yorkshire farmer, another a World War II RAF pilot and a third to have been a girl who died young in second-century Greece.

Checking details as best he could from Canada, Fisher became convinced the "ghosts" were what they said they were. It was only when he returned to England to visit his mother that he found that, although the area of Yorkshire described by the farmer was real, no farmer of that name had ever lived there. Similarly, the RAF squadron described by the second entity *had* existed, but no one of his name had ever flown with it. Finally, the town the Greek girl had described *did* still exist in modern Greece, but it had not existed during the second century, when she claimed to have lived there.

Returning to Canada, Fisher confronted the "ghosts", only to be shouted at and threatened by the farmer. The RAF pilot apologetically said he couldn't talk about the matter because he was just due to reincarnate. The Greek girl, for whom Fisher had built up a special affection, refused even to talk to him. He concluded, like John Keel, that whatever these entities were – they were not what they claimed to be . . .

A sceptic will point out that many of the fantastic claims made in John Keel's *The Mothman Prophecies* are unsubstantiated and unsupported by any evidence other than Keel's own word – including, of course, all the "prophecies" themselves.

Certainly the strange sightings around Point Pleasant and, of course, the Silver Bridge disaster are all on public record. However, the bridge collapse might have been what the enquiry said it was – a tragic accident. The UFOs might have been natural (if as yet unexplained) atmospheric effects and the Mothman, the MIB, the slaughtered pets and the poltergeist hauntings might all have been the result of the sceptic's favourite fall-back explanation: mass hysteria.

If, on the other hand, we take Keel at his word – and it should be remembered that he is one of the most respected paranormal investigators in the world – then perhaps we can consider some rather less empirical explanations.

Was Apol a projection from Jane's or even Keel's subconscious mind? Certainly the fact that Keel only ever spoke to Apol through Jane in a trance suggests this. In which case, we might conclude that the subconscious is able to "see" into the future, and that prophets are simply those people who are in touch with their subconscious selves.

Or perhaps we are surrounded by non-corporeal beings who are adrift, so to speak, from time as we know it. Perhaps – when they manage to "materialize" themselves for brief periods – they are able to pass on predictions of future events.

In either case, if we rely on the evidence of Keel's *The Mothman Prophecies* and Fisher's *The Siren Call of Hungry Ghosts*, it is clear that we should never fully trust such doubtful intelligences.

Chapter 24

9/11

On the morning of 11 September 2001, two hijacked Boeing 757 passenger jets were deliberately crashed into the twin towers of New York's World Trade Centre. The first plane struck the North Tower at 8:45 a.m., the second hit the South Tower at 9.06 a.m. Both of the 110-storey (1,350-foot) skyscrapers collapsed within an hour and a half of the first impact. The death toll caused by the destruction of the twin towers has been estimated as 2,811 people.

At 9.40 a.m., a third hijacked Boeing 757 struck the west side of the Pentagon building in Washington DC – the nerve centre of the US Military – killing 189 people.

At 10.37 a.m., the fourth and last hijacked plane crashed in open countryside near Shanksville, Pennsylvania, killing all 44 on board. A mobile phone message from a passenger just before the crash said that he and some others were going to try to recapture the plane from the terrorists.

It has been speculated that, if the hijackers had not crashed the Shanksville plane prematurely, they would have tried to crash the jet into Camp David – the presidential rural retreat in Maryland. American President George W. Bush was not in residence at the time, but Camp David is the place where the historic peace accord between Egypt's President Anwar Sadat and Israeli Prime Minister Menachem Begin was signed in 1978: a hated symbol of Arab–Israeli co-operation to Moslem fundamentalists.

The destruction of Camp David – the place of presidential meetings with foreign heads of state over five decades – would also have been a powerful statement against the intrusive power of US, pro-Israeli diplomatic tactics in Middle-Eastern affairs.

The official death toll for what has come to be known simply as "9/11" (i.e. September 11 2001) – including the 19 suicide hijackers – was 3,044 people.

It is known that the hijackers were Islamic fundamentalists. The *Al-Qaeda* terrorist network, headed by the Saudi Arabian outlaw Osama bin Laden, is strongly suspected of being behind the 11 September hijackings, but (as of this writing in March 2003) conclusive proof has yet to be offered in open court.

What quickly became known as the "Attack on America" shocked the world and emotionally traumatized the USA. No such large-scale attack on the North American homeland had taken place since the British invaded the East Coast during the War of 1812.[1] Decades of American security – some might say complacency – came to an end in the instant the hijacked jet hit the North Tower.

Naturally, once the initial shock of grief, rage and fear had worn off, many Americans asked whether this catastrophe had been foreseen by anyone. Some Christian fundamentalists pointed to the Bible – and specifically The Revelation of St John the Divine, which predicts the destruction of several cities during the "Last Days" – but no specific Biblical prediction could honestly be said to fit 9/11.

After religion, many turned to that great guiding force of modern life: the Internet. As usual, many on-line cranks claimed – after the fact – to have been fully aware of the coming atrocity, but

[1] An inconclusive and pointless conflict brought about largely by accident. Interference by British and Napoleonic navies with neutral American shipping drove the US Congress to issue a threat of war to both nations. France immediately apologized but Britain, because of a bureaucratic mix-up, failed to meet the deadline. The British, hard-pressed by Napoleon, could only afford to send a small invasion contingent. However, the over-confident Americans lost the Battle of Bladensburg (nicknamed the Bladensburg Races, because the US leaders had to flee on horseback) and were forced to end the war in 1814 with a mutual agreement (the Treaty of Ghent) that effectively promised that both sides would forget that the whole embarrassing conflict had ever happened.

It was during the War of 1812 that the British raided Washington DC and torched many public buildings. The presidential residence was not totally destroyed, but was so badly smoke-damaged that the building had to be painted white to disguise the black marks. It thus earned the nickname "the White House".

none could offer any proof that they had known anything before the event.

However, one Internet rumour gathered a following and was soon being quoted in national newspapers. Nostradamus, it was claimed, had specifically predicted the destruction of the World Trade Centre in the following poem:

> In the City of God there will be a great thunder,
> Two brothers torn apart by chaos,
> While the fortress endures,
> The great leader will succumb,
> The third big war will begin when the big city is burning.

Readers of this book will doubtless spot the telltale detail that shows this "Nostradamus" prediction to be a fake: it has five lines, and therefore is not a quatrain.

In fact, it turned out to be a misquotation from a college thesis which had been published on the Internet by a Canadian undergraduate called Neil Marshall. As part of this sceptical dissertation – titled "A Critical Analysis of Nostradamus" – Marshall invented a quatrain to show just how easy it is to attribute historical events to portentous sounding rubbish:

> In the City of God there will be a great thunder,
> Two brothers torn apart by chaos,
> While the fortress endures,
> The great leader will succumb.

He goes on to say:

What does "City of God" mean? It could be Mecca, Medina, Rome, Jerusalem, Salt Lake City or any holy city, depending on your religion. What do I mean by thunder – a storm? War? Earthquake? Lots of stuff can be described by thunder. There are a lot of two brothers on this world (I think the number runs among the billions). And "fortress endures" what? Besiegement, famine, etc.? What "Great Leader"? How will he succumb? To what?

Marshall has a valid point, of course. We have already noted that Nostradamus-interpretation is singularly prone to the "Rorschach inkblot effect". This can lead the reader to see predictions in Nostradamus' quatrains that are based mainly on their own inclinations and obsessions, rather than on events and developments that can be supported by historical evidence.

On the other hand, we have also noted a number of quatrains where the Seer of Salon gave strikingly accurate predictions – the date of the Great Fire of London and the fame of Louis Pasteur, to name but two. It would be absurd to simply discount such amazingly precise predictions as simple coincidences.

So, *did* Nostradamus predict the 9/11 atrocity? The answer, as usual, is a matter of personal interpretation, but one of the quatrains does seem a close match:

Century VI, quatrain 97
> *Cinq et quarante degrés ciel bruslera,*
> *Feu approcher de la grand cité neufve,*
> *Instant grand flamme esparse sautera,*
> *Quant on voundra des Normains faire preuve.*

Translation:

> The sky will burn at forty-five degrees,
> Fire approaches the great new city,
> On the instant a great scattered flame leaps up,
> When they will want proof of the Normans.

The first line suggests two different interpretations, both centring on the ambiguous phrase "forty-five degrees". In conjunction with the words "the sky will burn", it initially sounds like an angle of view from the ground – i.e. "the upper atmosphere will burn" or, perhaps, "a very tall building will burn."

The other possibility is that Nostradamus was referring to the cartographical degrees – either latitude or longitude. If we were talking about anyone else, we might forget longitude, as it had not been accurately measured in Nostradamus' day. However, since he apparently foresaw the introduction of the Gregorian calendar, he might also have had some foreknowledge of longitudinal matters.

The longitude of forty-five degrees runs through or near a number of cities; for example, Antananarivo in Madagascar, Mogadishu in Somalia, Baghdad in Iraq and Volgograd (formerly Stalingrad) in Russia. All these, at one time or another since Nostradamus' day, have suffered burning skies – usually as a result of war or, in Antananarivo's case, mass human burnings.[2]

However, since no city on the forty-fifth degree of longitude can be described as both "new" and "great" (as stated in line two), we can probably settle on latitude as the more likely explanation.

There are many possible cities sited around the forty-fifth parallel, which runs through northern China, southern Russia, southern Europe and the northern United States. For example, the description in line three of "scattered" fire is reminiscent of the Great Chicago Fire of 1871, when high winds spread flames faster than they could be put out and 17,500 houses were destroyed in a single night.

However, the use of the phrase "great new city" in line two has convinced most Nostradamus scholars that the seer was talking about New York. Of course, this interpretation ignores the fact that New York City is actually closer to the forty-first parallel – some 200 miles south of the forty-fifth parallel – but the similarity of the names is generally enough to allow this inconvenient fact to be quietly forgotten.

The description of fire approaching the city in line two adds an air of suspense to the quatrain: whatever is going to cause the terrible conflagration is obviously going to come from outside the "great new city". This line used to make Cold War period commentators think of intercontinental ballistic missiles, but the approach of the hijacked jets of 11 September also fits this phrase.

Line three certainly creates a strong visual link to 11 September. It is highly reminiscent of the shattering explosions, caught on

[2]The insanely xenophobic Queen Ranavalona I (who ruled Madagascar from 1828–61) often held mass executions in Antananarivo – killing hundreds of people at a time by boiling them alive in pits, burning others at the stake and hurling yet others off a high cliff. The "crime" of most of these unfortunates was simply to be in the wrong place at the wrong time. Ranavalona has been called "the nineteenth century's Caligula", but the comparison is flawed. She ruled longer and killed many more people than the Emperor Caligula ever did.

numerous cameras, as the aeroplanes hit the towers of the World Trade Centre.

Finally there is line four and what is possibly a classic Nostradamus wordplay. "Proof" is described as being demanded from the "*Normains*". The English/American translation of this word is "Normans" – the Norse conquerors who successfully invaded first northern France, then Britain, Ireland, Italy, Sicily and the Holy Land, but who had ceased to exist as an unadulterated ethnic group long before even Nostradamus' day.

An explanation of the word "Normans" could be a contraction of the phrase "*North Americans*". Of course, as of this writing, the US authorities have yet to offer conclusive proof as to who was responsible for the 9/11 atrocity – a possible explanation of the line.

However, to believe that "*Normains*" means "North Americans" demands that we believe that Nostradamus both knew of the word "America" (as we have seen, it was hardly in use in his day) and that he would have uncharacteristically created a word puzzle utilizing English rather than French, Latin or Greek.

As usual, the reader must decide for themselves if Nostradamus actually foresaw this event, was describing some other event(s) or was simply pulling the collective leg of history.

With Nostradamus being his usual, enigmatic self, we have to look elsewhere for authenticated predictions of the 9/11 attack. They are however, at the time of this writing, rather scarce on the ground.

It has been pointed out that the 3,000-plus fatalities directly attributable to the 9/11 atrocity is actually a fairly negligible number when compared to, say, the number of people who die during frequent natural disasters worldwide – like earthquakes, floods and famines – or that died virtually every day during the two world wars. During 2001, 37,795 people – more than ten times the number killed in 9/11 – were killed in car accidents in the US alone.

There are two main reasons why 9/11 has had such a significant impact on world opinion. The first is that it was an act of terrorism that took place in supposedly one of the most secure cities belonging to the most powerful nation on the globe. The second is the world witnessed the catastrophe as if we were all there in the flesh. Satellite broadcasting meant that almost every community on the planet – that had access to electricity and at least one television – witnessed 9/11 happen almost exactly as New Yorkers in distant buildings saw the destruction of the World Trade Centre.

It is a trait of modern human intelligence that we empathize with people we do not know or share interests with;[3] the sight of *any* human suffering traumatizes us. As a result, 9/11 became a personal tragedy to the entire planet, and there are at least two documented cases of it being predicted by people who lived thousands of miles away from the site of the catastrophe.

Australian psychics Scott Russell Hill and Rosemary Walter predicted the correct time period for 9/11 in 1996. The pair were comparing their own predictions with those of Nostradamus on their weekly Adelaide radio show, *Psychic Saturday Night*, when Hill said:

> The last time Nostradamus was spoken about was when the World Trade Centre was bombed. My strongest feeling is that if the World Trade Centre has been attacked once, it could be attacked again.

Hill's psychic partner, Waller, then added that they both believed such an attack would come in 2001: "The key months to look for will be September, October and November, and it will be unexpected."

As with many psychics, both Hill and Waller had suffered childhood traumas, after which both began to have clairvoyant episodes. In Waller's case, she survived a severe car crash at the age of five. Hill, at the age of seven, had fallen off a pier, knocking himself semi-conscious against a boat as he fell. His father dived in and saved him, but not before the drowning boy had what he later described as a "near-death experience".

The *Psychic Saturday Night* show had several other notable successes in 1996. That September, Hill mentioned Britain's Princess Diana:

---

[3]A trait that many of our ancestors – for example, the Roman crowds cheering the sight of people being eaten alive by wild animals in the arena – notably failed to exhibit.

She's just had her thirty-fifth birthday . . . I don't think she'll reach forty . . . I had a dream [about the cover of a woman's magazine] and she wasn't on it. Instead there was a picture of the Eiffel Tower and my initial thought was, "Why isn't Diana here [on the cover]?" And I thought: "Well, because she's dead" . . . [Diana's death will be] connected to Paris or France, or something to do with the French.

Of course, Princess Diana was killed in a car crash in Paris on the night of 31 August 1997.

In further bad news for the British monarchy, Scott Hill also predicted that Prince William, Diana's oldest child, was in grave danger of dying in a skiing accident, and that the next British king would not be Prince Charles, but his younger son, Prince Harry. This would seem to indicate that Charles will either be removed from the succession (perhaps because he wishes to marry the divorcée, Camilla Parker Bowles) or that Charles may not outlive his mother, the present queen.

During the same evening's broadcast, Hill predicted: "The Concorde [supersonic passenger jet] is going to have a disaster . . . a terrible explosion . . . there's going to be loss of life . . . it's in France."

On 25 July 2000, an Air France Concorde was taking off from Paris's Charles de Gaulle Airport when smoke and flames were seen pouring from the port engine. Immediately thereafter, the jet crashed into a nearby hotel, killing all 109 on board and four people on the ground. It later turned out that runway debris – possibly pieces of punctured tyre – had flown up and damaged the engine during take off.

Another psychic also predicted both the 2000 Concorde crash and the 9/11 World Trade Centre atrocity. David Mandell was an art lecturer at London's Guildhall University but, on retirement, became a full-time painter, specializing in depicting his strange dream visions.

Born in 1933, Mandell had precognitive dreams from his early boyhood. At the age of six, in 1939, he told his parents that he had dreamed that, on the outbreak of war with Germany, all the locals would have to go to a particular local farm to be given ugly masks. On the outbreak of the war in September that year, the shipment of gas masks for the Watford area was distributed from the predicted farm.

Later in the war, Mandell told both teachers and classmates that two bombs would fall on specific spots in the local park. The next morning there were two craters in the park, just where David had foretold they would be.

"Some of the parents said I must be in league with the Devil," Mandell later ruefully recalled. His own parents were not much better; as strict Welsh Baptists, they regarded David's precognitive episodes with some alarm.

Mandell continued to have precognitive dreams in his adult life, and claimed to always be able to differentiate normal dreams from his dreams about the future, because they were "vivid, longish and nearly always in colour. [In the precognitive dreams] I have a particular sense of place, even if I have never been there."

In the 1980s, Mandell hit upon a method of proving that he foresaw events before they happened. The morning after a likely dream, he would paint a general image of what he had dreamed. He would then take this down to his local bank in Sudbury Hill, North London, and would get a member of staff take a photograph of the painting next to the bank's calendar clock.

Many of what Mandell called his "major event dreams" tended to be symbolic. For example, on 14 October 1987, he dreamed about Hawker Hurricanes – the World War II British fighter planes. He painted a picture of a flight of Hurricanes and took it down to the bank the next day, although he could not guess what a vision of these obsolete fighters might mean: an accident at an air show perhaps?

Two days later, southern England was hit by hurricane winds of up to 110 miles per hour. The winds did millions of pounds worth of damage and killed sixteen people. Such powerful storms are almost unknown in England. Even a few hours before the hurricane hit, weather forecasters had little or no inkling that it would happen.

Other Mandell dreams were rather less allegorical. In February 1988, he dreamed about two pleasure boats colliding. The following August, a Thames pleasure boat called *The Marchioness* was struck by a cement freighter – 51 people were drowned.

On 12 July 1997, Mandell took a picture titled "Concorde

Crash" down to his local bank to be photographed next to the calendar clock. It showed a delta-winged jet streaming flame and, quite distinct in one corner of the picture, a French flag. As we have already seen, the world's first Concorde crash took place outside Paris on 25 July 2000.

During the early morning of 11 September 1996, Mandell dreamed of New York's Statue of Liberty. Then he saw the two skyscrapers of the World Trade Centre collapsing, as if "embracing". On waking he drew a picture of two flaming skyscrapers in the moment of collapse, and had the usual confirming picture taken at his bank at 4.19 that afternoon.

Exactly five years later, the twin towers were smoking heaps of debris.

There is another "prophet" worth noting in connection with the 9/11 catastrophe.

Cyril Richard "Rick" Rescorla was born in Cornwall, England, in 1939. He enlisted in the US Army in 1963, and fought in Vietnam with distinction. On leaving the army, he successfully applied for US citizenship, married and took a law degree. In 1985, he was made head of security for the international investment firm Morgan Stanley – the post was based in the Morgan Stanley offices in the World Trade Centre.

In 1990, Rescorla called in a friend from his army days, Dan Hill, to help evaluate potential terrorist threats to the twin towers. After an extensive study, the pair agreed that the underground car parks, if bombed, could be a threat to the stability of both buildings. The report was duly sent to the New York Port Authority – who had built and owned the World Trade Centre – but nothing was done about it.

On 26 February 1993, a massive bomb, hidden in a parked van, went off in the underground car park beneath the World Trade Centre. The aim was to undermine the support pillars and bring down one or both of the towers.

Fortunately, although the explosion displaced 6,800 tons of concrete and support beams, the damage was not enough to cause a collapse. However, six people were killed in the bomb blast and over 2,000 were injured. If the plot had worked, the 50,000 people in the towers would not have had time to evacuate before the buildings fell.

Four Moslem fundamentalists were later found guilty of the bombing.

Rick Rescorla, as director of security, co-ordinated the evacuation of the twenty floors of Morgan Stanley employees in the South Tower, and was officially noted as the last person to leave the building.

Following the World Trade Centre bombing, Rescorla continued to warn that the twin towers were a major target for terrorist attack. However, he no longer thought that the chief threat came in the form of a bomb in the underground garages – the New York Port Authority had finally acted on his 1990 suggestions and had greatly increased building security. The great threat, Rescorla now warned, came in the form of a suicide air attack.

Speaking in a television interview in 1998, Rescorla stressed why he thought suicide terrorists were the chief threat in the post-Cold War world:

> Terrorist forces can tie up conventional forces and bring them to their knees . . . Just one man willing to give his life for what he believes in, chooses the time and place and there is no way that [security forces] can be a hundred percent alert.

Despite his previous army background, Rescorla was in little doubt that America's "cavalier actions" in foreign countries were to blame for the increasing threat of international terrorism. He warned that if America and her allies continued to act as the US had in Vietnam – as if they were above international law – they would face a greater and greater backlash from people who suffered as a result of US foreign policy. Such people, in a state of increasing desperation and hatred, would be more and more likely to give up their lives in order to hurt their perceived enemy.

On the morning of 11 September, Rick Rescorla was at work in the South Tower when the hijacked 757 hit the North Tower. The Port Authority officials, fearful of a stampede, told those in the South Tower to stay where they were, but Rescorla immediately told Morgan Stanley personnel, and anyone else who would listen, to start making their way to the ground.

Rescorla continued to organize the evacuation, giving instructions and singing morale-boosting songs through a bullhorn, after the second hijacked 757 hit the South Tower. He was last seen alive, having escorted nearly 3,000 people to safety, heading back into the building to look for stragglers. He died in the subsequent collapse.

Rick Rescorla never claimed to be a precognitive psychic. He was simply a man who knew what he was talking about and made warnings based on sensible ideas and logical extrapolations. It is a moot point as to whether, if listened to, his warnings might have prevented the 9/11 horror, but his 1990 prediction could certainly have prevented the 1993 bomb attack on the World Trade Centre.

The reader of this book will have seen, again and again, that precognitive visions might have prevented disasters *if* they had been heeded before the event. They will also have seen that most such predictions are too vague or, in the case of prophets like Nostradamus, too deliberately opaque to be of much use before the event.

It is perhaps true, as Nostradamus claims to have believed, that history is preordained; that "as it is written, so it shall be". However, to give up trying to prevent future disasters on this basis is plain nonsensical. H. G. Wells, speaking of the possible immutability of the future in his novel *The Time Machine*, said: "If that is so, it remains for us to live as though it were not so." Anything else would be a counsel of despair.

We may never be able to act on the predictions of Nostradamus, Edgar Cayce, the West Virginia Mothman or The Revelation of St John the Divine, but we *can* listen to men like Rick Rescorla – perhaps the true prophets of our scientific age.